THE NEW YORKER THEATER

and Other Scenes from a Life at the Movies

THE NEW YORKER THEATER

and Other Scenes from a Life at the Movies

TOBY TALBOT

Columbia University Press   NEW YORK

Columbia University Press

Publishers Since 1893

New York   Chichester, West Sussex

Library of Congress Cataloging-in-Publication Data

Talbot, Toby.

The New Yorker Theater and other scenes from a life at the movies / Toby Talbot.

p. cm.

Includes bibliographical references and index.

ISBN 978-0-231-14566-4 (cloth : alk. paper) — ISBN 978-0-231-14567-1 (pbk. : alk paper)

ISBN 978-0-231-51982-3 (ebook)

1. Talbot, Toby. 2. Talbot, Daniel. 3. Motion picture theater owners—New York (State)—
New York—Biography. 4. New Yorker Theater (New York, N. Y.)—History. 5. Motion
picture theaters—New York (State)—New York—History—20th century. I. Title.

PN1998.3.T3424A3   2010

791.43092—dc22

[B]   2009019806

∞

Columbia University Press books are printed on permanent and durable acid-free paper.

This book is printed on paper with recycled content.

Printed in the United States of America

c 10 9 8 7 6 5 4 3 2 1

p 10 9 8 7 6 5 4 3 2 1

References to Internet Web sites (URLs) were accurate at the time of writing. Neither the
author nor Columbia University Press is responsible for URLs that may have expired or
changed since the manuscript was prepared.

For Dan

CONTENTS

FOREWORD

MARTIN SCORSESE

This is a book about the love of cinema. You can find it on every page, in every photograph, and in every reproduction of schedules and ledgers and suggestion "Guest Books.

Let me flash back to the year 1960, the year that Dan and Toby Talbot opened The New Yorker. At that time, love of cinema meant dedication to cinema. In a sense, the world was separated between people who liked to go to the movies to pass the time and people who went for the same reasons that lovers of dance would go to see a Balanchine performance, that lovers of literature would spend their weekends scouring the bookstores, that lovers of painting would mount the steps of the Metropolitan Museum or The Museum of Modern Art to commune with Tintoretto or Cézanne.

The barrier between these two points of view was formidable. I was eighteen years old in 1960, and believe me, the idea that movies were to be taken seriously was a minority opinion, at least in my world. You would get it from all sides. The people around you would laugh when you were affected too deeply by a picture. Devotees of literature and the fine arts, when you had occasion to run into them, would scoff at the idea of cinema as an art form. And even certain people who did take it seriously would single out a few masterpieces (little if anything at all from Hollywood apart from *Citizen Kane* and some Chaplin films) amidst a sea of junk, and claim that it was an art form that had yet to realize its potential. I suppose this is the way it always goes when attitudes change.

And that's what made it exciting. I knew what I was seeing up there on the screen, what I was feeling there in the theater. The fact that it was almost a secret, something special, something that was shared by just a few people, made it even more powerful.

When I left home to go to school at NYU, the actual distance was negligible, just a few city blocks. But it also felt vast, like crossing the ocean. When I got there, I met other people who shared my love of film. We would go see everything. We would look at everything new from all around the world, and we would also look at older pictures with new eyes, pictures we always loved, by people like Hawks and Hitchcock and Lang and Ford. It was all part of the same moment—*Breathless* and *Scorpio Rising* and *The Searchers* and *The Band Wagon* and *Shadows* and *Before the Revolution* and *Vertigo* and *8 1/2* and *High and Low*. We would congregate at the Thalia or the Bleecker Street Cinema or The New Yorker, and at the first- and second- and third-run theaters all over town. Every new screening, no matter what quality the print was, whether it was a new picture or one we'd already seen dozens of times, was some kind of affirmation. These moving images projected up there on the screen—this was who we were. It was what we wanted, and somehow, in a way we couldn't even begin to articulate, it *described* the world as we saw it. I could imagine how it must have felt to be present at the unveiling of Rembrandt's "The Night Watch" or Piero della Francesca's frescoes in Arezzo, but I *knew* what it felt like to watch Antonioni's *L'Avventura* for the first time, and then leave the theater and walk into what seemed to be an altered world.

Even during that precious time, The New Yorker was a very special place. It was a place of communion, where the customers, the owners, the programmers, and the filmmakers all seemed to be part of the same family. Dan and Toby were right there on the front lines, showing films, making films, distributing films, sticking their neck out on pictures by Godard and Bertolucci and Fassbinder and Straub and Huillet and Oshima and Sembene. Reading this book is a little like reading a legendary tale. Something was created in those years, a real *consciousness* of cinema. Dan and Toby were right there at the center of it all.

The New Yorker is gone now. So are the Metro and the Cinema Studio. So, sadly, is New Yorker Films. And that time is also gone, passed into history. But the spirit of the time is very much alive. Anyone who lives in America and cares about cinema and its history, no matter how old or young, owe something to The New Yorker and to Dan and Toby Talbot. Once you've read this marvelous book, you'll understand why.

ACKNOWLEDGMENTS

I want to thank Jennifer Crewe, Associate Director and Editorial Director of Columbia University Press, for her encouragement, and Bruce Goldstein and my copyeditor Roy Thomas for their attentive reading of the manuscript. And, always, our daughters: Nina, Emily, and Sarah.

THE NEW YORKER THEATER

and Other Scenes from a Life at the Movies

REEL 1

The Theater

Genesis of the Theater

"What kind of work is running a movie house?" my father-in-law asked. Who knew? Not us, until we opened the New Yorker. It ran through the sixties and early seventies: a golden age in cinema, turbulent in politics— French New Wave on our screen, '68 uprisings at Columbia University. An Upper West Side hub became, as Bernardo Bertolucci dubbed it, "a kind of wild cinema university, like Henri Langlois's Cinémathèque in Paris." We were young film buffs, learning as we went. Not knowing where we were going. The theater is gone, but its marquee still glimmers in my mind. As we shaped it, it shaped us. Movies, moviegoers, our own lives unspooled on one ongoing reel. The New Yorker became our anchor, where time and place converged. I thought it would go on forever.

Flashback

What were we up to before that venture? Flashback to June 1958: One fine morning, with two small daughters and twelve cartons of Beech Nut baby food, we picked ourselves up and headed for Spain. Torremolinos, Marbella—what voluptuous names. The S. S. *Guadalupe* sat anchored at a downtown West Side pier. Dan's Aunt Yanka, a refugee diva from Warsaw, sent me off with a gauzy white nightgown, like that bestowed at a bridal shower—it kind of felt like a honeymoon. Dan's parents had a glum look. It was their daughter-in-law's idea, scheming Spanish professor and translator, to lure their son abroad—that's what they thought. Dan, in fact, employed as Eastern Story Editor for Warner Bros., yearned to escape the nine-to-five world. As a child, when I got headaches my mother claimed I read too much. And when sad, that I thought too much. At our departure, she declared: "That's the craziest thing I heard in my life."

The ship, owing to low tide, didn't budge for hours, reluctant it seemed to depart. We were the only American passengers on a rickety vessel minus ballast, along with some pensioners returning to spend their golden years in *la patria*, and the fish in the galley making their rank return to Spain. All got seasick, save our nursing infant Emily, and Raúl Castro, brother of triumphant Fidel, heading now for Spain "to visit his aunt" in Asturias. Raúl (current president of Cuba) whiled away his afternoons shooting at sea gulls, blasts that sent our four-year-old Nina flying to my skirt.

On sighting land, after a bumpy seven-day crossing, I felt like dropping to my knees as had Columbus when his ship landed in Hispaniola. In July 1958 we disembarked in Santander on the northern coast of Spain. "Are you setting up a business?" demanded the Customs Official in black, three-cornered hat, eyeballing Dan and myself as he pried open each of those cartons with Beech Nut baby food jars lined up like little soldiers awaiting orders. We headed south to the small, then unknown coastal village called Torremolinos, and set up house in a stone cottage in the Bajondillo, the fishermen's quarter in the lower part of town. To warm a baby's bottle we lit a coal stove, and to keep the ice-box cold, ascended steep steps to the upper village for a block of ice. In the market, when a vendor was asked if the fish was fresh, in all honesty he told me: "No señora, it was caught during the night."

Thirteen months later, that little band of footloose adventurers boarded the *Queen Elizabeth* bound for Manhattan, minus the baby food. Who in that village of Churriana, where we finally settled, where autos gave way to burros, would *dream* of feeding their baby anything but fresh fruit and vegetables? The villagers had resourcefully deployed the cunning Beech Nut jars for storing nails and screws. We returned broke, recovering from infectious hepatitis—the *gayle zach*—the "yellow thing"—as my mother promptly diagnosed it in Yiddish. I learned a new term: *bili rubens*—hallmark of hepatic conquest.

Dan, recalling that day (one year after our marriage) when he got fired as a book editor, wanted never again to work for anyone else—*chutzpah* buoyed by a wife, daughter of a gambler. In his early thirties by now, his Curriculum Vitae incorporated editor at Fawcett and Avon paperback houses (where he edited the *Partisan Review Reader*); multi-anthologist (*Mountaineering* paid our first obstetrician bill, without his ever having climbed a mountain), editor of *Film: An Anthology* (an essay collection that included Erwin Panofsky, James Agee, and Pauline Kael, and used to this day in classrooms); Eastern Story Editor for Warner Bros.; creator of a small, offbeat textile venture, fabrics packaged in paperback format, one yard of percale for an apron, two of broadcloth for a skirt, three for a fat woman, and distributed in suburban Long Island Five and Ten Cent stores. Those were the days when ladies stitched—I myself sewed our daughters' dresses and Dan's shirts. My mother cut and packaged the goods in a Canal Street firetrap that eventually burned down, whisking away in flames my father-in-law's black market stash hidden in a desk compartment. Dan was a man of parts and I part of those parts.

We found a second-floor apartment in a brownstone on 90th Street between West End Avenue and Riverside Drive, overlooking a Greek Orthodox Church. While figuring out where to go next, he became the film critic for the *Progressive Magazine*, a liberal political monthly, and I began teaching Spanish Literature at Columbia University, eking out a supplementary bread-and-butter sustenance as a translator. In 1958 Noonday Press had published my translation of Ortega y Gasset's *On*

Love: Aspects of a Single Theme, and now Dr. Félix Martí Ibáñez, a psychiatrist exiled from Franco Spain and founding editor of *MD* magazine, commissioned me to translate his encyclopedic essays—on José Martí, the temples of Cambodia, Machu Picchu, you name it. That man could write faster than my Remington—letter *t* partly missing—could transcribe. The magazine thrived, free copies distributed to physicians, and Dr. Ibáñez, so pleased with my work, was most generous in fees.

Ensured of a modest income, we began fantasizing about opening a bookstore in New Hampshire, and one December day trekked up to Hanover to explore. On that long, snowy drive, we began reciting movies we longed to see again, like children wanting a tale repeated no sooner than read. With each mile on the odometer, the litany progressed. Soon it got narrowed to British films: *Brief Encounter*, *The Red Shoes*, *The Man in the White Suit*, and *I Know Where I'm Going*, we called out in unison—the last, Michael Powell's 1945 tale about a headstrong Wendy Hiller on the verge of marrying a rich man but getting distracted by a dashing flyer—small on plot, but witty and juicy. We knew not where we were going, but wanted juicy. And that's when Henry Rosenberg came along.

One day my sister and brother-in-law casually mentioned that their accountant was thinking of buying the Yorktown Theater on Broadway between 88th and 89th Streets. Maybe we should talk. On a February evening in 1960 Mr. Rosenberg came for dinner: mustached, navy blue suit, white-on-white shirt open at the neck, an engaging smile—the look of a smooth entrepreneur in a silent flick. He and his partner, a Syrian named Jack Jamil, owned a number of stores on Broadway that sold rugs, electronics, and assorted *tchotchkes*, but he also had a chain of Spanish movie houses. And there begins the tale.

How the Theater Got Its Name

In 1934 Broadway had eighteen movie theaters between 59th to 110th Street, only ten then functioning: the Regency at 67th Street, the Loews 83rd, the Adelphi (now the Yorktown) between 88th and 89th, the Symphony and the Thalia at 95th, the Riverside and the Riviera on 96th, the Midtown at 99th, the Edison at 103rd, and the Olympia at 107th. Most were "flea pits" or "toilets" in movie house jargon, with lumpy seats, poor sight lines, musty odors, and scuttering roaches. Former picture palaces—relics of palmier days—had been converted into TV studios and supermarkets. The Yorktown marquee perennially promised TWO BIG HITS irrespective of what was playing, while the Red Apple to the right announced *FRYERS AND BROILERS 39 CENTS PER POUND*, and Joe Rosen's Butcher Shop to the left brandished strings of kosher salamis on lustful hooks.

But by the early sixties, the Upper West Side began undergoing change. Young couples in the arts and professions were moving into old brownstones and apartment buildings. It was the only place in Manhattan where one could find a large, roomy flat at an affordable rental. Nobody then was thinking Harlem, Williamsburg, Staten Island or, God forbid, New Jersey. This was a harbinger of other unfashionable neighborhoods getting developed: Soho, Noho, Chelsea, Tribeca, Park Slope, Boerum Hill and, yes, Harlem and Williamsburg.

The Upper West Side, some two square densely populated miles, was definitely under-screened. And Dan came up with an idea: he convinced Henry to allow him to experiment a while, converting the Yorktown into a revival house, Dan himself managing it. Well, Henry was not born yesterday: a practical fellow, he was not given to throwing money down the drain, no less on an "art house." Dan's salary was to be $125 a week, plus one-third of the profits. If the theater failed to turn a profit after the year was up, Henry figured, that spot could always be added to his Hispanic chain.

On March 7, 1960, Rosenberg's office issued a release: "Brandt's Yorktown Theater (900 seats) has just been purchased by Arjay Enterprises, Inc."

Oh Henry! We were ready to roll. Four neon letters salvaged from the Yorktown morphed into the New Yorker.

How did the theater come by its name? In the early thirties, my Uncle Harry, ingenious and dapper, a sometime bootlegger in the heyday of

Prohibition and a fellow with *chrain* (or "horseradish" as the Yiddish expression goes), who drove a cobalt blue Buick and smoked Havana cigars ignited by a silver lighter matching the pattern of his wife Rosie's tenth anniversary compact, decided under counsel of her cardiologist to move to Miami's beneficent climate. Though its coast was sheer swampland, it occurred to Uncle Harry that what its beaches needed was a hotel. Surely others, aside from *his* family, would be migrating south to escape the cold. Uncle Harry was a quick mover. Within a year, mangrove marshes got drained and the New Yorker Hotel rose on 1415 Collins Avenue. One of the earliest hotels in Miami Beach, it was a proud Art Deco structure pictured on the postcards sent us by Uncle Harry, Aunt Rose, and cousins Moe and Yetta. Sybaritic South Beach was far in the wings. As a parting gift, Tante Rosie bequeathed me her compact, an anticipatory gift of adulthood for an eight-year-old, and I was heartbroken when it got lost in the Málaga airport in 1959. But in tribute to the gods of Enterprise and the Recycling of Letters, we named our offspring the New Yorker.

An Art Deco relief of Diana the Huntress and her hound hung above its marquee. At night, yellow and green lights—sometimes a letter missing—lit up the block and on a rainy day painted the sidewalk. You handed the cashier $1.25, swung past the turnstile, entered a mirrored lobby, and turned to ogle the overhead banner of black-and-white photos of Greta Garbo, Humphrey Bogart, Bette Davis, Cary Grant, Katharine Hepburn, Peter Lorre, and company. On August 10, 1960, when Gloria Swanson in white ermine, white limousine, and black chauffeur showed up to see *Sunset Boulevard*—about a star dreaming of a comeback for millions who'd never forgiven her for deserting the screen—she lit up on finding herself in that stellar company and promptly checked her aging self on the mirrored wall, still angling for the best profile.

Opening Programs

Our first show on March 17, 1960, was *Henry V*, starring Laurence Olivier and a chorus advising its audience "to eke out our performance with your mind." What better counsel for the rapture of art? Co-featured was *The Red Balloon*, a fantasy about a Parisian boy's friendship with a red balloon, and then soaring into the heavens. The program ran for three weeks. As people lined up, we too were soaring! Shortly before noon, we stood in the empty theater, hall dark and quiet, seats unoccupied, screen blank, an air of stillness pervading an Edward Hopper kind of space. Moviegoers began drifting in, seats filling. The screen came alive.

That initial Friday evening of operation, *Henry V* and *The Red Balloon* drew over two thousand moviegoers, and within three months audiences came flocking, not just from our neighborhood but, as guest books revealed, from the five boroughs, New Jersey, and Connecticut. The two-week total for that first twin bill was over $10,000. Soon theaters around the country were copying our programs.

Item—June 1960: by *New York Post* critic Archer Winsten: "The New Yorker is a sizeable theater and can hold many people comfortably. At present it seems to be by far the most exciting film theater in town, not just for what it shows but for the departures and promise of its future. Obviously, it's the only theater with new and fresh ideas."

"Imagine the courage it took to launch a movie house," critic Phillip Lopate remarked in 2008. "Dan had no illusions of being gifted at business," I replied, "but somehow he managed to develop mature business judgment." One learns by doing, said John Dewey. And, as Nathaniel Hawthorne declared, unemployment may lead to the next step. Hawthorne himself, "decapitated" from a three-year post as Customs Surveyor when his party lost power, said that "the moment when a head drops off is seldom, or never, I am inclined to think, precisely the most agreeable of his life. Nevertheless, like the greater part of our misfortune, even serious contingency brings the remedy and consolation with it, if the sufferer will but make the best, rather than the worst of the accident which has befallen him." The life of the New Yorker lay like a dream before us.

"Get yourself some real work. Study to be a pharmacist," Dan's father persisted—doctor, dentist, or lawyer not prescribed. For a son hooked on Proust, Joyce, Kafka, Rossellini, and Fellini, professional Dog Walker was equally unlikely. *Make a living* is what he meant. Pursue a profession, or some useful trade, where not apt to be fired. Nor were writer, critic, or editor on Dad's list. Where had his own studies in philosophy and language at Cracow University landed him? It was the Depression. You did what you had to do. He became a textile jobber; he became a worrier, mindful of the cost of a loaf of bread. Why mention that Dan, while attending New York University, had moonlighted as a soda jerk and taxi driver just to hole up in spare time with the *Partisan* and *Sewanee Reviews*? Why mention that Carl Theodor Dreyer could pursue his art through income derived from managing the Dagmar Movie Theater in Copenhagen? Why mention that James Joyce in 1919 came up with the brainstorm of opening a movie house in Ireland and, aided by some Trieste businessmen, transformed a Dublin building—the numbers went south, the scheme was a flop, and the whole thing shut down that very year. Anyhow, who in the world when asked as a kid what he wants to be when he grows up pipes up with *exhibitor*? Two years later, in 1962, we purchased the lease from Rosenberg, assisted by my parents, who withdrew their little nest egg from the bank, as did our parsimonious friend, the writer Chandler Brossard, who withdrew *his* last $6,000, without examining the "financials."

Following that first three-week program of *Henry V* and *The Red Balloon*, the second bill was Carl Theodor Dreyer's *Day of Wrath* and Marcel Pagnol's *Harvest*: austerity and abundance. Next came Orson Welles's *The Magnificent Ambersons* and Robert Frank and Alfred Leslie's *Pull My Daisy*, a quirky Beat Generation riff shot in Leslie's loft in 1959 and narrated by Jack Kerouac of the mellifluous voice: odd film couples from the word "Go"! Ginsberg's *Howl* and *Kaddish*, Kerouac's *On the Road*, and the poems of Gregory Corso and Lawrence Ferlinghetti had been published by then. On September 5, 1957, Gilbert Millstein, reviewing *On the Road* in the *New York Times*, called it "the most beautifully executed, the clearest and the most important utterance yet made by the generation Kerouac himself named years ago as 'beat.' " But in 1958, when Millstein brought two Columbia buddies in checked flannel shirts to our living room, who could have foreseen what Ginsberg and Kerouac had in the works? *Pull My Daisy*, an ode to the Beat Generation, had a rich cast including Allen Ginsberg, Gregory Corso, Richard Bellamy, Alice Neel, and Larry Rivers. The twenty-nine beatific minutes at a surreal dinner party with a bishop and a working-class family were, well, fresh as a daisy. Even so, one customer wanted his money back. He thought we were showing *Please Don't Eat the Daisies*. "You wouldn't catch me going in there with a ten-foot pole," Dan overheard one passerby say to another. "They play such crazy shows. But such lines at the box office!" The program sold over 7,300 tickets during its two-week run and had people cheering from their seats.

As a revival house, we showed American movies along with others that had English subtitles at the bottom of the screen, the kind of films our kids' friends didn't care to see, even without paying. To this day I find it exhilarating to slip into our movie theater *for free*—and without waiting "on line"! On Monday the Andrew Sisters might be crooning "Don't sit under the apple tree with anyone else but me," while on Tuesday Emil Jannings would weep for his unattainable Blue Angel, and on Wednesday hyper Harpo, boozy W. C. Fields, or deadpan Buster Keaton might be doing their stuff. I, onetime acrobat and tap dancer, was smitten by Keaton's rubber-band stunts, and loved standing in back of the theater when we played a comedy, listening to the laughter—a crowd's laughter more restorative than attending church or temple. "Make 'em laugh, make 'em laugh," enjoins Donald O'Connor in *Singin' in the Rain*. And in Preston Sturges's comedy, *Sullivan's Travels*, a chain-gang audience in a dirt-poor rural African-American church escapes their confinement by roaring over the antics of Mickey Mouse and Pluto. I could always locate Dan by his bursts of laughter as he sat in the audience watching W. C. Fields.

Our audiences were viewing Hollywood movies as art, not just popular entertainment. Screwball comedies, gangster flicks, musicals, and westerns—films of the '30s and '40s that we'd gorged on as kids—shared our silver screen with Murnau, Eisenstein, Griffith, von Sternberg, Lubitsch, and Renoir. The theater became a cocoon for young people getting schooled in film. "That's where I found my education," says Peter Bogdanovich. That's where Vittorio De Sica's *Shoeshine* got paired with Alfred Hitchcock's *Strangers on a Train*, Stanley Kubrick's *Paths of Glory* with Orson Welles's *Touch of Evil*, Joseph L. Mankiewicz's *All About Eve* with John Huston's *Treasure of Sierra Madre*, and Robert Bresson's *A Man Escaped* with Jacques Becker's *Casque d'Or*. The theater had a policy of no policy. We thought of it as our living room, playing movies *we* wanted to see. For two days and nights, ignoring Hollywood censors, the Maltese Falcon bedded with Hedy Lamarr—nostrils flaring and breasts quivering—and no one fainted! Unlike the "thematic" programming of most exhibitors—two musicals, two westerns or two social films—ours was fragmented. Opposites attracted, and our audiences—including Morris Dickstein, then a young Columbia student—found that exhilarating.

A Family Store

In a scene in *Annie Hall*, Woody Allen is standing on line with Diane Keaton inside the New Yorker (to see *The Sorrow and the Pity*) and is getting bent out of shape by a pontificating pseudo-intellectual in front of him. When the pseudo drops the name of Marshal McLuhan, Woody triumphantly produces the *real* McLuhan from behind a review stand in the lobby. McLuhan promptly denounces the puffed-up pseudo as knowing nothing about his work. "If only life were like this," Woody says to the camera.

In real life, the place was a family store. At lobby center stood an elderly man, eyes alert, hands slightly quivering—a sentry of sorts. That was my father, Joseph Tolpen. At the left, presiding over the candy stand, was my mother Bella. Posted nearby were framed photos of directors and current reviews by New York critics. Three red and gold banquettes from the erstwhile Roxy Theater flanked the area: "They look like the settees you'd find in a bordello, don't they?" Dan quipped to a reporter. The inner lobby door had a black-and-white Jules Feiffer mural of an audience glued to an invisible screen. Slipping through that rabbit hole, you entered the dreamworld of Movieland.

In its anonymous velvety dark, one had a sense of being alone, though right alongside sat a CUNY or New York University student, some director or would-be director, a star or has-been star, or any enthusiastic dyed-in-the-wool cinephile. Could be Zero Mostel, Vincent Canby, Jonas Mekas, Andy Warhol, Alfred Kazin, Robert Wilson, or a neighbor come out of the cold in winter or the heat in summer. In the dark, as they say, all cats are gray. All privy to what Jean-Paul Sartre called "the frenzy on the screen." Or what art historian Élie Faure described as "the commotion experienced on observing the relationship of a piece of black clothing to the grey wall of an inn." *Commotion*: collectively being moved by a moving image—each spectator viewing the same screen, each devising his or her own dream. Had Don Quixote attended a movie theater and seen *The Battleship Potemkin*, rather than burying his nose in books of chivalry, what phantasmagoria might have erupted.

Struggles and Obstacles of an Art House

Now for some shop talk. Dan would open each morning, select and order films, and make sure there was enough toilet paper in the bathrooms— movie theaters are forever running out of *that*. I, movie-house matron (required by law, with or without a reserved children's section), was properly licensed as such with a City Hall badge attesting with X-ray proof that I was tuberculosis-free (though never did I don a white uniform like ladies of yore). Mornings we screened films and at home chose intermission music—Vivaldi, Mozart, or Bach.

Even with no sweet tooth, it was hard to resist Bella's pantry of M-and-M's, Good 'N Plenty, goobers, chocolate raisins, Mounds, Baby Ruth, O'Henry—delectable names rolling off your tongue—all neatly arranged under sparkling glass. For those with a yen for something cold, she might offer a frozen Milky Way or Dixie cup. Neither Dan nor I are, or ever were, popcorn fans. Ugh, that smell, that ruminant munching. But howls of protest downed any notion of its elimination, and Bella insisted that hers was always fresh and *without* butter.

The orchestra of the New Yorker had a carved ceiling and red velvet walls graced by a sylvan Art Nouveau nymph. Our plush burgundy velvet seats, one thousand of them, were purchased for a dollar apiece from the old Roxy Theater when that glorious cinema palace came down. The New Yorker wound up with only nine hundred seats, the rest we stored. A cubby hole on the first floor beneath the stairwell served as manager's office, overseen by a photograph of Alfred Hitchcock, pudgy and dressed to the nines, alongside Dan and myself, in front of our marquee. A storage room next to the office held cleaning supplies and toilet paper. Our kids found the storage room spooky, a menagerie of stuff jumbled together—scraggly wet mops with witchy hair, shelves of bulbs staring out of empty sockets, and the odor of damp and detergent.

The stairway led to a balcony of 150 seats, a men's room, and a ladies' room. The male retreat became a favored haunt for cruising gays—a Columbia colleague of mine found those intersecting glances and titillating eyes irresistible. Certain movies were a gay draw—Mae West and Tallulah Bankhead made for a big turnout. Our friend, the artist Tomi Ungerer, hesitated before entering the men's room. A staunch Alsatian male, he was no prude himself and, in the long tradition of Roman, Renaissance, and Japanese erotic art, had depicted humans coupled and in threesomes, *doing it*—with updated prehensile machines. An audacious artist, his offbeat children's books have been admired here and abroad, and his paintings and drawings hang in the Louvre. But still.

A small staircase from the balcony led to the projection booth, on it a sign: *DO NOT ENTER. Entry Prohibited by Law.* Dominating the booth was a huge Century projector with a Peerless carbon arc lamphouse, framer, exhaust, and sound system. A carbon arc gave off a more intense light with a softer glow than today's lighting systems, but was prone to burn out during a reel (leaving the screen dark, with the soundtrack going) and, if the projectionist wasn't paying attention, elicited catcalls from the audience. No longer are those carbon arcs in use. A stack of empty reels alongside patiently awaited 20-minute changes. It takes a certain breed of man to be a projectionist, a person who doesn't mind sitting in a dim, airless cubicle under the constant whir of the machine and of carbon lights that provide light for the image. Sequestered from all eyes, cut off from any sense of nature and the outside world, his only audience contact is a small window to peer at the screen. From home he brings a brown paper bag sandwich and from the lobby vending machine gets a Coca Cola. A film is pulled into place inside a projector by pins entering and withdrawing from sprocket holes. The image on the screen may jump a bit, but a projectionist must not jiggle or doze. Ever alert to changing the reels, he dare not read or sleep. When Buster Keaton in *The Projectionist* dozes off in his booth for a few minutes, things run amok, and in an ensuing dream sequence, he jumps straight into the film on the screen.

Projectionists belong to Local 306. No one else, heaven forbid, ventures to touch the machines. Membership in the union, like taxi licenses, passes from father to son. One day, when our projectionist failed to appear for a morning screening, our assistant manager José López went up to the cubicle, threaded the machine, and got it going. The dilatory fellow showed up five minutes later and went into a fury, threatening to report us to Steve D'Inzillo, the tyrannical head of the union, a fellow with a handlebar mustache and a Gary Cooper gait, who sired a son at eighty-five. The theater opened at noon and closed at midnight, and three projectionists covered the 90-hour week. One of them, Melvin, liked to jerk off during Marilyn Monroe movies. I've forgotten the names of the other two.

Common wisdom holds that to start a new enterprise one must develop a business plan describing concept, felt need, competition, individuals involved, five years of financial projections, etcetera. We had none of those. Who knew what would happen in the next few months? It's not like being pregnant for nine months. But who's ever prepared for *that*?

Who's ever prepared for any new undertaking? Nothing is more hopeless than a scheme for merriment, declared Samuel Johnson. "Our aim at the New Yorker," said Dan, "is to present films that won't embarrass the eye or ear. If we make enough money to sustain the kind of programs we envision, fine, and if we get clobbered, maybe the next best thing is to go in for burlesque."

In the first six months, films long unseen were shown: Buster Keaton's *The Playhouse* and *The Boat*, Charlie Chaplin's *Easy Street*, *The Cure*, and *The Immigrant*, Max Reinhardt's *Midsummer Night's Dream*, Billy Wilder's *Sunset Boulevard*, and René Clément's *Forbidden Games*.

What a moment in cinema! The three B's: Buñuel, Bergman, Bresson (like Bach, Beethoven, and Brahms), all operating at full steam; with Fellini, Visconti, Pasolini, Godard, Truffaut, and Chabrol at our beckoning. That's what movies are and how they'll always be, we thought, awaiting the next with bated breath. *Going to the movies* in our *own* movie house was a fantasy come true: *seeing* the audience, being *part* of that audience, having *created* that audience.

In 1960 the New Yorker drew about seven hundred patrons on Friday nights and close to a thousand on Saturdays and Sundays. The theater grossed around $350,000 that year, which meant that we'd succeeded well enough financially to remain open: we had found an audience.

In the sixties, cinema and politics marched in tandem: post–Cold War, post–Joseph McCarthy, atomic bomb embedded in everyone's psyche (Dan's cousin built a fallout shelter on Long Island and a friend contemplated moving to Canada). The era witnessed three presidents with ambitious agendas and facing momentous events: John F. Kennedy's New Frontier, Peace Corps, Cuban Missile Crisis, and ultimate assassination; Lyndon Johnson's War on Poverty, the Tonkin Gulf Resolution leading to the Vietnam War, and the pivotal Tet offensive, with Richard Milhous Nixon reaping the aftermath and putting his own spin on things. The upheavals of the spring and summer of 1968 saw Martin Luther King's assassination in April, Robert F. Kennedy's in June, racial rioting in American cities, and the disastrous Democratic Convention in

Chicago, with police intervention. It was an era of massive civil rights struggles and, overshadowing all, the Vietnam War. We staged antiwar demonstrations in Central Park and a candlelight march on Broadway. A World War II veteran marched on crutches; our four-year-old daughter sat atop Dan's shoulders. "Keep her away from the flame," I begged. The country was burning; we were killing our heroes—John Kennedy, Robert Kennedy, and Martin Luther King Jr. Busloads of youths rode south for demonstrations and sit-ins while others rocked to the Beatles and the Rolling Stones, read Dr. Timothy Leary, dropped acid, became flower children, joined counterculture communes. A neighbor invited us to a New Age weekend at Esalen in Big Sur, California, to take the baths and liberate our psyches. People guffawed at seditious Lenny Bruce, read Philip Roth's *Portnoy's Complaint* (whose mamela surpassed all others), and witnessed on television the racial battles in Detroit, Watts, Haight-Ashbury, and Washington, D.C. On arriving one morning at Columbia University, three subway stops away, to teach Latin American literature in Hamilton Hall, I found the building occupied, graffiti scrawled on its walls. The student demonstration had begun. But the SDS—Students for a Democratic Society—declared our New Yorker a "liberated zone."

I used to feel guilty about going to a screening first thing in the morning, while others hurried to office, factory, and school. What a way to start the day—grown-ups playing hookey. You enter the dark, only to emerge blinking an hour or so later into blinding glare, beeping horns, flesh-and-blood creatures bustling about. Now *that* was Reality—enough to give you the bends. But, said George Balanchine, non-reality is the real thing. And watching movies, nursing an infant in darkness, and greeting on-and-off-screen characters became ours. A merging of real and reel, actuality and illusion.

Down the aisle I'd glide, stealthy as a thief savoring loot in a prospective coffer, steps muffled by zigzag carpet lines as familiar now as the cracks on my bedroom ceiling. Darkness and theater aroma beckon, nymphs on the red velvet walls sway in their timeless dance, tiny exit lights glimmer like magic lanterns pinned against the dark. The screen billows in chaste whiteness—pre-movie shuffle of coats, handbags, and umbrellas; candy wrappers unfurl; glasses emerge as heads lean this way and that for the best sight line. Finally silence falls. Eyes roam the becalmed sea of a blank screen. Passengers await departure. House lights go off. Credits go on. We sail forth into dreams. I'm my 10-year-old tap dancer self in blue satin bra and skinny shorts with silver sequins à la Ginger Rogers in *The Gay Divorcee*. I'm Charlie Chaplin tucking into a boiled, scruffy shoe, carving it delicately like succulent chicken, twirling laces on my fork like spaghetti, and nibbling the nails of its soles like bones. I'm Katharine Hepburn sailing down river with Bogart in *The African Queen*, I'm the mother in Yasujiro Ozu's *Tokyo Story*, I'm Joan of Arc, I'm Nanook of the North, I'm King Kong! In Borges' tale *Nadie Hubo en El*, Shakespeare is in search of Shakespeare.

What is a movie? Mere celluloid ribbon some 12,000 feet long, passing before our eyes at twenty-four frames per second, at which speed, says Jean-Luc Godard, cinema discloses truth. Each time we close our eyes, we lose sixty seconds of light. "Camera! Action!" shouts the director. Viewfinder composes shot, camera moves in. Yet a shot in the end hinges on the flick of a wrist, and film on persistence of vision. You have a story, chronological or not, and perhaps a notice that characters and events are not based on actual ones. But, insists the director Pedro Almodóvar, everything that isn't autobiographical is plagiarism. For where does a story come from? Take Dickens, Tolstoy, Bellow, or Roth: their characters are not some abstract concoction but a version of their author—plus a leap into imagination. No need to read Bellow's biography, just read his novels. Art is in the details, and a good story overshadows a good fact. But film is not just a story—neither Dreyer nor Sternberg dwelt on plots. *Historia* encompasses story *and* history, and in life's free market, fact and fiction interchange. Readers and moviegoers yield to dreams, daydreams, and fantasies, as do authors to make-believe characters. Henry James, attending a dinner party, would notoriously snatch the first line or two of a situation or piece of gossip from his dining partner, then sign off and take over from there. Give him the *donnée* and away he went.

I'm writing about an actual place with actual people. But memory, with its ways, fashions unreliable narrators, prey to blurring, distortion, hindsight, and regret. As one remembers, disremembers, and recollects, images and scenes bleed through as palimpsest messages. Phantom faces rise to the surface like the names of the deceased in a dwindling Rolodex whose cards I haven't the heart to remove. Images flash through the turnstile of my mind, not necessarily in chronological order. Kaleidoscopic movie plots juggle with crossover characters: "What are you doing here?" Peter Lorre demands of Marilyn Monroe. "Eat your spinach!" Popeye the Sailor Man tells Tarzan. Frames get reshuffled, spliced, distilled, transformed, edited out. Two films run simultaneously in my revival house of memory. In one, I'm in my mother's house, in another in a movie house; in one, I'm a Girl Scout learning the art of knots, in another making love. Superimposed on a projected film, another mentally unspools. "Film, unlike the novel or drama, or ballet or opera, is not a metaphor for reality or a distillation of reality, but rather like a city, or a battle operation, in an incessant barter and quarrel and romance with reality," said Robert Warshow. Tell me a story. Tell me a history. Tell me a movie. Tell it slant, said Emily Dickinson.

What is my subject? Call it persistence of vision: time, place, our personal lives all intertwined. Moment and milieu are stitched together like a patchwork, we part of that pattern. My father would sing a Yiddish song: *vas is gevein is gevein is nicht du*—what was is not what is. Over and over he sang it as we walked in the park, as he whittled a design on a young branch, or wove in and out of the rooms of our apartment. Its imprint was there when we got home—as is the New Yorker.

The theater became an Animator—a cinema mecca, Jules Feiffer called it. One picture bestirred another, one moviegoer another. "There's nothing out there to see!" some may grumble nowadays. "Oh yeah?" Jimmy Durante might say. Movies, a hundred years young, have a sturdy past—from Méliès' magic lantern, the Lumière Brothers, F. W. Murnau, Fritz Lang, D. W. Griffith, Josef von Sternberg, to Orson Welles. Who can resist a retrospective of Roberto Rossellini, Jean Renoir, or Yasujiro

Ozu? Or ignore the Taiwan or Korean cinema, or Zhang Yimou? Or thrill to discovering a new director from Senegal, Mexico, or Turkey? Who can resist sitting in a theater, sharing a *frisson* with others? Who can resist getting out of the house and getting *out* of oneself?

Where to begin? Where to end? Has any history an absolute beginning or end? When is that *punto final*? On concluding *Don Quijote*, Cervantes wrote *he escrito. I have written.* That's it. But literature is news that stays news. And our lives, like a horse's rein or rubber-band ball, go on and on, each event, each moment acting upon the next, and being acted upon. The day before giving birth to me, my mother went to the movies and saw a revival of *Dr. Jekyll and Mr. Hyde* with John Barrymore. Did that *commotion* bestir the next? At her death in 1978, I sat down and wrote a book about her, calling it simply *A Book About My Mother*. Were our common cells while I gestated preparing for that? Does an ending reside in its beginning, beginning foreshadowing end? Rubble often makes the best building material, goes a Palestinian saying. Did the New Yorker seed the way for our Cinema Studio in 1977, the Lincoln Plaza Cinemas in 1981, and the Metro in 1982? Looking backward, this is my take on that original era.

Obtaining "product," to use exhibitor lingo, was an ongoing struggle. Our guest books clearly indicated that patrons weren't just interested in plots. A burgeoning movie culture thirsted to see everything from *Intolerance* to *Singin' in the Rain*. Disappointments began when hunting down prints. Aging ones from the thirties and early forties, from *Scarface* to *The Big Sleep*, were dropping out of circulation. Dan and Pauline Kael, who programmed and ran a prestigious twin cinema in Berkeley, phoned each other weekly, tagging the whereabouts of prints that studios denied having. She told Dan about a print of *Sunset Boulevard* sitting in a Texas depot. Dan confronted Paramount and subsequently booked it. It was one of the more successful runs at the New Yorker. As for new films, distributors were understandably leery of booking what represented an investment of thousands of dollars into an untried location, a place with no track record. Better wait until a spot opened up in one of the mid-town theaters. Most upsetting was the crass, callous, short-sighted commercialism of the major companies, or of the TV crowd, such as MCA, who'd bought the rights to old movies. Even when we wanted to rent a picture, pay for it, and pay to have prints made, they looked at Dan as if he was some kind of nut—too much trouble, not a million dollar mainstream deal. Movies were just merchandise—not art.

Poor exhibition practices were rampant. Screens ought not to be programmed by those who know little about movies, yet most exhibitors never saw what they showed. Moreover, cinema is a spectacle and all elements count. Despite good programming, if the air-conditioning breaks down or projector bulbs go dim, what about the audience? A theater cannot be run by absentee management. Dan was concerned with every detail, minded the store seven days and nights of the week, and set up a cot in a small room adjoining the projection booth. Some nights, the children would ask: "When is Daddy coming home?"

Matinees

What goes on in a movie house before its doors open? The manager will arrive at around ten, turn on all the electricity, including house lights. He checks if the place has been properly cleaned during the night, that bathrooms have sufficient towels and flushers all work, that show-time recordings are current, and that the previous day's receipts have been dropped off by the night manager into the chute at the Hanover Bank on Broadway and 95th Street. By now, the cashier and usher will have arrived. The usher opens both exit doors to see that alleys are clean and front sidewalk swept. Once the manager verifies that the cashier has proper change—singles, quarters, dimes and nickels, and a $200 bank—he retrieves calls left on the tape, orders supplies, and speaks to distributors. At about 11:30 the projectionist appears, threads up the film, studies the time schedule (for the night manager may have made certain changes), and checks for an ample supply of carbon arcs to clamp inside the projector and ignite the film on the screen (some may have burnt out), and exciter lamps to control sound. At around 11:45, moviegoers begin lining up. The manager will remain for a while with the cashier to see that the first show runs smoothly and to answer patrons' questions.

Our manager's office was the lost-and-found. Though small in space, large was its bounty. Umbrellas and eyeglasses, and more umbrellas and eyeglasses, orphaned gloves and earrings, dentures, scarves and hats, a diaphragm in a discreet ivory case, paperback books—mysteries and best sellers—and an offbeat manual, *Sayings of the Ayatollah Khomeini*, which gave precise instructions to the Shiite faithful on how to wash and pray, which way to face when voiding, what to do when someone hurts your camels, and a stern admonition: "If a man during fasting period masturbates and brings himself to ejaculation, that fast has been broken." And further down: "Clapping one's hands or jumping during a prayer makes it null and void."

Who goes to the movies early in the day? We had unemployed actors, a cop/part-time opera singer from Brooklyn, a farmer from upstate New York, a New Jersey architect between jobs, a blind man from our block, elderly retirees, blue-haired women living on fixed incomes, not to mention the Belgian from Great Neck who left home each morning with dispatch case and gray flannel suit, giving his wife the impression that he had a full-time job, even inventing office tales and handing her a "paycheck" each Friday, drawn from a bank account set up by his rich parents—wife never suspicious. Every once in a while, he and Dan would link up at the Lyric or some other 42nd Street fleabag movie house, for a Melville, Walsh, Franju, or Preminger.

My earliest exposure to movies was at matinees when I was maybe five or six—well, not quite. There was of course that evening before giving birth, when my mother watched *Dr. Jekyll and Mr. Hyde* and sat enthralled as a benign doctor turned into a hideous creature with apish features, canine teeth, hirsute arms and hands. Wielding a stick, the monster ran amok, leaped on desks, hurled vases at pursuers until, breathing his last, he reverted from Hyde to Jekyll. Women pregnant with their firstborn notoriously fantasize giving birth to a monster with six fingers, one eye, and who knows what else? Small wonder that Jekyll and Hyde induced my mother's first labor—a rapid one. But Jekyll and Hyde didn't trigger nightmares in me, though the fleeting image of a phantom attic woman in *Jane Eyre* produced a pounding headache. *The Good Earth* is the first film plot I can recall. Based on Pearl Buck's novel (never read), it tells of Chinese peasants (Luise Rainer and Paul Muni) devoted to their land and suddenly besieged by a swarm of locusts. I felt sorry for those poor people, and lucky that we had no such plague on Pelham Parkway, and wondered how the forces of Nature could be your enemy. Subsequent university courses like "Man Against Nature, Man Against Man" made me wonder about that even more. *The Good Earth* became a prelude to Hitchcock's *The Birds*.

At the RKO Pelham in the Bronx, we kids got our money's worth (twenty-five cents) with newsreels (the *March of Time*), cartoons of Felix the Cat, Popeye the Sailor Man, or Betty Boop (sometimes referred to as Petty Poop), a chapter in the adventure serials of Flash Gordon, Dick Tracy, or Tarzan, plus a double feature—western, thriller, melodrama, comedy, or musical. No air-conditioning but the air got cooled by a fan, and so overheated were we by Errol Flynn, Tyrone Power, Clark Gable, so levitated by Fred Astaire, so besotted by Ann Sheridan and Linda Darnell, and so overwhelmed by Martha Raye's bosom (our own little buds mere polka dots), that no cooling system could have reduced our bodily thermostat.

Every Saturday, in bobby socks and saddle shoes, toting a brown paper bag lunch (often a sandwich from Friday night's chicken dinner—matzoh balls not included), we headed for the matinee, quivering when the identifying logo of the RKO tower and the opening notes of Beethoven's Fifth came on, or when MGM's roaring lion cast his head aside and gave way to a moony expression. Nothing mesmerized us like *going to the movies* for *moving pictures.* Something we did *without* parents—willingly being kidnapped. Once the movie was over, we stayed to see the beginning again, and maybe the whole thing. I discovered that you could see something a *second* time, and it would be better. The films of the thirties and early forties seeded a sense of genre: screwball comedies (*Mr. Deeds Goes to Town*), burlesque (Marx Brothers), dance-and-vaudeville (Astaire, Rogers, and the Ziegfeld Follies), crime and gangster films (Jimmy Cagney in *Public Enemy*, George Raft in *Scarface*, Paul Muni in *I Am a Fugitive from a Chain Gang*, and Edgar G. Robinson in *Little Caesar*—"Mother of God, is this the end of Rico?"). Life was not all one long Busby Berkeley spectacle. There were guys who did bad things, yet you *cared* about them. "The gangster is what we want to be and what we are afraid we may become," said Robert Warshow.

I began leading the lives of Katharine Hepburn, Ida Lupino, Joan Crawford, and Barbara Stanwyck, all of whom won out over Alice Faye. I envisioned myself as a Rosalind Russell career girl. Flat-chested me was wowed by buxom Lana Turner and Ann Sheridan (the "Oomph" girl), and I took a fancy to Gene Tierney's overbite and Bette Davis's mesmerizing eyes. Myrna Loy, William Powell, and Cary Grant offered a nascent hint of irony; Dick Powell, Nelson Eddy, Jeanette McDonald, and Tyrone Power one of kitsch; Al Jolson and Eddy Cantor, a pinch of schmaltz. Child actors Jane Withers, Roddy McDowell, and goody-goody Shirley Temple left me cold—on my report card, I didn't mind pairing an A for academic achievement with a C in conduct. Nor did my mother faint when summoned by the teacher to discuss my chatty ways. If I had a runny nose, she advised: "Stay home from school—you'll be a teacher a day later." In bed, I found the maroon leather-bound *Book of Knowledge* with its Book of Wonder and Book of Golden Deeds to be healing companions. Yet hardly ever did I miss a day of school and never a Saturday at the movies.

Those Saturday matinees provided a thrifty babysitting arrangement. A matron in starched white uniform and sturdy white shoes patrolled the aisles, less our guardian than protection for grownups against rowdy boys with spitballs and peashooters. We emerged on a cloud into the dusk, giddy and overdosed on pistol-packing men and slinky-gowned women (always accompanied, it seemed, by men in jaunty blazers, ascots, and top hats), gliding in and out of salons, cocktails in hand. In our house, a bottle of brandy lasted a year, appearing for colds and ritual occasions; and the wine shared with guests came from grapes stomped in the bathtub (the very tub where every few years my mother refreshed our goose-down pillows). On Saturday night we listened to the Top Ten popular songs on "Your Hit Parade." A string of first lines ran through my head. I can still sing *Boohoo, you got me crying for you-hoo* or *Tippy-tippy-tin, tippy-tin,* or *Chatanooga Choo-Choo*. And it doesn't take much for me to break into a tap dance. On Sundays, *Let's Pretend* radio fairy tales replaced Hollywood glamour, but the radio was just a little box and the movies a grand screen. With the radio you were *at home,* vulnerable to Brush your teeth, Run a bath, Bring in the milk (delivered daily), Throw out the garbage, Get that cockroach! At the movies we were liberated of Demand, Time, and Season. We would enter at glaring daylight and emerge into chiaroscuro twilight or the dark of a winter night. On entering, our eyes needed time to adjust to that dim hall with maroon walls. The street might be cold, but the movie house was nice and warm. Came summer, at a small outdoor theater on White Plains Road with wooden benches, we saw Charlie Chaplin, Fatty Arbuckle, Harry Langdon, Harold Lloyd, and assorted pie-throwers doing their stuff. It was there that I first laid eyes on Ninotchka—Garbo, pale, long-necked, ethereal—and asked my mother to tweeze my eyebrows. Decades later, from the velvet Roxy seats at the New Yorker, I greeted them all like long-lost relatives.

Brief Encounter

"How did you meet?" a new friend may ask. I draw a deep breath, having told and retold this tale countless times. Thank goodness, Dan isn't present for the recitation. Early one summer evening in 1949, walking along the Bronx River and headed for Howard Johnson with my friend Roslyn Rosenbaum, I crossed paths with Ernie Zimmerman, a high school chum accompanied by *his* friend. Like several of my "red" schoolmates, Ernie was a member of the Young Communist League, and lived in the

Amalgamated Housing Cooperative, popularly known as the "Coops" on Allerton Avenue in the Bronx. He sold the *Daily Worker* at our Christopher Columbus High School, and distributed pamphlets studded with Marxist-Leninist names and passwords: ruling class, dictatorship of the proletariat, Togliatti, Thorez, the New Masses. His brother Sol had fought in the Spanish Civil War with the Abraham Lincoln Brigade, and passed on to us songs like "Viva la Quinta Brigada." Well, Ernie introduced us to Dan and I introduced them to Roslyn and off we went our opposite ways. The next morning, Dan phoned.

Yes, we met by accident. As for choice, who remembers which of Howard Johnson's twenty-eight flavors I chose that day. Ortega y Gasset, following Stendhal, describes that first encounter as "crystallization." Something clicked: Dan's voice, his prominent chin and steady gaze, his bushy eyebrows, his passion for books and classical music. I fell in love and have lived over half my life with that Other.

A translator tinkers in words. *Adios*, said when crossing paths with a person without pausing to chat, compresses hello and goodbye. Hail-to-you and God-be-with-you merged thereby like the tissue-thin arrival/departure sides of a railroad schedule. Flaubert in a letter to Louise Colet remarked that never did he see a cradle without envisioning a grave. Interrogations, with like duality, show an inverted question mark at the outset of a sentence and an upright one at the end. A child's "Why?" is invariably followed by another Why. Exclamations, as well, have that inverted mark preparatory to what E. M. Forster called the "credible surprise." What if Dan and I hadn't crossed paths that particular evening, at that particular hour? *Beshert*, they say in Yiddish, foreordained—or just plain luck. What if my friend Roslyn and I had taken the Pelham Parkway bus to Howard Johnson and never crossed paths with Ernie and Dan? What if a train is missed and one dismounts at the wrong station, as happens often in dreams? What if one brushes past someone with whom a life may be spent? What if one doesn't run into someone it might be good to know, like Henry Rosenberg? What if an opportunity is not seized?

People want to know how a story begins and ends. If I were writing a novel, would it begin in 1949 when Dan and I met? Or in 1950 when we married? Or with our felicitous encounter with Henry Rosenberg in 1960? "A story has no beginning or end: one arbitrarily chooses that moment of experience from which to look back or from which to look ahead," said Graham Greene. And Henri Bergson: "A melody is composed of single notes which follow each other in sequence. A melody has no dimension in time, because the first note is made an element of the melody only because it stands in definite relation to all other notes down to the last. Hence, the last note, which may not be played for some time, is yet always present in the first note as a melody-creating element. The last note completes the melody only because we hear the first note in it." Our New Yorker was the beginning of a love affair, a trial run, running time unknown. If one doesn't take risks, nothing happens.

A date for Dan and me meant going to the movies. In the dark of a theater, we held hands, watched Alfred Hitchcock's *The Lady Vanishes*, Jean Renoir's *The Rules of the Game*, or Fellini's *La Strada*. At home, we held hands and read André Gide's *The Counterfeiters*, James Joyce's *The Dubliners*, and Franz Kafka's *Metamorphosis*. In 1950 we moved into our first apartment in a row house in Sunnyside, Queens. Apartments then as now were hard to find. Ours got pegged by my cousin while we were honeymooning in New Smyrna, Florida, on a plantation draped in Spanish moss. Our neighbors were a Bulgarian émigré couple. Mr. Bukowski, tall, mustached, and dignified, worked for Voice of America, and pale, childless Mrs. Bukowski, ever pining for her homeland, taught me how to make moussaka. Dan and I would walk across the 59th Street Bridge to the Beverly Theater and with hero sandwich in hand watch British movies. On 42nd Street, between Seventh and Eighth Avenues, there were perhaps a dozen grungy movie houses, where we saw old comedies, westerns, newsreels, and even "art movies." It was a way of catching up with the thirties and forties. At East Side theaters like the Paris, the Sutton, and the Normandie we saw first runs, devouring every Ingmar Bergman close-up and flashback. Bergman's melancholy and theatricality excited our imagination as Godard's free-wheelingness would in the '60s. At the Sutton we saw *Hiroshima Mon Amour*, at the Normandie *Symphonie Pastoral*, at the Little Carnegie *Last Year at Marienbad*, at the Paris *Devil in the Flesh* and *Children of Paradise*. And at the Thalia on 95th Street off Broadway, we rediscovered *Shoeshine, Paisan, Open City*, and whatever we could. In time, they would all be revived at the New Yorker.

Some of our early education had taken place at the Stanley Theater on Irving Place, which showed classic Russian cinema. Pudovkin, Dovzhenko, and Eisenstein relayed urgent news of the Bolshevik Revolution. There we saw Grigori Chukrai's *Ballad of a Soldier* and Mikhail Kalatozov's *The Cranes are Flying*. An American couple, loyal members of the Communist Party, had been awarded an exclusive license on Russian films and distributed them under the Artkino banner. At the expiration of their lease, they moved uptown to 43rd Street and Eighth Avenue. When that theater got triplexed into a male porno house, the films ran at the 55th Street Playhouse on Seventh Avenue, until that too met its porno fate.

As a book editor at Gold Medal Books, Dan was earning $55 a week while I, cultural editor of *El Diario de Nueva York*, brought home $25. Meager though the salary, it was my first and possibly best job. The only *gringa* on the staff, I got to do everything from writing an entire cultural page on *any* subject I chose—from José Martí, Pablo Neruda, and Federico García Lorca—to soliciting and writing advertising copy for language schools, serving as liaison with the New York City Board of Education in its nascent bilingual program for that early wave of Puerto Rican migration, informing recent urban dwellers that the rural habit of tossing garbage out the window didn't apply in New York City. *El Diario* got its money's worth, and I got mine. From a Puerto Rican patriot, I learned about the struggle for autonomy of PIP (Puerto Rican Independent Party), I learned about activism. One day this sad-eyed reporter, abandoning politics, published a poem dedicated to *La Mujer en el Vestido Verde*, referring to my Kelly-green dress, self-sewn shantung with cap sleeves and cut on the bias.

Our first flat had a dumbwaiter and white enamel stove with side-by-side ovens. At a Connecticut country fair, we purchased a white rabbit and named him Gig. Bunny could make no graceless move but, unable to resist gnawing on the books we read to each other and unresponsive to saltpeter purchased at Macy's Pet Department, the horny fellow would chew his way out of the cage Dan had built and mount me in the middle of the night. I didn't keep kosher as my parents did, but when *milechdik* and *fleishedic* (dairy and meat) rubbed against each other, I envisioned an earthquake. We bought succulent lamb breasts at nineteen cents a pound, Penguin paperbacks for a quarter or thirty-five cents, a Chilean wine for three bucks, and a ticket to the Beverly for less than a dollar. We managed.

Walking to Work

We've been Upper West Siders since the late fifties—when it "wasn't the place to be." Bums loitered a block away from canopied West End Avenue buildings with white-gloved doormen. Hookers, eyes heavily kohled, posted themselves quite aptly at Party Cake Bakery before a display of rugelach and hamantasch to turn a trick with passing drivers ("Wanna have a party?"); heroin addicts transacted from scruffy side-street brownstones; and roosters engaged in cockfights on those sooty stoops. Upper East Side mothers refused to allow their darlings to cross town to play with classmates on the wrong side of the tracks, though they themselves might taxi over to Daisy the Dressmaker on Amsterdam Avenue, or to Murray's Sturgeon Shop (still there) for an appetizing fix of schmaltz herring or half-a-pound of Nova, sliced thin.

Our first Manhattan flat was in a brownstone on 90th Street between West End Avenue and Riverside Drive. Its second-storey rear window overlooked not some grisly Hitchcock murder scene but the Greek Orthodox Church on 91st Street and West End Avenue. Gregorian chants accompanied meals and served as metronome to the two-cents-per-word tapping on my portable Remington. On the floor above lived the sociologist Nathan Glazer, co-author with David Riesman of the *The Lonely*

Crowd. In 1961 we moved down the block to our current Riverside Drive apartment, where our third daughter Sarah was born.

The neighborhood felt like a village. At Benny's corner luncheonette, I'd pause with my stroller for a hot coffee plus a fresh orange juice for our daughter. Everyone there wanted to chat or just exchange a few words with acquaintances. Benny, in white sailor cap, was expert in moving your car to the other side of the street to avoid a parking ticket while you were at work. And he didn't mind holding my ground tenderloin and lamb chops in his refrigerator should Joe Rosen the butcher close before I returned from Columbia, teaching *Axolotle,* Julio Cortázar's tale of a man so entranced by the *quietude* of tiny lizards in an antequarium that ultimately he metamorphoses into one. In the rush of motherhood, movies, and shuffling of classes, how I envied that quietude. Benny became my unofficial bank (no waiting on line), cashing my monthly check and pitching in if I ran short at Daitch's Supermarket. Monday morning, spotting me down the block, he'd reach into his pocket or cash register and have the precise amount ready by the time I came through the door. But early in the day, receipts being scant, he'd vanish through a trap door to his basement cache, popping up a moment later, à la jack-in-the-box, with crisp green bills.

At the Tiptoe Inn, hefty Zero Mostel might drop in after his show (Eugene Ionesco's *The Rhinoceros*) for blintzes and sour cream. At Steinberg's Cafeteria, Isaac Bashevis Singer debated with cronies while contentedly downing rice pudding and sipping tea in a glass through a lump of sugar. At Daniel's Cigars, Dan procured his Havanas under the table from the eponymous proprietor. And at Mike's Fish Store on Broadway and 91st Street, my mother got whitefish, pike, and live carp for Friday's gefilte fish, shielding the children from the fatal beheadings. Columbus Avenue boasted a glazier, locksmith, tarot card readers, storefront Pentecostal church with window painted in reds, greens, and yellows, and botánicas with little wooden saints and herbal cures for rheumatism, indigestion, romantic obstacles, and malevolent spirits. Throughout the sixties, many a once pink side-street brownstone, now sooty, got marked with a big white cross for demolition—like that under the death head on a bottle of poison. Some windows were blocked with metal plates, as if they were blind, while others were simply gaping holes. One day, a sign on Broadway Hardware read: I'VE BEEN DISPLACED. Banana Republic became its replacement—instead of hammer or broom, one could now outfit oneself in Safari gear. Coach Handbags and Victoria's Secret would follow in time. How many bras does a woman need? Dan asks.

Many friends lived nearby: Judy and Jules Feiffer, whose "Sick, Sick, Sick" cartoons appeared in the *Village Voice*, were a block away; Carol and Jack Gelber, who read us an early version of *The Connection*, lived on 95th and West End Avenue; editors Linda and Aaron Asher were in the Belnord on 86th and Broadway, as were Arlene and Ned Polsky, author of *Hustlers, Beats, and Others*, a classic work on pool rooms. On 101st Street and West End Avenue resided *Commentary Magazine* editor Norman Podhoretz, soon to publish *Making It*, a blunt look at power that raised many hackles; and nearby were Murray Kempton (columnist for the *New York Post*), novelist Chandler Brossard, social critic David Bazelon, psychologist Leslie Farber, Madelaine and Pete Martin (with whom we later opened the New Yorker Bookstore). At the Podhoretz's, Les's brother Manny, the curmudgeon critic, might show up with Patricia Patterson, his wife-to-be, and with Nicholas Ray, cult figure of the French New Wave, much admired by Manny. New York intellectuals, they engaged in heady discussions into the night.

Our daughters attended local Riverside Church and Montessori nursery schools, then P.S. 166 on 89th Street opposite the Clarement Stables, one of the few places in the city to offer a whiff of horse manure, a smell I happen to relish. Saturdays they hung out at the candy stand with their grandmother—Bella to them. From an early age, they mimicked Charlie Chaplin's walk, Mae West's "Beulah, peel me a grape," and Groucho Marx's "I could dance till the cows come home, but on second thought would rather dance with the cows when they come home." Or a customer in W. C. Field's *The Pharmacist* who, asked if he wants to take a postage stamp with him or have it delivered, replies: "D'ya think I'm gonna lug *that* home?" They mimicked Gene Kelly *Singin' in the Rain* and dressed up like Carmen Miranda in *The Gang's All Here*, flamboyant tutti-frutti hat drooling with bananas that magically turned into a bright yellow pyramid sprouting from her head. On Columbus Day 1961, escaping my mother's eyes, they watched *Freaks*, without freaking out. In a final scene, the freaks take revenge on a beautiful trapeze artist (played by Olga Baclanova) and her lover, who've tried to kill a midget for his fortune, crawling after her with knives and turning her into another freak; yet those macabre images struck them as less spooky than mysterious sounds heard at night from a closet with its door slightly ajar. In broody moments, I sometimes worried about the effect Movieland might have on their young lives. Did they see it as a cartoon bubble, a fantasy overshadowing their own reality?

Broadway was a 24-hour street, where an insomniac could buy a bagel or a kiwi at any time of day. Like New York harbor, where confluent fresh and ocean waters yield myriad plants, fish, and birds, Broadway street life was highly diverse. In 1960, émigrés from Hitler's devastation relaxed on Riverside Drive benches while Orthodox Jews with sidelocks, black sateen frock coats, broad-brimmed hats, and *tallis* strolled arm-in-arm along the Drive. The fringes of the shawl or *tallis*, my father told me, represent the 368 *mitzvahs* or good deeds man may accomplish. But what good deed, I wondered, could compensate for Hitler? Nearly half a century later, on Succoth, Passover, or Sabbath, one sees like figures, hurrying to or from a *minyan* in a brownstone basement synagogue, then slowly walking back, followed now perhaps by a Latina mother, baby snuggled to her breast. And if streets were named after trees, ours might well be Linden. Came spring, my mother's elderly Polish neighbor, a refugee who took in a well-bred boarder to make ends meet, would emerge with her basket to collect its fragrant blossoms for tea.

Our city kids mounted the Civil War cannons at the Soldiers' and Sailors' Monument, straddled the lions on the steps of the 42nd Street New York Public Library, embraced the totem pole at the Museum of the American Indian on Broadway and 155th Street, patted the dinosaur in the Museum of Natural History opposite Central Park, gazed at the stars in the Planetarium, roamed the Cloisters of Fort Tryon Park. Manhattan was their Disneyland.

Grouted into a supporting column of our present kitchen (which I hope never to leave) are twelve ancient Persian tiles, blue and viridian. In our back closet-cum-attic hang mini-skirts, long skirts, Marimeko smocks sewn for daughters to be passed on in time, and a flowered black challis dress worn by my mother the year she died. It holds her smell and I can't imagine never smelling her again. On Pelham Parkway in the Bronx, where I grew up, moving yielded reward. A new apartment brought a month's concession (those extra $54 were not, as they said, chopped liver), a fresh coat of paint, crisp window-shades, striped awnings, and a squeaky new linoleum. My family—non-movers—stayed put at 2045 Holland Avenue.

Dan's mother, unlike mine, underwent an almost annual itch, moving seemingly a source of energy and renewal. From perch to perch she flitted, migratory bird rearranging her nest with starched dotted Swiss curtains in the kitchen and organdy in the bedroom. Dan may have inherited that gene. In 1973, when I mourned the sale of the New Yorker, he replied: "Had we not sold that, there would never have been a Cinema Studio, a Metro, or a Lincoln Plaza." Each theater begat the next—but it took a while to forgive him.

One day, Rabbi Zusya, the Hasidic leader of Hanipol, began studying the Talmud. His disciples, noticing him the next still dwelling on that first page, assumed he'd stumbled on a difficult passage. Though astounded several days later at finding the master still engrossed in that very same place, they dared not query him. At last, one summoned the courage and asked why he did not proceed. The reply: "I feel so good here, why go elsewhere?"

Our *here* is the westernmost rim of Manhattan. A blustery wind charges up and down 90th Street, piercing eyes and ears and sticking nostrils together. Pounding fists thump at our panes, and air seeps in beneath the cracks in the window. Certain evenings, before windows got double-glazed, guests might sit bundled up in winter coats. On the frosty glass, our daughters exhaled their breath and learned to write their names. Boris, our doorman from tropical Santo Domingo, adores the cold and icy wind. But on a gusty day, awaiting the No. 5 bus on Riverside Drive (Manhattan's most beautiful trajectory, winding from the Cloisters to Washington Square), I cling to the lamppost lest like Mary Poppins I be blown away or tossed about like a thrashing leaf.

The days and seasons unfold on my thirteen-storey screen. On Riverside Drive one is ever aware of Manhattan being an island. Certain days you can smell the river. Certain days you're fogged in. Each morning from my window seat, over grapefruit and coffee, I observe the sky of the day: a pale firmament inscribed by gulls and framed by cumulus clouds, images ever moving. Never is the sky empty, said Walt Whitman.

Vague ships glide beneath the George Washington Bridge five miles north. A yellow barge drops anchor, and a freighter bearing coal and oil plies upriver—an island once purchased by the Dutch from the Algonquin Indians for $24, and still engaged in commerce. The playground, as yet unoccupied, will soon bustle with kids on the swings and monkey bars where our own once played. A baby carriage on the gleaming steps of the Soldiers' and Sailors' Monument evokes the massacre scene in Sergei Eisenstein's *Battleship Potemkin* in which a carriage precariously rolls down the Odessa Steppes—anxiously I search for the mother. Fiery sunset demands closing the shutters until that borderline hour of twilight when day and night and river and sky merge. Silhouetted trees fade away, landscape dissolves into a nocturnal screen. The Soldiers' and Sailors' Monument looms phantom-white against an inky sky.

In spring, metallic shards splice the Hudson. Cherry trees flush the hills, pregnant women blossom, and a cluster of Japanese gather beneath its branches to pay obeisance. In autumn, russet and gold festoon the trees as observant Jews gather at the riverbanks to cast away their sins. Snow simplifies all. Trees, slopes, river, parked cars, everything turns white. Miniature Breughel-like figures dash out like zealots to baptize the chaste fleecy slopes, and the eternal Hudson slogs along under bluish-white floes, bringing to mind D. W. Griffith's *Way Down East* and Lillian Gish stranded on a floating sheet of ice. The seasons unfold: *Early Spring, Late Spring, The End of Summer, An Autumn Afternoon.* Quintessential Ozu.

Cinephiles

In the early sixties a group of cinephiles would gather at our place to discuss starting a Filmmakers Cooperative for distribution of independent cinema. Among them were Jonas and Adolfas Mekas, George N. Fenin, Bill Everson, Herman G. Weinberg, and Andrew Sarris. When Adolfas's *Hallelujah the Hills* opened at the New Yorker, audiences were ready for his liberated style. Jonas became a critic for *Film Culture* and the *Village Voice* and went on to distribute avant-garde films through the Anthology Film Archives. Everson and Fenin ran the Theodore Huff Society and on Sunday mornings at the theater showed rare and obscure American and British movies to a select group (Everson's living room was stacked with these prints). Weinberg, film critic for *Film Culture* and *MD* magazine, also subtitled foreign films. Sarris wrote for the *Village Voice.*

The theater became a hangout for film buffs from all walks of life: Columbia students Phillip Lopate and Morris Dickstein; critics Vincent Canby, Pauline Kael, Manny Farber, Richard Schickel, Eugene Archer, Andrew Sarris, Jonas Mekas, Parker Tyler, Stanley Kauffmann, Dwight Macdonald, and Susan Sontag. The first day Ms. Sontag showed up with her seven-year-old son in a cowboy outfit, she asked Dan for a press pass—and got it (the only one who ever did) and always she occupied the second row. Cinephiles tend to have their favorite spots as well as hours. I myself am an aisle-person; Phillip Lopate, a late-afternooner, as I recall, sat in the middle; Manny Farber hovered in back.

"The New Yorker myth," said Sarris, "was born not simply out of scholarly input, but because Dan initiated a dialogue with the audience. Dan believed an audience is always as intelligent as you want it to be. It was a lot of fun holding discussions in the lobby. It was kind of a salon. There was much excitement and enthusiasm." Peter Bogdanovich recounts how Dan was the first to petition Chaplin to have his films shown at the New Yorker. He and Dan came up with a trailer that said, "Would you like to see *Modern Times*, *City Lights*, *The Kid*?" and the audience broke into applause when they saw the titles—"If you do, please sign the book at the back of the theater." Chaplin was sent ten books full of signatures, and in 1964 they were re-released at the New Yorker.

Future film critic Jim Hoberman, then a high school student, took the subway from Fresh Meadows on weekends to see the Marx Brothers and "thirties" stuff. Photographers Richard Avedon and Diane Arbus became regulars (at one point Arbus asked Dan to put her in touch with Mae West to take her picture), and musical archivist Miles Kreuger came to record musicals. In those pre-video days, he was recording the soundtrack of the musicals on probably a portable reel-to-reel recorder, the only way a die-hard movie buff could then "own" a movie. Jules Feiffer caught up on the thirties and forties: "I was blown away by how Hollywood handled the Depression. High entertainment gave the audience a sense that they could survive—'We're in the money, we're in the money.' And the noir and sci-fi films mirrored the fear factor of the Cold War."

Bruce Goldstein, repertory program director of New York's Film Forum since 1986 and founder of the specialty distributor Rialto Pictures, in a note recalls going to the New Yorker when he was about sixteen. The movie was *Gold Diggers of 1933*, and he remembers being impressed by the hand-painted program notes outside:

> The theater was dark and dank, a mingling of smells that telegraphed "old theater" to me right away—a smell I grew to love. I recall the lighting fixtures: amber sconces that gave off as much light as a handful of fireflies. I remember people stumbling in the dark for their seats; I distinctly remember one man lighting a match to find empty seats.
>
> It may have been the first time I ever saw an old movie without commercials, and in 35mm, and uncut. I remember that particular movie

had lines like "stop looking at me with those bedroom eyes"—it was the first time I realized that even old movies were censored for TV in those days. But what I loved most about the experience was that the theater took me back to 1933. The New Yorker itself was like a time machine—no other theater, not even the Thalia, did that for me.

That first New Yorker experience had a profound impact on my life, for better or worse: my whole career has been devoted to getting better 35mm prints of classic films and I have made a genre out of "Pre-Code" movies, films made before the enforcement of the Hollywood production code—I was first made aware of this era with that screening of *Gold Diggers*.

Most of our audience were ordinary moviegoers wanting to dream and feel the breath of others. The theater served as a barometer to critical and popular taste and helped to shape the sensibilities of a new generation. The New York film scene in the sixties was indeed remarkably fertile. Cinema 16, founded by Amos Vogel and his wife Marcia in 1947, ran until 1963. At its height, it boasted 7,000 members. Its programming was eclectic. On Sunday mornings, one might see Flaherty, Grierson, and Cavalcanti along with a film on psychology and psychiatry, biology, chemistry, art appreciation, or literature. There I saw *Two Men and a Wardrobe* by Roman Polanski; there I saw John Cassavetes, Nagisa Oshima, Jacques Rivette, Alain Resnais, Man Ray, Stan Brakhage, Maya Deren, James Brougton, Kenneth Anger, Sidney Peterson, and Bruce Connor. Vogel kept meticulous notes on 3 x 5 index cards of every film he ever screened and catalogued them in a small room in their apartment in Greenwich Village. Over a Swiss fondue, often in the company of Eastern Europeans—filmmaker Ivan Passer, screenwriter Yvette Biró, novelist George Konrád—we'd discuss the state of filmmaking in Soviet-occupied Hungary, Czechoslovakia, and Poland. Despite censorship, important films were emerging. Vogel's subsequent *Film as a Subversive Art* insists that most of the images around us are worn-out, riddled with commercialism, and pernicious in their banality.

In 1963 Vogel and Richard Roud started the New York Film Festival at Lincoln Center. Relatively small, the festival offered no prizes but was intended to be a "festival of festivals." Roud, a Francophile, had gotten to know Henri Langlois during the 1950s while working for the British Film Institute, as well as the innovative New Wave directors, and he championed the films of Jean-Luc Godard, François Truffaut, Alain Resnais, Agnès Varda, Jacques Rivette, F. W. Fassbinder, Sergei Parajanov, and Dusan Makavejev, among others. As director of the New York Film Festival from 1969 till 1987, he kept in close touch with Dan and me, tipping us off to films that might be of interest to us for distribution. In 1963 we saw Alain Resnais's *Muriel*, Chris Marker's *Le Joli Mai*, and Luis Buñuel's *The Exterminating Angel*. In 1964 we saw Jean-Luc Godard's *A Woman is a Woman* and *Band of Outsiders*. There we saw Rainer Werner Fassbinder's *Merchant of Four Seasons*.

Sarris and Archer became evangelists of the *politique d'auteur*, formulated in 1954 by François Truffaut in *Cahiers du Cinéma*, a yellow-covered journal founded by the legendary critic André Bazin. Contributors were Jean-Luc Godard, Claude Chabrol, and Eric Rohmer, cineastes under thirty who launched the Nouvelle Vague on modest budgets without beautiful sets and costumes or high literary tone. The director/*auteur*'s personal vision was regarded as the core of a film, and cinema's mission was to represent the world from that personal vision. Chronological story mattered less: Godard claimed that he wanted to make films that had a beginning, a middle, and an end, but not necessarily in that order. Mise-en-scène superseded montage as a truer representation of continuity and respect for unity of space; and in-depth shots, with foreground and background in full view, were favored. Jean Renoir, Robert Bresson, Max Ophüls. Jacques Tati, Alfred Hitchcock, Howard Hawks, Orson Welles, and certain Hollywood B movie directors like Sam Fuller and Budd Boetticher fell into the *Cahiers* canon. Our audiences applauded the French New Wave: Godard's *Breathless*, Resnais's *Hiroshima Mon Amour*, Truffaut's *The 400 Blows* and *Jules and Jim*, Claude Chabrol's *Les Bonnes Femmes*, and Eric Rohmer's *Claire's Knee*. They were seeing something fresh—and I couldn't keep away.

Monday Nights: Special Series

Monday nights at movie theaters are typically slow. So we decided to start a film society. On April 18, 1960, and successive Monday evenings at 7:15 and 9:15, movies were shown by subscription or single admissions. Programs got plotted in a small room adjoining the projection booth by Dan and two young film buffs—Marshall Lewis and Rudi Franchi. Marshall had started a film society in Philadelphia (and later programmed the Bleecker Street Cinema), and Rudi ran the Abbey Film Society at Fordham University (subsequently becoming an authority in memorabilia, antiques, and movie posters). All had program notes written by aficionados and movie mavens such as Bill Everson on *The Golem*, Jonas Mekas on *Shor*, Eugene Archer on *Sabotage* and *The Little Match Girl*, Jules Feiffer on *Gold Diggers of 1933*, Terry Southern on *A Star is Born*, Robert Brustein on *Never Give a Sucker an Even Break*, Jack Gelber on *Foolish Wives*, Chandler Brossard on *Dead of Night*, and Harold Humes on *The Last Laugh* (in lieu of *writing* notes, "Doc" Humes personally delivered them in synch with the film), and Jack Kerouac on *Nosferatu*.

Arthur Kleiner accompanied five silent films on the piano: D. W. Griffith's *Intolerance*, Erich von Stroheim's *Greed*, Fritz Lang's *The Last Will of Dr. Mabuse* and *The Cabinet of Dr. Caligari*, and Carl Theodor Dreyer's *The Passion of Joan of Arc*. We bought a used Steinway for Kleiner, an émigré from pre-Hitler Austria, who was a full-time pianist at the Museum of Modern Art and also composed for George Balanchine and Agnes de Mille. He played musical scores for nearly seven hundred silent films, some of his own composition, adaptation, or arrangement: *The Birth of a Nation*, *The Cabinet of Dr. Caligari*, *Un chien andalou*, *Metropolis*, and *Battleship Potemkin*. After having finished the magnificent four-hour score of *Intolerance*, Mr. Kleiner's fingers were bleeding. We became good friends with this diminutive, courtly gentleman, and he escorted our daughter Emily to the Steinway Piano Company on West 58th Street to select her first piano while she was studying at the Mannes School of Music. That Baldwin spinet from the Steinway Piano Company followed her for decades from apartment to apartment and from state to state.

We began a Special Series of one-week bills. Bette Davis drew tribes from East Side, West Side, and all around the town. An Emil Jannings series included *Variety*, one of Marlene Dietrich's favorite films: a melodramatic tale about a trapeze duo, a cuckolded husband, a murder with impressionistic lighting, expressionist imagery, and exuberant camera work. Dietrich was still getting requests for prints of the film from directors all over the world, among them Orson Welles, Luchino Visconti, and Alain Resnais, whose heroine in *Last Year at Marienbad* appears swathed in feathers like Dietrich in Josef von Sternberg's *Devil is a Woman*. "The feathers were von Sternberg's idea," said Dietrich. "In the films we made after *The Blue Angel*, plots became less important, the decor more elaborate and the effects harder and more expensive to achieve. In *Devil*, our last film together, I was completely covered and draped by nets. The purpose was not only to make the surface beautiful, but to use the power of suggestion on the audience. Mae West used the same principle and kept her body covered. Sex was in the eyes and in the audience's imagination." Marlene should know: In *Shanghai Express*, she informs Clive Brook that "it took more than one man to change my name to Shanghai Lil."

When we announced a Mae West festival, calls came from around the country. The president of one club arrived with a gaggle of friends and phoned daily for audience reaction. Mae West was one lady who knew how to put herself together, strut her hips, and dish out repartee with a drawl. A fan, as a token of appreciation, gave us a list of some of her *bons mots* with an accompanying photo.

"Come up and see me some time when you have nothing to do and want someone to do it with."

"When I'm good, I'm very good—when I'm bad, I'm better."

"It's better to be looked over than overlooked."

"It's not the men in my life that count—it's the life in my men."

"Goodness, what lovely diamonds," someone remarks, and Mae answers, "Goodness had nothing to do with it, honey."

Diane Arbus, who attended the festival, received a commission from *Harper's Bazarre* to do photos of Miss West and Mae agreed. She dwelt in a house with a mirrored bathroom in Santa Monica, California, and saw very few people (life as Sex Queen certainly hadn't left her destitute—rumor had it that she had seven million in the bank, disproving the theory that only good girls win), and that's where Arbus did the shoot. Eighty-five-year-old Mae—undulating satin garments, sequin swirls, frothy accoutrement, and looking somewhat grotesque—all got published. Mae, less than pleased, registered her displeasure in a letter to Dan. Nonetheless, for several years after our Mae West Festival, she sent us Christmas cards, proper missives with Mary and Child.

The most successful film in our series was *Triumph of the Will*, which hadn't been shown in the United States for years. On the evening of June 27, 1960, a line formed around the theater, students from Columbia University eager to see that legendary film of the 1934 Nazi Party rally, shot in the Nuremberg Stadium by Leni Riefenstahl with unlimited funds. Hitler descends from the clouds, moves through the streets, and before seig-heiling multitudes, launches into his brainwashing tirades. There was such an overflow we had to hold an impromptu midnight screening. Isaac Bashevis Singer, who happened to be passing by with a young woman, unaware that it was the murderous Führer drawing crowds, beamed: "How wonderful to see people line up for culture and not for bread."

A Phone Call

One day, Dan received a call from Singer, who lived in the Belnord on Broadway and 86th Street, one of those fine courtyard buildings on the Upper West Side, constructed in 1909, where Zero Mostel and our friends the Ashers and the Polskys also lived. In Isaac's rambling apartment, a canary chirped from its birdcage at a sunny window, overlooking the courtyard where its master took his daily promenade. The building was a few blocks from Steinberg's Cafeteria where every afternoon Isaac and his tea circle, a group akin to the Spanish *tertulia,* congregated at the same place at the same time *to talk* and pick up the threads of yesterday's conversation. We'd met Isaac shortly after having read his sublime "Gimpel the Fool," a story published originally in Yiddish in 1953 in the *Jewish Daily Forward,* discovered by Irving Howe and translated by Saul Bellow for *Partisan Review* in 1961. This tale of a simpleton, enraptured and cuckolded by his wife Pesha, is as lush in detail as a strudel studded with nuts and raisins. Our meeting took place at a *Partisan Review* reception, attended by Philip Rahv and William Phillips, its founding editors, and Cecil Hemley, poet and co-founder, with Arthur Cohen, of Noonday Press. I'd expected a kind of Polish Jean Gabin but found myself shaking hands with a bald, bespectacled gent in proper suit, and no more than five foot three. Papery-pale, near albino skin rather like Andy Warhol's, and eyes transparent blue as the puree marbles I played with as a kid. Unsexy, but clearly responsive to the curvaceous young women with whom he was shaking hands and lots of play in his eyes. "Gimpel" launched the career of a writer born in the Polish shtetl of Radzymin, son of a Hasidic rabbi, younger brother of the writer I. J. Singer.

On that phone call, Isaac asked Dan if he could give his wife Alma a job as cashier at the New Yorker. An author clearly fared better with his demons and dybbuks in an empty apartment. No spot was available, but Alma found a job on the fourth floor of Lord & Taylor selling chic garments, a post held until they moved to Miami a couple of decades later.

At one point, we invited Isaac for dinner. Knowing him to be an avowed vegetarian, I deliberated on the menu, settling on a ratatouille, a lentil potage, and a verdant non-carnivorous stew. Hearty fare all could share. If memory serves, our friends Arthur Cohen (novelist, Hebrew scholar, and rare book collector) and Cecil Hemley with his wife Elaine Gottlieb (short-story writer and sometime translator of Singer) were at that table—all Singer fans. No one commented on the food. Oh well, when Claude Chabrol came for dinner as I recall, there were no compliments for my painstaking dishes—in the French way, perfection was expected. But, sniffing the Bordeaux Dan had so carefully selected, impish Chabrol looked up: "Pas un vin idiot." Towards the end of Isaac Singer's dinner, Isaac spoke up: "In the mid-sixties, I became a vegetarian for health reasons, the health of the chicken. But, to tell the truth, the smell of a sizzling steak makes my mouth water."

Singer's "Zlatah the Goat" enchanted my children. His stories and novels of Jewish folklore and shtetl life were replete with imps, golems, and erotic desire, down-to-earth housewives wringing the necks of chickens while worrying how to find a husband for a plain-looking *meezkeit* of a daughter, *meschugeneh* Upper Westsideniks, and retired Miami folk. Those stories of love and old age haunted us all. I read them in English, but could hear them in Yiddish. In 1978 he won the Nobel Prize.

Peter Bogdanovich

Peter Bogdanovich got off to a fast start. Shortly after the New Yorker opened, a young man of around eighteen showed up. "I'm Peter Bogdanovich," he said. "I live across the street from you and want a free pass and a job—not as an usher or doorman but as a *consultant*." By then, he had written a monograph on *Intolerance* for the Museum of Modern Art and could rattle off the names of stars, directors, and films.

At age fifteen, he'd studied acting with Stella Adler and, at nineteen, managed to raise enough money to stage an off-Broadway production of Clifford Odets's *The Big Knife*. Brash, self-confident, impressive, he began hanging around the theater, at times trailing Dan home. How could I say, Peter, we're about to sit down at the table? Innuendos were not part of his repertoire—and he *was* engaging. Soon he asked to write program notes for our Monday Night Special Series, the first on his revered Orson Welles, mimeographs he sold at a nickel apiece from a bridge table in the lobby. Nobody bought them and we started giving them away for nothing. Peter's salary was $15 a week and rose to $35 when he began helping to program our series of "Forgotten Films," featuring directors like Howard Hawks and John Ford, whose critical reputations were just beginning to emerge. "We chose films we ourselves wanted to see," Peter recalls. "Most were from the '30s and '40s and from Warner Bros. I had to cut short my first trip to Hollywood not to miss the series of pictures I was running. It was twenty-eight movies in fourteen days, and I saw every one of them."

Peter's father Borislav painted temperas of Orthodox priests with icons representing their order. In the manner of old Byzantine fresco masters, he mixed his own colors with egg yolk and powdered pigments. Though he himself was from a prominent Serb family, at the onset of World War II, fearing for the safety of his Jewish wife Herma, he picked up the family and fled. Their apartment on West 90th Street was a labyrinth of dark corridors lined with his paintings and Peter's film books. Anna, their young daughter, and Nina were the same age and would play together while Herma and I shared Simplicity patterns for pinafores and smocks. Boris taught Anna to read by his own ingenious system: *A* is a tent with a crossbar, *B* is a bar, etcetera. By age three she *was* reading, but when I took our children to St. Agnes Public Library, Boris refused to have his child join us: "I don't want Anna taking out books handled by who-knows-who."

The Bogdanovich livelihood was precarious. Only years later did Boris begin selling his dark, thickly painted canvases. Herma was the breadwinner. In a small room of their apartment used as her studio, she gilded frames for the Metropolitan Museum of Art. Many evenings after seven, she and I would run into each other at the corner Daitch's Supermarket, when it was at its emptiest; she'd finished her day's stint, and I myself was freer. Never did she begrudge having to support the family. "Boris is an artist," she said time and again. This large handsome aristocrat of intense black eyes and proud mustache never left the house in wintertime, but in balmy May would emerge in white linen suit and Panama hat. Such was Peter's stock.

His first wife, Polly Platt, was of the New England Platts. The young couple lived on Riverside Drive and 105th Street: Peter's film library and a Singer sewing machine occupied most of the space. Polly adored Peter, sewed his shirts, typed his *Esquire* pieces on Jerry Lewis, John Ford, Humphrey Bogart, Jimmy Stewart, and Fritz Lang, and helped pack up his library when in 1964 he decided to head for Hollywood in a 1951 Ford jalopy purchased for $150. They headed west with their one-eyed mongrel and a huge TV in back, having shipped his books on ahead.

Peter's first film, *Targets* (1968), made for under $125,000 and produced by Roger Corman, showed the influence of Hawks, Welles, and Hitchcock. It's about a psychopathic killer and co-starred Boris Karloff and Peter. This extraordinary film explored the relationship between the inner world of the imagination and the outer one of violence and paranoia, both relevant to contemporary American traumas. When we visited Peter and Polly in Van Nuys, a suburb in the San Fernando Valley, they were living in a tract house in the middle of nowhere. One evening they took us to the posh home of Bert Schneider, where we met Larry McMurtry, author and screenwriter of Peter's *The Last Picture Show*, a brilliant study of life in a small Texas town during the 1950s. Peter subsequently made *What's Up Doc?*, *Daisy Miller*, and *Paper Moon*, among others, and married Cybill Shepherd, star of *The Last Picture Show*. Director, actor, and film scholar, when in New York he stayed at the Plaza Hotel and was driven around in a limousine.

Events of 1968

On June 5, 1968, Robert Kennedy was shot and killed. This only two months after another national tragedy: the murder of Dr. Martin Luther King on April 4th. Less than three weeks later a different sort of theater was happening at Columbia University—one to have startled its ex-president, General Dwight D. Eisenhower, whose august portrait hung in Butler Library. Arriving for class one warm April morning, I found students sprinting on the cornice of Hamilton Hall, graffiti splashed on its facade, and the Dean's office occupied. The student uprising had erupted: anti-authoritarian, anti-establishment, anti–Vietnam

War (the draft, ROTC, classified defense research), anti–neighborhood encroachment (longtime Harlem residents threatened with eviction to make way for a prospective gymnasium), plus the issue of Open Admissions, closely linked to racial injustice. The university was but two blocks from Harlem, yet few black students were visible on campus. Despite Martin Luther King's "I had a dream" and President Johnson's "We shall overcome," Harlem was "up there" and Columbia "down here." Intellectuals took positions, the faculty split: Sidney Morgenbesser, Frederick W. Dupee, Steven Marcus, and Kenneth Koch supportive of the students, as were Jules Feiffer, Jack Gelber, Ned Polsky, and many of our friends. "Don't rebel against what the university offers you," Herbert Marcuse had advised, but Western classics and Core Curriculum notwithstanding, there was plenty to protest against. "For a brief period, the university turned into a microcosm, a laboratory for direct democracy in society as a whole," said Morris Dickstein, who'd pursued his undergraduate work at Columbia and taught in its English Department from 1966 to 1971. The SDS, acronym for Students for a Democratic Society, organized the demonstrations. Mark Rudd, its president, an A student in my Spanish Literature class, never betrayed his extra-curricular activities, passing out political fliers at high schools.

In the early sixties the SDS, with some 80,000 to 100,000 members, fantasized a violent overthrow of the government. In 1969 and 1970 part of the organization threw bombs and held up banks. By late 1967 the Black Panthers, founded by Huey P. Newton and Bobby Seale in Oakland, California, were a force. The party had a fairly reasonable and ambitious program for social change and empowerment of African-Americans (employment, education, decent housing, social justice, and political representation), but was branded as a shadowy revolutionary organization and a threat to national security, as were the Weathermen (later the Weather Underground Organization), who became the self-appointed vanguard of the fissured, dying SDS.

In 1968 a Latin American conference at Columbia got suddenly disrupted. As I watched half-blind Jorge Luis Borges being led to the lectern, half-a-dozen students barged through the door. "Borges is a fascist, a Peron supporter." Borges, renowned writer and chief librarian of the Buenos Aires Library, who lived less in politics than in his labyrinthine tales, stared blankly ahead. No matter—the conference went adrift.

Black students, prominent in the uprising, asked white radicals to abandon Hamilton Hall shortly after its seizure. Determined to separate out, the students brought in observers, among them Kenneth Clark and Stokely Carmichael, who called for "Black Power." Students milled around and marched in front of the library, arms linked, singing "We shall not be moved." Two days later, mounted police with billy clubs began chasing students and bystanders across the lawn and backing them up against the stone walls of the library. The intervention had been well planned and foreseen: in fact, Jules Feiffer noted the presence of Abe Rosenthal of the *New York Times*, ready to turn in copy. More brutal interventions would recur during the 1968 Democratic Convention in Chicago. Again, to quote Dickstein: "While handling the black students in Hamilton Hall with kid gloves—afraid Harlem would erupt—elsewhere the police let loose with wanton brutality and a good deal of unnecessary damage to the university itself. It set back Columbia's fund-raising and created a financial crunch in the '70s. The overall effect, not unwelcome to the SDS, was to cripple the moral legitimacy of the administration and to radicalize the large moderate mass of students."

Why did the cops, labeled as *pigs*, behave this way? Clearly there was a distinction between blue-collar cops and privileged kids. Officers gazed in awe at Low Library's regal rotunda while a few yards away a flippant young radical poet puffed on a cigar, his feet on the president's chair. Pier Paolo Pasolini (*Accattone, Mamma Roma, The Gospel According to St. Matthew*), himself a radical, objected to the term "pigs"—the police, he said, belonged to the working class. What were the hopes for a peaceful solution? "Ah, the Revolution! What art. There's never been a more pitiful period," exclaims a character in Gustave Flaubert's *Sentimental Education*.

The '68 eruption, a great watershed in our history, was the dynamic approach by a new generation aspiring to be anti-establishment, anti-bourgeois, and New Left. But in the end, however, it failed to generate the yearned-for revolution. The political engagement and drive for social justice that rattled the university in the 1960s and '70s evaporated. To some traditionalists that period grates, and disputes often spill into the nation's political discourse. "The '60s were just a terrible time for the country," says former Attorney General Edwin Meese 3rd. "It was the age of selfishness. It was the age of self-indulgence. It was the age of anti-authority, an age in which people did all kind of wrong things. That was the start, really, of the drug problem in the United States." This view of the sixties—hippies, love beads, Woodstock, Elvis Presley, the Beatles—overlooks civil rights, the assassinations of John and Robert Kennedy and Martin Luther King Jr., Open Admissions, university encroachment on "blighted" neighborhoods, military priorities. Ultimately, clarion calls for change of the capitalist system or the social structure for the most part went out of style; the current generation is not so ideologically driven, and subject to the pressures of market conditions and careerism. When I discuss the sixties with students, or show documentaries relating to the Chicago Riots, say, or Mai Lai veterans, or the Bay of Pigs, it seems Ancient History. And Angela Davis, Mark Rudd? Who were they? What is in the past seems to have vanished, but continues to flicker nervously in our minds. Civil liberties, economic disparity between rich and poor, militaristic priorities and authoritarian encroachment are not of the past.

Paris, not to be left behind, underwent its own '68 events. In May 1968, as Dan and I checked in at a cheap hotel in Paris, a block away at L'École des Beaux-Arts, students marched with banners: *La Lutte Continue!* Demonstrations had shut down the Sorbonne on May 3rd. Three days later, students battled police in the Latin Quarter and, on the weekend of May 10th and 11th, marched through Paris, ripped up paving stones, and barricaded themselves in the Latin Quarter. The student agenda was social and cultural: *L'imagination au pouvoir*—"so that man can become himself," as the Appeal from the Sorbonne of June 13–14, 1968, declared. The police responded with tear gas.

Numerous cineastes participated in the demonstration: Louis Malle, Jean-Luc Godard, François Truffaut, Claude Chabrol, Agnès Varda, film critic Louis Marcorelle, and Marin Karmitz, who ran a triplex theater and a left-wing bookstore in the Bastille quarter. All were responding to the shutdown of the Cinémathèque Françoise, archive and shrine, though Columbia students claimed *their* uprising had ignited it. The Cinémathèque, founded in Paris in 1936 by Henri Langlois and George Franju, had played an important role in the early development of cinephiles and young directors of the French New Wave who spent innumerable hours in dark screening rooms viewing millions of feet of old and new films. Godard, Truffaut, Chabrol, and Demy proudly called themselves "Children of the Cinémathèque." It housed a vast collection of nearly 60,000 films, many rare, as well as stills, film books, and original documents on the history of cinema, collected from every available source.

Langlois's reputation had spread worldwide. During World War II he saved hordes of prints by hiding them from the Nazis in his own bathtub and in the bedrooms and basements of friends. After 1945, the Cinémathèque operated under the auspices of the government-supported Centre National du Cinéma, but following a dispute in 1968 involving Langlois's anarchic working methods, the subsidy was withdrawn and the Minister of Culture, André Malraux, announced his intention to remove Langlois from his post. *Aux armes, citoyens!* came the battle cry. Pressured by demonstrators and threats by famous directors to refuse permission for screening their works at the Cinémathèque, Malraux backed down. In 1970, when Henri Langlois welcomed Dan and me into the Cinémathèque, his manic enthusiasm matched its staggering collection. Metal cans were stacked up in library, corridors, and courtyard, impervious to rain pelting the cans—in "joyous disarray" as he likewise described Georges Méliès' abandoned studio in Montrieux. Langlois and Mary Meerson, his devoted associate and companion, seemed equally unfazed.

In 1968 Godard privately showed us footage shot in the Peugeot factory where assembly-line production of automobiles began with flat-steel plates and wound up as four-wheeled vehicles. In true cinema-verité fashion, he asked workers that earnest question: "What is it you want most?" *Liberté, égalité, fraternité* was not their reply. They wanted washing machines and television sets and automobiles—like everyone else. The Cannes Film Festival of 1968 collapsed during those chaotic events.

Kids

Raising children in the sixties was no easy matter, streets not always safe and drugs rampant—84th Street between Amsterdam and Columbus Avenues was a dangerous block. Our friend's daughter was taking a six-week Saturday course in martial arts protection against assailants. A sign posted in a subway car read: "We are entering chain-snatching season. Women are advised to carry a hatpin and to use it decisively—aim at eyes, temples, ears, and Adam's Apple." City kids had city smarts: street-savvy, seven-year-old Sarah cautioned me against eye contact with a spaced-out subway drug addict undergoing a bad trip and looking as if he might keel over. I thought he needed help. "Mommy, don't stare," she cautioned. Teenage Nina, coming home late, told us not to worry—she knew to walk in full view in the middle of the street and not on the sidewalk, where some lurking mugger or rapist might spring from a shadowy doorway.

As enlightened parents, we'd read Dr. Arnold Gesell's *Child Development I* and *Child Development II* telling us what to expect at such-and-such time. It was reassuring, it was disheartening. Weren't our progeny *special*, not just cut from the same mold as everyone else's? Hadn't all their baby food been mashed from fresh vegetables? Hadn't they read everything from *Goodnight Moon* to *The Little Prince*? Hadn't the television set been closeted for years? Hadn't they gone on nature walks at the Bronx and Brooklyn Botanical Gardens? Hadn't they studied recorder and piano and guitar at the Mannes School of Music? Hadn't they learned to swim at age three, and studied ballet and modern dance? Hadn't they had braces on their teeth? But, in light of such fatalistic forces, how could we make their lives special? Benjamin Spock's counsel was to be permissive, feed on demand, and allow your child self-expression. Though we shared many of the political and social goals of the sixties, and had smoked a joint or two ourselves, as parents the celebration of drugs, casual sex, and break-down of authority was unsettling to say the least—the shoe transferred to another foot. A neighbor on the fifth floor of our building spoke of his extraordinary LSD trips; pot and acid could be bought on the side streets. Kids could get hooked.

One afternoon at the New Yorker, a young man on LSD climbed the stairs leading to the balcony, undressed, flung his clothes down the steps, and began ranting. He rolled down the stairway, broke his spine, and became a vegetable. In his wallet we found his name and address and phoned his father. This gentle, mustached man in a nice suit arrived, face flooded with sorrow. "Eight years ago, I brought my family from Greece so our children would have a better education." We scooped up the clothes and helped him into a taxi.

Public schools were in decline. Private schools had smaller classes, higher academic standards, and seemed safer. But Nina from the word *go* refused to attend one. Though many of her classmates, on graduation from junior high, attended Dalton, New Lincoln, Brearley, or Trinity, she wouldn't hear of a school for "rich kids." No use arguing that many were on scholarship. From an early age she *knew* what she wanted to do, which was to paint. Diligently she created a portfolio and was accepted into the High School of Music and Art. Its students were gifted and precocious in more ways than one, and at neighboring City College pot vied with politics. Who knew what to expect from those young adven-turers of the sixties? LSD, heroin, cocaine? The father of one of Emily's best friends was a pothead. A classmate, a talented young violinist, over-dosed on LSD and wound up indeterminately in the hospital. Secretly and ashamed, I found myself searching Nina's drawers for cannabis, pipes, pills, diaphragms. When she and some friends closeted themselves in her bedroom after school, I sniffed for the slightest whiff of pot. She had two younger sisters in the next room—they too had noses. We lived with anxiety, yet found it hard to blow the whistle. Mixed messages, mixed boundaries. Words didn't come. My own parents had never been on top of my case. Unlike my friends, I was never given an allowance, simply asked for what I needed. But how many windows did my father, a window-cleaner, have to shine to purchase our winter coats? My mother never asked who are you going out with, or where did you go and what did you do? She relied, presumably, on my rearing. Not that she had trouble finding words. What was on the lung was on the tongue. At age thirteen, when I got my first period, she came out with it, bluntly. "Whatever you do, don't come home with a bastard."

One balmy morning, I set out for a stroll with our little pug Sancho, who Dan sometimes referred to as Edward G. Robinson. These leisurely ramblings are one of Manhattan's great pleasures. Walk a few blocks and you find yourself in a new neighborhood, with its own newspaper stands, tradesmen, and activities. Our own Upper West Side had several new independent merchants. A Lebanese stationer on Amsterdam Avenue, a Pakistani news vendor on Broadway, a Korean fishmonger on 96th Street, and a Dominican seamstress on Amsterdam Avenue had joined Broadway's Austrian chocolatier, Brooklyn-born Benny, and Russian Zabar's. I loved those solitary, free-floating strolls: Nietzsche said that the only ideas of any value are those born during walks. Dan's Eureka moment for *Point of Order*, the film he and Emile de Antonio made on the Army-McCarthy trials, came to him like that. Two children's books I wrote sprang from a detour on 93rd Street between Columbus and Amsterdam Avenues. The spicy odor of black beans, chicken, and plantains drifted through the windows of a brownstone along with a cha-cha radio melody. Sancho pulled on his leash, definitely drawn to that enticing smell. On the stoop sat a little girl looking, well, very stranded. She was about ten, our daughter Sarah's age. Sancho began sniffing her shoes, finding kitchen crumbs perhaps. Startled, she drew back, but I assured her that he loved children. "What's his name?" she asked, timidly patting him. When I told her, responding perhaps to my Spanish inflection, she answered: "Soy Maria." And there it was, the title for a children's book. *I Am Maria* appeared the following year. And as if that wasn't enough, in parting she asked if I'd be passing again. I told her I would. She broke into a smile: "Mi casa es tu casa." It became the title of *another* book: *My House is Your House.*

Guest Books

Patrons from the outset began filling the 300-page ledgers in our lobby with their names and miscellaneous remarks, some enlightening, some maddening. There were thousands of film requests, but also entries on dreams, passions, and artistic ideas. The zealous and the impatient sometimes used different penmanship to create the impression that their obscure object of desire had a popular following. We have several hundred tomes.

"This is a wonderful debut," wrote someone in the first week. "But could you grease the seats?" How could we grease the seats? They would stain people's clothing and we might get sued.

"Get rid of noisy vending machines." Good idea, whereupon machines got banished to the outer lobby where they clanked and gushed to no one's unnerving.

"Bring back Jean Renoir's *The Golden Coach* and the popcorn machine." In total accord, Dan and I had banished popcorn for a while but were persuaded to bring it back. *The Golden Coach* needed scant persuasion.

March 10, 1961: P. Adams Sitney, avant-garde critic, requested in script that virtually covered the page: "Luis Buñuel's *L'Age d'Or* (if you can get it!!!), *The Great Dictator*, and more Chaplin." But, directly below, another patron replies: "Who needs red-rat—Chaplin? I for one am not interested in his political life. I like his work as a performer. But to me a movie house is to enrich art, not to have a political discussion."

"Please show *Queen Christina* (Garbo), *Zero de Conduite* (Vigo), and *Germany Year Zero* (Rossellini)" wrote Susan Sontag one week. A week later, on April 24, 1960, she added: "Pagnol's *Les Lettres de Mon Moulin*, von Stroheim's *Queen Kelly*, *Prix de Beauté* with Louise Brooks, Visconti's *Senso* and *La Terra Trema*, Tod Browning's *Freaks*, Carl Theodor Dreyer's *Day of Wrath* and *Joan of Arc*, *Grand Hotel*, *Queen of Spades*, *Les Enfants du Paradis*, and

Harvest." From the looks of it, Ms. Sontag was ready to sign on as co-programmer. Indeed, we were on the same wavelength.

W.H. Auden requested any Carole Lombard film, *City Lights*, *Les Visiteurs du Soir*, any Jean Harlow film, and early Marilyn Monroe films.

On March 10, 1961, Twyla Tharp asked for *Pinnochio*, *Snow White*, *Gulliver's Travels*, *Wizard of Oz*, *The Outlaw*, *Casablanca* (again, every six months), Dreyer's *Day of Wrath*, and *Farewell to Arms* with Jennifer Jones and Rock Hudson.

On June 2, 1961, Robert Downey asked for Chaplin's *Monsieur Verdoux*, *The Great Dictator*, and *King in New York*, *Anna Christie*, *Mata Hari*, *Ninotchka*, *The Wizard of Oz*. His son, Robert Downey Jr., *played* Chaplin (astonishingly well) in Richard Attenborough's *Chaplin* (1992), so the son probably saw the films first at the New Yorker. Downey Sr. astonishingly ended with "Please show some early Eddie Cantor films like *Whoopee*."

"Let's concentrate on Eisenstein and Pudovkin for the next two or three weeks, but we could do without *Alexander Nevsky*," said a patron. And directly below, an adversarial "The damn fool who wrote the above wouldn't know a classic if he saw one."

On December 12, 1966, the historian Peter Gay asked for *Twelve Pearls in a Crown*. We guessed he meant *Les Perles de la Couronne/Pearls of the Crown* (1937), which traces the history of seven matched pearls given to Catherine d'Medici, then passed down to Mary, Queen of Scots; but we never could find that film.

"Improve the sound system and fix the seats," signed John Simon. "Right on both accounts," Dan replied. But, on the very next page: "Can anyone stop John Simon from mumbling during the show?" No one could.

The guest books were a psychic ledger with no dearth of advice to the management:

"Please do not pay any attention to the lunatic fringe that requests such horrors as Brigitte Bardot films and early Cinemascope."

"*Henry V* was a big disappointment, much too talky." And, penciled in the margin alongside: "Hear, hear"—followed yet by another scrawl: "Boob!"

Customers spoke to each other in the guest books as viewers in 42nd Street movie houses were given to talking to the screen. "Don't trust that broad! I told you not to trust her."

Incensed at some of the comments, Dan felt compelled to answer back in a column reserved in the ledger for our own replies. Responding to a sarcastic remark about Lionel Rogosin's *Come Back Africa*, he wrote, "Idiot." To a request for *Sink the Bismarck!*, he retorted, "This film stinks." But when asked for Val Lewton films, he wrote: "Yes, they're very good," and thereupon embarked on a search for *Cat People, I Walked with a Zombie*, and *The Body Snatcher*. To a request for some earlier Chaplin pictures, he replied: "By all means, but they're difficult to obtain."

On January 14, 1967, Joan Baez wrote: Thank you for a lovely evening.

There was an obvious hunger for film. Our patrons were as interested in *who* made the film as in what it was *about* and *who* was in it. They cared about visual style and wanted to follow a director's body of work. But detective work was often necessary to satisfy requests. One writer asked for a picture with Sterling Hayden—he couldn't remember the name of the film—where Hayden tries to hold up a racetrack while killing a horse in a race. Dan filled him in: *The Killing*.

An early comment was inscribed in feminine backhand: "Dear Management, we love you." (For sample Guest Book pages, see pp. 263–311.)

Things That Bug an Exhibitor—and an Audience

One enters a movie house anticipating solitude, insularity, respite from the din of the world. Ah, to feel private in a public place—alone with one's dreams, yet not lonely. Briefly you are somewhere else, communing with characters more real than Mr. So-and-So next door, and discovering in a myriad cast links to your own existence. Nothing must break that magical spell.

So inured are New Yorkers to the daily wallpaper of Noise that beeping garbage trucks, construction work drills, even wailing police and ambulance sirens may not register. But in the quiet of a theater, auditory invaders cannot be ignored: *Whisperers, Snorers, Rattlers* of candy-wrappers and newspapers; *Munchers* (human ruminants, of popcorn and pretzels); *Coughers, Sneezers, Snifflers* (hankies unable to muffle the sobs and moans triggered by weepy scenes); *Guffawers* (outbursts outlasting everyone else's and sometimes for something not even funny); *Kickers* (feet thumping the seat ahead without missing a beat; *Commentators* (with run-on explanations and plot interpretations, all brilliantly parodied by Mel Brooks in his short *The Critic*); *Subtitle Readers* (aiding a companion presumably illiterate or, God forbid, blind); *Predictors* (foreseeing the end five minutes into the plot)—*mea culpa*: Dan calls me Rapid Transit for guessing that plot in five minutes or so.

Don't think that's it! Sociologist Erving Goffman in *The Presentation of Self in Everyday Life* has expounded brilliantly on public behavior and transgressions. Theaters inevitably have their host of offenders: *Smokers* furtively lighting up, inhaling, puffing, and scattering their butts for ushers to pick up; *Picnickers* tiding the show with Kentucky Fried Chicken or hamburgers with the works (french fries, onions, pickles, and ketchup)—enough to make a woman in the early months of pregnancy retch; *Gum-stickers*—bane of theater owners—depositing their leavings under seats or on the floor; *Sombreros*, with high-crowned hats that obstruct the view of the person in back; *Fidgeters* bobbing this way and that as in a ping-pong match; *Imperialists* draping their outer garments on the adjacent seat or the one in front, waging silent battle for total occupancy of the shared armrest and casting dirty looks at anyone who asks if that seat is occupied; *Sheriffs* refusing to stand up for a latecomer who gropes for a seat in the dark; *Bullies* arriving late for a movie—after the credits have gone on—loudly asking that you move behind the tallest person in the theater so that they, dear husband and wife, can sit together. But what bugged us most were *Sneakers*, flinging their hippo Addidas or Nikes on the seat ahead—*our beautiful red velvet Roxy seats!* Up and down the aisle Dan would march, minus cane or club, grinding his teeth yet ever polite: "Could you please remove … ?" No theater, of course, is invulnerable to *Knee-rubbers, Gropers,* and *Pickpockets,* though ours was relatively free of those Ultimate Invaders. Finally, there are customers who want their money back—after having seen the entire film. They *didn't* like the movie.

One problem remained ever unresolved: *Pigeon shit*. Our marquee became an *irresistible* depository for our plump fellow urbanites, plumed in ethereal lavender and pewter. There they were, strutting and flapping, with that endless capacity for defecation (the average pigeon producers more than twenty-five pounds of droppings a year). Those Picasso doves—symbols of peace—were indefatigable besotters of our neon letters. Dan, immaculate in his ways, couldn't take it. In scholarly fashion he scoped the problem, and as with any household snag (being less than a technological whiz), out came his reflex battle cry: "Consult the Yellow Pages." But, *oy vey*, all avian strategies failed. Specialists descended with nets, spikes, overhead grid wires, camphor, dummy owls, buzzers, and hummers. All acoustical approaches failed, for just as sleeping pills eventually lose their force, so ruses get figured out.

Whoever invented the term "birdbrain"? Heroic pigeons of yore carried battle messages at top speed. During the imprisonment of Queen Marie Antoinette, it was a pigeon that passed messages to her from her advisers outside Paris. And it was a pigeon that delivered the results of the first Olympics. Their homing instinct, related perhaps to the magnetic field of the earth, remains an unsolved and awe-inspiring mystery. How not to admire those romantic *palomas*, mating for life, sexual act relatively gentle and consensual? Moreover, both male and female pigeons produce crop milk for babies—two coming every four weeks! But alas, that instinctual gathering in large flocks and *staying put* became our undoing. We became their Home Sweet Home. Of an afternoon, more pigeons might occupy the marquee than moviegoers inside. And unfortunate the head on which a dropping landed! Glancing up at them, massed ominously and with intent, I envisioned Hitchcock's blackbirds in *The Birds* swooping down on terrified humans.

"How about hitting those bloated buggers with a sling shot?" suggested a friend. Out of the question, for my aim is unreliable. Besides, some pigeon fanciers or defense group would undoubtedly soon be fulminating on behalf of our cooing kin. "How about hiring a pigeon poacher to scatter seeds and net them, then take them out of state and sell them for sport or food," recommended some wise guy. Overhearing this, a chum reminded him that the Department of Environmental Conservation could arrest and convict the poacher. "How about pigeon pie?" recommended a culinary neighbor. "But mommy," says our little daughter, "they're pretty!"

The world is beset by pests, albeit not born as such. When a creature becomes a pest—moles, wolves, grubs, deer, sparrows, cockroaches, carp, lamprey, *pigeons*—people are out to get them. In centuries past, when Old World cathedrals became encrusted by pigeon droppings, certain clever clericals devised a falconer's solution to preserve architecture by dispatching vicious hawks on flocks of harmless birds. Recently, I've been told of a new "recipe" for eliminating this nuisance by egg oiling—oiling considered humane for it's applied only to eggs in early stages of development. The method keeps air from passing through the shell, preventing the embryo from developing. Maybe oiling is the way to go—a kind of pigeon abortion—though it sounds a bit complicated. Once, I tried stationing some pigeon fanciers across the street, providing them with bread and challah crumbs from Party Cake in the hope that the birds would decide, à la guide *Michelin*, that the repast was worth a detour. Nothing, however, deterred those city-savvy critters. Down they swooped from some unseen perch, zoning in on their target to deposit their load. After the movie, a dreamy-eyed viewer might emerge to behold a tableau of purple pigeon dribbles on the sidewalk. "Like Jackson Pollack splatters," remarks a passerby. "Pigeon poop!" squeals a kid.

Hardy and disease-resistant, these feral creatures are one of the least-endangered species on earth, though pest control companies have done an excellent job of convincing the public that they are the Enemy. Subway notices warn: *Pigeon droppings cause sixty diseases. Someone has to clean it up!* Not long ago, a London mayor, calling the pigeons "rats with wings" (quoting Woody Allen from *Stardust Memories*), made it his mission to eradicate them from Trafalgar Square. Yet our potion of one part detergent to four parts vinegar failed to obliterate the mess. With pigeons one must get to the root of the problem and not the excretions themselves. An ingenious friend suggested applying glue to the surface. Pigeons don't *permanently* stick to the stuff, he assured me as I envisioned an installation of petrified pigeons, yet the experience is sufficiently annoying that they don't come back. Another proposal was to strew popcorn laced with LSD, to disorient them forever (*that* source indicated that LSD could be medically procured). Twenty-five years later, at our current Lincoln Plaza, the problem persists. Since our marquee is flat, their chosen site is a ledge over the staircase where people enter and exit. But we haven't given up. And if anyone who reads this has a solution to pigeon poop, kindly phone the theater at 212–757–3458. (Pigeon *Poisoners* need not call.)

Furthermore: anyone on a cell phone, PLEASE TURN IT OFF! That includes those who think nothing of checking their e-mail during the film (and emitting an infuriating bright light) in the middle of a packed audience.

Payoffs

"There's a price for everything in our society," a fellow-passenger on a plane once remarked, and as Karl von Clausewitz, the military strategist, once pointed out, morality has nothing to do with money, power, or politics. All cities in the world experience corruption, and who knows, but the commerce of large ones might collapse without an intricate system of payoffs. Higher levels of corruption may exist in Mexico City, São Paolo, Cairo, and Palermo, but Manhattan was by no means innocent.

Dan learned this bitter truth within hours after opening the New Yorker. Given the number and myriad complexities of city codes, it seemed unavoidable. If city officials wanted to pull out all the stops, the place might come to a halt. Let's say a hapless young man drifts into the occupation of fireman or cop so as to retire at an early age, and (since all aren't Boy Scouts) a twenty-year stint may offer endless opportunities for little hits here and there. These little scores spiced up the week. It all boiled down to a question of slipping the right amount to the right guy at the right time. The New York City Fire Code has over 1,000 pages with thousands of written specifications pertaining to public places and public assembly. Those specs were the nuts and bolts of violations and could, unattended, lead to fines and ultimate shutdowns.

Dan got introduced into the byways and intricacies of corruption while operating the New Yorker. When at first he came across this racket it upset him. Why should he have to put a fixer in some beefy palm because Mr. Uniform gave him the glad-eye? But when hit with violations— all twenty—he coughed up. A very small gratuity could persuade the guy to *overlook* once or twice, but Mr. Uniform kept coming—after all, he too was in business. Dan found himself spending more time curing violations than in programming and promotion. While trying to fall asleep at night, his brain was besieged by cops, firemen, stairwells, doors, balconies, and fire escapes, a new arsenal that began crowding out Dreyer, Hawks, Godard, and Sturges. There must be other ways. He considered speaking to our lawyer Robert Montgomery (really!) about this problem but realized that our dear friend was the straightest of arrows and nothing would come of such a conversation. There remained but one solution. Consult a corruption *maven*.

Rolando Martin immediately came to mind. A Cuban superintendent, he lived in the same building on 89th Street as our friends Sally and Chandler Brossard, occasionally did odd plumbing and carpentry jobs at the theater, and sometimes sent a Cuban immigrant looking for work. This short, squat man with the build of a Basque wrestler, an everglade of shiny black hair, and an ebony mustache two inches high, acted as fence for various transactions at Benny's Luncheonette, and he also had the knack of converting a $35 parking ticket into $17.50. Stored in one corner of his basement was a bevy of hot goods. In another he held hot poker and blackjack games with a group of fellow-loving *aficionados* of cockfights in New Jersey's Cuban neighborhoods. Rolando was a born fixer. A student of the workings of corruption, he could size up a deal in the blink of an eye.

In short order, he taught Dan some tricks of the trade. A bank night-drop in a police car warranted two dollars. A fireman on a few minor violations could be headed off for fifteen. But a license renewal at the downtown Fire Department was pricier, a caper that had to take place at Fire Department headquarters and *in person.* One day Rolando accompanied Dan downtown and ran him through the ropes. Several hundred firemen, seated at desks a few feet apart in a vast open room, like in Orson Welles's *The Trial,* presided over license renewals and violations. Rolando, before entering and approaching one of those desks with our application, performed a kind of origami, tucking a neatly folded $20 bill into an inch-wide cardboard matchbook between matches and back cover. With a wink at the fireman, he purred: "Smoke?" A silent signal flashed from eye to eye.

"Sure, why not?"

"Here, use these matches."

Punto final.

But one day a major problem arose. A fire inspector came up with a significant violation and wrote up a fault on the iron fire escape outside an exit door. The cost of replacement was prohibitive, over $10,000. Nothing was truly wrong with the fire escape, but the inspector pointed to a few rusty sections and claimed iron corrosion. All that had to be done was to paint these with Rustoleum, but he claimed that the entire fire escape was damaged and gave us two weeks to replace it. Dan studied the face of this well-dressed, articulate man in his mid-thirties and divined that he couldn't be bought off for twenty, fifty, or even one hundred dollars. The guy came across as the real thing, an honest-to-goodness sheriff out to nail us. Whereupon Dan asked the inspector if he would please wait a few moments so he could speak to his maintenance man. Immediately he fetched Rolando, who quickly sized up the deal, walked with the inspector into the alleyway, chatted, took his name and home phone number. After the inspector had left, Rolando told Dan that this honcho could be bought off but he wasn't exactly sure for how much. Well, Rolando had a contact man in the Fire Department whom he would phone. Two days later, all was organized. The fee was five hundred dollars. Dan gave Rolando the cash, Rolando painted the fire escape with Rustoleum. A week later the violation was cured.

Distribution

Bernardo Bertolucci

In 1964 we saw a film at the New York Film Festival that we loved and immediately wanted to show. It was *Before the Revolution* by Bernardo Bertolucci. We wrote to the producer, asking to launch it at the New Yorker, but were told that he sought nationwide distribution, not just a run at an Upper West Side art house. Since no one cared to distribute the work of a 22-year-old unknown, to show it we'd have to bite the bullet, import a bulky steel canister with a 35-millimeter print from Italy, and circulate it nationwide. What did we know about Distribution? And, what did we know about Exhibition until we began exhibiting? What does one know about anything until embarking? We put up a $500 advance against percentage and opened *Before the Revolution* in the summer of 1965. Before we knew it, we found ourselves in distribution.

An excerpt from Archer Winsten's review in the *New York Post*, July 27, 1965:

Before the Revolution is the work of a young Italian director who, at the age of 22, drew heavily upon his life in Parma, his loves both sacred and profane, his Marxist teacher, the death of a blonde art-cinema friend, and his own thought processes to distill this tightly packed, rambling, very youthful picture. If Bertolucci lives up to this promise and comes through with great work, this picture will bear study as the raw material.

A Talleyrand quotation introduces the film: "He who does not live in the years before the Revolution cannot understand what the sweetness of living is." Set in 1960 and loosely based on Stendhal's *The Charterhouse of Parma*, it recounts the rites of passage of young Fabrizio through love and politics, including an affair with his beautiful, neurotic, sexually charged aunt, played by Adriana Asti. Nostalgia for the present, for the beauty of life *before* the revolution prevents the young idealistic Fabrizio from living his Marxist ideals. Incurably bourgeois, he falls in with those of his class. Among the memorable scenes are a brilliant night at the opera with social classes layered in tiers, and a gorgeous panning shot of Fabrizio circling a fountain in Rome at the parting from his aunt.

Never parsimonious in praise or criticism, an exultant Pauline Kael declared: "*Before the Revolution* doesn't widen the screen, it makes you widen your eyes. The world has opened: it is the power of art." Equally smitten after viewing Bertolucci's *Last Tango in Paris* at the New York Film Festival, she compared that film with the premiere of Stravinsky's *Sacre du Printemps*. Bertolucci was subsequently nominated for an Academy Award as best director for *Last Tango in Paris* and in 1987's *The Last Emperor* won two of that film's nine Oscars (for directing and co-writing).

Cada loco tiene su tema goes a Spanish saying—every madman has his obsession. Truffaut contended that a filmmaker's entire world is contained in his first film. Bertolucci's ode to love, politics, and cinema prevails in *The Conformist*, *1900*, and *The Dreamers*. *The Dreamers*, inspired by Jean-Pierre Melville's adaptation of Jean Cocteau's novel *Les Enfants Terribles*, is about two youths and a young woman holed up in an apartment, reveling in lovemaking while demonstrations rage in Paris streets. Sex alternates with snippets of Sam Fuller, Nicholas Ray, Godard, Truffaut, and Bresson. "*The Dreamers* is not a historical film," says Bertolucci: "I'm so much about the present. The only way to do a film about the past, for me at least, is to do it as if the past was where we actually lived at the moment. The only time the camera can speak is the present." Shortly after *The Dreamers* opened, I asked him if Jules Feiffer's panel—which we had given to him after the New Yorker closed—still hung in his apartment. He smiled: "Of course."

Another of Bertolucci's splendid films is *The Spider's Stratagem* (1970). Based on a short story by Jorge Luis Borges, it premiered at the New Yorker on January 12, 1972, and ran for four weeks. A young man arrives in a sunny, somnolent Italian village to investigate the murder of his father, a dedicated anti-Fascist, assassinated some thirty years before in a box at the opera house during a performance of *Rigoletto*. In the piazza, he discovers a monument dedicated to his father, yet the townspeople greet him with suspicion and hostility. Slowly, and through encounters with his father's former mistress (the beautiful, aging Alida Valli), he learns that his father was not a hero but a penitent traitor who contrived his own death in order to give the anti-Fascists a martyr. What began as an Oedipal search for the truth evolves into a study of consequences. In a haunting scene the young man departs the village, and walking along the railroad tracks, he stoops and presses his ear to the metal rails as if incorporating the reverberations of that mystery. The film was gorgeously shot by the cinematographer Vittorio Storaro.

In the spring of 1966, we visited Bertolucci's apartment in the Trastavere in Rome. He and his beautiful girlfriend Paola were dancing an Astaire-Rogers number while watching a dubbed version of *Top Hat* as *bolliti misti* simmered on the stove. We became fast friends, met his parents and brother Giuseppi, and visited the family home outside of Parma, where *Before the Revolution* was filmed. His mother Nina, a cultivated Australian woman, prepared the best veal tonnato I ever tasted, and his father Attila, a renowned poet, had translated Proust's *Remembrance of Things Past* and written occasional film criticism in the forties. Bertolucci introduced us to Pasolini, Alberto Moravia, Moravia's wife Elsa Morante, actress Laura Betti, and Gianni Amico. Gianni, a music devotee enamored of Latin America, made *Tropici* (1969), which entered the Cinema Novo canon. It tells of a poor migrant family's voyage from the barren Northeast to São Paulo, a typical theme of the odyssey of countless rural migrant families who wind up in urban shantytowns and provide cheap manpower for modern technology. Nelson Pereira dos Santos treated this theme masterfully in *Barren Lives* (1964), based on Gracilano Ramos's modernist novel, *Vidas Secas.*

One hot afternoon, we drove to Moravia's beach house in Fregena, less than an hour from Rome. As we sat on the sand, some people came by and plunked themselves down right next to us. "Let's move," Moravia grumbled from under his bushy brows. This Jewish man, who had hidden in the mountains from the Nazis and witnessed plenty, needed space. A man of habit, he wrote every morning and, as film critic for *Corriere della Sera*, attended movies—both good and bad—every afternoon. When we accompanied him, he bought us ice cream from the vendor who marched down the aisle at the beginning of the film announcing her *gelato, dolci,* and cigarettes.

Moravia invited us for Easter Sunday lunch. We headed over with Bertolucci and Paola. Already present and sipping wine were Pasolini, Marco Ferreri and his wife, and we were joined by the writer Dacia Maraini (Moravia's girlfriend), who lived one floor below. Succulent pascal lamb, baby peas, and a *torte siciliana* were served. Ferreri was Italian but had been working in Spain. We'd played his *El Cochecito* (1960) more than once, a droll film about a healthy, wealthy man who has everything *except* what fellow-cronies have—a wheel-chair—whereupon he pulls all sorts of pranks to get that strange object of desire. The black humor and surreal touches were sheer Spanish. Ferreri's *Dillinger is Dead* (1969) is a small masterpiece about a designer of industrial masks, played by the great Michel Piccoli, as he tries to escape the captivity of household objects. *La Grande Bouffe* (1973) is yet another anarchic Buñuel-like swipe at materialism in which four middle-aged men (Marcello Mastroianni, Michel Piccoli, Ugo Tognazzi, and Philippe Noiret) decide to commit group suicide by eating themselves to death. The film, an assault on grossness, is gross—and sublime.

At that lunch, Pasolini sat to my right. How I wished that my Italian exceeded *"Dov'e?"* and *antipasto misti* so that I could read his poetry and novels in the original. His films "reached" me politically and spiritually. *Accattone* portrays the sordid existence of a pimp in a squalid section of Rome. *Mamma Roma* (1962) is about a Roman prostitute (Anna Magnani) aspiring to a middle-class life. Though grim, there is much compassion (with Marxist, and mystical, overtones) shown for the proletariat. That Easter repast was not given to religiosity but to the buzz of ideas and cinema. I remember the vast Sicilian Easter tart; if only I could remember what we talked about!

One evening Gianni Amico and Bertolucci organized a party at Gianni's apartment. Everybody was drinking wine and beer, smoking pot, dancing, having a ball. It was a party! The bell rang. Jean-Marie Straub and Danièle Huillet were in the street, waiting for keys to be thrown down. "Shh-sh," said Bertolucci. "Get rid of the pot. Put the drinks away. The Straubs are here!" Joints got flushed down the toilet and windows flung open to expel the fumes. And there was Straub in white shirt at the door: a stark eminence, an intense purist.

Born in Alsace in 1933, he studied literature at Strasbourg and Nancy, ran a film society in Metz where he made the discovery of the abstraction of Robert Bresson's *Les Dames des Bois du Boulogne*, and in the mid-fifties in Paris was assistant on several films, including Jean Renoir's *French Can-Can* ('55), Jacques Rivette's *Le Coup de Berger* ('56), and Robert Bresson's *Un Condamé à Mort S'est Échappé* ('56). Loathe to fight in Algeria, he renounced French citizenship and moved to Rome. He and his wife and collaborator, Danièle Huillet, now lived in a small room in an old apartment building off the Tiber River. Many regarded them as the most uncompromising, radical voice in modern cinema. Eschewing "dull and boring naturalism," their aim was to bring the viewer into an active and thinking relationship to the film. Their works, minimalist and complex, emphasize the struggle between word and image.

Machorka-Muff (1963) is a short film, based on a Heinrich Böll story about the revival of militarism in Germany. *Nicht Versöhnt / Not Reconciled* (1965), perhaps their greatest work, is a 51-minute film about the effects of Nazism on Germans after World War II. *Chronicle of Anna Magdalena Bach* (1967) is a Marxist interpretation of the life and work of J. S. Bach, portrayed by the great pianist, Gustav Leonhardt. The Straubs have filmed works by Corneille, Brecht, and Schoenberg in modern settings. So rigorous and uncompromising are their later films as to make spectators fly to the exits. I remembered Godard's remark: "I look forward to the day when I make the kind of films that result in my being the only spectator left in the theater."

Jean-Marie and Danièle lived their lives in Spartan fashion. Shortly after the release of *Chronicle of Anna Magdalena Bach*, they came to New York. On this, their first visit, there were two things they wanted to do: visit Harlem and the Metropolitan Museum of Art. Not so uncommon: Harlem had a certain, almost iconic reputation in Europe, for jazz, violence, and drugs, and who of course did not want to visit the Met? The four of us drove up to 125th Street and wove in and out of the area. After a while Jean-Marie turned to us and declared, "It's not as bad as Cairo." It was a comparison that had never occurred to me, but on recalling the City of the Dead, that cemetery-village in Cairo where squatters cohabited with the deceased, I might have to agree. Still, Cairo was Cairo and Harlem Harlem. Next stop: the Metropolitan Museum of Art. And there they knew precisely what they wanted to look at: Cézanne. We ascended the escalator to the second floor and the Impressionists gallery. As to a lodestone, they halted in front of *Still Life with Apples and Pears*. And there they stood for half an hour, just looking at *that*, almost entering the frame. At dinner that evening in a modest Italian trattoria in Greenwich Village, when the meal was over, Jean-Marie stared at the bread basket, worrying about what would happen with the leftover bread. Would it go to waste?

Jean-Luc Godard

What can I say? *Breathless* indeed left me breathless on first viewing—a *moving* picture alive with *movement*, rushing sound, images, and jump cuts, Mozart and jazz riffs! A familiar American gangster-style movie, its "hero" (Jean Paul Belmondo), a Parisian cool cat, steals cars for a living, murders a cop, and recommences a love affair with a pretty American girl (Jean Seberg), who squeals on him to the police. Certain images were unforgettable: Belmondo with cigarette dangling from the side of his mouth (some young viewers took to doing it), an iris shot of Belmondo gazing coyly at Seberg through a rolled-up magazine, a protracted bedroom scene between the two self-destructive lovers, and an uncompromising end. Susan Sontag declared it a masterpiece. This was the French New Wave. And waiting in the wings (or already causing a sensation) were films from Resnais, Truffaut, Chabrol, and Rohmer!

Sometime in the sixties, our friend Claude Nedjar brought Dan to Jean-Luc Godard's apartment in Montparnasse. Claude, a good friend and jolly fellow, knew everyone in the industry. He was working for Louis Malle's company, NEF (Nouvelle Éditions du Film), managing productions and overseeing Malle's Pagoda twin theater in Paris and twin theaters in Munich. Despite the warm day, Jean-Luc was clad in a tweed suit and knitted tie. Quite formally, he shook hands with his visitors—a powerful handshake—then led them into a clean, well-lighted, uncluttered space, what one might expect from a well-bred son of a Swiss physician. The place was sunny but without glare, not warranting those dark glasses eventually associated as Godard's typical gear, but allowing him to scrutinize without being fully exposed. He subsequently said that the color values of black-and-white films are those obtained with dark glasses. Noted to be hermetic and taciturn, he struck Dan as gentle, civilized, and attentive. He spoke softly, solemnly, a slight rasp to his voice, and to the point. A clefted chin lent a sense of definitiveness. Ever alert to hands, Dan reported that Jean-Luc's were small and "good."

Godard's role was pivotal in the New Wave of young cinephiles who wrote for *Cahiers du Cinéma*: "Film is a revolutionary art because it is the sensation of movment," he declared. By the time he and Dan met, he had made five films: *Breathless* (1959), *A Woman is a Woman* (1961), *My Life to Live* (1962), *Le Petit Soldat* (1962), and *Les Carabiniers* (1963.) Breaking with the traditional dramatic and visual way of suspenseful storytelling, he leaned more towards exploring themes than to spinning plots or probing psychology. In *My Life to Live*, a placard announces what is about to happen. Some called him an essayist—*essayer* suggesting an attempt. Typically, he employs fragmentary techniques, staccato editing, dissociative word and image, master shots or close-ups with little in between, and playful references to pop culture—traffic signs, neon, advertisements, cartoons, exploration of signs, and references to earlier films and techniques. The term *Godardian* entered the cinema lexicon. Some complained about his didacticism, simplistic politics, and tricky maneuvers. Godard—polemicist, philosopher, and poet—took risks.

On that July afternoon, before lighting his own Gauloise cigarette, he offered one to Dan, who declined—not for being a nonsmoker, but rather preferring Lucky Strikes or Havana cigars, when lucky enough to get them. The Cuban embargo was in full force, and cigars sometimes arrived via Claude. Dan looked forward to them like a kid to candy. Born in 1930, Godard was just four years younger than Dan. How did it feel, Dan wondered, to be legendary at that age? Claude's raucous manner failed to lighten the occasion. Jean-Luc was not about to make small talk, particularly with a Distributor, no less an American one. Not that he was anti-American. He admired the great days of Hollywood's '20s and '30s, through the mid-forties, the creativity and artistry of American directors such as Alfred Hitchcock and Howard Hawks, and loved the Russians and neo-realists. Dan jumped straight to the point. "I love your work and would like to distribute anything you make." Yes, Godard knew that Dan was the distributor of two of his early works (*Les Carabiners* and *Le Petit Soldat*). That was OK with him, but as Dan reports, "it didn't get a rise out of him." He worked for a fee, didn't own the negative to most of his films, and never focused on what happened to his films *after* they got made. All he needed was money to make the next. In due course, in addition to *Les Carabiniers* and *Le Petit Soldat*, we distributed *Tout Va Bien, Letter to Jane, Two or Three Things I Know About Her*, and *Hail Mary*.

In 1964 our "Godard and More Godard" series included *Breathless, Vivre Sa Vie, Masculine Feminine, A Married Woman, My Life to Live, Alphaville, Band of Outsiders, A Woman is a Woman*, and *Contempt*. Addicted as I am to black-and-white movies, *La Chinoise* (1967) prompted a category of "Redness in Films" to include Antonioni's *Red Desert*, Kieslowski's *Red*, and Zhang Yimou's *Raise the Red Lantern*. Once when asked by a critic why there was so much blood in *Pierrot le fou*, Godard replied: "That is not blood, but red." Grace Borgenicht, an art gallery dealer, aware of our two painter daughters, advised us that "red sells."

Godard's view of American film ultimately changed. Movies, he said, were profit-driven and made by lawyer-types or agents. When both he and Dan received the New York Film Critics Award for Lifetime Achievement, Godard in typical no-show Jean-Luc fashion sent a telegram saying he wished there were more film people like Dan Talbot. With growing interest in video, he asked Dan to withhold his royalties and apply them towards purchasing equipment on 47th Street. Calling from his home in Rolle, Switzerland, he read aloud a video shopping list and asked Dan to handle his video productions. But much as Dan admired them, he turned him down. "As a theater man, I was too accustomed to the look, texture, and power of the 35mm image," he said. Godard appreciated this. Dan offered, however, to act as agent at no fee, making an arrangement with a small video distribution company that had expressed interest, and Godard insisted that this company work through Dan throughout the licensing period. Dan got him an advance, listed his 26-hour video film in our catalogue, and referred clients to the "Electronic Arts" section.

Godard was cooperative in publicity campaigns. He came to New York to work with us on ads, posters, and trailers for *Every Man for Himself* and helped design the poster. Very easy to work with, he was precise, firm, and knowledgeable, and always knew what he wanted. Generous with other filmmakers, he provided "short ends" (leftover parts of rolls of film) for Jean Eustache's *Le pere Nöel a les yeux bleus* (*Santa Claus Has Blue Eyes*), and when Eustache ran 20,000 francs in debt, Godard agreed to cover his costs and become the film's nominal producer. Godard is passionate, naïve, glib. You'll hear it all. Godard is his own man. He revolutionized filmmaking. Godard is a pleasure to watch.

Ousmane Sembene

Even as novice distributors, we began receiving work from young filmmakers. In 1965 we stood with our friend Louis Marcorelle (subsequently film critic for *Le Monde*) outside the narrow doorway of a small, shabby hotel on the Left Bank in Paris. Marcorelle wanted to introduce us to Ousmane Sembene, director of *Borom Sarret*, which had just won the Jean Vigo Prize at the Tours Film Festival (where Marcorelle headed the jury). A recommendation from Marcorelle deserved a salute. Down the steps descended a spry black man of around forty, pipe in mouth, who greeted us in Senegelese-accented French. The next day, in a small screening room, we viewed *Borom Sarret* and *Black Girl* and immediately put them into distribution. Sembene, the second director we distributed, is now regarded as "the Father of African Cinema."

Over coffee, in the adjoining café, we learned a bit about this individual whose education had taken place in the University of Life, as he put it. From the age of fifteen he worked as a fisherman, mason, mechanic, dock worker, and union activist. In the mid-1950s he began writing fiction and eventually published ten books, largely in French, many translated into English. His short stories and novels are politically and socially engaged: *Le Docker Noir* deals with a black dockworker, and *God's Bits of Wood* with the epic landmark strike of 1947–48 in Africa. In 1965, in the wake of Senegalese independence from France, Sembene, in light of the widespread illiteracy in Africa, turned to fiction. To this day only 40 percent of Senegelese are literate.

He studied cinema technique at the Gorky Film Studio in Moscow under Mark Donskoi, returned to Dakar, spent twenty years in Paris, and then toured Africa. "I wanted to know my own continent. I went everywhere, getting to know people, tribes, cultures. I was forty years old, and I wanted to make movies. I wanted to give another impression of Africa. Since our culture is primarily oral, I wanted to depict reality through ritual, dance, and performance." He regards cinema as "night school" and makes his films in indigenous languages rather than in French, thereby triggering a revolution in African filmmaking.

In *Borom Sarret* (1963) a young black in Dakar sets out with his horse and cart through the dusty medina for a day's work, his path ridden with obstacles. A young woman ready to give birth needs transportation to the maternity hospital, a legless beggar appeals for alms, a grieved father besieges to be driven with his dead infant to the cemetery, and, finally, a policeman halts the cart on the border of the affluent black bourgeois section of Dakar (which forbids horse-drawn carts), fines the driver, and confiscates the cart. Twenty minutes long and sparely made, *Borom Sarret* conveys life through the youth's eyes as he speaks to other characters or expresses his thoughts to himself. He returns empty-handed; his wife gives him the infant, saying: "I'm going to the city. We must eat." She will sell her body.

Tauw (1970) is a short film about a youth who, in order to get on a dock for a day's work, must buy a gate-pass with a hundred francs— which he doesn't have. *Black Girl* (1965), the first African feature-length film and winner of the 1966 Prix Jean Vigo for Best Direction, tells of a young girl from Dakar who, hoodwinked into working as a nanny for a French middle-class family in Antibes and virtually imprisoned as a housemaid, ultimately commits suicide. The power and economy with which Sembene films her life and her death (the latter in three stunning shots), and her strictly moral revenge, offer a stinging indictment of colonialism. Students, seeing those short films, immediately wanted to read about Senegal and to read Sembene's fiction.

Screenwriter, producer, director, and occasional actor (often adapting his own fiction), Sembene has made a dozen features, among them *Emitai*

(1971), *Xala* (1974), and *Moolaadé* (2004). The formal end of French colonial rule in 1965 did not produce an end to social injustice and drastic economic imbalance, and Sembene speaks of the "imperative of social and mental liberation, of Africa decolonizing itself to survive." His later films often denounce the callousness and chicanery perpetrated by the African petit bourgeoisie. In *Xala* he takes a humorous look at polygamy, traditional African medicine, and the contrasts between urban and rural life. *Emitai* and *Moolaadé* tackle the question of women's lives in contemporary African villages. *Emitai* conveys their social power as retainers of ancient myths, rituals, and struggle towards emancipation. *Moolaadé* (2004) is a rousing polemic directed against the still-common African practice of female genital cutting—termed "purification"—which fifty-two African countries still practice. It has been determined that 50 percent of childbirth deaths occur amongst women who have been subjected to that barbaric process.

Sembene's films, albeit not blockbusters, are seen in China, France, the United States, and Africa. "I was born on the continent and am from the continent. I'm a participant and an observer of my society," he said, and bicycled from one African village to another, presenting his films on a makeshift screen. At the 2004 Toronto Film Festival, at age eighty-two, encircled by filmgoers in the courtyard-garden of the Toronto auditorium where *Moolaadé* had just been shown, he responded as filmmaker, pedagogue, and whistle-blower. More than forty years after his first film: populist and universalist—same pipe, same wit and irony—he still shared the same commitment to cinema and to his people. Our friendship with him has been a gift. Sembene, *je vous salue.* He died in 2007 at the age of eighty-four.

Point of Order

One day in 1960, walking along Broadway, Dan came up with an idea and rushed home with his Eureka: "Why not rerun the entire Army-McCarthy Hearings just as shown on television in the spring of 1954, charging one dollar per hour?"

Why not? I countered. Like millions of Americans at home, in barber shops and bars, he had watched every bloody second of Joseph R. McCarthy trying to "prove" that Communists had subverted the armed forces. "I have here in my hand … " intoned the junior senator from Wisconsin, and out came the dirty goods. Susan Sontag called those morning hearings with McCarthy's bullying, whining cruelty, the real *comédie noir* of the season. Eleven years after World War II ended, Western democracies and Eastern state dictatorships were in confrontation: during that Cold War, the climate of paranoia and uncertainty was extreme. It may be hard for Americans born after 1945 to envision the scapegoating and state of fear during the grotesque McCarthy reign from 1950 to 1954. The Hollywood Ten went to prison for contempt of Congress. Arthur Miller relied on the First Amendment's guarantee of free speech rather than the Fifth Amendment for protection against self-incrimination, which had kept many non-cooperative witnesses out of prison. Some of our friends were blacklisted. The Rosenbergs were sentenced to death. McCarthy the Red-Hunter, and right-wing demagogue, epitomized the hypocrisy and moral theatrics of the American political scene.

Dan, unemployed at the time of the hearings, tended our two-year-old daughter while I was conjugating the imperfect subjunctive with adolescents at East Rockaway High School and trying to infect them with Don Quixote. In between feedings, he guzzled every image of the insanity that mesmerized America for thirty-six days: a great political spectacle, an actuality unfolding in real time, a forerunner of TV's power to influence public opinion. McCarthy was out to track down Communists in the State Department and in the Army, but Dan viewed the hearings as a kind of *High Noon* spectacle. No one could have cast it better: McCarthy, demonic, histrionic, grinning, with a rasping, nasal voice and W.C. Fields gaze, forelock bobbing over balding pate; sidekicks G. David Schine and dapper Roy Cohn, smart-aleck city kid, coaching mid-Western yokel Schine, and whispering with cupped hand into Joe's hairy ear. Evil lurked on sniper Joe's face in his posse after left-wing traitor "jackals." "He understood the perverse appeal of the bum, the mucker, the Dead End kid," said Richard Rovere in his classic study, *Senator Joe McCarthy*. Army counsel Joseph N. Welch initially treated McCarthy as a clownish rube, but, finally, when McCarthy deviously attacked Fred Fisher, a young lawyer in Welch's law firm, Welch accosted McCarthy with the outraged, now famous: "Have you no sense of decency, sir, at long last? Have you left no *sense of decency?*" It was the beginning of McCarthy's end. The smear campaign failed. On camera, we witnessed the "give 'em enough rope" scenario of public destruction. The tube might distort and obscure, but could also serve as a weapon in fighting demagoguery and revealing the truth. McCarthy never unearthed a single Communist who worked for the State Department.

"Call me Dee, everyone does," said Emile de Antonio when we met in 1960. Chino pants, a large fold of belly under button-down blue oxford shirt overriding the belt of his pants, testified to abundant beef and bourbon. As artist's promoter, he'd been steering Andy Warhol from ladies shoe ads for I. Miller into pop American iconography while representing Jasper Johns, Robert Rauschenberg, Frank Stella, John Cage, and Merce Cunningham before their renown. In that initial meeting, he proposed that we launch *Pull My Daisy*, which he was also representing. We found the 29-minute film irresistible and paired it with *The Magnificent Ambersons* in our second New Yorker program.

If one were to choose a single adjective to characterize an individual, for Dee it would be BIG. Hefty, expansive, ebullient, extravagant, and charming, he had a raffish smile and, when drunk, could boom out the words of Horst Wessel's Nazi anthem. Powerful, intelligent, and gallant, he easily captured front-center. But also he was impulsive, paranoid, and unpredictable, given at times to an "Only the Shadow Knows" laugh, which prompted keeping my guard up against some barbed remark that never came. At a small dinner party at our house, he and our friend Chandler Brossard took one look at each other and understood immediately that there wasn't enough room at our table for two kindred egos.

Words were exchanged, fists rose. Chandler saved the day and departed. Next morning, Dee sent a bunch of roses.

Before he promoted artists, it was unclear how Dee made his living. Born in 1919 in Scranton, Pennsylvania, the son of Lithuanian and Italian emigrants, he'd grown up in comfortable circumstances and entered Harvard in 1936. There he claims to have shared a class with John F. Kennedy and to have fallen in with radical leftist friends in the John Reed Club and the Young Communist League. But with Dee one never knew what was mythology or fact. In short order, he got expelled from Harvard after drunkenly setting fire to an elevator and spraying a policeman with an extinguishing hose. At Scranton University, he became further involved with working-class radicals and intellectuals, and in 1942 enlisted in the Marines but was expelled after three months for lack of training discipline. Though disciplined in work, Dee was ever resentful of conformism. Then, so he said, he worked as a riverboat captain. During the war, he retained his leftist associations, and by 1943 the FBI had a complete file on him. Resuming his studies in the forties, he pursued philosophy and English at Columbia University. In 1949 an inheritance from his father allowed him to live in a suite in the Plaza Hotel—Dee always liked "good," and the good life had arrived. In the mid-fifties, through the International Communist League, his connection with painting was formalized and he befriended, advised, and represented the aforementioned painters. "I've begun a new business: artists' agent," he wrote to his sister-in-law in 1956.

Dee referred to himself as an American Marxist—not a Marxist American, but an American Marxist. This helped him score with women; his ability to discourse on Hobbes and his riverboat Marxism disarmed young and middle-aged alike. A classy *Vogue* model as well as a gifted adjunct professor of English at Hunter fell under his spell. He married six times. Rumor had it that some of his wives provided for him. Once Dan received a call from Dee from a hotel room in Manhattan saying that he had just returned from some mission in London and was screwing an airline stewardess he had picked up on the flight home. He even put her on the phone. That man never had jet lag. Dee traveled among the liberal rich, who found him charming, even quaint. He *was* charming, magnetic, a good storyteller with excellent diction and a fine baritone voice. When seeking a narrator for *Berimbau*, a documentary I was making on mankind's earliest musical instrument, I chose Dee. You *wanted* to listen to that man, you wanted to build blazing fires on the beach with him and dig into one of his thick barbecued porterhouse steaks.

In 1960, shortly after we'd opened *Pull My Daisy*, Dan described his Army-McCarthy idea to Dee, who went gaga. That saga was a perfect vehicle for his American-Marxist curriculum. And what grabbed him was Joe McCarthy's anarchic spirit. He and Dan approached a television network that owned a complete set of the 16mm kinescopes of the thirty-six days of the 1954 hearings. The network asked for $100,000 for the rights, which today might be worth half a million dollars. No problem, said Dee, and in short order he approached Eliot Pratt, a liberal member of the old rich Yankee Pratt family. Over and above this $100,000, an additional $100,000 was to be given for the making of the film. In the deal with Pratt, there was to be a fifty-fifty split after the film had recovered all its costs. Dan and Dee took no salary. They screened the kinescopes, all 188 hours, in our living room. The room was a mess, cans of film strewn everywhere. As freighters carrying coal and oil silently sailed by on the Hudson, notes were taken of scenes that might be used. Suddenly, after hours of boredom, out came McCarthy's shout: "Point of Order!" Anticipation of those explosions was extraordinary. *Point of Order* became the title of the film. There was no voice-over commentary or manipulation of footage other than the reduction of 188 hours to 97 minutes.

There were scenes of sheer surrealism, such as the 45-minute conversation about a strawberry sundae at the Colony Restaurant. The form of the film evolved over a three-year period. At a certain point, seeking a professional film editor, Dan and Dee flew in from Hollywood Irving Lerner, an independent director with a left-wing point of view. The four of us drove to Tina Fredericks's East Hampton house for a weekend. Tina, daughter of the publisher of Rowalt Books in Germany before it was taken over by the Nazis, had worked as a fashion editor at *Harper's Bazaar* and, recently divorced, was Dee's friend. An intelligent woman, she became one of the most successful real estate agents on the East End of Long Island. While she prepared gourmet meals, Dee went out with his gun to shoot marauding rabbits. The three men spent Friday and Saturday evenings drinking bourbon and playing poker, but when Lerner quoted his high fee, Dee and Dan realized it would not work out. They asked around town and came up with Paul Falkenberg. German-born, stout, with monocle on a black string, he had worked with Fritz Lang on *M* and G. W. Pabst on *Diary of a Lost Girl* and edited various documentaries with Lewis Jacobs. He was given eight hours of potentially usable raw material plus a basic outline. Seven sections encapsulating the key moments in the hearings were to be winnowed down to less than two hours. For several months Falkenberg scraped along on a rickety Movieola. But Paul was further to the left of Dan and Dee. When down to two and a half hours, he inserted a scene of a May Day Parade in Moscow—to make an "ironic" statement about Communist infiltration in the Army. At this point he was fired. The last thing Dan and Dee needed was a Stalinist point of view. In the end, Robert Duncan, a young production editor, was hired and worked closely with Dan and Dee.

Dan and Dee exchanged ideas easily, were never competitive, worked well together, and differed only on the ending of the film. Since both were steadfast in their positions, they decided to flip a coin. Dee won and insisted, when it came time for film credits, that he be designated as director. There was in fact no direction of live people, just editing of footage and, save for the ending, the film was jointly made. But Dan agreed to the credit, regarding it as pretentious and knowing that he himself had no intention of ever embarking on another film. Filmmaking—a combination of money, art, ideas, technology, people, psychology, manipulation—is full-time work. By the time *Point of Order* reached the can, they were heavily in debt. In the end, the film wound up being financed by the New Yorker Theater's weekend box office receipts, which Dan brought to Movielab every Monday morning for processing.

One day Dee came up with the idea of screening the film for an audience of senators and congressmen in Washington, D.C. Social critic David Bazelon (his uncle a judge on the Court of Appeals) was living in Washington and had been hired to do some consulting on the film and to help organize the screening. Several hundred spectators showed up, including many members of Congress. The response was overwhelming. By 1964 Senator Joseph McCarthy was a certified villain—an archetypical demagogue, so mischievous as to refute any right as elected official or man of good faith. As the credits rolled at the end, Dan's face turned red with rage—both his credits had been removed by Dee. Outside, on the building's steps, I stood fuming at this violation. On the sidewalk Dan began denouncing Dee, who simply stood silent, blushing, finger caught in the cookie jar, showing sheepish remorse but offering no explanation. Dan's credit was restored and eventually he forgave this lapse.

Point of Order got sold to Continental Pictures, the distribution arm of the Walter Reade Organization. Dan and Dee were paid a large advance, enough to repay Eliot Pratt, though they themselves received no money and had worked for three years without pay. The film opened at the Beekman Theater in Manhattan to powerful reviews and ran for four weeks, a long period at that time for a documentary. It played spottily around the country without success.

Two unexpected things happened prior to the opening. Dee had an interview with the *Harvard Crimson* about the film. In it, he referred to Paul Falkenberg as a Stalinist, whereupon Falkenberg sued Dee and Point Films, the production company. They wound up paying a sum of money to Falkenberg and Dee wrote a retraction in the *Crimson*. A week before the film's opening, Dee and Dan arranged a private screening for Roy Cohn at the New Yorker Theater. Dee thought they could get some yardage out of it in the press. At the end of the screening Roy said: "I'm going to sue you guys. The film is false." When the episode was reported to *Variety*, one of Dan's statements was quoted: "We don't care if he sues, we've got insurance." Next day, a telegram came from their insurance carrier canceling the policy. But as it happened, one of the members of the Board of Directors of the insurance company was George Plimpton's father, and Dee, who knew George, got him to prevail upon his dad to reinstate the policy.

Over the following ten years Dee made numerous documentaries, often planning and consulting with Dan. He pioneered a new form of documentary which consistently advanced a left-wing political view. Avoiding the mainstream direct or cinema verité approach as well as standard voice-over narration, he often used "radical scavenging," as he called it—a collage technique that fused network footage (often obtained surreptitiously, which he calls the "real history of our time") with interviews in order to make damning critiques of media-clouded post–Cold War America. He labeled his work "the theater of fact" and today would be pleased to be known as a gadfly, a troublemaker, and progenitor of Michael Moore.

Among his films are *Rush to Judgment* (1967), a rebuttal to the Warren Commission's "lone assassin" conclusion on the assassination of John F. Kennedy; *In the Year of the Pig* (1968), a penetrating history of the Vietnam War; *America is Hard to See* (1968), a detailed chronicle of Eugene McCarthy's quixotic 1968 presidential campaign; *Millhouse: A White Comedy* (1971), a devastating chronicle—compiled from newsreel and TV footage and interviews with various commentators—on the public career of Richard Milhous Nixon; and *Painters Painting* (1973), a non-academic survey of modern art with canvases and conversations featuring Willem de Kooning, Jasper Johns, Robert Rauschenberg, Robert Motherwell, Jackson Pollack, Andy Warhol, and others.

In 1971, New Yorker Films—our distributing company—was lodged in one small room in a building that adjoined the theater. At street level was Joe Rosen's kosher butcher shop, a beauty salon, a dress shop, Benny's Luncheonette, and a leather goods store run by a short man with a thick Honduras cigar perpetually sticking out of his mouth. On the side street was Sol the tailor, and upstairs Lynn Oliver's Studio for musicians, where Dizzy Gillespie, Les Brown, Zoot Sims, and many others came to practice—their loud horns and foot-stomping shook the building and our office like a boat in a storm. Sally Brossard and Carol Gelber were the secretaries, while an anorexic British boy did the shipping, and I'd pop in to do my bit.

Running a film distribution business was so difficult it put Dan's soul into a funk. As beginners, we had to fight hard for outlets around the country to play our "off" films. When Emile de Antonio's *Millhouse: A White Comedy* got Dan on Nixon's "Enemy's List," all our lefty friends on the Upper West Side were immediately envious. "How come you got on and not us?" one asked. It so happened that the success of *Millhouse* made up for the minus-zero income from Straub, Bertolucci, and Chris Marker.

Sometime during the third week of its run, Dan got a visitor: a tall, lanky fellow, named Ullalawicz, formerly a New York detective and one of the Watergate burglars. He pronounced the word *film* as "fil-um" and wanted to talk about *Millhouse.* Dan said that he couldn't see him right away but he could go down to the theater, watch the show for an hour, and then come by to chat. Along with *Millhouse* we were also showing Robert Bresson's masterly *Pickpocket*, as part of a ten-week series premiering ten foreign and American independent films. Bugged by the poor caliber of film reviewing, Dan held no press screenings and charged one dollar at all times in order to encourage the audience to take a chance on these films. Each was to open on a Sunday to avoid opening day reviews. In a full-page ad in the *New York Times*, he attacked the critics (Pauline Kael helped write the text).

Pickpocket has a balletic ten-minute sequence in which three pickpockets (one played by Martin Lasalle, the others by professional pickpockets) ply their trade, working their marks in a railway station and on a train. Wallets, wristwatches, and jewelry fly all over the place. All the regular New Yorker Theater pickpockets showed up—not to pick pockets but to study the wrist action of their fellow artists.

It is easy to spot a pickpocket. In they come—thin, quick, with tracking-shot eyes until they locate their mark. My father knew them all. The way we dealt with one was to let him know we knew by posting an usher nearby. The usher would stare at the fellow, at which point he usually left. If not, the precinct was called, a few plainclothes men would arrive, and the pickpocket was arrested—by law in New York a pickpocket with a record is not allowed to be in a public place among many people.

So, anyway, here was this New York City gumshoe Ullalawicz, standing in back of the theater, mesmerized by the film. And guess what? His pocket was picked! Running up to our upstairs office, he shouted: "Hey, what kind of place do you run here?"

New Yorker Films

Our first catalogue appeared in 1971 with Dan's introduction:

> New Yorker Films is a new film library with a somewhat unique origin. It began as an extension of the New Yorker Theater, a repertory cinema in New York City long devoted to exhibiting the best New Cinema and important film documents, alongside classic revivals. Given the commercial instincts of most American film companies, it became necessary for the New Yorker to directly import (as well as exhibit) many important films deemed box office risks by the regular distributors. In the last three or four years the number of major films from Europe and the Third World overlooked by commercially motivated distributors has increased sharply. Hollywood is now supplying product to the small art cinema that used to show mostly foreign films: the exhibition market for truly independent foreign films (as well as American films made outside the industry) is as marginal today as it was before *The Seventh Seal* and the French New Wave created the art film syndrome of the late fifties and early sixties.
>
> There are very few theaters willing to show the most original and important films being made today. Film documents providing alternate sources of information on political subjects are deemed too

controversial. Narrative features from countries like Brazil or Senegal are judged too obscure. Personal works by such modern masters as Bresson or Skolimowski are too "difficult". New discoveries of classic genius, like the present re-discovery of Ozu, are considered best confined to the Museum of Modern Art. Hence the focus of New Yorker Films is on 16mm distribution to colleges and film societies, where there should be considerable interest in the New Cinema works and political documentaries offered in these pages.

As a translator, I know that it is easier to interest a publisher in an established classic rather than a new foreign author. With little trouble, I persuaded Noonday Press in 1958 to publish José Ortega y Gasset's *On Love: Aspects of a Single Theme*, and Frederick Unger to publish *Compassion* by Benito Pérez Galdós, the renowned nineteenth-century novelist. But publishers, anticipating unpromising sales, are reluctant to undertake a new foreign work since it entails absorbing permission rights from the author or estate or other publisher and paying a translator's fee. Hence, the United States publishes fewer translations than most European countries. Resistance to subtitled foreign movies is similar, in light of few national outlets. Yet most of our directors *were* from abroad: Roberto Rossellini, Robert Bresson, Jean-Luc Godard, Jean-Marie Straub, Ousmane Sembene, Chris Marker, Bernardo Bertolucci, Agnès Varda, Louis Malle, Bo Widerberg, Jerzy Skolimowski, Yasujiro Ozu, Kenji Mizoguchi, Akira Kurosawa, and Susamu Hani, plus German and Russian silent film classics.

Among the Independent American films and filmmakers were John Korty, Shirley Clarke, Emile de Antonio, Robert Frank, *Nixon's Checkers Speech*, *Interviews with Mai Lai Veterans*, *Far from Vietnam*, *An Interview with President Allende*, *Brazil: A Report on Torture*, and *Lenny Bruce on TV*. Many of these films reflected political events. Chris Marker's *Cuba, Battle of the 10,000,000* (1970) covered the period of the 1969–70 Zafra, the sugar harvest which was to have exceeded ten million tons but proved a bitter disappointment. In *Fidel* (1971), Saul Landau, sharing jeep and tent with Castro, accompanies Castro on a five-day trip through El Oriente province, during which he speaks of his guerrilla days in the Sierra Maestre, his cruel childhood, local problems, and listens to the needs of villagers. Castro speaks frankly of Cuba's problems, stemming from underdevelopment and the American blockade. There are newsreel inserts of the Bay of Pigs, and flashbacks showing Fidel and Che in the mountains during the guerrilla campaign. In an attempt to remain objective, Landau interviews political prisoners and Miami-bound members of Cuba's vanishing bourgeoisie.

In the early seventies, Dan and I were invited to a Latin American Film Festival in Havana. Intrigued by the achievements of the revolution, we were eager to see for ourselves what life there was like, and were particularly interested because José López, our assistant manager, had arrived from Havana several years back. Yet, not to be beholden, Dan insisted on paying our own way. Having gone to Cuba in the fifties after graduating from college, this was to be my second trip, and I began describing the beauty of the island, the Hotel Nacional in Havana where I had stayed then and where we'd be staying now (shimmering chandeliers, mahogany appointments, veal scallopini embellished with a slice of lemon and served in the garden by the fountain).

Owing to the blockade, it was impossible to fly directly from New York. One had to go via Mexico or Miami. At the Miami airport, we spent a few hours with the López family. In 1961, at age fourteen, José Jr. had arrived in New York on the Peter Pan Airlift from Havana. His father, proprietor of several pharmacies, hoping for a restoration of democracy, was an early supporter of Fidel Castro and had raised money for the rebels while they were in the hills. But now, disillusioned with the new regime, he wanted his son out of the country. I recall, on my first trip to Havana in the mid-fifties, those squalid shacks from the airport to the Malecón seawall of the city, with children begging in streets not far from posh country clubs replete with Johnny Walker, hookers, barbecues, and bidets. Small wonder the need for a revolution—who could not protest Fulgencio Batista's corrupt regime? But José López Sr. had had reason to change his mind.

On seizing power in 1959, Castro centralized the government, removed moderates, suppressed the news media, jailed dissidents, and finally confiscated "bourgeois" ventures, including López Sr.'s pharmacies in Havana and Santiago. Ideology was ideology. Private property had to go, private opinions had to go. Reform precluded dissent. Foreseeing that youth would be brainwashed, López dispatched his son on that Peter Pan Airlift, to be received in New York by his uncle Rolando Martin. The ultimate plan was for the entire family to leave. When young José arrived, Rolando asked Dan to give the teenager some work.

Barely speaking English, he started as an usher. This was his first job. He rose to be assistant manager, while Dan became a surrogate father and my parents surrogate grandparents. As my father's Parkinson's condition worsened, José would accompany him home, help him to undress and get into bed. In the ripeness of time, young cashiers from Hunter, City College, and Columbia—writing dissertations on Joyce, Durkheim, or Freud—provided a trove of lithesome young women. This one or that one? José would question my mother. One day he showed her a gold-and-blue striped tie purchased from Brooks Brothers, in which he planned to propose to Alicia, a beautiful, traditional, Dominican young woman in the stamp of his mother. Ultimately, José became office manager of the New Yorker Distribution Company. We have worked together to this day.

In 1962, José's father, mother, and sister crossed the ninety miles to Miami in a small vessel, traveling light and carrying just a little suitcase for a presumed weekend stay. Never again would they set foot in Cuba. One winter morning before the theater opened, when Dan happened to be in the lobby, a man in a camel hair coat and wearing a gold signet ring appeared. Rolando had sent him to ask for a job. A movie house, albeit large, is small in staff: projectionist, manager, cashier, ushers, and night porter. Dan, in his usual chinos and sneakers, looked this elegant man up and down and, somewhat embarrassed, told him the only slot available was for a night porter. Without a blink, Mr. López said "I'll take it." For seven years he cleaned the theater until he, his wife, and daughter moved to Miami. Cold winters were not to his liking—he referred to the snow as white mud. "Thank God, my son is in good hands," he said on parting years later. Now, in the Miami airport, seeing us off for Cuba, he remarked: "If a ninety-mile bridge were built from there to Miami, it would be flooded with people leaving." I hoped not.

We flew in an iffy one-engine plane and arrived in time for Fidel's welcoming blitz against Yanqui imperialism. No matter, we'd come to see films. The light bulb in our room was bereft of fixture, toilets of covers, and breakfast was a sickly frankfurter with watered-down coffee—mere quibbles in light of what the population got. Rationing was severe, and in this agricultural land burlap sacks in groceries held wizened potatoes. Colonial buildings were blistered and unpainted—*abandonados.* Soviet aid had not filtered down. Yet education was free, as were transportation and medical care; nurseries and day care centers were luminous and well-staffed; Cuba was training good doctors. And those were the things that counted. Not to mention that ice cream in the park was affordable.

But the atmosphere embittered the bite. Visitors with money might order *mojitos* and horsemeat stew in the very same restaurant attended by Ernest Hemingway. With money one could take a cab, though idle drivers might pass you by—no incentive: they didn't keep the fare. The streets had been "cleaned up"—not a prostitute or homosexual in sight. Subversives had been jailed, or gone into exile. Nestor Almendros, the prominent cinematographer, was one who'd left, and in 1984 he and Orlando Jiménez-Leal directed *Improper Conduct,* a chilling indictment of the systematic persecution of writers, dissidents, and homosexuals. The novelist José Guillermo Cabrera Infante had also left for England. But tourists could go to La Tropicana for a floor show with a flamboyant lineup of feathered chorus girls.

One day Dan and I were sitting in a square near a school and a church which, like all others, had been closed down. It was the recess hour. A curious boy, spotting us as foreigners, approached the bench and sat down alongside. We told him our names, he told us his, glancing furtively all the while over his shoulder in case he was being spied on. By age ten, he knew to be careful, having incorporated self-censorship. Who knows, even a neighbor, concierge, or school teacher might denounce him or a member of his family as "subversive." Jacobo Timerman's *Cuba: A Journey*, which I translated in 1992, cited many examples of this inner network. The bells for the church on the square tolled for no one. When the schoolbell rang, he hurried off but gazed at us long and longingly.

There is a strong pro-revolutionary, propagandist component in most of the films of the early Castro days, the decade spanning 1959 to 1969, widely considered the golden age of Cuban cinema. One of the greatest of the period is Tomás Gutiérrez Alea's *Memories of Underdevelopment* (1968), adapted from the novel by Edmundo Desnoes, about a bourgeois intellectual adrift in post-revolutionary Cuba. The time frame switches from the Bay of Pigs era to the 1980 Mariel boatlift, when the hero at the last minute refuses to join. *Memories* is a brilliant exposé of the contradictions inherent in the response of Cuba's progressive bourgeoisie to the revolution. The protagonist is trapped in a bleak existential position. Another film of that period is Humberto Solás's *Lucia*, which traces the dramatic history of the island by examining the lives of three women called Lucia. It begins with the struggle for independence from Spain, proceeds to a bourgeois intellectual presenting a scathing criticism of the excesses of 1930s glamour, and concludes with the passions aroused by political revolution.

Dan and I did not remain to the end of the festival. Having paid our own way, we felt free to leave and spent an entire unnerving day at the consulate getting permission to do so. As our rickety plane rose to the sky, we were glad to get the hell out of there. It was painful to see the heavy price being paid for Castro's attempt to do what other Latin American societies failed to do. No one in Havana was abandoned in the streets; old and young had medical care; illiteracy was eliminated. Posters everywhere read *Todo por el Porvenir*—Eveything for the future. What lay in store was hopeful.

Cinema Novo and Latin American Films

Cinema Novo was an organized cinema movement of Brazil, and ultimately of the Third World. Glauber Rocha, its leading theoretician and film-maker, said: "Brazil is such a varied and big country, its culture such a challenge, that I often think that Brazilian is not merely a nationality. It is a condition. Latin America is being shaken by a revolution, and for a few of us the cinema is a political arena." The basic aim of Cinema Novo was to make films that authentically reflected Brazilian culture, making them quickly and cheaply for widespread distribution. Brazil's commercial cinema had been largely colonized by American capital and Hollywood aesthetics. Typical were kitsch musicals, crude melodrama, and movies that exploited the false image of Brazil as a tropical paradise à la Carmen Miranda, often taking place in happy/sunny Rio de Janeiro. But Brazil's indigenous culture survived in the Northeast, in unique Afro-Portuguese ways and with feudal landowners. Its vast arid *sertão* (parched backlands), with draught-ridden migrant workers, bands of *cangaceiros* (rebel bandits), and crazed holy men, served as the epic backdrop for the early Cinema Novo films.

Glauber's *Barravento* (*The Turning Wind*), in black and white, is set in a small fishing village on the Bahian seacoast whose inhabitants live in a superstitious past that hampers self-expression and progress. Glauber Rocha acknowledges his debt to the neo-realism of Rossellini and the operatic strain in Visconti. Alberto Moravia compared its theme and content to *La Terra Trema*. But Rocha, a spokesman for change, had a political message.

We met him at a Soho loft party. Short, thin, olive skin, with jet black hair, he had a delicate face and delicate hands and a deep, resonant voice. Aside from his native Portuguese, he spoke French, English, Spanish, and Italian. The occasion was a *feijoida*, Brazil's national dish made with manioc, beans, and assorted, unidentifiable parts of a hog, accompanied for this gathering by chunks of peasant bread, whiskey, and pot.

Seated across the room was a black musician in African attire playing an instrument that resembled a large hunting bow—I remembered having seen one in *Barravento* where two men in a *macumba* ceremony perform a kind of shadow dance, accompanied by the instrument. Someone next to me, who introduced himself as Affonso Beato, asked if I'd like to meet Nana, the musician. A tall man, with penetrating eyes, Nana spoke no English—I spoke in Spanish, he in Portuguese. So taken was I by the *look* and *sound* of the *berimbau*, I decided on the spot to attempt a film.

The next Tuesday, at eight in the morning, Nana, Affonso Beato, and I met on the balcony of the New Yorker. With Affonso behind the camera, and walls behind Nana draped in black, we shot and recorded his music. And how he played! Aside from ritual African chants and *capoeira* melodies of slave origin, he performed his own original compositions—Nana could make music with a matchstick against a wall. By the time the theater opened at noon, our footage was shot. In the following months, in Columbia's Butler Library stacks, I researched the instrument and unearthed old engravings from musty tomes.

The *berimbau* is a one-stringed musical bow classified as a percussion instrument. It is struck by a small stick (*vaina*) and resonated with a gourd. The instrument derives from the hunting bow millenniums ago. I envisioned an African hunter, resting one day on a log, idly fooling around with his bow, then picking up a stick and starting to strum. Delighted by the extracted sounds, he hurries home, picks up one of his wife's harvested gourds, and applies it as a resonator. In the sixteenth century, blacks seized as slaves from Angola by Portuguese landowners brought their *berimbaus* to Brazil and on them played traditional songs, accompanied by seemingly innocent, but actual warrior dances.

In the next few months Affonso and I edited the footage in the Mayles Brothers' laboratory on Broadway and 46th Street. Every now and then, he'd offer a joint, assuring me that I didn't have the makings of an addict. A 20-minute film resulted, Nana playing and Emile de Antonio narrating. It opened at the Fifth Avenue Cinema. Nana went on to become an international figure, Affonso returned to Brazil and became a noted cameraman who worked with Martin Scorsese among others.

Incantatory and magical is the *berimbau*. Like the cave paintings of Altamira and Lascaux and other expressions of early art, it both transmits and triggers culture. The primitive *berimbau* became a modern chamber instrument, capable of improvisation and subtle modulations. Once plucked in an ancient forest, it is now played and danced to by young men in today's markets. Go to Bahia and you'll see them.

In the late seventies, Glauber, fleeing the military junta, moved to Paris. When Dan and I visited him, his career was going nowhere. He missed Brazil, and was smoking dope day and night. One evening, when the three of us went to Pruneau, a three-star fish restaurant, he had to be helped up the stairs. The maitre d' took one look at his woolen poncho, Brazilian fedora, and feverish eyes and gave us a funny look. But having reserved, we got seated—in back. Shortly after, Glauber moved to Los Angeles. Feeling better, he was working on a new script and had found an offbeat Hollywood producer to raise the money. But paranoid and longing for his country, he ran adrift. About a year later in San Francisco, while Dan was visiting our two good friends Mel Novikoff, America's premiere exhibitor of quality films, and Tom Luddy, programmer of the Pacific Film Archive, he heard that Glauber was ill and imagining that people were trying to poison him. Dan went down to Los Angeles and bought him a one-way ticket to Brazil. A few weeks later, in a hallucinated moment, he denounced Dan as a CIA agent. After some months, a long correspondence ensued between Dan and Glauber, who was contemplating running for president of Brazil. He died in the late eighties.

The Cinema Novo peaked with Rocha's *Black God, White Devil* and *Terra em Transe* (aka *Land in Anguish/Earth Entranced*), Nelson Pereira dos Santos's *Barren Lives* (*Vidas Secas*), Gustavo Dahl's *O Bravo Guerreiro*, Carlos Diegues's *Ganga Zumba*, Ruy Guerra's *The Gods and the Dead* and *The Guns*, Walter Lima's *Plantation Boy*, Joaquim Pedro de Andrade's *The Priest and the Girl*, Leon Hirszman's *They Don't Wear Black Tie*. *Barren Lives* won the Palm d'Or in Cannes in 1963. They were all premiered at the New Yorker, and in the zeitgeist of the sixties our audience identified with them. Other political films from Latin America emerged. *The Hour of the Furnaces*, made in 1968 and directed by Fernando Solanas and Octavio Getino, was a three-part documentary on the liberation struggle in Argentina during the sixties, a struggle not uncommon in countries with a powerful entrenched elite.

In 1974 I translated for UNESCO *The First Stages of Modernization in Spanish America* by Roberto Cortés Conde. A daunting translation, it presented an unfamiliar lexicography of economics: input, output, gross national product, etc. So laborious were those endless columns of numbers and percent signs, I felt at moments like flinging my manual Remington out the window. In those pre-computer days, backspacing, deleting, or correcting a misspelling was not an option. Each use of White-Out produced a mess that required retyping. Finally meeting the deadline, I delivered my misery, not at all confident of the finished product—an imposter tackling terminology. Surely the publisher would call in short order to tell me there were "problems." A few weeks later, a call did arrive. Was I ready to take on volume two? No, thanks. Yet the task, though onerous, was enlightening. The economic colonization of the Americas, begun with the conquistadors, endured for centuries through foreign investment—British-refrigerated railroad cars for shipping beef in Argentina, oil investments in Mexico, bananas in Central America, etc. Latin America has undergone a sad history. Monocultures (rubber and coffee in Brazil, tin in Bolivia, sugar in Cuba, coffee and bananas in Central America) arrest economic diversification. Dictatorships flourish, indigenous populations suffer, the disparity between the privileged and poor grows—side by side in Rio, they live in different spheres of existence.

In the early seventies I gave a course at the Fifth Avenue Cinema: "Latin America as Viewed through Film," sponsored by the Center for Inter-American Relations in conjunction with the New School. The 273-seat theater, an art house at 66 Fifth Avenue in Greenwich Village (and originally known as the Fifth Avenue Playhouse), premiered films of high quality, such as Satyajit Ray's *Pather Panchali* and Pasolini's *Accattone*. The feature films in my course included *Los Olvidados* (Luis Buñuel), *The Hour of* the *Furnaces* (Fernando Solanas), *Barren Lives* (Nelson Pereira dos Santos), *Black God, White Devil* (Glauber Rocha), *Big City* and *Ganga Zumba* (Carlos Diegues), *The Priest and the Girl* (Joaquim Pedro de Andrade), *The Courage of the People* and *Blood of the Condor* (Jorge Sanjinès), *Os Fuzis/The Guns* (Ruy Guerra), *Tropici* (Gianni Amico), *Earth Entranced/Terra em Transe* (Glauber Rocha), *Memorias del subdesarrollo/Memories of Underdevelopment* (Tomás Gutiérrez Alea), *Reed: Insurgent Mexico* (Paul LeDuc), and *Aguirre, the Wrath of God* (Werner Herzog). Leading historians, political scientists, sociologists, and literary critics came and discussed political and social issues.

The blurring between fiction and nonfiction films was quite evident. Back in 1947, André Bazin, the French film critic, said that every film is a social documentary. Buñuel's *Los Olvidados* (1950), inspired by newspaper reports of Mexico City slum kids, depicts a gang of gutter punks who literally pull the ground out from a legless man and rob the blind. "All characters are real," states the movie's prologue. But about an hour into the film, Buñuel's surrealistic touches sneak in: in a dream sequence, 13-year-old Pedro imagines his mother offering him a glistening slab of raw meat, subsequently snatched away by the gang leader. In Buñuel's earlier *L'Age d'Or* (1930) there was a similar overlap of documentary and fantasy. And his 1932 *Las Hurdes (Land without Bread)* was a stark documentary depicting impoverished Castile. Hector Babenco's *Pixote* (1981), like *Los Olvidados*, chronicles the lives of street children in São Paulo and the hellish school to which they are sent. As in Italian neo-realism nonprofessional actors are used whose real lives resembled those of the protagonists in the film. Tragically, its young protagonist, Fernando Ramos Da Silva, was killed at the age of nineteen by Brazilian police.

When we showed Gillo Pontecorvo's *The Battle of Algiers* (1966) at the New Yorker, you sensed the urgency of those revolutionary cells plotting their actions against the French and you could practically *smell* the casbah. It is a meticulous, documentary-like dramatization of events that actually happened, featuring many of the Algerian participants playing themselves (especially the main terrorist, played by Saadi Yacef). Columbia students came to see it more than once. Robert Kramer's *Ice* (1969) is a gripping political fiction of a nationwide revolutionary offensive (Dan, by the way, had a bit part as a Secret Service agent). "Revolutionary cinema does not tell stories," said Jorge Sanjinés, the Bolivian director. "It is a cinema that makes history." Cuban filmmakers were equally at home with fictional and nonfictional documentaries to express reality. *Memorias del subdesarrollo* has strong elements of documentary within the script: newreel footage intercut with narrative. When subtitling Paul LeDuc's *Reed: Insurgent Mexico*, I took pains to transpose extracts from John Reed's book—he himself had noted the fine line between onlooker and participant. Stage by stage in the film, the viewer enters into the true realities of the Mexican Revolution: skeleton mountains, organ cactus, bands playing in dusty plazas, starving peons dying for liberty, land, water, and schools.

Documentaries seek to transmit direct images of reality "without a mask, as a world of naked truth," as Dziga Vertov put it. While in Chile to interview Salvador Allende, Saul Landau and Haskell Wexler had the opportunity to speak with a group of exiled Brazilian political prisoners who testified to the tortures received at the hands of the military/police specialists. The documentary that resulted was *Brazil: A Report on Torture* (1971). The men reenact the most common tortures, explaining the mechanics of such brutal instruments as the *pau de arara*—"Parrot's perch." Their descriptions spare no details, yet invite no false sentimentality. It is the *concreteness* of documentaries that fascinate. *The Brickmakers* (Martha Rodríguez and Jorge Silva) tells of a shantytown family in Colombia that earns its living making handmade bricks; Helena Solberg-Ladd's *Double Day* is about women working in agriculture, manufacturing, and domestic service part of the day and as mothers and wives the rest of that day; Raymundo Gleyzer's *The Land Burns* is about the marginal rural poverty of Brazil's *sertão* (Gleyzer became one of the 30,000 "disappeared" during the rule of the Argentine junta); and Gabriela Samper's *Los Santísimos Hermanos* deals with a messianic death cult in Colombia. Students were intrigued. I was hooked. When the theater building became part of the New School for Social Research, that course evolved into one I currently give at the New School: "The Human Condition Seen through Film." The course, alternatively, might be called "Openings" in its attempt to "open" students to significant political and social issues and to *active* viewing.

"It's just a documentary" used to imply something cut and dry and droning. But Dziga Vertov's *Man With a Movie Camera*, Alain Resnais's *Night and Fog*, Leni Riefenstahl's *Triumph of the Will*, Marcel Ophüls' *The Sorrow and the Pity*, Louis Malle's *Phantom India*, Errol Morris's *The Thin Blue Line*, and Claude Lanzmann's *Shoah* do more than document actuality. They convey fact *and* feeling. In *Nanook of the North*, Robert Flaherty was untroubled by a mixture of documentary with fiction. Jean Rouch, as well, broke the false line drawn between documentary and drama. In 1959, the year before his own breakthrough of *Breathless*, Jean-Luc Godard contended that all great fiction films tend toward documentary. No work, students soon realize, is objective. Bias, received opinions, and point of view come into play. "All the news that's fit to print," declares the *New York Times*. "*Sez who ?*" they say in the Bronx. Or, as an Andalusian villager put it, "Yesterday's newspapers serve to wrap today's fish." There are documentaries from A to Z—anorexia to zoology—and in a large class some student invariably has had a personal encounter with a given topic. For others, it will be news. Unfortunately, as revealed in discussions and critiques, what happened the day before yesterday may for some be news.

In 1981 I translated Jacobo Timerman's *Prisoner Without a Name, Cell Without a Number*. Timerman, editor and publisher of *La Opinión*, an Argentine newspaper comparable to the *New York Times* and *Le Monde*, had dared to criticize his government's policy in the "dirty war" of the seventies against left-wing dissidents and suspected "subversives," which resulted in the arrest and "disappearance" of hundreds of its citizens. In his Sunday edition, he published the names of the *desaparecidos* . On April 15, 1977, Timerman was kidnapped by military authorities and held captive for thirty months. The book describes his captivity, torture, and interrogation. I learned a new lexicography for "softening up" the prisoner for a session with the "machine"—"a chat with Susan," as they called it.

That testimony became instrumental in advocacy of human rights. But, unfortunately, some of those torturing techniques, still not outmoded, have been employed by our own government.

When I met Timerman in New York in September 1979 at the home of his childhood friends, Dora and Amnon Issacharoff, he was a traumatized man, stripped of citizenship and expelled from Argentina. Years later, over a drink at the Algonquin bar, he took out a magazine article written by William Styron, "Darkness Visible," which described Styron's own suicidal depression, and read aloud a passage: "For those who have dwelt in depression's dark wood, and known its inexplicable agony, their return from the abyss is not unlike the ascent of the poet, trudging upward and upward out of hell's black depths and at last emerging into what he saw as 'the shining world.'" Dan and I became good friends with Timerman. This self-educated, worldly, and pragmatic man, who during the Peronista regime managed to straddle necessary fences, turned out to be an avid moviegoer with a keen eye. He liked nothing better than to discuss the latest movie he'd seen at our theater. What he said was witty and shrewd. What hovered in his soul was eternal.

Earlier, in 1979, I had translated another Argentine novel, by Humberto Constantini, a writer living in exile in Mexico City. *De Dioses, Hombrecitos y Policías* (*The Gods, the Little Guys and the Police*) is about the terror in Argentina during the Dirty War. Most of the characters and deeds in the novel were invented though the story emerged from real circumstances. Ordinary people—a circle of amateur poets—are carted away in unlicensed black Ford Falcons (like the one that nabbed Timerman) and tortured by a sinister group of government-supported para-police. Luisa Valenzuela, another Argentine whose work I translated, described in her short stories and novels the pervasive atmosphere of fear and paranoia generated during that era. Coups, dictatorships, kidnappings are an old Latin American story. That story has not ended. *¿Qué hacer?*

One day in 1971, Glauber Rocha showed up at the New Yorker office with a short, skinny kid in a brown leather hat who was looking for a job.

His name was Fabiano Canosa. Since we were in one of our film distribution cash crunches, there was no job, but Dan hired him anyway. Canosa proved enthusiastic and eager to learn. But, as it turned out, he was constitutionally unable to show up at 9:00 A.M. A night soul, he stayed up till early morning, rolling and smoking joints with fellow Brazilians, playing samba tunes, and singing American songs, of which he was a master historian. "Dan," he said, "I love you, I love New Yorker Films, and am willing to work until midnight, but not early in the morning. Can't we work something out?" Somehow we did, for close to two years.

Fabiano always needed money. Brazilian visitors were continually crashing his place and, generous to a fault, he could never refuse compatriots. He mothered them, fed them, provided whiskey and pot. Dan managed to get him a side-job as a producer's representative, with a staggering fee of $1,000 per week, to line up American films that this producer could resell in Brazil. After eight weeks, Fabiano was fired and told Dan he needed a raise of a thousand dollars more a week. Then, hired by Joseph Papp, he directed a cinema program at the Public Theater—but Papp's successor decided to discontinue the film program at the Public and that was the end of that. Canosa is a walking cinema encyclopedia with total recall of countless films. And he knows where to find every print. He has programmed festivals in São Paulo and Rio de Janeiro and could do so anywhere in the world. He is universally loved. Viva Fabiano.

One day Dan said "Let's go to Rio." The Barretos had invited us to their seaside home in Buzios, two hours outside of Rio, a Brazilian version on a smaller scale of the Hamptons. The Barreto family is a cottage film industry: Luiz Carlos (cameraman for *Vidas Secas*) at the helm, his wife Lucy producer and office administrator, her mother an assistant. Years later, their sons Bruno and Fabio became filmmakers (Bruno's *Dona Flor and her Two Husbands* played for months at our Cinema Studio), and their daughter Paula (who married Brazil's most famous soccer player) began to run their office.

In Buzios we talked about *miuras* (pronounced "meeyouras"), a term invented by the Italian director Gianni Amico, director of *Tropici* and aficionado of Brazilian culture, to describe films of quality appreciated mainly by cinephiles but—and this was the determining factor—doomed at the box office. The word actually refers to unfulfilled sexual activity between a bull and a cow. Gustavo Dahl's *O Bravo Guerreiro*, for example, and most of Brazil's Cinema Novo, were *miuras*. As to the films of Straub–Huillet or the early ones of Phillipe Garrel, the term was simply inadequate. A new word needed to be coined, unless you said *miura-issimo*. We sometimes said *miureen* with emphasis on *een*. This was our private and affectionate denomination. New Yorker Films (and later its DVD offshoot New Yorker Video) specialized in *miuras*, films not yet part of any canon but which liberated and invigorated one's sensibilities and consciousness. Such was Brazil's Cinema Novo.

Catalogues

A stack of New Yorker catalogues sits at one corner of my stainless steel desk. At the other end, in magisterial solitude, rests a black leather tome bound in burgundy with all the New Yorker Theater programs from 1960 to 1973: Exhibition and Distribution on the same stage. Chaste white is the cover of that first catalogue, published in 1971, yet undated—timeless as it were. On its cover is a black silhouetted skyscraper of Manhattan with a caption: New Yorker Films. This would become our logo, appearing on all subsequent catalogues, and on the screen of all New Yorker releases. I smile when an audiences applauds, on seeing it. The following catalogue, bright Kelly green, appeared in 1976–77. The theater had been sold by then and we were devoting ourselves wholly to distribution. An alphabetical column of directors flanks the right side of that catalogue—innovators of classic films in the sixties and seventies. That column moved to the back cover the following year, to be replaced by a still from a newly released film. Much discussion went into choice of color and image.

Independent filmmakers figure prominently in our first catalogue: John Korty's *Funnyman* (1967), shot on location in San Francisco; Shirley Clarke's *The Connection* (1961), about eight junkies waiting for a fix, and *Portrait of Jason* (1967), about a black homosexual male prostitute; Robert Frank's *Me and My Brother* (1968), about schizophrenic Julius Orlovsky, who lives and travels with his brother Peter and Allen Ginsberg; *Pull My Daisy*, and *Conversations in Vermont*, about Frank's two teenage children, Pablo and Andrea, at the school-commune in Vermont. In New York, Robert and his wife Mary, a painter and our daughter Nina's mentor, lived with their children, Pablo and Andrea, in the Belnord on 86th Street. Mary's attic studio overflowed with sketches, paintings, and miniature clay figures—fugue figures and dreamscapes inhabited her work. Robert, solemn, stolidly Swiss, captured plumb reality in his renowned photography collection *The Americans*. The beef liver and onions he served us was down-to-earth.

That first catalogue is sheer sixties: *Nixon's Checkers Speech*; *Lenny Bruce on TV*; *Paris Uprising: May 1968*; Robert Kramer's *Ice*; *Interviews with Mai Lai Veterans*, directed by Joseph Strick and documenting as few films have the matter-of-fact, yet haunting, experiences of soldiers who participated in that massacre. And I am suddenly reminded of that indelible, iconic photograph by Nick Ut that appeared in the *New York Times* of a fleeing child hit by napalm who has torn off her clothes.

Rossellini and Bresson are its first entries. My mind wanders. When did we first see *Open City*? And *Paisan*? Was it 1947 when they were released at the World Cinema on Broadway and 54th Street? Will Dan remember? When did we play them at the New Yorker? We met Rossellini himself in 1970. By then he had abandoned his neo-realist films about the working class, had made the much-admired more detached, philosophical *Voyage to Italy* (1954), and begun addressing dialectical films. Roberto was ever reinventing himself, ever questioning the relationship between moving images and the world. Godard, when asked if he were to name a master, said it was Rossellini. He admired that man's will to independence. And perhaps his pedagogical streak.

We premiered Rossellini's *Socrates* in 1970. Rather than "entertain" the spectator, he now enlists us in the "human stories" of such figures. The film recounts the period from the Spartan Conquest of Athens in 404 B.C. to the death of Socrates in 399 B.C. Dialogues provide dialectical examples of Socrates' mode of reasoning and his ideas on madness, eloquence, death, justice, politics, rhetoric, beauty, knowledge, and the immortality of the soul. Far from a traditional film biography— melodrama and spectacle rejected—it pursues Rossellini's "pedagogic" phase in which he thought that "history, taught visually, can go beyond dates and names. Abandoning the litany of battle, it can surrender to its social, economic, and political determinants. It can build not on fantasy, but on historical knowledge, situations, costumes, atmosphere, and men who had historical significance and helped the social developments by which we live today. … Through their human qualities, they can become the embodiment of action." Rossellini's studies of St. Frances, Louis XIV, St. Augustine, and his 1958 film *India* adhered to that approach. How I wish I could tell him that his daughter Isabella has become a friend and enrolled in my documentary film class.

Traveling to the Ledger on the other side of my desk—this shared surface—I open to find myself at October 5, 1960, with *Weddings and Babies*, directed by Morris Engel. Morris and Ruth Engel (Ruth Orkin) were Upper West Siders and lived with their son and daughter on Central Park West. His first film, *The Little Fugitive*, which appeared in 1953, is about a seven-year-old Brooklyn boy who, mistakenly believing he has killed his older brother, runs away to hide in Coney Island. Made on a budget of $30,000, it was shot on location with a lightweight 35mm camera. Impressive in its intimacy, it went on to influence other independent directors, among them John Cassavetes and François Truffaut, who drew on its childhood themes and production techniques to create *The 400 Blows*. In an interview for the *New Yorker*, Truffaut told Lillian Ross: "Our New Wave would never have come into being if it hadn't been for the young American Morris Engel, who showed us the way to independent production with his fine movie, *The Little Fugitive*." *Weddings and Babies* (1958) is the more autobiographical story of a photographer whose artistic ambitions are thwarted by his fiancée's dreams of domesticity. When we visited the Engels, Ruth was snapping pictures of their children and taking photos from their window overlooking Central Park. Morris was a street photographer, her photos were of the hearth. I found it easy to identify with that tug between Work and House.

Engel's films set me to thinking about other independent films of that period. Shuffling back a few pages to April 28, 1960, I arrive at *Come Back Africa*, directed by Lionel Rogosin. It is a dramatized documentary about the plight of a dislocated Zulu family in Johannesburg, South Africa, partly shot with a concealed camera to avoid scrutiny by the authorities. In 1956, Rogosin had used his own money to direct and produce the documentary *On the Bowery*. Both films are in black-and-white, raw, and have a powerful effect. In the early sixties we met Rogosin, more or less at the same time as we met Barney Rosset and Arthur Cohen. What the three shared in common was having come from wealthy families. Yet rather than clip coupons they poured their funds and energy into bold political, social, and literary projects: Rogosin with documentary films; Rosset as the risk-taking publisher of Grove Press (confronting American courts with D. H. Lawrence's *Lady Chatterley's Lover* and Henry Miller's *Tropic of Cancer*), the *Evergreen Review*, and sometime film distributor (*I Am Curious Yellow*); and Arthur Cohen, co-publisher of Noonday Press, one of the first to publish Machado de Assis, the great nineteenth-century Brazilian author of *Dom Casmurro*, *The Posthumous Memoirs of Brás Cubas*, and *Quincas Borba*, untranslated until then into English.

Back to the white catalogue: on page 24, Agnès Varda's *Les Créatures* (1966). Varda, sometimes called the "Grandmother of the French New Wave," laughs at this—there's nothing grandmotherly about this woman, who still seems the youngest of the New Wave directors. *Les Créatures* focuses on a mysterious island in Brittany where allegory, science fiction, and a dose of the supernatural all bubble merrily. A novelist (played by the delicious Michel Piccoli) and his pregnant wife (Catherine Deneuve), mute as a result of a car accident, inhabit an eerie island house. He is writing a novel whose progress parallels the birth of the baby. This film about creativity juggles illusion and reality: the writer's story becomes the film's own plot, the villagers they encounter become its inspiration, and at the same time, the couple's love seems nurtured and even enriched by the absence of dialogue. It is definitely not a grandmotherly film.

One day in June 1966, shortly after our release of *Les Créatures*, Agnès Varda waves us into her house at 15 rue Daguerre in Montparnasse, five minutes from Boulevard Raspail. We follow her through an outdoor passage into a courtyard to say hello to Jacques Demy. They are a complementary couple in this garden of earthly delights: Agnès roundish, earthy, and voluble; Jacques slender, ivory-cameo delicate. His films create magical worlds: *Lola* (1960), *La Baie des Anges* (1964), and *The Umbrellas of Cherbourg* (1967), which won the Palme d'Or at Cannes in 1964. Our children saw *Umbrellas* three times during its two-day run at the New Yorker, enchanted by its vivid palate of indigo, saffron, olive, and aquamarine, Michel Legrand's music, and Demy's lyrics. In Cannes, shortly after Jacques died, Agnès premiered *Jacquot de Nantes*, based on his life from when he was a kid fiddling with a camera. It is an unsentimental film tribute, with Jacques himself given a film credit.

Agnès Varda is unclassifiable as a filmmaker. An autodidact, she worked initially as a photo-journalist for TNP (Theatre National Populaire), and in 1954 wrote and directed her first film, *La Pointe Courte*, a reportage of two lovers visiting a small village near Marseilles. In the deconstructed style of William Faulkner's novel, *The Wild Palms*, the film presents us with one character's face in profile, the other staring into the camera—a forerunner of Bergman's *The Silence* and *Persona*.

"Agnès is a true artist," Bertolucci remarked one evening in our living room sometime in the late sixties. Indeed, she knows how to look. When we go to an Alexander Caldwell exhibit at the Guggenheim, her eye picks up the minutest detail in a mobile. At a flea market, she spots an antique ceramic doll which will wind up in her garden and a Mexican broach on her blouse. Yes, Agnès knows how to look. The concept of gleaning, or collecting, a portion of crops on a farmer's field for the needy is not new. Agnès is a gleaner of images. Everything is material, everything usable, as shown in *The Gleaners and I*. With a photographer's eye, she gives gleaning a new life. Foragers of every stripe transform the castoffs of others. A man feeds himself from what people leave on their plate—and looks quite healthy!

There is nothing ivory-towerish about this practical person. She has converted a building adjacent to her residence into a film laboratory used by herself and rented out to other filmmakers. Ousmane Sembene has edited several of his films in that space. A hands-on filmmaker: she *makes* the film and *makes* it work. *Manos limpias* —the proverbial "clean hands" of Spanish nobility—is not up her alley. When *The Gleaners* was launched, she herself delivered flyers to the theater. At a special showing at the New School, she arrived from Paris just three hours before the evening performance. To avoid traffic, I insisted on taking the subway. But we happened to get on the wrong train; unfazed, she followed me to the right one. We arrived in the nick of time to a full audience at Wollman Auditorium. One question followed another. After an enthusiastic ovation, imagining how tired she must be from the trans-Atlantic flight, I announced "We have time for one last question." Indomitable Agnès glowered at me: "And why a *last* question?"

Varda alternates between fiction and documentary. I adore her documentary *Daguerréotypes*, about shopkeepers in her quarter. "Chance is my best first assistant," she says. "I want to go on writing in straight, cinematic terms and, of course, directing the camera eye. Pure, complete cinema. That is my passion." Her best-known films are *Cléo from 5 à 7* (1961), *Le Bonheur* (1964), *Vagabond* (1985), *Jacquot de Nantes* (1991), and *Les Glaneurs et al Glaneuse/The Gleaners and I* (1999–2000.)

As I sit at my desk, meandering through catalogues, night falls. The blue-black river is the color almost of a mussel shell. Sailboats sit anchored not far from shore—their spindly masts so very white. All is motionless, not a ripple on the water. A large vessel wends its way into the frame: a Circle Liner taking tourists around the island. My eyes track its path until slowly it moves into peripheral view and disappears. The nocturnal vision brings me into the opening shot of Bresson's *Four Nights of a Dreamer*, a *bateau mouche* gliding down the Seine around the Pont Neuf.

We are Bresson devotees. His films grace our catalogues: *A Man Escaped* (1956), *Pickpocket* (1959), *Une Femme Douce* (1969), *Four Nights of a Dreamer* (1971), and *Lancelot of the Lake* (1974). In February 1970 the New Yorker did a retrospective of his work, including one of my favorites: *Au hasard, Balthazar*. *Notes on Cinematography* (1975) is a slender book of aphorisms often in my purse—to be read on the subway or in a doctor's office. Bresson's aphorisms invite repeated readings just as his films invite more than one viewing. He is often referred to as a patron saint of cinema, not only for the strong Catholic themes in his oeuvre, but for his convictions. Jean-Luc Godard declared: "Robert Bresson is French cinema, as Dostoevsky is the Russian novel and Mozart is German music." Bresson strove to make films "express the ineffable," what he called "interior movement." Everything considered false or unnecessary is removed. His actors do not *act*, but are vessels in this distilled reality. Many of his aphorisms are in my journal:

My movie is born first in my head, dies on paper, is resuscitated by the living persons and real objects I use, which are killed on film but, placed in a certain order and projected on the screen, come to life again like flowers in water.

There is only one way of shooting people: from near and in front of them, when you want to know what is happening inside.

Cinema is an attempt to create a new language of moving image and sound. ... What is for the eye must not duplicate for the ear.

When one violin is enough, don't use two.

A Man Escaped, released in 1956, was a critical and popular success in Europe but a total failure in the United States. We revived it several times at the New Yorker. It is based on a newspaper narrative by resistance leader André Devigny on his escape from a Nazi prison in Lyons just hours before he is to be executed. The film constructs from his most external acts the drama within—with no sense of boundaries between the physical and spiritual. Bresson minimizes the facts of prison life by concentrating on his character's solitude and the objects for escape— the spoon Fontaine has to steal and then shape into a cutting tool; the grate he must transform into a hook; the bedding he must braid into rope. It is not a "hot" film, not ingratiating. As in all his films, Bresson refuses to let his actors "act." He demands that they strip themselves of gesture and facial expressions and speak almost in a monotone. Yet the minimal images, spare commentary, the few bars of Mozart's C Minor Mass are mesmerizing. Even Pauline Kael declared, "The Bresson hero's ascetic, single-minded dedication to escape is almost mystic. I know that all this makes it sound terribly pretentious and yet, such is the treacherous power of an artist that sometimes even the worst ideas are made to work."

In 1983 a 76-year-old Bresson invited Dan and me to a private screening in Paris of his latest film, *L'Argent* (it turned out to be the last of the fourteen he made). He stood in back of a small screening room to assure that the projection be no less than perfect—maniacal about detail, he awaited our response.

L'Argent was adapted and updated from a short story by Tolstoy. A young man unsuccessfully asks his father for an advance on his allowance. Goaded then by a friend, he passes a forged 500 franc note at a photography shop. The shopkeepers thereupon pass the bill on to Yvon, an unsuspecting deliveryman, who is arrested and sent to prison. Unable to find another job due to his tainted employment history, Yvon descends into a life of crime, despair, and eventually, murder. The pursuit of money leads to the destruction of his soul. In *L'Argent* every action leaves a trace, nothing is superfluous.

When the lights went on after the screening, Bresson was still standing in back: broad forehead, shock of white hair, clairvoyant eyes, erect in a yellow sweater. What does one say to a master? To a perfectionist? "He expresses himself cinematographically as a poet would with his pen," said Jean Cocteau. The projection had been perfect, but Bresson was ready for a concrete conversation, whereupon we discussed an opening at the Cinema Studio. Vincent Canby reviewed it in the *New York Times*: "Original and fascinating … a ruthless tale of greed, corruption and murder (by) one of the most rigorous and talented filmmakers of the world."

The next morning the Hudson River appears motionless, small craft slumbering. At the steel desk, resuming my ramblings, I turn to the green catalogue and find Louis Malle. We had met him in the late sixties through Claude Nedjar, the manager of Malle's distribution and production company, when we began going to Paris to acquire films. At that time, Malle turned over to us *Elevator to the Gallows* (1958), *The Lovers* (1958), *Zazie dans le métro* (1960), and *The Fire Within* (1964). *Elevator to the Gallows*, his first feature, and arguably the first New Wave movie, is an archetypical Hitchcockian noir film about an aging war hero and the boss's wife (Jeanne Moreau), who contrive to murder the inconvenient husband. It had music by Miles Davis. *Zazie* is a freewheeling take on Raymond Queneau's argot-filled novel about a foul-mouthed 11-year-old girl visiting her drag-queen uncle in Paris. It's a book both Dan and I loved, and the film captures Queneau's punning style through sight gags, film parodies, and visual games. My favorite of that period is *The Fire Within*, an account of the last forty-eight hours of a dissolute playboy, relentlessly heading for suicide. *The Lovers*, a tale of adultery between a fashion-obsessed provincial wife (Jeanne Moreau) and a brusquely unhypocritical young man, created an uproar when it opened at the Paris. Its steamy over-the-top eroticism set me to giggling and Dan banished me to the rear of the theater.

In 1969 Malle asked Dan to distribute *Phantom India*. A seven-part documentary, six and a half hours long, it is culled from four months of travel in 1968. The first part, *The Impossible Camera*, defines Malle's relationship to the subject matter, stressing his identity as a Westerner, an outsider observing another culture. Like James Agee in the introductory passages of *Now Let Us Praise Famous Men*, he conveys a sense of humility, characterizing himself as an intruder, a plunderer. The visit was made in '68 and seems to be a self-questioning of his own origins and the momentous nature of '68 events.

"Sometimes, India staggers you," Malle laconically remarks. "The reality is not as simple as it may appear." Nor were Malle's life and work that simple. Scion of a famous sugar family, he was given to wearing bluejeans, frequenting Cuban-American eateries on Amsterdam Avenue, and chewing gum. *Phantom India* takes in both urban and rural, sophisticated and primitive India—Calcutta, Madras, Kerala, Bombay. It reflects on art, religion, politics, the caste system, racial and religious minorities, and Indian commercial filmmaking. In the dying city of Calcutta, fishermen and peasants toil, and women laboriously hand-shape bricks for the construction of an immense tourist hotel. Alongside ancient temples and awesome natural beauty, people are dying of hunger. A separately released 90-minute feature, *Calcutta*, which grew out of the same trip, aroused the ire of the Indian government for its display of the city's grinding poverty. Malle's commentary is soft, diffident, winning. Gary Arnold of the *Washington Post* called it one of the greatest documentaries ever made and certainly the greatest travel documentary.

When the commentary begins, it often seems uncanny. Malle echoes one's own first impressions and apprehensions, then proceeds to complicate them with contrasting data. It's amazing the number of times Malle seems to anticipate our responses and questions. We have the illusion of traveling with a personal friend.

Phantom India was shown, section by section, as a second feature in a 1972 series of new films. Some of the sequences capture fantastic sights. One of the strongest belongs to an early passage of unflinching natural history—dogs and vultures gathering to feed off a dead water buffalo while a farmer plows his fields in the distance. Malle lingers over the feeding, bringing the camera gradually closer to the corpse and the dogs and the birds, until they are individualized and memorialized in a strange, affecting way.

From time to time, Malle confided with Dan over his intended projects. In 1982 he asked him to read the script of *My Dinner with Andre*, unsure of whether he wanted to make the film. Dan read it in one sitting with great excitement, urged him to make the film, and even got the French film company Gaumont to invest $50,000. When he showed Dan a rough cut, Dan had no suggestions to make; the film was perfect, he thought. It covered areas of malaise and doubt that would touch many people. After a slow opening at the Lincoln Plaza, twelve weeks into the run the film took off. Word-of-mouth rocketed it into orbit. It played for fifty-four weeks and went on to another hundred cities.

Wealthy as Louis was, black beans and rice were not beneath him. But when we visited him at his large manor on the outskirts of Cahors, his brother Bernard, an erudite bibliophile, descended to the wine cellar to fetch a 1982 Bordeaux to accompany the truffle omelette made by their brother Vincent. Louis and Dan had a harmonious relationship. They enjoyed bumping into each other, at a Dreyer screening for example at the Museum of Modern Art. He often sought Dan's opinion of certain films playing in town, and was pleased when their tastes coincided. Never complacent in his career, Malle alternated between documentary and fiction, ever anxious as if each film were the first.

By the seventies the French New Wave was in full swing—Godard, Truffaut, Chabrol, and Rohmer. Some lesser known directors also appeared in our green catalogue, filmmakers who shunned the traditions of orthodox cinema and created unorthodox works. Jacques Rivette was one of the most eloquent of the young cinephiles who gathered at the Cinémathèque. In 1963 he took over the editorship of *Cahiers*, succeeding Eric Rohmer, who had succeeded André Bazin. Rivette trumpeted American cinema and the comprehensive mise-en-scène of Erich von Stroheim, Roberto Rossellini, F. W. Murnau, and Fritz Lang. His own legendary black-and-white film, *L'Amour Fou* (1968), ran for over five hours, with ingenious interplay between 35mm and grainy 16mm footage. Partially improvised by the actors, it shows a theater group preparing to stage Racine's *Andromaque* and the ensuing conflict between the producer (Jean-Pierre Kalfon) and the actress, his wife Claire, playing Hermione (Bulle Ogier). Claire walks out because she objects to the intrusive presence of a documentary movie crew filming the rehearsals for television. At one point, she reads from Hermione's lines, which echo her feelings about her husband: "Where am I? What have I done? … / What madness seizes me? / Aimlessly, I wander through the palace. / I do not know whether I love him or I hate him … "

The Mother and the Whore established Jean Eustache as one of the most innovative post–New Wave directors when in 1973 it won the Special Jury Prize at Cannes. James Monaco wrote in the *New York Times*: "It may well be the most important film of 1973." Like his contemporaries Rivette and Rohmer, Eustache revitalized the function of the actor in modern French cinema. *The Mother and the Whore*, shot in black and white, has very little action and no flashy editing. It is composed almost exclusively of talk—monologues, dialogues, stories, confessions, conversations. Jean-Pierre Léaud, on screen as Alexandre for almost 215 minutes, is an accomplished mock-philosopher. At age thirty, he has no visible means of support, wears long flowing silk scarves (sometimes two at once), smokes Gauloises down to the end, and reads Proust aloud in existentialist cafés. He is a master of "hanging out." Eustache declared: "Why can't cinema be the art of reflection rather than that of action? It's an art of images, I agree. But somebody's face and voice is also cinema."

The New Wave, however, was not simply French. There were European counterparts—harbingers of future careers: Alain Tanner in Switzerland, Bo Widerberg in Sweden, and Jerzy Skolimowski in Poland. Bo Widerberg became known in the United States through *Elvira Madigan*, having already gained a following in Europe through his first feature,

Raven's End (1964), which was praised by Vincent Canby and Andrew Sarris. It's about a bright young man, a would-be writer, drowning in his father's failure, who finally breaks away from home to make his own place in the world. It is a cry against the all-encompassing inertia of lower working-class life. Polish Jerzy Skolimowski's *Identification Marks: None* (1964) and *Walkover* (1965) depict characters who suffer a more modern alienation—not from work (they do not work), and not from poverty, because they know how to hustle. They are alienated from a society informed at every level by a dull and repressive bureaucracy.

In Germany, a major new cinema sprang up in the seventies: Rainer Werner Fassbinder, Volker Schlondorff, Werner Herzog, Wim Wenders, and Jean-Marie Straub. *A Free Woman*, co-written by Schlondorff and Margarethe von Trotta, released in 1972, was considered by some as the first masterpiece of the women's liberation movement. One Sunday in 1970 we visited Volker and Margarethe in their modest apartment in Munich, where he screened for us *Baal* (based on a Brecht play) and *The Sudden Wealth of the Poor People of Kombach* (1970), which is based on a true story about seven peasants who, in 1821, robbed a tax collector's wagon and were subsequently caught, tried, and executed for their crime Those not informed on, or who didn't reveal themselves by conspicuously spending money, gave themselves up to extirpate their sins. The thieves, according to the director, were doomed from the start "by the structure of society, which made it impossible for the disadvantaged to see through their situation and to change it. Superstition and religion, edifying public school nonsense, and a paternalizing conception of justice make poor people into bungling simpletons who are even taught to laugh about their own clumsiness, that is, to accept it as God's will. That is to say, they seek their salvation in irrational beliefs." That afternoon, we drove to Marienbad. The grand austerity of the park was a dramatic contrast to that peasant world.

Werner Herzog is one of the most passionate and prolific of German directors. His protagonists are outsiders: his theme obsession. In settings as far-flung as an Aegean valley filled with windmills, a God-forsaken Wisconsin truck stop, the rim of a volcano about to erupt, and the heart of the Amazonian jungle, Herzog films individuals who live outside "normal" bourgeois society. Dwarfs, deaf-mutes, a demented conquistador, the world's greatest ski-jumper, a cannibalistic tyrant, super fast-talking auctioneers, and maniacal preachers people his films. His first feature film, *Signs of Life* (1968), is about three bored German soldiers assigned to guard a munitions dump on the Greek island of Cos, off Crete, and the gradual descent into madness of one of them. *Even Dwarfs Started Small* (1970) shows an uprising in an asylum as a microcosm for crumbling bourgeois values. Like Varda and Malle, Herzog has shuttled between documentary and fiction. One of my favorite Herzog films is *Land of Silence and Darkness* (1971), a feature-length documentary about a middle-aged German woman, deaf and blind, who tries to help fellow-sufferers. Neither sentimental nor depressing, it explores the incommunicable nature of people, the idea of man being his own handicap. One morning in 1977 Herzog read a news item of a volcano in Guadalupe about to erupt and one man who had refused to evacuate. Fascinated by this man and his view of death, Herzog packed up his camera and went to Guadalupe. The volcano was spewing toxic fumes but, to the bafflement of geologists, never blew up. We premiered Herzog's *Aguirre, the Wrath of God* (1974) at the Cinema Studio. It is about a band of conquistadores in Peru in the mid-1500s searching for the mythical city of El Dorado. Its exotic Amazon setting and Klaus Kinski's manic, over-the-top performance drew large audiences. In Paris it ran continuously for eighteen months. *Stroszek* (1977) is to Herzog what *Ali: Fear Eats the Soul* is to Fassbinder. It tells of three oddly-assorted Berlin misfits who follow the American dream to a forsaken truck stop, Railroad Flats, Wisconsin. The title role is played by Bruno S., the Berlin streetsinger and former mental institution inmate whom Herzog had previously used to play Kaspar Hauser. The memorable conclusion of *Stroszek* involves a flaming truck, an amusement arcade, an Indian chief endlessly circling a ski lift, a frozen turkey, a single gunshot, and a dancing chicken.

Wim Wenders's *The American Friend* (1977), which premiered at the Cinema Studio, is based on Patricia Highsmith's thriller *Ripley's Game*. Widely considered the major revelation of the 1977 Cannes festival, it established Wenders, along with Fassbinder and Herzog, as one of the major figures in German cinema. The story centers on an ordinary Hamburg resident (Bruno Ganz) employed by a manipulative American art dealer to work as an assassin for a French gangster. Hollywood mavericks Sam Fuller, Nicholas Ray, and Dennis Hopper appear in the film. It includes two remarkable action scenes, one in a Paris metro station and another on a speeding train. Nicholas Ray, a close friend of Wenders, watched the film more than once. In 1979, Wenders made *Lightning Over Water*, a painful film about Ray when he was very ill.

Alain Tanner

Alain Tanner's first film, *Charles Dead or Alive* (1969), put an almost nonexistent Swiss cinema on the international map. The film begins in Geneva, Tanner's least favorite city—"full of banks and American spies with their children." It tells of an aging conformist who suddenly drops out of life and emerges a madman. *La Salamandre* (1971) was written in collaboration with the English writer John Berger as was *The Middle of the World* (1976) and *Jonah Who Will be 25 in the Year 2000* (1976). In *La Salamandre* Bulle Ogier gives a hilarious performance as Rosemonde, the spacey, defiant heroine who shoots her guardian-uncle because he bores her. She travels from job to job. Her first job consists of slipping condom-like casings over an industrial nozzle that ejects macerated sausage meat. The finished product looks like an enormous penis. She walks off the sausage job when her boss criticizes her hair as messy, leaving the machine to spurt out endless yards of innards. Later, working in a shoe store, she gets herself fired when she deliberately caresses the legs of every customer, male or female. Like the salamander, Rosemonde can endure fire and survive. A defiant lady, she refuses to succumb to the view of her held by two suitors trying to write a story about her. The film had a good run at the Cinema Studio.

Jonah Who Will be 25 in the Year 2000 tells the story of eight veterans of 1968, stranded between revolution and accommodation. Tanner's interest in the drop-out continues: In *Messidor* (1979) he recounts the exhilarating, terrifying odyssey of two female hitchhikers, children of Swiss security and plenty, into a world of accident, crime, and flight. *In the White City* tells of a sailor (Bruno Ganz) who jumps ship in Lisbon to wander the steep streets and alleys of the ghostly "white city." Tanner the Swiss Man rebels against the stodginess and security, the "cleanliness" of his society.

One weekend, he visited us in our home in Watermill, Long Island. He had no interest in swimming in the ocean, and was aghast at how often we showered and bathed—all that water not good for the body. Though his films had a spontaneity, a naughtiness, a frothiness, his own movements suggested slowness. "When I go into my office, the first few hours I just pace back and forth," he told me. There was no need to entertain this guest. Not keen to go swimming, or pick beach plums for jam, or take long walks, sitting and talking sufficed. But when it came to punctuality, his Swiss-clock mentality prevailed. Driving him to Kennedy Airport to catch his flight back to Europe, we got snagged in traffic. "There's plenty of time, don't worry," I kept reassuring him. And there was. (Though I must confess that my getting-there-at-the-last-minute syndrome—arriving *juste*—is a thrill.) Tanner became increasingly edgy as his watch ticked away, we moving at a snail's pace. He began sweating, eyes darting at the cars jammed in the next lane. Jaw clenched, he stopped talking, and when I turned on WQXR to relieve the tension, he gazed at me with a look of near hatred. We were in a pileup of cars like in Godard's *Weekend*. Enmeshed in a nightmare of Sunday drivers, this measured observer lost control. With more than minutes to spare, I dropped him off at Departures. With barely a backward glance, he dashed through the revolving door.

Jack Gelber

When I was a kid, a friend accused me of reading the dictionary. I still like doing that. One word leads to another like in the old library system of card catalogues—when you scanned for a desired item, one card rubbing against another, and brought you to new places and ideas. Now as I thumb through our New Yorker catalogues, one film leads to another, one director to another. How can I omit talking about Jack Gelber?

We saw his play *The Connection* before having met him, though he and his wife Carol lived with their children, Jed and Amy, but a few blocks away on West End Avenue. The production, put on by the Living Theater in a rundown theater on Eighth Avenue and 14th Street, was the freshest play we'd seen in years—its language hit you in the gut. It is about eight junkies waiting for a fix in a Greenwich Village loft. More than just a slice of life with guys rapping, jiving, blowing cool jazz, it was a provocative theatrical experience, the proscenium barrier between a complacent voyeuristic audience broken by a taunting actor. Robert Brustein gave it a rave review in the *New Republic*:

> The most striking thing about the work is its Spartan honesty. The only false note of the evening is struck by your own conventional expectation, conditioned by phony drama and sociological indoctrination. … *The Connection* forms the basis for a brilliant theatrical occasion, and it lives in that pure, bright, thin air of reality which few of our "good" playwrights have ever dared breathe.

Gelber's career was thereupon launched. In the 1961 film, directed by Shirley Clarke, an actor (Roscoe Lee Browne) and his camera stand in for the actor-in-the-orchestra, and a "film about making a film" is written into the screenplay. A savage text and an inventive camera, all taking place within a single claustrophobic set, produce an edgy mise-en-scène.

We and the Gelbers became good friends. When we entered distribution in a tiny office above the theater, Carol became our secretary.

They were a loving, symbiotic couple and great travelers—Spain, Scotland, Honduras, the National Parks. We joined them, bird-watching in Sarasota, Florida, and gathering shells on Sanibel Island. Jack's curiosity roamed wide, his cultivation totally unpretentious. Never did I hear a malicious remark from him. When my mother accompanied us to *The Connection* in that 14th Street theater, her response was *nebech*—compassion for its fallen characters. The last time I saw Jack was in May 2003 at the New School where both of us were teaching, he Dramatic Writing, I Documentary Film. It was 12:40 as I was going up the elevator to the fourth floor when the elevator stopped on two. The door opened and I saw Jack at mid-distance—that lively, kind, bearded face. It was one of those startled, happy moments of spotting a friend. My class, however, was about to begin and there was no time to get off. We smiled and waved. Jack died two days later. He was waving goodbye.

Nagisa Oshima

Nagisa Oshima, universally considered to be the most important force in modern Japanese cinema, is often called the "Godard of Japan." He sees himself as being *in* Japan but not of it. An innovative director, he broke with the studio that launched his career. His most active years were spent worrying about specific Japanese issues: responsibility for the war, racial prejudice against Koreans and other foreigners, colonial attitudes toward Okinawa, and a series of political wrong turns in Japan's postwar history. *Diary of a Yunbogi Boy* (1965) is a 24-minute black-and-white film about a ten-year-old Korean boy, typical of the many who roam the streets of Asia. Abandoned by his mother, he peddles chewing gum, herds goats, shines shoes in the battle against starvation. Lonely, he draws his mother's face from memory, and then a pigeon, wishing he could become that pigeon and "fly around the sky to look for Mama." *Yunbogi* is a "short" slim in production values yet so moving and hard to forget. Will this child become a revolutionary? How will the viewer incorporate this cry?

Many of Oshima's greatest films are inspired by true stories, including *Violence at Noon* (1966), a fractured portrait of a serial rapist and the two women who love him; *Death by Hanging* (1968), a Brechtian screed against capital punishment and Japanese xenophobia; and *Boy* (1969), a coming-of-age tale about a family that forces its eldest son to fake traffic injuries. The subject of *The Ceremony* (1971) encompasses the entire history of postwar Japan. "Ceremonies are a time when the special characteristics of the Japanese spirit are revealed," said Oshima. As one of the family members of the powerful Sakurada family in the film observes: "We only see each other at weddings and funerals." Elaborate flashbacks delve into the family's past—a whole spectrum of relatives, Communists, war criminals, and businessmen: indeed, the family becomes Japan. What starts out looking like one of those long and formal Japanese sagas spins into a nightmare of incest and inversion. The long cycle of weddings and funerals begins to blur together, most notably on the hero's surrealistic wedding night, consummated in a coffin. "All families must be disinfected," declared Nagisa Oshima.

Satyajit Ray and Ismail Merchant

Satyajit Ray is India's greatest filmmaker and, with Renoir (whom he worked with on *The River*), Mizoguchi, Rossellini, and De Sica, one of the masters of humanist cinema. In 1995 we presented nine of Ray's films at the Lincoln Plaza Cinemas. They were restored for this major release through the efforts of the Merchant and Ivory Foundation. *The Apu Trilogy* is based on Banerjee's classic autobiographical novel and hauntingly scored by Ravi Shankar. It traces Apu from birth to early manhood and simultaneously expresses India in transition. *Pather Panchali* (1955), the first of the trilogy, is a dense mosaic of Bengali village life seen through the boy's eyes. In elemental black-and-white images, it recaptures childhood, harsh poverty, death. I was deeply moved when I first saw it, have seen it time and again, and showed it in my class as an example of the fusion of documentary and fiction. *Aparajito* (1956) and *The World of Apu* (1959) take Apu through the modern city streets and schools of Benares to the University of Calcutta, beyond self-consciousness to the destruction of his egotism, and the rebirth of feeling.

"Call me Ismail," said Mr. Merchant when *Shakespeare Wallah* opened at the New Yorker in 1965. Bombay-born, Ismail Noormohamad Abdul Rehman became a brilliant businessman and a good friend. In 1961 he and James Ivory (his future lifetime business partner) formed Merchant Ivory Productions in order to make English-language theatrical features in India for the international market. He came up with a scheme to finance MI productions by persuading various American studios to use money in their rupee accounts that could not legally be repatriated because the Indian government had frozen them. *The Householder* (1963) and *Shakespeare Wallah* (1965) thus came about, with a remarkable triumvirate team (Merchant, Ivory, and prize-winning author/screenwriter Ruth Prawer Jhabvala), spanning over forty years. Merchant was hugely energetic. He was a charmer and persuaded fine actors to work cheap. An astute businessman, he oversaw fifty-three films. *The Householder* and *Shakespeare Wallah* remained my favorites until *The Remains of the Day*, based on Kazuo Ishiguro's novel, with Anthony Hopkins's subtle performance. Merchant-Ivory films have even made money—a rare occurrence for art house movies.

One evening Dan and I went to their East Side apartment. Jim greeted us at the door. Ismail emerged from the kitchen—dark, handsome, with glowing eyes, and holding a bottle of chardonnay. As he filled our glasses, I complimented his beautiful embroidered white batiste purdah. Sniffing the fish roasting in the kitchen, Ismail disappeared, presumably to check on it. He returned, this time in a pale blue purdah, and presented me with the white one I had admired. Immediately I thought of that Spanish admonition not to admire some item another was wearing. Dinner was delicious: striped bass marinated in yogurt and spices, curried spinach, a basmati rice pilaf, and chocolate cake. I am indebted to Ismail for his friendship, his cuisine, and to the Merchant and Ivory Foundation for restoring Satyajit Ray's films.

It would be selfish not to share the marinade recipe: In a blender combine ½ cup yogurt with 1 small onion, 1 clove garlic, 1 teaspoon grated fresh ginger, ½ teaspoon ground coriander, ½ tablespoon cardoman seed, ½ teaspoon turmeric, 1 teaspoon chile powder, and a pinch salt. When all is blended, coat 2½-pound striped bass (or red snapper, sea bass, etc.) and place in refrigerator for half an hour or more. Bake in 350-degreee oven for about forty-five minutes (until translucent).

Jacques Tati

One day in August 1970, Jacques Tati phoned from the Waldorf Astoria where he and his party were staying. He had an idea. When Tati had an idea, one saluted. We invited them for lunch the next day at Gino's, a favorite haunt of ours on Lexington Avenue and 62nd Street, waiters all Italian, food lusty Sicilian. The New Yorker had played all of Tati's work. In his films, it is neither rain nor shine that holds him up, but just about everything else. There's no story, no stars, no close-ups—just visual gags galore, as in Chaplin or Keaton. "In real life we don't stand on top of people's noses," he insisted. *Jour de Fête* (1949) is a silent film about a long-legged, slightly pop-eyed village postman bicycling on his route and bumping into every corner—a send-up of the ever-reliable mailman, come rain or shine.

"Hulot is an inclination to be," said André Bazin, and *Mr. Hulot's Holiday* (1953) is about a gangly bachelor (Tati) vacationing at a seaside resort in Brittany. The lobby is an island of calm, dialogue at a minimum. One hears the wallpaper patter of summer folk solemnly going about the business of enjoying themselves—until our man blows in, triggering a series of mishaps involving a waiter, a tin kayak, and more.

After the success of *Mon Oncle* in 1958, Jacques Tati became fed up with Monsieur Hulot. He inched toward a new kind of cinema: a supremely democratic film that would star "everybody," in which the wonders of modern life relinquish their functionality and become a ravishing backdrop to pure human delirium. Tati's journey took ten years in all. A massive set known as Tativille was built in Saint-Meurice, at the southeast corner of Paris. One hundred construction workers made two buildings out of 11,700 square feet of glass, 38,700 square feet of plastic, 31,500 square feet of timber, and 486,000 square feet of concrete. Tativille included its own power plant and approach road. Building number one featured a working escalator. The result of Tati's exploration: ignominy and bankruptcy. But he was secure in the knowledge that with *Playtime* [1970], as his film about everybody came to be called, he had made a masterpiece. (Walter Reade program brochure, December 29, 2004–January 5, 2005)

Anyway, the following day that August, Tati arrived with bells on, gangly body enveloped in a dapper white suit, plus wife and secretary. We ordered a bottle of Chianti. Tati's patter and jokes flowed faster than the wine—this was a voluble fellow, not the silent one of *Jour de Fête*. A one-man orchestra, every part of his body punctuated a barrage of words. Long arms flailed like a windmill in wild gesture; head bobbed on a rubber-band neck; a flash card of expressions darted across the face of this marionette free of strings. Wife sat silent, contriving a faint smile at jokes undoubtedly heard a thousand and one times. The younger woman, secretary and co-handler of Tati (his exuberance required more than one), smiled indulgently.

Tati's idea was to open *Traffic* in a "special" way. He himself, 6' 3" in white gloves and uniform with gold-starred epaulets, would manage the queue that formed outside the theater. "Of course," he said, waving his arm like a baton, "the line will be enormous!" Dan and I exchanged glances. We couldn't believe our luck: to have the Amazing Tati—creator of *Jour du Fête, Mon Oncle, Parade, Mr. Hulot's Holiday*—this genius who wrote, directed, and acted in his own films offering himself as guardian of our line! A total role reversal: cinema Tati—bungling, bumping into walls and people, capsizing from bicycle, totally accident-prone, and unfit for the absurdity of convention—now in real life, *controlling* a line. His strategy on maintaining a steady queue in Paris was to have people buy a ticket, enter the theater, then emerge and rejoin the line. He described the current scheme in detail—marquee, the color of the lights, even the trailer. We were talking to a pro. Finally, he began describing the "deal." Not unlike other great comedians—Fields, Chaplin, Groucho Marx—Tati had a keen interest in money, though his films inevitably went over budget due to his policy of absolute control. With arms gyrating faster and faster, and speech increasingly fevered, he began explaining the intricacies of his proposal.

Just at that moment, the uniformed waiter emerged from the kitchen, balancing a big plate of spaghetti marinara. Unsure of whose order it was, yet hesitant to interrupt the rambunctious scene, he glanced at me discreetly. I signaled it was Tati's. As the waiter leaned over to deliver the steaming dish, Tati's arm hurtled up, hit the bottom of the plate, and the whole squirming, scarlet mess fell on his shoulder, sauce streaming down and dripping on his neck. Dan's eyes, normally large, turned outsize. It was one of those believe-it-or-not situations, a scene straight out of a Tati "everything amiss" movie. The waiter broke into an effusion of Italian, reminiscent of the waiter in *Mr. Hulot's Holiday*, while Tati's wife and I, like emergency nurses, applied our napkins. The jacket—a disaster—was carried into the kitchen, and another came forth, the sort held in reserve for customers who arrived without one. Of course, it was too short for Tati, reaching just to his navel, wrists dangling inches out of the sleeves. His wife's composure was broken. This apparently was the only suit Jacques had in his luggage. Tati looked unfazed. Like Mr. Hulot, there was an almost philosophical acceptance of the random chaos and absurdity of life.

After lunch, like solicitous parents sending a child off to school, we set Monsieur and Madame Tati and their companion into a taxi, and agreed to meet at the New Yorker the following day. The phone rang when we got home. In congested traffic, their taxi had had a small incident and banged into another taxi. (Had their driver been distracted by some Tati schticks?) The drivers insulted each other, exchanged license plate numbers and insurance carriers, and finally the Tatis (like the mail in *Jour de Fête*) were delivered to their hotel. But an hour and a half later we got another call. A thief had broken into their room and stolen all their money, which Madame Tati had hidden in a garment. She announced that they would be returning to Paris on an evening flight. It was a Tati script: Life is a series of annoyances, everything capsizing, nothing going as planned. But nothing surprised Tati.

Yasujiro Ozu

German, with its knack for piling prefix and suffix to stem, has a word for deriving pleasure at someone else's misfortune—*schadenfreude*, or malevolent pleasure. There should be one to express envy of someone viewing a sublime work for the very first time. If I were asked, What keeps your marriage going? my answer might be (just to say something), Uh, we never have breakfast together. Dan takes his yogurt and cereal at our seventeenth-century Spanish trestle table in the dining room, overlooking the Hudson, while I sip my espresso in our kitchen cove. The *New York Times*, delivered with a thud at our door at seven, gets divided. On opening a new film, we turn immediately to the Entertainment section—its review can make or break it. But, seeing and re-seeing certain films together is a moment of communion.

Vladimir Nabokov claimed that the only real readers are those who reread—a dictum that holds true when applied to certain films and certain directors. Yasujiro Ozu, Jean Renoir, Robert Bresson, and Satyajit Ray never go stale, for humanity is their raw material. There was a time when I longed to visit Tegucigalpa, Pernambuco, Patagonia, and Cambodia. But on our very first visit to Delphi, Dan got so turned off by the bustling hordes he took pictures of the tourist buses! Henry James, no slouch himself in voyaging, decided in the end that he traveled best in his head. My own travel lust has not yet died. Our daughter Nina and I traveled to Chichén-Itzá and scaled the jungle mounds in Tikal. Once I even managed to convince Dan to visit the Roman baths in Slovakia. But now, though I may never get to Patagonia or Estonia, there are endless films to see and see again.

Certain moments in life are indelible—first love, first childbirth, first reading of Walt Whitman, first words and steps of one's child, last gaze of one's mother—all having little to do with actual journeys. One such moment was Ozu's *Tokyo Story* (*Tokyo Monogatari*). Donald Richie, then film curator of the Museum of Modern Art, brought it to our attention. Steeped in Japanese culture, Richie eventually settled in Japan and became an ex-officio anthropologist of its society. After screening the film one morning in 1969, we immediately took it on for distribution, along with eight other Ozus. *Tokyo Story* opened at the New Yorker and ran for seven weeks.

Its story is simple as can be. An elderly couple (Chishu Ryu and Chieko Higashiyama) travels to Tokyo to visit their two busy married children, only to find themselves tactfully dispatched to a hot springs resort. Seated on a parapet, they gaze at a passing train—life is passing, and their faces wordlessly express its ebb and flow. In the end, they return home and the wife dies. The widowed husband (Ryu, whose face was to become as familiar as a close relative) gazes stoically ahead. Spare and condensed as a haiku verse, *Tokyo Story* conveys, within a daily framework, life's inner eruptions and universal predicaments. Spanish avails itself of two verbs for "to be": *ser* signifies permanence, *estar* temporality. "*Je est un autre*," Baudelaire declares—"I am someone else," expressing, as does Ozu, our transient existence.

What transpires *between* viewer and screen counts as much as to what is *on* the screen. As life unfolds in an Ozu movie, we reflect on what is in store for us. "Too slow, too static," complains a friend to whom we send a tape. For sure, the pace is deliberate: camera pitched at eye level, few movements, dissolves, or fades; clean lines, right angles, and frames within frames to emulate the geometric qualities of a Japanese interior. Ozu's stories are ordinary: same actors, no melodrama. Images, gestures, words, and pace convey emotional resonance. Small changes occur with "pillow shots," as Ozu called them, of passing trains, empty side streets, wind-rustled trees—typical punctuation shots and silences, no suspense—the viewer is unburdened by What Comes Next, as if there were a next. "I ran to Death and Death greets me as fast / And all my pleasures are as of yesterday," said John Donne. What century? The day before yesterday, one might say. When Fray Luis de Léon, sixteenth-century poet, theologian, and dean of Salamanca University, was expelled by the Inquisition, he returned to his rostrum years later, gazed out at his students, and picked up the thread, "As I was saying … "

Ozu's *Late Spring*, made in Japan in 1949, never had a commercial run in this country until its premiere at the New Yorker twenty-three years later. It was then little known, even though some of his films had won major international prizes and been called masterpieces. Not until 1969, six years after he died, leaving behind more than fifty films, did Ozu gain any appreciable notice here—a comment on the exposure lag of foreign films in the United States.

End of Summer (1961), Ozu's penultimate film, describes the disintegration of a close-knit family, and by extension the traditional society to which he was so attached. The charming old patriarch, having broken the rules long ago by keeping a mistress and fathering a daughter by her, decides in his old age to rekindle his extramarital affair and get to know his "other" daughter. His tragicomic antics shame and distress his legitimate family, a household of three daughters and various in-laws helping to run the family business, a small brewery. He dies and leaves no spiritual heirs. The final montage, discordant, and unlike anything else in Ozu, shows the funeral and the artifacts of cremation with an abrupt finality. "Isn't life disappointing?" someone remarks in *Tokyo Story*. *Desilusión*: disillusion; disappointment. Life embodies both. One expects the lives of their children to be exceptional, having been so well-tended and nurtured. But as said in Yiddish: Everyone gets chicken pox and measles. Or, as Matthew Arnold put it: "The bottom line seems to be that most people manufacture their own misery out of the difference between what they expected life was going to be and what it turns out to be." Could be bad teeth, a limping gait, depression, Alzheimer's—who knows what will be inherited?

The seasons that figure predominantly in so many Ozu titles—*Late Spring*, *End of Summer* (known also as *Early Autumn*)—express transience, life's ever-changing continuum. "Why can't things stay as they are?" laments Nuriko in *Late Spring* (1949). In that great work, a widowed professor approaching retirement (Chishu Ryu) lives with his daughter Nuriko (Setsuko Hara). She is happy, but he fears his needs are keeping her from marrying. A busybody aunt (Haruko Sugimura) finds an appropriate fiancé for Nuriko, allowing the professor himself to remarry (she has a candidate in mind for him as well). The film ends with an image of the father peeling an apple. The peel drops away, falls to the ground, expressing ineffable loss—the permanent earth, grazed by volatile feelings.

I can enter an Ozu film at any point and recognize it as Ozu, as with Bresson, Fellini, or Antonioni. No need to be told by a guide: this is a Gothic cathedral, this Frank Lloyd Wright, this Gaudi. *Espíritu*, like the polysemic German *sein*, unites multiple meanings: soul, mind, breath, sense, interpretation, the unnamable essence of human beings. All apply to Ozu's films. Ripeness is all, said King Lear. At different viewings of *Late Spring*, I am alternately daughter and parent. Who has not experienced the tug between filial bond and pressing life—a parent with Parkinson's disease, a child with a high fever and earache? As our lives change, so how we view it. Ozu's work is transformative. No sooner have I finished reading a story to my granddaughter—canny and keen listener—than she looks up and says Again. Each year, Dan and I exchange silent vows over *Tokyo Story*, knowing we will grow old, and possibly (hopefully not) become a burden to our offspring before our lives come to an end. One of us will be widowed—selfishly I pray not to outlive my steadfast movie companion.

Dreamland

I sometimes dream about characters in movies. Nocturnal visitors, they enter when I'm asleep and at times when sleepless. Like shadow figures they appear, mingling with others from other movies, other countries, other centuries. I find it not hard to envision meetings that have not taken place but might have. These characters all existed but simply had no opportunity until now to run into each other. Yet all seem to know who everyone else is. It is one grand party, but I am no eavesdropper, for in this silent movie they do not talk. I am simply a languid host, enfolded by darkness, body soft and yielding between sheet and blanket. A slab of light penetrates a corner of my bedroom window like the beam of a projector, and the rustle of cars on the West Side Highway becomes the steady breath of an audience. I make no effort, in this cinema trance, to introduce anyone to anyone else. They are on their own. Sometimes I doze off. When I awaken, one or another may have sneaked off, and another may have entered. Like a projectionist fallen asleep at the machine, I try to rewind. But truants must be caught on another night.

The guests wander about as in a cocktail party. Over in one corner, two men huddled beneath a cloak gaze steadfastly into flickering candles—Toshiro Mifune and Masayuki Mori from Akira Kurosawa's *The Idiot*. Almost rubbing elbows with them is Charlie Chaplin, facing the blind flower girl who, with sight restored, stares incredulously at her pitiful savior. Just then, two slick jewel thieves—Miriam Hopkins and Herbert Marshall from *Trouble in Paradise*—zero in on unsuspecting Kay Francis, while avuncular Charles Ruggles and Edward Horton simply stand by. Now, *who* is that crashing in? Why, the Marx Brothers—Groucho, Harpo, and Chico up to their usual pranks. Then, no surprise—it *is* open house—W. C. Fields shuffles in like a penguin and heads straight for the booze. How *many* times will those guys show up? But how many times did they appear at the New Yorker? And how many times did we play *The Treasure of Sierra Madre*? Come to think of it, why are Fred Astaire and Ginger Rogers not here? Or Giulietta Masina and Marcello Mastroianni, who Fellini once cast as Ginger and Fred. Oh, how I'd love to see Marcello's smile. But maybe I'll see them all later.

Problems of Distribution

We entered distribution as greenhorns, no one having taught us its ABCs. We fell in love with Bertolucci's *Before the Revolution*—paid $500 against percentage. Next came Chris Marker's *Koumiko Mystery* and a few others here and there, but we weren't yet really involved in Distribution. Dan simply made a pass at them for they were the kind of films clearly not viable for theaters around the country, but which *we* wanted to play—it was like buying yourself a gift. Even though it was a business, we never cared about the money; it was always about the song.

One of the things Dan had prided himself on in the first decade was never to repeat a program at the theater, no matter how successful. But in the early seventies, when he did, and found himself at the same time possessing the rights to some fifty titles, he felt compelled to make a decision about his commitment to these films. Distribution is much different from exhibition and involves an enormous amount of detail: keeping records, making reports, collecting money.

In 1973, a year that witnessed "sensational" business, Dan sold the theater to the Walter Reade Organization. I resisted this, was even angry at having to put my signature to the closure. "Why can't things stay as they are?" I heard my inner voice, echoing Nuriko in Ozu's *Late Spring*. But Dan had accomplished what he wanted to do at the theater and now wanted to immerse himself in the affairs of our distribution company. Distribution was a struggle, its eternal problem the ferocious economics. A German film in the seventies might command a maximum advance guarantee of $35,000, while French and Italian pictures could go as high as $100,000. The average price for a film that had commercial potential was $50,000, but a risky project could command substantially less than $20,000. The advance is the least part of distribution—prints and advertising costs comprise the bulk of the expenditure. For Donald Rugoff, to open a new foreign film in the seventies in one of his fancy East Side theaters cost in the vicinity of $35,000 just to say hello. Today it is closer to minimally $100,000 to open a film in New York. And then, so much depends on reviews. Critics can make or break *most* films. The power of the *New York Times* is formidable, and mass market films pander to the tabloids, with distributors culling for quotes: Captivating. Haunting. Touching.

A major studio can spend many millions just for the pre-opening campaign and opening week, for pictures that may never draw. What has it grossed? That is the question. People in the business are students of the industry and keep tabs on the numbers like a veteran gambler playing his ponies. Will it have "breakout"? They track the ad campaigns. Scour for selling reviews. Soaring production costs require a film to make a lot of money in the first month of its release, if it is to be profitable at all. This favors the blockbuster over the low-budget film, though even blockbusters may turn out to be flops and a "small" film—a sleeper—may surprise everyone. The theatrical run for movies, like the shelf-life of books in bookstores, has become shorter and shorter. Many films are designed to go directly into DVD shortly after their theatrical release. And radical directors in the mold of, say, Nagisa Oshima suffer from the increasing timidity of art house taste.

In the sixties, it cost $4,500 to operate the New Yorker for a week, discounting advertising. If we took in only $1,500 that week, we could lose our shirt. No one knows what will work. You buy what you love. In the seventies, we loved Fassbinder and loved Herzog and began distributing their work. Who knew that *The Marriage of Maria Braun* would be a greater success in the States than it was in Germany? That it would run for fifty-four weeks? Tanner's *Jonah Who Will be 25 in the Year* 2000, with a box office gross of $800,000 and a distributor's net profit of $300,000, set a record. "Distribution is not a business, it's a casino," as Dan once told a gathering at a film awards dinner.

You can go broke overnight. "We'll break even" is a hopeful prognosis with a director's first film to play, even a second. What we do is minimize our risks by starting slowly—we open with two prints, on a modest budget, and wait for critical and audience response. If it has a chance of taking off, we back it up with more money; bring in an internegative and spend more on promotion. But commitment to a director means supporting each film as part of an oeuvre, a work-in-progress of a singular and distinctive voice. Easy for critics to bludgeon awkward attempts, easy to pat a crowd-pleaser, easy to praise a masterpiece. For the record, the *New York Times*'s Bosley Crowther panned *Citizen Kane* and *Monsieur Verdoux* at the time of their release. *The Magnificent Ambersons* was likewise drubbed and *The World of Apu* flopped at the box office.

Dan considers the distribution business almost like a book publishing operation.

> The principles and approaches are the same: Your print costs resemble the production costs in book publishing, the advertising is the same, and both survive on their hits. You need one big hit or a few medium-sized hits to carry on, and there's a thin line there of compromise. A publisher can't print everything he secretly admires, knowing its audience is limited. He'll go broke.

"Oh, I don't think this Bergman [ditto Fassbinder, Wenders, or Herzog] is as good as his last," mutters a moviegoer. When a new Woody Allen movie opens, I like to stand in back of the theater to see what it takes to make a smart aleck New York audience laugh. As Fassbinder had, Allen turns out a new film every year. When asked why he didn't pursue a more leisurely pace, Fassbinder replied, "That's the way I do them." Lucky for us, since he died at thirty-six. Lope de Vega, the sixteenth-century dramatist, one of the greatest in Spain's Golden Age, was dubbed a "monster of nature" in light of his fifty-six plays. Not all were perfect. But wasn't it Jimmy Durante who said, "Nobody's poifect"? Some tribes weave a deliberate imperfection into a rug to reflect man's imperfection.

The age of the "stand alone" distributor is virtually past. Astronomic bids get reeled off by those who don't have to dig into their own pockets: Sony, Miramax, New Line, Fine Line, Lionsgate became the new kids on the block for art films. At one Cannes Film Festival, Harvey Weinstein told sales agents that he would pay 10 percent more than the highest bidder. When Dan and I first ran into him in 1986, he was little (metaphorically speaking, for Harvey was never little) known. It was at a small

Moroccan restaurant where our friend Claude Nedjar had brought us for couscous and pastries made by the owner's mother. Harvey learned fast, and in 1998, when Dan refused to play a Miramax picture at the Cinema Studio, Harvey threatened to "destroy" him. They shouted at each other. Dan stood firm. Next day, Harvey sent over a case of Dom Perignon, with a love note.

Will we ever break out of the mold of the Profit Motive, the Commercial Imperative, the Bottom Line? As of 2008, 95 percent of American screens were controlled by less than five or six major circuits: AMC Theaters, which absorbed Loews; the Regal chain, which absorbed United Artists; National Amusement; the Marcus theaters; and the Pacific theaters. The remainder is small, with only fifty to one hundred screens. And then there are those like ourselves who have only one theater: the Lincoln Plaza in New York. In forty-seven years of exhibition, Dan has never signed a contract with a distributor. Every booking—and there have been thousands—has been done orally. In our business, an oral contract has the force of a written contract. Dan's ideal contract with a director would include the title of the film, the names of the parties, and a picture of a handshake.

We've had the good fortune to be involved as distributor and exhibitor of a score of films that endure in memory: Krzysztof Kieslowski's *Decalogue*, Rainer Werner Fassbinder's *Ali: Fear Eats the Soul* and *Berlin Alexanderplatz*, Andrei Tarkovsky's *The Sacrifice*, Satyajit Ray's *Apu Trilogy*, the Dardenne Brothers's *La Promesse* and *Le Fils*, Hirokazu Koreeda's *After Life*, Werner Herzog's *The Land of Silence and Darkness* and *The Enigma of Kaspar Hauser*, Theo Angelopoulus's *The Traveling Players*, Ousmane Sembene's *Borom Sarret* and *Moolaadé*, Yasujiro Ozu's *Tokyo Story*, and Kenji Mizoguchi's *Sansho the Bailiff*. These works inform and nurture the soul and remain our compelling imperatives.

A Last Hurrah

On May 6, 1972, we premiered what one journalist called a kind of Last Hurrah in America for independently made foreign films. In that 1972 series were Alain Resnais's *Je T'Aime, Je T'Aime*, Uwe Brandner's *I Love You, I Kill You*, Alain Tanner's *Charles Dead or Alive*, Barney Platts-Mills's *Bronco Bullfrog*, Ruy Guerra's *The Gods and the Dead*, Susan Sontag's *Brother Carl*, Yasujiro Ozu's *Late Spring*, and Louis Malle's *Phantom India*.

The premieres were to have no spotlights on opening night, no limousines parading the marquee, no pedestrians to stare at international celebrities outside the theater on Broadway and 88th Street. Nor were patrons offered a series of all new films. Another unusual aspect of the premieres was the first serial showing of Malle's *Phantom India*, its six-hour length divided into seven 50-minute segments. Each film played an open-ended run and lasted as long as business warranted. Resnais's *Je T'Aime, Je T'Aime* ran for a week. The series was an artistically gratifying, economically hazardous adventure.

To quote Dan at the time: "Ten years ago you had an art house movement in America. There were close to six hundred art houses around the country that devoted themselves largely to foreign films. There's been a tremendous decline, having dropped from six hundred to very close to zero. They've gone over to commercial product and play what's box office. You get burned a sufficient number of times on less commercial films and you're not going to get burned again."

Shoah

The *New York Times* was never more useful to us as one Friday morning in May 1985. Over breakfast, we read an article by Richard Bernstein about a nine-and-a-half-hour film on the Holocaust opening in Paris. It was called *Shoah* and directed by Claude Lanzmann. That name was not unfamiliar. In 1973, at the New York Film Festival, we'd screened a documentary he made on Jewish identity, twenty-five years after Israel became a state. In direct dialogue, Lanzmann talked with Jewish émigrés, intellectuals, dock workers, police, prison inmates, and the newly arrived. The title of the film, *Pourquoi Israel*, wasn't meant as a question, but rather as a reply or explanation from various viewpoints. Its premier at the

New York Film Festival was just three days after the Yom Kippur War began. We also remembered him as editor-in-chief of *Les Temps Modernes*, an intellectual journal named after Charlie Chaplin's famous film and founded by Jean-Paul Sartre and Simone de Beauvoir. In one of her journals, Beauvoir describes the travels the three took together and the subsequent, more intimate seven-year relation she had with Lanzmann. Also, our friend Lia van Leer, the director of the Jerusalem Cinémathèque, had mentioned *Shoah* while it was in progress.

After both of us had read the *New York Times* article, Dan turned to me: "Can we hop a flight to Paris tonight?" I had a class to teach in an hour and a half, and another on Monday. "Why not?" I said. Dan put in a call to Lanzmann to ask if we might see *Shoah* on Saturday morning and meet with him. At seven P.M. we climbed into an Air France plane with a return ticket for Sunday night—I could make my class. "You can't be at two weddings with one bottom," my mother liked to say. Sometimes you could.

We arrived in Paris, tired and stiff from our coach-class trans-Atlantic journey. A pillow and sheet was what I fantasized, followed by a croissant and a strong espresso. "Je suis désolée, madame," the concierge told me. Our room was not ready. Depositing our overnight bag in the lobby, we sought a café for that much-needed caffeine and phoned Lanzmann, who arrived very soon. A dark handsome man of around sixty, he had penetrating eyes, disheveled hair, and an anxious manner—a burlier version of Claude Raines (plus a shopping bag full of reviews, all raves). Returning to our hotel, we popped some Benzedrine pills to counter jet lag and drove with Lanzmann in his red Rover to the Monte Carlo Theater on the Champs-Élysées, one of the three cinemas premiering the film in Paris.

A bomb had been set off several weeks before at an Israeli film festival, and now, wherever the film played, there was police protection. On that bright sunny morning, at the Monte Carlo, a couple of detectives frisked every patron at the door. Inside, two plainclothesmen monitored the crowd, walkie-talkies pinned to their ears. Dan and I as a rule, almost religiously, refuse to screen a film with the director present. But now, with a print in various languages, without English subtitles, and time so limited, we sat with Lanzmann behind us, whispering the English into our ears. The film opens with a poignant reenactment of Simon Srebnik, one of only two survivors of the Polish village of Chelmno (Isaac Singer's fabled *shtetl*), following Lanzmann's command to sing as they float downriver in a boat, just as the Nazis forced him to do as a 13-year-old. The landscape is bucolic and makes me think of my father rowing with my sister and me on a Sunday along the Bronx River. I see my father's eyes and high cheekbones in the face of this "witness." The voice of the adult man echoes with the pain of the bar mitzvah boy, whose voice perhaps has not yet deepened. Now the peasants in the village only remember him as a young singing lad, completely erasing the circumstances in which he was forced to sing.

As other human voices disgorge their memories, Dan and I fall into their past, eerily overlaid by the whispered voice behind us. It is a requiem, it is a *kaddish*. Searching pans track the neatly tended, tranquil landscapes of Poland where death camps once stood. There are no charred bodies, no piles of scavenged eyeglasses, shoes, dentures, or dolls. There are only those voices, and gazes, and a demonic litany of place names—Treblinka, Auschwitz, Chelmno; and Michael Podchlebnik (the other survivor besides Srebnik, out of 400,000 murdered at Chelmno), Abraham Bomba, Filip Muller, along with former members of *Sonderkommando* teams forced to observe the last moments of thousands of their fellow Jews at Treblinka, then Auschwitz. We are there with Franz Suchomel, deputy commando of Treblinka ("No, Herr Lanzmann, you are mistaken, we only processed twelve thousand people in a day, not fifteen!"); with Polish peasants admonishing Simon Srebnik that "the Jews were paying for having sinned against Christ"; with Jan Karski, the aristocratic former courier of the Polish underground, who is brought to tears as he recounts his visit to the Warsaw Ghetto shortly before the Germans destroyed it; and with Itzhak Zuckerman, a former leader of the Zionist Fighting Organization in Warsaw, who survived the destruction of the Ghetto, became an alcoholic, and died of a damaged heart shortly after his interviews with Lanzmann. The interviews were shattering. I couldn't help thinking about my mother's village of Dynav in Poland, invaded by the Germans in 1939, where her entire family, including a beloved 80-year-old grandmother, was dragged to the edge of the forest and shot—the very forest where my mother as a little girl had gathered wild mushrooms. I couldn't help but remember Hitler's crazed voice on the radio, which I heard as a child, announcing his demonic scheme. I couldn't help but remember my mother's pale face as she heard it too. I couldn't help but remember all the packages of clothing and delicacies wrapped and posted, and the money sent for a new roof. Which Polish peasant was now living under that roof? At the end of the first part of *Shoah*, we had no words but arranged to meet with Lanzmann that evening for dinner. He asked if he could bring his *amie*.

Exhausted, but too agitated to sleep, we wandered around Paris for a while, then found a bench at the Luxembourg Gardens. It was the end of the day: Parisians safely relaxing on benches, *les enfants* sailing their little boats on the pond, young couples embracing. It seemed more unreal than the world we had just left—the world of *Shoah* (Hebrew for "annihilation"). How unlike Alain Resnais's haunting *Night and Fog* it was, with those starved prisoners in striped clothing, yellow stars, fuming smokestacks, piles of corpses, mounds of orphaned shoes and eyeglasses; how unlike the stock or fictionalized footage shown on television and theater screens.

That evening we learned a bit about Lanzmann. The Yiddish *landsmann* means "someone from your village"—a kinsman. Somehow, already, I felt bonded with this man who had confronted this mighty truth. Though Jewish, his family was not religious. But when the Nazis invaded France, they moved to the French town of Clermont-Ferrand, to hide from the German occupiers. As a young adult, Lanzmann joined the French Communist Party and resisted the Nazis, thus vulnerable to the Gestapo. After the war, he continued his study of philosophy in Germany, and while there, began his career as a journalist. His first piece unmasked the persistence of Nazism in Germany's supposedly de-Nazified university system— already he was an inquirer. He then wrote for the French newspaper *Le Monde* and was the first Frenchman to travel through East Germany, which he did (illegally) after being denied a visa. His interviews in *Pourquoi Israel* had prepared him well for the conversations with victims and perpetrators in *Shoah*. Soon after, Lanzmann befriended Sartre and de Beauvoir and took up his position at *Les Temps Modernes*.

We were eating in Le Dôme in Montparnasse, Lanzmann's favorite restaurant. A man of habit, he ate there regularly, always ordering a dozen oysters on the half shell, grilled fish, and a red Bouzy wine from southern France. This was a man of appetite. Dressed in a navy blue suit, white shirt, and gray patterned tie, you might mistake him for a family lawyer. Up close, there was a restless, searching gaze. His *amie*, Odette, pretty and in her forties, was obviously much in love with Claude. As we began talking about the film, she remarked (rather glibly I thought) that, being so young, that era for her was all history. *Why* did that remark put me on edge—fatigue, a sense of absurdity in sipping a nice wine after the horrors just seen (corroborating Dan's notion that despite what horrors viewers see, they go home, make themselves a martini, and make love). I jumped on the poor woman. "How old are you?" I asked. "Forty-two," she said. "Well, you're middle-aged," I pointed out. She stared at me blankly, as if that cold mathematical fact had never occurred to her. The men said nothing. Nevertheless, Odette and I became friends, and years later, after Claude had left her for someone (younger?), she phoned me in New York, desolate. I did what I could to console her: "You're a young woman. You have your life ahead."

That evening Lanzmann described the genesis of *Shoah*. In 1984, after he had finished *Pourquoi Israel*, an Israeli friend suggested that he make a film on the Holocaust. It took Lanzmann twelve exhausting years to finish. There were multiple obstacles: depletion of the start-up money received from Israel, round-the-globe tracking down of Holocaust survivors, physical dangers (Lanzmann once beaten to a pulp outside of Munich by a gang of neo-Nazi toughs), condensing 350 hours of testimony, discarding what didn't fit into the narrative, and attempts to find completion money in America.

The next day we screened Part Two. Enter the perpetrators: ex-Nazis unrepentant of the horrifying efficiency of the camps. Franz Suchomel, a former SS Unterscharführer at Treblinka, carefully describes, for the sake of "history," the procedures at Treblinka. Lanzmann painstakingly records the step-by-step machinery of the mass extermination of the Jews from the mouth of murderers, all of whom deny actually doing it or seeing the killing. With a certain pride Suchomel cites facts and figures: 12,000 to 15,000 a day gassed at Treblinka, not the exaggerated figure of 18,000 that the Jews reported. The entry operation, when things were running smoothly, took approximately two hours, from the arrival of the boxcars carrying the Jews until they had been incinerated in the ovens. At one point, in the interest of history, Suchomel sings for Mr. Lanzmann the Treblinka camp song, including the phrase, "All that matters to us now is Treblinka / It's our destiny." Employing duplicity, pseudonyms, false identification papers, and a concealed camera, Lanzmann secretly filmed these former Nazis without disclosing the true nature of his project. At one point in the process, the son of a former Nazi discovered Lanzmann's equipment, took the film footage, and beat Lanzmann so badly that he was hospitalized for a month.

Other detailed recollections emerge from a man in charge of railroad traffic control for trains going to and from the camps; from a railroad engineer in a cap riding past a village, leaning out, and by a hand-slitting-throat gesture indicates the fate of his passengers; from a Polish peasant woman who smilingly admits that her life is better without Jews; from peasants standing in front of a Roman Catholic Church where Jews were held until they could be hauled off to the gas ovens.

In another memorable scene, Abraham Bomba, a survivor of the Treblinka camp, stands in a busy Tel Aviv barber shop, cutting a customer's hair and answering the questions of the offscreen interviewer. Asked about the details of his routine as one of the sixteen or seventeen barbers assigned to cut the hair of women about to be gassed, he replies: "In

Treblinka all feeling was impossible." Yet, when relentlessly questioned by Lanzmann, he breaks down and cries, saying he can't go on. "You must," Lanzmann insists. "You know it." And, scar tissue ripped away, the unspeakable is spoken. He begins to remember in detail a friend of his, another Treblinka barber, who found himself confronting his wife and daughter in the "undressing" room (also the hair-cutting room) just outside the gas chamber.

As we emerged from the Monte Carlo Theater into the glittery Champs-Élysées, all I could hear were the searing words of a survivor: "At that time, had you been able to lick my heart, you would have been poisoned."

Shoah is a *shanda* on the human race.

The day after the screening of Part Two, Dan met with Lanzmann and his lawyer. Without haggling, they worked out the terms of a distribution deal. We learned subsequently that two other American distributors had shown interest in the film. One was Roger Corman of New World Pictures, who had produced and distributed mainly action films—horror movies, westerns, crime stories—as well as hired many first-time directors, among them Peter Bogdanovich, Martin Scorsese, and Monte Hellman. Corman seemed an unlikely choice, however, and even less likely was another interested party of rather dubious reputation. The next day we sat with Lanzmann at a little café table strewn with correspondence and debts.

We returned to New York and Dan immediately began working on the film, ordering one brand-new 35mm print. The first person we screened it for was Lucjan Dobroszycki, an important historian and archivist who worked at the YIVO Institute for Jewish Research in New York. His groundbreaking book, *The Chronicle of the Lodz Ghetto, 1941–1944*, had been published in the States in 1984, a year before *Shoah* opened. We'd met him through Elie Wiesel, but as it turned out, he was an Upper West Sider who loved movies and with his wife frequented the New Yorker and then the Cinema Studio. A word-of-mouth campaign had to be started and Lucjan was an ideal choice. Like Simone de Beauvoir, he called it a masterpiece.

We held many screenings during the summer of 1985, all at a professional screening room in the Gulf and Western Building at Columbus Circle, where the Trump International Hotel and Tower now stands. Irving Howe, Philip Roth, Cynthia Ozick, Alfred Kazin, Elie Wiesel, Robert Brustein, Albert Goldman, Morris and Lore Dickstein, Daniel Stern, Georges Borchardt, and many other friends were invited. Borchardt, after seeing Part One, could not return for Part Two. A French survivor of the war, he found it unbearably painful. Over the summer, Dan and Lanzmann were in close consultation. They became close friends.

Distributing a nine-and-a-half-hour film in America proved a mighty challenge. Dan hadn't the vaguest idea as to whether it would succeed. But, consumed, he wanted it to work as no other film we'd ever distributed. He tried to get a pre-opening "event" screening at Lincoln Center but failed—the cost of renting its hall there was prohibitive. But by the time we were ready to open *Shoah* at the Cinema Studio in the fall of 1985, many screenings had been held and there was a buzz on the film.

In 1976 we had taken over a theater on the east side of Broadway and 66th Street. It had only one large auditorium of six hundred seats and catered to a Hispanic audience. We changed its name from the Studio to the Cinema Studio and split the space into two theaters, one with 300 seats and the other with 185, the economics of our business dictating such a move. Initially, Dan had trouble getting the films he wanted from distributors since the theater had no track record for foreign and independent films, but luckily, as distributor *and* exhibitor, we showed our own films. But after Fassbinder's *The Marriage of Maria Braun* ran one full year and Ermanno Olmi's *Tree of Wooden Clogs* for many months, distributors took notice and we had a steady flow of "product." By the time *Shoah* opened, on October 23, 1985, the theater had a following.

In that morning's *New York Times*, Vincent Canby wrote:

Shoah is unlike any Holocaust film ever made. This isn't a conventional documentary composed of newsreel footage from the archives. The images of *Shoah* prompt no preconditioned responses. Everything is of the present—the faces of the "witnesses" as well as the tranquil, neatly tended landscapes that were once death camps. Where railroad tracks leading to Treblinka had been, now there is only a path through the forest. That path suggests the roadbed of the River Styx.

Elie Wiesel, in the *New York Times*, responded as a *survivor*; *Shoah* triggered hidden memories:

> These trains which ride, day and night, across occupied Europe, I remember them. The barbed wire of Auschwitz, the watch towers, the lead ceiling pushing down on merciless earth, I knew them. The march at midnight, toward the platform and the selections; separation, last words, mute cries, suppressed sobs, the fear of hunger which is as keen as hunger: all this is in the film and in my memory.

After *Shoah* opened, we brought Lanzmann to New York for interviews. With the notable exception of Pauline Kael, an old friend and at that time the foremost film critic in the United States, the press was virtually unanimous in its praise. Kael considered the film to be "logy and exhausting right from the start," and found herself "squirming restlessly when it went on for an hour or longer," her attention slackening. She objected to Lanzmann's method of questioning, to the "long camera movements, repeated ritualistically," to the film's lack of moral complexity. But Gene Siskel extolled *Shoah*'s moral value, and the film even won praise from Pope Paul II. According to Roger Ebert, "What is so important about *Shoah* is that the voices are heard of people who did see, who did understand, who did comprehend, who were there, who knew that the Holocaust happened, who tell us with their voices and with their eyes that genocide occurred in our time, in our civilization."

Dan responded to Kael's review with a three-and-a-half-page single-spaced letter in which he attacked her for *her* moral obtuseness in not understanding the urgent, poetic interviews with some of the survivors of the biggest catastrophe in Jewish history. "The critics around the country are right. I think that you are wrong. You're often on target but some forces outside of film criticism prevented you from experiencing this work in a whole way."

There were lines around the block on opening day, and often on the weekends. Lanzmann, visibly moved by what he saw, draped his arms around Dan and wept. The film ran twenty-six weeks at the Cinema Studio. The audience, mostly an older crowd, was conservatively dressed and unlike the hip regulars who often frequented the theater. They were, in effect, coming to a secular *shul* to watch a film about the most devastating event in Jewish history. Still, several young people, children of survivors, came up to Lanzmann: "Our parents never talked about this. Now we know."

The film grossed $729,290 during its run, an unprecedented figure for a film of this length. Phones rang off the hook at New Yorker Films. Dan began organizing openings around the country and devoted one full year to the theatrical distribution of *Shoah*. He did all the selling, launching, and publicity himself, wearing several hats that had been on a rack for a few years. The cost of distributing this film was staggering; each of the six subtitled prints cost $15,000.

The usual pattern of distributing a foreign film in America is to open in New York City, sometimes in Los Angeles on the same day, and then a few weeks later to fan out to all major cities. With *Shoah*, Dan hit upon another strategy. Since he was working with only six prints, he tried to target cities with large Jewish populations such as Chicago, Los Angeles, Cleveland, and San Francisco. Unable to afford lengthy runs due to the wear and tear on prints, Dan selected an exhibitor in each city on the basis of his ability to do strong marketing and to reach a large Jewish audience. Each exhibitor was restricted to a two-week run. Instead of the usual percentage arrangement, the film was sold for a very high flat rental rate—a minimum of $20,000 and often more, depending upon the size of the city and its Jewish population. Since the picture could be shown only a limited number of times in a two-week period, the exhibitor was allowed to use the film as a fund-raiser for a Jewish nonprofit organization in his city. Also the exhibitor would pay for 100 percent of all advertising and publicity. In this way, New Yorker Films had an assured film rental with no expenses beyond the print and shipping costs. Jewish groups in every city desperately wanted the film and put their money and shoulders behind it. A competition surfaced among these groups for the privilege of playing it.

The largest theatrical event after New York City took place in Chicago. Dan gave the film to an organization that held frequent cultural events. His point man was Rabbi Joel Pupko, a local "cultural swinger" who drove around Chicago in a convertible and had staged many events over the years. On the phone he sounded thin, bearded, and wired. He spoke show-biz lingo—"heads" (audience), "hires" (critics), "toilet" (an inferior theater)—read *Variety*, and was schooled in theatrical grosses around the country. He talked rapidly, thoughts tripping over his tongue. Dan never met him but felt he knew him well, having run into such whirling types before. Dan hit upon the idea of playing the film in a 2,000-seat auditorium in Skokie, a suburb of Chicago that had more Holocaust survivors than any other city in America. He and Pupko *hondled* gently over the deal—percentages, number of shows, fees, and the like. We didn't travel to Skokie: Rabbi Pupko, Dan's alter ego and juiced up for the event, choreographed everything. They spoke to each other five, six, seven times a day, and when we sent Lanzmann to Skokie to attend the showing, Rabbi Pupko took him in hand, and Dan and Claude spoke to each other daily. Claude couldn't get over the effect it had on such a large body of survivors. Subsequently, he went to other cities to "defend" (as the Europeans say) the film. Claude, a strong personality, didn't suffer fools gladly, but he behaved well. The showings in America were larger and grander and wider than in any other country in the world, and we sensed his gratitude.

The film played in over a hundred cities and towns. It was one of the most successful films in the history of our company. While it was playing, we embarked on a plan to get it shown on the PBS network. In order to do so, money had to be raised. Dan enlisted Sue Weill, a high-level executive at WNET in New York, to help us. Sometime before she got on board, Claude and Dan met with a prominent financier. He had read that we'd taken the film on and asked if he could buy a 35mm print. We turned him down but remembered his call when the financing of the PBS broadcast came up.

That he granted Claude and Dan a meeting was no small matter. Wealthy people were flocking to him at the time, begging to invest their money—the minimum amount accepted was rumored to be $10 million. Dan heard that Henry Kissinger, ever alert to a smart investment, had visited him with several lawyers to check him out. He was known to be generous, which proved to be true. Claude and Dan had a rendezvous with him and his wife at the bar in the Algonquin Hotel. They were both excited by Lanzmann and his film and offered to help in any way possible. When told that $1.5 million was needed to cover the costs of the PBS broadcast, they promptly offered to hold a fund-raiser in their mansion in Mount Kisco, New York.

A week later Dan and I accompanied Claude to their home, along with Henry Orenstein, a warm and colorful Holocaust survivor and self-made man in America who, shortly after *Shoah* opened, over lunch at the Four Seasons, handed Claude a check for $25,000 in gratitude for having made such an important film, and to help pay some of his debts accumulated over the twelve long years of research and production. Entering the mansion's large living room, we noted the Renoirs, Matisses, and Cézannes on the wall. Along with others of wealth in the room, the gathering was attended by billionaire investor Carl Icahn as well as a member of the Bronfman family and some prominent film director. Henry Orenstein spoke passionately about the film. He and his brother in their teens had hidden for years in the forest after the Nazis entered their Polish village. Our host pledged $200,000, and others joined in. We were still short of our goal, but with Sue Weill's help and the generous contributions of many individuals, we managed to put the necessary money together within a few months.

We embarked on the distribution of *Shoah* not thinking of its commercial possibilities, and prepared personally to guarantee all losses. It was an emotional undertaking. To our surprise, the film was a considerable commercial success. Lanzmann was gratified by this, though much of his earnings went toward reducing the debts incurred while making the film. He hoped to live on the balance so that he would not, as he put it, "die in misery." The profits from the film that New Yorker Films made did not go into mink coats or champagne parties. We plowed what we got back into a slate of new films, all of which went down the tube, so that two years after the success of *Shoah*, we were back to square one. But for us, the biggest reward was the national PBS airing of the film in 1987. Over ten million people saw it.

When I showed the film in my documentary film course at the New School, a student did some research and reported: "The prisoners are to be transported to Germany, secretly. These measures will have a deterrent effect because (a) the prisoners will vanish without leaving any trace (b) no information may be given as to the whereabouts of their fates." This quotation came from Hitler's now notorious Night and Fog Decree, which pertained primarily to political prisoners. Any information about the Jews was to be totally effaced. Claude's film ensured that Hitler's final plan to erase the memory of those he exterminated would not succeed.

Shoah is the definitive work on the Holocaust. Lanzmann's powerful camera zooms in on the geography of faces and places with a high sense of drama. These are not ordinary interviews. They are more like confrontations between an angry, probing filmmaker and damaged souls. His relentless traveling shots from automobile and railroad train are like search engines into hitherto unknown landscapes. He is not at all interested in morality or "history." It is both a film about the relation between witnessing a catastrophe and a systematic refusal to historicize the subject. One sees this refusal in the absence of documentary footage of the liberation of the camps by the Allies. "Image kills imagination," Lanzmann has said to explain this sparsity. He is an adamant critic of the film industry's commodification of the Holocaust with films like *Schindler's List* and Roberto Benigni's *Life is Beautiful.* "Holocaust is not a fairy tale, it is not digestible."

Sometime in November 1985 a rabbi and his wife came to the Cinema Studio to see Part One of *Shoah.* They drove fifty-five miles from Livingston, New Jersey, to see the film. It was doubtful that either were moviegoers. When the film ended, the rabbi lingered in the lower lobby, just outside the auditorium. Ushers were guiding people out and, once everybody left, they went to clean the hall in preparation for the next showing. An usher politely asked the rabbi to leave. When Dan saw the rabbi still lingering, he interceded and told the usher to leave the man alone. The rabbi then went to the back of the auditorium and, facing a wall, body rocking back and forth, he prayed. He was blessing the theater.

On Location

New Yorker Bookstore

In 1965 we opened the New Yorker Bookstore, with Peter Martin and Austen Laber. Pete was the illegitimate son of Carlo Tresca, the anarchist leader who masterminded several strikes in this country in the 1930s. Pete grew up under the aegis of the American Communist Party and once showed Dan a large photo of his father, smoking a cigar and playing cards with a colleague on a wooden box, surrounded by several hundred strikers, most wearing red Alpine hats. Pete's aunt was Elizabeth Gurley Flynn, a Communist Party leader in the United States.

We met Pete in the early fifties. He had just left San Francisco, having co-founded with Lawrence Ferlinghetti the City Lights Bookstore, birthplace of the Beat movement and of the literary magazine *City Lights*. Only five issues were published—Manny Farber, Pauline Kael, David Riesman, Pete Martin, and Parker Tyler among its contributors. Pete, by then a confirmed alcoholic, didn't get along so well with Ferlinghetti and in one of their fights he shouted: "Here, keep the fucking bookstore. Give me a dollar. I want out." He came East, married Madelaine, a member of the Doubleday family, and also a charter member of the grape. They had an apartment in Gramercy Park, and to assure that the rent got covered—being drunk every day—Madelaine paid three months' rent in advance. Pete took a job editing sex magazines.

One night we ran into him at a jazz session in the loft of the painter, David Young. Located in the flower district at 821 Avenue of the Americas, near 28th Street, it was the kind of place that got going after midnight when musicians had finished their nightly gigs and came to jam. Zoot Sims, Bob Brookmeyer, Dave McKenna, you never knew who might show up. One night a white-haired Dutchman arrived. It was Willem de Kooning, surrounded by various acolytes. W. Eugene Smith, who shot the legendary series of Spanish post–Civil War photographs for *Life* magazine, lived in that building and was a regular. And there was Pete, a surrealist interpreter of news, spinning goofy tales of the day's events, putting on them an anarchist spin that made you see through and around the events. He and Dan became sometime drinking buddies and talked about opening a bookstore some day in New York—it was something Dan and I had long dreamt of doing. "Let's raise a glass on that one," said Pete in his gravelly voice. Clink. Then off we went to Spain.

But two months after the New Yorker Theater opened, Dan and Pete spoke more concretely about their plan to do a bookstore. He told Dan he'd just inherited $10,000 from his Aunt Elizabeth, enough to get something going in those days. Then he and Madelaine disappeared, and we hadn't the foggiest notion where, until one day we received a postcard from Moscow. Friends of his Aunt Elizabeth had invited him to spend some time in Russia. The red carpet had been rolled out and in no time at all, amidst vapors of vodka, Pete and Madelaine blew the $10,000 in Moscow. Our book venture went off the radar.

Our friend Austen Laber, who lived in our building, likewise had a notion of starting a bookstore. In 1965 (two years after we'd bought out the New Yorker lease from Hank Rosenberg), Laber found a group of ten to buy the taxpayer that housed the theater, six stores, and loft space on the second floor. Now there was a place for the bookstore, and Pete, Dan, and Austen formed a partnership, each owning one third of it, Pete taking a modest salary.

Well, a bookstore needs shelves. Therein enters Manny Farber, whom Pete knew from *City Lights* and we through Chandler Brossard. Farber, film critic for the *New Leader*, who made his living as a carpenter, was in big trouble. Though he had a loyal following, the editor Sol Levitas didn't like the way he wrote and wanted to replace him. He found his prose jerky, inverted, elephantine—that way he had of pinning down objects and characters in American movies. Also Manny suffered from deadline-itis and simply couldn't get his manuscripts in on time. Ever revising and rewriting, he'd deliver them to Levitas at the printers just as the machines were clamping down on paper. I'd known Sol Levitas from the fifties, having translated articles for the *New Leader* by Spanish Civil War refugees in southern France. We were also close friends with his son Mike and daughter-in-law Gloria. Dan liked Manny's work and put in good words to avoid his dismissal. But Manny had other problems. His marriage had broken up a year before, and there were money matters.

Pete and Dan invited Manny to sleep in the bookstore while constructing its shelves and tables. Manny, whose view of life and art never moved along straight lines, built shelves such as none other in the history of bookshelves. Books flew out of the walls from tilted-angle shelves, didn't rest on them but jumped out at you (like his film criticism, which didn't adhere to conventional "white elephant" lines but to ant or termite-like trails—critical terms he coined for his 1962 essay, "White Elephant Art vs. Termite Art"). For three months, he dwelt in the store, and when it came time to stack the shelves, Pete ordered the stock. We specialized in film books and radical books, posters, stills, periodicals, and works related to the arts. While stocking the shelves, all of us—Pete and Madelaine, Dan and I, Austen and his wife Jeri—held a book party. Pete was the showman: "Which section shall we put a book on the assassination of JFK?" we asked. "Science fiction," he replied. Pete had odd juxtapositions—*Commentary* rubbed against *Mad Magazine*. He hired a few hippie kids to work the store, but only *he* knew where every book was in a bizarre system that transformed the Dewey decimal system from drill-like order into planned chaos. That's how Pete saw the world. During the first month he and Austen spent a lot of time in the store. Business was good. The place caught on, was always crowded. People in the neighborhood loved it. It became a hangout for many writers.

We live in the age of the image. Most people get their news from TV as those in the Middle Ages got stories from tapestries. The rates of illiteracy in the United States are high, but on the Upper West Side people were still reading. Pete showcased books of young neighborhood authors. Phillip Lopate remembers bringing him his books to sell and though he never saw a cent he was happy to have exposure. The store carried poetry and little magazines and added a line of newspapers. Isaac Bashevis Singer came daily to pick up the *Forward*, where his stories originally appeared.

But Austen and Pete *did not* take to each other. Austen, a control freak of sorts, couldn't take Pete's ways and started making suggestions. Pete, who wore a suit and tie daily, tucked a 3 x 5 index card in his upper jacket pocket, on it written GET AUSTEN LABER OUT. He showed us the card. "*Basta!*" said Dan to Austen, and they agreed to let Pete own the store and repay their investment with no interest at his convenience. It took twenty months.

Dan, aside from being Pete's friend, now became his landlord. Pete and Madelaine rented an apartment with a balcony on a high floor in the Normandie on 86th Street and Riverside Drive and encircled it with a high railing to assure not tipping over at party time. The two would come to dinner at our house, a liquid repast for Pete, who merely jiggled the food around on his plate. Of an occasional afternoon, Pete and Dan might drift off to Wilby's, the bar up the block, owned and run by four brothers who'd escaped from the Nazis. Pete, a barroom raconteur of bulbous nose and ruddy complexion, held forth with his interpretation of world and domestic news—a cross between W. C. Fields, Will Rogers, and Bakunin. His sayings were like cartoon blurbs from Felix the Cat and the Katzenjammer Kids. A cartoon aficionado, he read them aloud with great glee.

Business at the bookstore peaked in five years and then went into decline. Pete continued drinking heavily and couldn't stand the business end of the store. Certain penurious customers stole books, as did some of his help. Eventually, costly works on art and cinema had to be put in upper reaches. Debts mounted. Book deliveries went on a C.O.D. basis. He fell six months behind in his rent. Dan, who was managing the real estate, took it upon himself to say nothing to his partners for he was prepared to make good if Pete stuck them with the rent. But clearly there was no solution to salvaging the bookstore, and Dan urged Pete to go into Chapter Eleven. At first he resisted, feeling honor-bound to pay off all his creditors and keep the store going. But when the hole of debt grew deeper and deeper—by now around $50,000—he threw in the towel, sold off whatever he could, and closed. It was a mournful day. Pete and Madelaine left their Upper West Side apartment, rented a house in Oyster Bay, Long Island, and we didn't hear from them for a while. Then one day an envelope arrived, in it a check for seven months' rent owed us. Subsequently they moved to San Francisco, where Madelaine's married daughter was living. Within two years both died, six months apart, of cirrhosis of the liver.

Box Office

From time to time I would relieve a daytime cashier for her break. This task I relished, the hour sped by. Like a stationary camera, I observed the flow of the street—seeing but not being seen. "An author must be like God in the universe, present everywhere and visible nowhere," said Gustave Flaubert, and André Bazin likened the camera to an individual spectator without partiality. In the frame of the box office window I'm privy to multiple close-ups (ticket buyers), medium shots (bag lady down the block), long shots (No. 104 bus), partial shots (a chain of nursery school children blocked by a parked truck, a woman with a walker cut off by a man entering the laundry, shirts slung on his arm). Moving vehicles and people produce random montage—purposeful walkers, racing skaters, an ephemeral sandwich man with some indecipherable message. It brings to mind a message intoned by my seventh grade teacher, quoting Samuel Finley B. Morse, the American inventor and painter: "Hurry, worry, and bustle are the ever marked symptoms of a weak and frivolous mind." But city life is ever in flux: in Honfleur, France, a banner waves over the city: *Une Ville Qui Bouge* ("A City on the Go"). Motion cannot be slowed down, nor the frame frozen. "Every shot," said film theorist Vlada Petric, "must be kinesthetic." At last a person in no hurry enters the frame. Hong Cho, the Korean grocer from down the block, walking like a sleepwalker, hands folded behind his back, is gazing at some inner film only he can see.

Figures familiar and unfamiliar appear: Hank our window-cleaner, with pail and squeegee (any time he straps himself to a window of our thirteenth-floor apartment, I dash to another room, envisioning my father as that dangling man); Mr. Fuller Brush Man (real name never known), toting a sample case such as the little black satchel carried by my childhood doctor on house visits; Peter Bogdanovich's father Boris in white linen suit, straw hat, and spats—must be Spring; Mary the Fancy Lady, as our children call her, dressed to the nines—fuchsia lipstick, white gloves and all; blue-haired Jenny, scooping the poop of her white poodle into a Bergdorf Goodman bag; Dan's Aunt Yanka, a Polish diva whose 15-year-old son was murdered by the *Einsatzgruppen*; and Jimmy the Three-Card Monte dealer, his lookout planted at the curb as Chicky-the-Cops.

Horns honk, mothers imprecate, a Julliard flutist plays her heart out for whomever will listen—sounds like Mozart. June the Bag Lady, in rusty old mink worn winter and summer, pauses there a moment, then treads to her Red Apple post. A rookie cop cases her, but intimidated by her Look, twirls his baton and retreats. From the corner of my eye, I catch a man in a red Turkish fez studying our marquee of *Journey Into Fear* and *Tiger Shark*. A young woman suddenly bumps into him, her tight tee-shirt reading *LIFE IS SHORT, BREAK THE RULES*, and as he jumps away, the tassel of his fez waves in consternation.

Here comes blind David Swerdlow, confidently circling his cane. I see him but he can't see me, nor do I hail him. On balmy days, seated at our street corner, he fingers Braille, wife knitting alongside. "My house is without mirrors," he once told me. Never has he seen his wife's face, and when she developed facial cancer and grew horribly deformed, he never saw that.

Now Raymond Freire staggers by—poor bleary-eyed fellow. Some called him the neighborhood drunk, though I viewed him as Michel Simon's tramp, saved from suicide by a bookseller in Jean Renoir's *Boudu Saved from Drowning*. This was not the first time that I found myself linking offscreen characters with screen doppelgängers. A seignorial Puerto Rican of lofty language, Raymond would occasionally run errands for Dan and quote Ben Johnson poetry. Hours he spent at the candy stand talking to Bella, making her laugh, tossing *piropos*, flowery phrases in praise of her beauty, youthfulness, and character—such a *buena persona*. On Valentine's Day, when he presented her with a candy box shaped like a silver heart, my father's eyes narrowed with jealousy. Just the other day, Raymond promised Bella to go on the wagon. Now, wending his way to the traffic isle, he lowers himself on the bench next to Dr. Zoltan Pollack, a Hungarian retired doctor, who lives in my mother's building. When we meet in the elevator, this gentleman doffs his hat (straw in summer, fur in winter), comments on the weather, and inquires about the family. His history is dramatic. Seized by the Russians in 1940 after having completed his medical studies in Budapest, he marched through freezing cold with a prisoner battalion until reaching a timber labor camp in Siberia where, as "house physician," he witnessed typhoid epidemics, the burial of prisoners, some so frozen the ground heaved in rejection; there he saw observant Jews on Yom Kippur lighting candles from sticks of wood. Dr. Pollack and Raymond sit side by side, part of what David Riesman called the "lonely crowd": individuals who regularly, and anonymously, pass each other, never colliding, never connecting. Raymond once said he's been alone so long he sometimes feels that he's lost his voice. Then he went on to remark that when Cervantes was a prisoner at Lepanto, he'd talk to the roaches and mice not to go mad. "Wherever man has lived there's a story to be told," said Henry David Thoreau. But Raymond knows nothing about this anonymous Dr. Pollack. Nor does Dr. Pollack know about Raymond's brutal childhood in Puerto Rico, of having stowed away in a freight boat at age twelve, of having been a valued bartender at Sardi's and classy hotels such as the Savoy and the Plaza, of having served the Queen of England aboard an ocean liner, of having suffered the DT's in a brownstone walk-up on 92nd Street between Columbus and Amsterdam Avenues.

Cinema verité filmmakers deliberately avoid intrusion on what transpires before their cameras—nor does the box office intrude. André Breton, however, claims the street to be the only valid field of experience, and each day I envision a box office short, with fleeting snatches of conversation on its soundtrack:

"Murray's is having a special on barley soup."
"Mommy, I don't want to go to school."
"Fanny, enough is enough. I've had enough."
"Jesus, the New Yorker is playing *Spellbound* again. *How many* times are they going to play it?"

Suddenly an adolescent in blue jeans furtively approaches the window— quite likely playing hooky early in the day. But rather than buy a ticket, he offers two books of Yeats's poetry for the price of one. I decline (saying I already own them, secretly wondering if they've been swiped from our New Yorker Bookstore), but when I invite him in to see *Brief Encounter* and *Spellbound*, he throws me a crooked look and darts away. On his heels comes a buddy, shoving a thick cut of sirloin steak wrapped in Red Apple plastic through the slot. "Lousy vegetarian," he snaps on being turned down, and spying Ivan the Panhandler posted at our billboard, thrusts the hot goods on *him*. Just then a Jehovah's Witness stations herself alongside Ivan and sets to railing against discos, videos, designer clothes, perversion, and pornography, whereupon, without a blink, Ivan passes the sirloin on to *her*. Sheer Chaplin.

Whatd'ya wanna be when you grow up, kids like to ask. Doctor, lawyer, Indian chief? Last on *my* list would be elevator operator or tunnel sentry, cooped up in a cage or walled in. Our cashier, however, loves her cubicle with its portable heater in winter and fan in summer, and her favorite pastime, like Balzac's and mine, is watching the human parade.

"Where's Mary?" I asked my mother one day. This woman, of uncertain age, maybe sixty or so, was a kind of neighborhood landmark. Ever dolled up, hair dyed black like her patent leather shoes, lips glossy red-purple and fixed in a perpetual smile, hat and gloves impeccably matched (unless the gloves that day were all-purpose white), she was ever raring to go. Mary didn't know my name, though I knew hers—everyone did. And I knew her ways. Each morning, she would sally forth towards Riverside Drive, while noon (that moment of shortest shadow, as Nietzsche put it) found her on Broadway. With determined pace and sense of destination, she did her rounds—72nd Street to 96th. In late afternoon, off she went again: window-shopping at Sylvia's Distinctive Half-Sized Frocks on Broadway and 89th Street, where West End matrons got outfitted in dressmaker suits, printed silks with matching jackets, and linen frocks with contrasting bindings; or stopping perhaps at the old-world Eclair on 72nd to meet some gent for tea and strudel. She was a mannequin on the go—mouth ajar, eyes popping as if in awe of the world. Now and then, she might perch like a parrot on the traffic isle of benches opposite the New Yorker. Never did she go to the movies.

I knew but the sketchiest details of her life, though seem to have heard that once she'd been the nurse of a well-to-do man whom she attended so loyally that he bequeathed her his modest fortune. On his death, she remained in his apartment, converting her legacy into bonds whose modest yield provided the wherewithal to dress like a queen and be a lady of leisure.

We remained familiar strangers: nodding, smiling, but never engaging. The fault was mine. Knowing that at the drop of a hat I might be in for a run-on conversation, I tried to give her the slip, even crossing the street once or twice at a glimmer of that blazing smile. Give an inch and they'll take a mile. But now, failing to see her for days and weeks, I missed her and found myself scanning Broadway benches, even inspecting the chalked outline of some unidentified traffic victim. One day, I asked Dr. Pollack, a kind of mayor of the block: Where's Mary? Had she moved to Miami, or having a fling in Las Vegas, or gone off to live with a niece in Arizona? What I secretly dreaded was what I learned. Mary was dead.

She seemed as everlasting as the Alianthus trees that nudge through pavement cracks. And now that she was gone I felt a twinge of remorse at having been so withholding, so *unneighborly*. How it would have pleased her to talk. Behind that mask and costume a real person might have emerged. "The most ordinary word, when put into place, suddenly acquires brilliance," said Robert Bresson.

Candy-Counter Tales

"What would you like?" Bella asks. Answers vary: "Something chewy, something creamy, something to see me through the show, something that won't stick to the teeth." A calorie-observant friend, quoting Oscar Wilde, says the only way to get rid of temptation is to yield to it. Another, on a perennial diet, buys something she doesn't like, not to be tempted or deprived. From time to time, I'll sit by the candy stand and observe the action. Bella gives no discounts, but should a young person not have enough to pay for a candy bar, she'd say, "Pay me later."

One of the candy-stand regulars was the budding musical scholar Miles Kreuger. A handsome young man, in his early twenties, with an ingenuous, winning smile, he lived on 92nd Street off Broadway in an apartment stacked with recordings from floor to ceiling. Often he would head for the projection booth to tape the score of Busby Berkeley's *Gold Diggers of 1933* or Jerome Kern and Oscar Hammerstein's *Showboat*, entrusting Chandor, his beloved Golden Retriever, to Bella. Like a mascot, the dog sat at the candy stand, Bella treating him to ice cream from time to time. One afternoon, when the theater wasn't busy, Miles took Chandor in and sat him down by his side. Along came a woman trying to climb over their seats in the dark. On passing Chandor, finding no dangling human legs, she let out a scream. Well-trained Chandor didn't utter a bark.

In 1972 Krueger founded the Institute of the American Musical housed in his home in Los Angeles. The Institute of the American Musical has catalogued two thousand early 78 rpm recordings of music from the American Musical Theater, with shows beginning in the mid-nineteenth century to 1940. Two hundred-sixty custom-made, acid-free storage boxes have been purchased to contain over 10,000 Broadway Playbills, which date back to 1836. There are spoken-word records by Sarah Bernhardt, Ellen Terry, and Julia Marlowe. If documentary filmmakers, theatrical producers, researchers, journalists, or performers need film stills, sheet music, recordings, photographs, or posters relating to Oscar Hammerstein II, Jerome Kern, Cole Porter, Richard Rodgers, Duke Ellington, Fred and Adele Astaire, Ethel Merman, Fanny Brice, Al Jolson, Eddie Cantor, Bing Crosby, Julie Harris, Ethel Waters, George Abbot, Busby Berkeley, or Leonard Bernstein, that's the place to go. Scholars can consult Krueger's *Showboat: The Story of a Classic American Musical* or *The Movie Musical from Vitaphone to 42nd Street*.

Manny Farber would often hang around. My father, Joe, watched that gawky eccentric going in and out of certain movies, gangster ones particularly—film buffs have their passions. Joe himself happened to be a fan of W. C. Fields and had seen our entire run of *It's a Gift, The Bank Dick, The Man on the Flying Trapeze, Never Give a Sucker an Even Break, My Little Chickadee, You Can't Cheat an Honest Man,* and *The Fatal Glass of Beer*. That anarchistic boozer of bulbous red nose, just barging through life, wasn't exactly a role model for my father: familial, filial, and frugal, Joe was ascetic and virtually abstemious, indulging only in an occasional glass of beer. But how he howled when Fields's daughter in *The Bank Dick* asks, "Don't ya love me, Pop?" And Pop, delivering his point with a smack, barks: "Of course I love ya." *What* did my father see in that habitual drunk, that misanthrope, that braggart—breakout against discipline, respectability, work, parents, wives, and kids? Joe was the oldest and only son in a family of five daughters, a sickly mother, and an improvident father, who bankrupted one butcher shop after another, and then needing his son to bail him out. The Tolpen family lived in a row house in Middle Village, a place in the middle of the world I thought, equidistant from everywhere and nowhere, to which we got in a trolley that crossed the Gowanus Canal. It was, in fact, on the edge between Brooklyn and Queens. My father indeed lived on the edge. As a window-cleaner, he might fall from a ledge any day, and as a gambler, go broke. He played poker, he played the Stock Market. He played not to break even or to win, but for the risk, the thrill. He played on perilous margins. When a dwarfish Western Union fellow in a red cap urgently rang the bell, his message brought only bad news—*Cover the margin or else!* To this day, the sight of a certain yellow puts me in mind not of Van Gogh, but of those telegrams. Joe would play poker all night before heading for some precarious ledge with chamois and squeegee. He had the strength of will to labor as a window-cleaner but not of mind to desist on the brink of ruin. My father's eyes were clear as water over stones, clear as the breakable glass he brought to a shine. When he cleaned ours, I feared getting absorbed in my book and taking my eyes off the panes, for then he might fall. At five in the morning, when he left the apartment, I never felt sure he'd return. Precious meant precarious. My sister and I were taught by mother never to lean over the windowsill. Other apartments had safety-guards, we needed none. When she laid pillows to air, I trembled lest she fall. When she was unhappy, I was afraid she might jump.

In a lull, while Bella would be checking her wares, I might drop in on a movie I'd seen more than once. On February 6, 1962, it was *Ninotchka* and I happened to be lucky enough to catch the scene where Garbo *laughs*. "What's so funny," my mother asked as I returned to the candy stand with a goofy smile. As I was about to answer, a patron approached, then another, leaving me to my thoughts. Just then an idea for a children's book came to me—the genesis of *Dear Greta Garbo*. It would be about a widowed grandmother, encouraged by her daughter to join a Senior Citizens Club with lectures and poetry, or work with clay for the arthritis in her fingers, or learn Tai Chi, but who instead answers a sign in the box office of a movie theater: WANTED CASHIER PART TIME. INQUIRE MANAGER WITHIN.

The candy stand was a crossroad of stories. Tales poured out like M and M's—of courtship, marriage, separation and divorce, offspring troubles, medical complaints, and ordinary neighborhood gossip. People needed to talk and how much easier to get things off your chest with a stranger. Bella never probed: rather private herself, she was not given to dropping in on neighbors to chat, going next door to borrow a cup of sugar, or confiding. "Dole out the skim of the soup but preserve its substance," I'd heard from her more than once, in *mamalushin*, the mother tongue—*la lengua del pecho* in Spanish, or the nursing tongue. Something about her encouraged divulgence—the expression in her eyes, says our Brazilian friend Fabiano Canosa, his own tearing up on invoking her image. "She was a *mensch*," he adds, a term perhaps picked up from her, though like all New Yorkers, he probably knew a handful of Yiddish words like *kvetch, schmatas, oy veyz mir*. Did Bella ever teach him *gazunte tsooris*, literally "healthy trouble," forbearance in the face of adversity? She herself had been through real *tsooris*—orphaned in 1918 at age ten, when her family, escaping pogroms, fled Dynav, their small Polish village in Galicia. In Czechoslovakia her mother died of influenza, leaving behind six children, my mother the oldest. Unable to accept a stepmother, Bella, at age sixteen, came to the States, alone.

That woman was no gossip. Tell her something and her lips were sealed. I may have inherited that trait; certain friends call me a clam, failing to pass on secrets confidentially told me by someone "in our circle." Delectable gossip is the spice of life, the subject of novels, they insist, and one even sports a *Proust Was a Yenta* button. But reveal something to one of these "novelists" and that item, you can be sure, will promptly be transmitted as in the game of Telephones, the message whispered from ear to ear and distorted in the end.

Several friends, unaware that the "candy lady" was my mother, would pour out their hearts, revealing confidences untold to me, speaking what they felt, not what ought to be said. Bella, nonjudgmental, was unfazed by revelation. "Everyone has his reasons," said Jean Renoir in *The Rules of the Game*. Listening, she gave no advice. D. was plagued with a symphony running through his head. Seventy-two-year old J. asks Bella if it made sense to get serious with someone of forty-eight. M. confesses to being bulimic. Once a floodgate was opened, I might then be confided in. Marriage was a big topic:

"I never got married, never wanted to get into it … "

"I awoke from a long sleep, my marriage … "

"I know it sounds silly but I'm getting married again—to the man I divorced last year."

"I'm leaving my husband—for another woman."

My dentist, whose wife had been in an Alzheimer's residence for five years, asks Bella if it's very wrong to go out with her friend? "They say it's bad to be alone. It is."

Young people had their own tales:

"Will my father have a heart attack if he finds out I'm gay?" worries a Columbia freshman, dreading a Christmas visit to the Connecticut homestead.

"Why are my parents so uptight?" asks a 36D 16-year-old knockout. "Tell me the truth, Bella, do you really think this sweater is too tight?"

And a mother wonders: "How can such terrific children become such irritating adults?"

Hospital stories vied with candy bars. One patron, a walking PDR and in seeming fine health, claimed to suffer from dyspepsia, insomnia, hypoglycemia, and hay fever. He was a symphony of hospital tales: "Did ya hear about Eddy's heart attack? *Oy veyz mir*, smoked like a chimney—they have him on three blood-thinners. And Skinny Lenny, remember him, the big spender from Washington Heights? Well, they opened him up for ulcer and found, you shouldn't know from it, the real thing. Aggravation, that's what did it, trouble with the kids, ate his *kishkas* out, who knows if chemo will help? And Jack, poor bastard, lasted less than two months after his bypass, went in his sleep without a peep. It should happen to all of us, no suffering. But doctor and hospital bills wiped out his family—surgeons and dentists, a regular swindle. I'm lucky, I tell my missus, with my little hiatus hernia. But everyone's got their problems, and there's a new simple operation for that. They do it through the, excuse me ... "

Commentators were given to verbal tics: This you gotta hear. Know what I mean? I can't believe it. You shouldn't know from it. Life is funny. Life is sad. Life is surprising. Life is disappointing. Life is a veil of disillusion, said Jean Renoir. Life, said Samuel Beckett, is a brief commotion. Life, said Pedro Calderón de la Barca, is a dream. Life is all of that, said Ozu.

Neighbors from 321 West 90th Street would drop by from time to time. Several were refugees whose living rooms had a mirrored credenza, porcelain, and worn Persian carpets. Dan's Aunt Yanka and Uncle Kuno owned a Steinway piano—she was a diva. And there was Mrs. Silver who lost her husband and two children in Auschwitz and, after years in a displaced persons camp, arrived in this country, remarried, and catered for homes. My recipes for nut cake and spinach timbale are hers. Dr. Pollack lived on the same floor as my parents and on his door at the left was a hammered *mezuzah*. One day I ran into him on the No. 104 Bus. "You look pale," he said. Indeed, I had a migraine headache. Whereupon he showed me the pressure points at temple and neck to relieve the drumming, asked about my blood pressure and offered to come and test it.

I accepted, welcoming an opportunity to find out more about him. He rang the bell, in one hand holding a small box of chocolates—an Old World visitor never comes empty-handed. In the other was a coil for measuring my blood pressure. It was low, I was told as we sat in the kitchen, and he advised me to refrain from standing up too rapidly as is my wont. As we sipped tea, music drifted in from the living room. He smiled: "Schubert's Sonata in B-flat." Weekly visits arrived with a small gift—a cake of soap and a bottle of lotion garnered from the Swiss hotel visited each summer, a strip of needlepoint, or beads from an Indian shop on Broadway. Sometimes Dan would join us for tea before heading to the theater.

Dubby (his real name Durwood Williams) was a sometime porter at the theater, but on passing, he would drop by. A tough-looking black, he carried a shiv tucked in his sock, ran numbers for a living, and tended his arthritic invalid grandmother up on "Twenty-fifth," as he dubbed 125th Street in Harlem. He fed and bathed her and bought her a color TV, getting around town on a Kelly green bicycle. At times, having cleaned the theater, he'd bed down for the night on its paisley carpet, where we'd find him the next morning at an early screening. Fiercely devoted to Dan, he warned of any fishy character who might be casing the joint for a stickup. Once or twice, he phoned in the middle of the night to complain in four-letter mother-fucking words about some uppity guys installing new seats during his shift. His mother, Zelda, was a slender, soft-spoken woman who day in and day out propelled a steam iron in the back room of a local dry cleaner. Bella dug his colorful language, intuitively understanding it, metaphors and all.

Dubby scrupulously studied our manager Paul, every detail of his black serge suit, white-on-white shirt, and patterned gray silk tie (trying to inject a note of formality in the informal atmosphere of the theater). One day, noting a pair of new patent leather shoes, he complimented them with feigned innocence and a note of irony unmissed by stolid Paul: "Man, them shoes say M-m-m." Clearly, the two were not kindred souls. Eventually, Dubby's provocations got him his walking papers. "But no hard feelings," he said. "Everything is everything."

One day he came to Bella: "I don't have to run numbers no more," he said, not specifying what activity had replaced it. Bella didn't ask. Months later, he showed up at the theater in tears. His grandmother had died in her sleep. Bella comforted him: "Everything is everything."

REEL 4

Film Critics

Manny Farber

The 1960s and '70s spawned a golden age in American movie criticism. Prominent were Manny Farber, Andrew Sarris, Pauline Kael, Vincent Canby, and Susan Sontag. Farber, a lanky, raw-boned, feisty fellow—the kind who looked poor—was in a class of his own. A maverick critic and painter, he knew his stuff. Over and over he would see a movie— soldier, gangster, or cowboy—slipping in and out our theater for particular scenes. My mother grew accustomed to his viewing pattern. At a particular moment—he *knew* which—he'd disappear to catch some telephone or cigarette shot in a Hawks, Walsh, Aldrich, or Wellman picture. Truth was in the details. How many times had he seen *The Big Sleep, They Drive by Night,* and *White Heat*? He and Bella dug each other's straight talk—no hype, no bloated clichés, no highbrow pedantry—and they enjoyed kidding around. I wish I'd overheard some of their conversations. His book *Negative Space* is dedicated to the New Yorker and to Dan's mother-in-law.

Farber was in contempt of certain Hollywood "problem pictures" and *cinemah* icons. He coined the term *termite art* (from his essay "White Elephant Art vs. Termite Art," 1962). Termite art is "the clever tunneling just under the surface of a terrain. It feels its way through walls. The three sins of white-elephant art: (1) frame the action with an all-over pattern, (2) install every event, character, situation in a frieze of continuities, and (3) treat every inch of the screen and film as a potential area for prize worthy creativity." Farber's essays appeared in the *New Republic*, *Film Comment*, the *New Leader*, *Commentary*, the *Nation*, and *Artforum* and were collected in *The Magic Lantern* and in *Negative Space*. His virulent anti-Europeanism underwent a radical change after his exposure to Godard, Chabrol, and Truffaut. "Now," Dan said smiling, "he writes incredibly glowing tributes to Straub and Herzog."

We saw him from time to time at his brother's apartment. Leslie Farber was former Chairman of the Washington D.C. School of Psychiatry, Director of Therapy at the Austin Riggs Center in Stockbridge, Massachusetts, and author of *The Ways of the Will* and *Lying, Despair, Jealousy, Envy, Sex, Suicide, Drugs, and the Good Life*). An exceptional therapist, intently engaged with patients, he was astute on topics ranging from anguish to pornography. Often present at those lively evenings at his home were David Bazelon (*Partisan Review* intellectual and nephew of Washington D. C. Circuit Judge David L. Bazelon), the Podhoretzes, and film director Nicholas Ray.

Manny's sensibility owed less to the literary values of critics like John Simon and Dwight Macdonald, more to action painters. He saw film as a compositional field—flow of images, sensuous surface, muscularity and propulsion, a director guiding a viewer into the subsurface of his work—his own paintings atomized particles in a fluid surface. He coined the term "underground" film to describe and reappraise the contemporary Hollywood "B" action movies (made by such directors as Howard Hawks, Don Siegel, and Sam Fuller), films ignored at the time by other critics but shown at outcast theaters like the Lyric on 42nd Street—broken seats, houselights left half on during the show, patrons talking back to the screen.

In his introduction to *Negative Space* Farber declared: "Space is the most dramatic stylistic entity—from Giotto to Noland, from *Intolerance* to *Weekend*." He describes three types of movie space: (1) the field of the screen, (2) the psychological space of the actor, and (3) the area of experience and geography that the film covers. For example: "Bresson deals in shallow composition as predictable as a monk's tonsure, whereas Godard is a stunning de Stijlist using cutout figures of American flag colors symmetrically placed against a flat white background. The frame of *The Wild Bunch* is a window into deep, wide, rolling, Baroque space; almost every shot is a long horizontal crowded with garrulous animality."

Farber derided ravishing technique for effect, and speaks against the evils of continuity—"the need of the director and writer to overfamiliarize the audience with the picture it's watching: to blow up every situation and character like an affable inner-tube with recognizable details and smarmy compassion." He had no trouble shooting down "problem pictures" with social messages, nor iconic art films like François Truffaut's *Shoot the Piano Player* and *Jules and Jim*, Antonioni's *La Notte* and *L'Avventura* (whose aspiration is to pin the viewer to the wall and slug him with wet towels of artifice and significance). The common denominator uniting apparently divergent artists like Antonioni and Truffaut, he said, is "fear, a fear of the potential life, rudeness, and outrageousness of a film."

Such railings echo Ortega y Gasset's *The Revolt of the Masses*, "masses" defined as people steeped in facility. *El señorito satisfecho* is someone who fails to exert himself and who lives by overworked cliché. Farber was a film critics' film critic: much admired by Pauline Kael and Susan Sontag, a model to Phillip Lopate, Kent Jones, Jim Hoberman, Donald Phelps, and a new generation of critics. "Manny was more like Stendhal," says Lopate, "changing from sentence to sentence, progressing in all directions. A kind of high-wire performer, a one-of-a-kind magician with lots of dependent clauses, starts a sentence, winds up elsewhere. He's an original prose stylist and this sometimes leads to complications. It isn't about this is good, this is bad, the least important part of a critic's work."

In 1970 Manny, who'd been teaching at the School of Visual Arts, joined the faculty of the University of Southern California in San Diego and took over its film department. An offbeat professor, he attracted a Columbia student of mine with austere Bressonian tastes (*Lancelot du Lac* being his favorite film), whose dream was to do graduate work with Farber. His dream was realized.

Andrew Sarris

We met Andrew in the early sixties, when he and Eugene Archer attended the New Yorker. Eugene, a gangly, preppy fellow from southern Texas, was a witty conversationalist who smiled little. At Columbia, where he and Andrew met, he was Phi Beta Kappa, and among his accomplishments, says Sarris, was the ability to type ninety words per minute. Andrew came from a middle-class Greek-American family—his father ran a boat rental business in Howard Beach. Voluble and disarming, he was a kind of boy-man with an easy, self-mocking laugh. Our three young daughters loved climbing over this huggable teddy bear on our living room chaise.

In 1960, while on the City Desk for the *New York Times*, occasionally reviewing films, Archer went to Paris on a Fulbright (and made an appearance in Eric Rohmer's *La Collectioneuse*) and Andrew went to visit his buddy. A steady at the Cinémathèque, Archer was an ardent reader of *Cahiers du Cinéma* where French New Wave critics were looking at American movies in a new way. He was shocked to discover that *Cahiers* critics were unimpressed by Huston, Kazan, Wyler, and Zinnemann. Sacrosanct were Howard Hawks and Alfred Hitchcock. "Archer and I thought we knew all about Hitchcock," says Sarris. "He was supposed to be fun, but not entirely serious. And Hawks, who was he? Why were the French taking him so seriously?" The progressive internationalization of Hawks now began, with Archer and Sarris's search for an answer to that question.

Through the fifties and sixties, Sarris wrote for *Film Culture*, the magazine started by Jonas Mekas, and from 1961 through the '70s for the *Village Voice*, the liberal-radical New York City weekly newspaper. He became identified as the leading proponent in the States of the *auteur* theory, and first used the term in an article published in *Film Culture* in 1962. A director's personal vision, he held, was the "authorial" voice in the best films: human intelligence applied to the camera. Like Manny Farber, Sarris confronted the objective core of a film: gesture, movement, the timing of a shot. A film was not just a matter of actors, cinematography, or dialogue, but rather a question of sensibility, of visual, verbal, or aural splendor. The *politique des auteurs* stressed the flowing mise-en-scène (deep-focused, often mobile long shots).

Sarris took Pauline Kael to task, with her credo of one-viewing/one-judgment—he appreciated re-viewing—the second "enhanced" look. He deplored her side-stepping of Resnais, Malick, Fassbinder, late Bresson, and asks: Why did she evade her Ten Best lists? He was somehow amazed when Pauline attacked him in her now famous "Circles and Squares." "I hadn't regarded myself as that important," he says. "I was just plodding along."

Turning his attention to Hollywood cinema, he treated it systematically and with intellectual seriousness, without the snobbery of many "film authorities." There were movies to be resurrected, genres to be redeemed, and directors to be rediscovered. Fourteen directors in his pantheon were Charles Chaplin, Robert Flaherty, John Ford, D. W. Griffith, Howard Hawks, Alfred Hitchcock, Buster Keaton, Fritz Lang, Ernst Lubitsch, F. W. Murnau, Max Ophüls, Jean Renoir, Josef von Sternberg, and Orson Welles. With his remarkable memory, he filled in the young novitiate Peter Bogdanovich on many of those plots.

The underlying problem for a fledgling auteurist, as we quickly learned when trying to program certain films at the New Yorker, was their unavailability. The aging prints Manny Farber had seen at the old 42nd Street theaters, films of the thirties and early forties, from *Scarface* to *The Big Sleep*, were dropping out of circulation. In 1961 Sarris and Archer, with Peter Bogdanovich, drew up a list of Hawks films and Dan launched a "Forgotten Films" season, screening twenty-eight classics, eleven of them Hawks. One Saturday when we showed *The Big Sleep* and *To Have and Have Not*, there were lines around the block. Hawks was on the map at last. "Film has everything," says Sarris. "It is above all an emotional medium. It allows you to focus emotionally on things you already know. Film is the art to which all other arts aspire. It produces the most sublime emotions." Small wonder that Ophüls, Mizoguchi, Renoir, Murnau fit his bill. Phillip Lopate, who studied with him, calls him a great humanist and teacher, his humanism tempered with skepticism.

Andrew appreciates women: "I'm a leg man," he jests, and has written keenly about Greta Garbo, Bette Davis, Margaret Sullavan, Ingrid Bergman, Irene Dunne, Myrna Loy, Norma Shearer, Jean Harlow, Barbara Stanwyck, Claudette Colbert, Katharine Hepburn, Carole Lombard, Vivien Leigh, Louise Brooks, Mary Astor, Anne Baxter, and Wanda Hendrix. How many girls does a man need to prove himself?

One day Andrew brought Molly Haskell to our house. She was working at the French Film office, holding the same job formerly held by Truffaut's right-hand woman, Helen Scott. The four of us became fast friends and at the 1984 Cannes Film Festival managed to squeeze in a tennis game or two and dinner. On the last night of the festival, we celebrated at a famed restaurant in Nice, dining on escargots, dorade, and soufflé glaceé. "See you in New York," we said in the lobby of the Hotel Splendid where we were all staying. Returning to New York, we learned that Andrew had collapsed the day after their return and been rushed to the Emergency Room of New York Hospital. He wound up in Intensive Care for three months with an undiagnosed ailment, semi-conscious, hallucinating. I spoke to Molly or her mother every day and asked our good friend and excellent physician, Jeremiah Barondess, to visit Andrew: "I was in the presence of a dying man," he reported.

Andrew did not die. Within a year of that traumatic experience, the four of us went to the Ziegfeld Theater to see a re-released restored print of *Lawrence of Arabia*. Usually "restored" means that the original glitches from the older print have been removed, but in this instance, an extra seven-minute scene removed by producers was finally restored and included in the new print. After the film, Andrew told us which of the deleted parts were now restored. As Dan's 95-year-old Aunt Yanka would put it: *die kop arbeit*—his head works, good as ever. Whoever consults Sarris's *The American Cinema: Directors and Directions, 1929–1968* will be all the wiser; whoever reads *Confessions of a Cultist: On the Cinema, 1955–1969* (more than one hundred reviews and essays), all the richer. Many subscribe to the *Observer* just for his reviews. His new work, *"You Ain't Heard Nothin' Yet": The American Talking Film, History, and Memory, 1927–1949*, is on my reading list.

Pauline Kael

For many years I could *not* forgive Pauline Kael for the hole she put in my sofa. Not that it was an elegant silk or velvet antique, just a *practical* ivory Naugahyde, purchased so our babies might pee on it without permanent stain. One swipe of the sponge with Formula-409, and any whiff of urine was gone. All gone, as kids say.

In 1961 Pauline came East. A native Californian and for years San Francisco–based, she'd written for *City Lights*, the San Francisco literary magazine, *Sight and Sound*, and *Film Quarterly*. Also, she had a radio column for KPFA in Berkeley, and cooked up spicy program notes for the Berkeley Cinema and Guild Theater, which she programmed and ran. Dan had included a piece of hers in his collection *Film: An Anthology*. When she and her young daughter Gina came to New York with her collection of Tiffany lamps and their frisky dog Corgy, Dan helped them to find an apartment on West End Avenue. For a brief period Kael reviewed for *McCall's* before winding up in her perch at the *New Yorker* magazine, which she held from 1967 to 1991. She became a cinema and neighborhood pal, dropping in of an evening with her daughter and talking about the latest movies. Raised on a California chicken farm, a philosophy student at Berkeley, she could talk about anything from Heidegger to fresh vegetables, and turned green when I presented a pâté laden with three different meats that I'd slaved over all morning. Ugh, so much *meat!*

So there we were one evening in the living room—children peacefully asleep, me relaxing on our olive-green recamier lounge, and 14-year-old Gina watching her mother's every move on the sofa. Pauline, with her usual bourbon in one hand, cigarette dangling in the other, took alternate sips of bourbon and puffs on her cigarette. Her arms flailed in excitement as we heatedly discussed—was it *Hiroshima Mon Amour*? As the bourbon decreased, the ash on the cigarette slowly mounted until, with one grand sweep of her arm, it *fell* on our Naugahyde sofa. Its pristine surface got marked with a *hole for life*! Most fabrics can be re-woven and cleverly re-stitched so that the wound is imperceptible—not so with Naugahyde. No reparation can heal its unforgiving plastic. "Oh, dear!" Pauline exclaimed in her high-pitched voice, trailing my look of horror to the neat little hole and, without skipping a beat, pursued her dismissal of the film. I just sat there. What could you say to someone who, like Boudu in Jean Renoir's *Boudu Saved from Drowning*, made messes and failed to be tamed by the female household?

Pauline, at five feet, was larger than my Naugahyde sofa. *Gutsy, gusto, gumption* are words that come to mind—along with salty, unsentimental, bawdy, brash, jazzy, feisty, passionate, ecstatic, scornful. How many words does one person need? A resolute heroine, she pursued personal freedom and applauded Catherine in *Jules and Jim* for being "part of a new breed—the independent, intellectual modern woman. Though determined to live as freely as a man and claiming equality, she employed every feminine wile to gain extra advantages and to increase her power position." Pauline was describing herself: petite, cheery, dulcet voice (interspersed with long-suffering sighs), proud of her legs, lover of clothes, coquettish—and a powerhouse. When she was good, she was very good; when she was bad she was horrid. She wrote with pizzazz and slangy freedom. Spoken language came alive. Like the kid in "The Emperor's New Clothes," she blew the whistle on "arty" *cinemah* and movies with puffy "production" values. *The Sound of Music*, *Last Year at Marienbad*, and *Blowup* fell equally under her guillotine. But when she loved something, she went for broke, as with *Bonnie and Clyde*, *Weekend*, *Last Tango in Paris*, *The Godfather*,

Mash, *The Garden of the Finzi-Continis*, and *Mean Streets*. She championed the work of Francis Ford Coppola, Steven Spielberg, Brian de Palma, and Robert Altman. There were older films she also loved, like Jean Renoir's *Grand Illusion*, D. W. Griffith's *Intolerance*, Preston Sturges's *Unfaithfully Yours*, and the Marx Brothers' *Duck Soup*. As David Remnick, editor of the *New Yorker*, said: "Kael broke down barriers between low and high cinema in her reviews, delighting in both the sublime and the profane." She went bananas when she heard movies described in hushed tones for their *creativity*, *illusion and reality*, *redeeming social message*. Movies were entertainment. Although she ridiculed the *auteur* theory with its insistence on the predominance of the director's personality, she was a longtime admirer of Jean Renoir, Orson Welles, Robert Altman, Jean-Luc Godard, and Satyajit Ray. Marlon Brando, James Mason, Barbra Streisand, and Jane Fonda were among her favorite stars. She wrote over ten books, including *I Lost It at the Movies*, *Kiss Kiss Bang Bang*, *Deeper Into Movies*—her titles super-sexy. Pauline fell in love with movies, and disciples ("Paulettes") fell in love with her. Even when off-the-wall, she was fun to read. She helped to shape American film criticism. I admire her passion, her pluck (having done odd jobs for herself and her daughter to survive, and at one point running a Laundromat in California), her valor in confronting Parkinson's disease when she lived in Great Barrington, Massachusetts.

A decade or so later, when our little girls were long continent, we gave away the Naugahyde sofa, and the hole went with it. How can I not forgive someone who, in her review of Satyajit Ray's *Devi*, said: "We see his characters not in terms of good or bad, but as we see ourselves, in terms of failures and weaknesses and strengths and, above all, as part of a human continuum—fulfilling, altering, and finally accepting ourselves as part of this humanity of experience—there is only so much we can do."

Pauline died on September 3, 2001.

Vincent Canby

More people have read Vincent Canby's reviews than those of many other movie critics. As senior critic of the *New York Times* from 1960 to 1993, he appeared almost daily, writing longer analyses for the Sunday Arts and Leisure section. For six years, he worked at the show business trade paper *Variety* as reporter and critic. His reviews and essays ranged from the French New Wave, European modernism, Hollywood blockbusters, to American independent filmmaking. He maintained a curiosity and openness, heralding Jean-Luc Godard, Rainer Werner Fassbinder, Spike Lee, Woody Allen, Jane Campion, Ismail Merchant and James Ivory. He was also a playwright and novelist. Among his works are the novels *Living Quarters* (1975) and *Unnatural Scenery* (1979) and the plays *End of the War* (1978), *After All* (1981), and *The Old Flag* (1984). Canby did not blow whistles, he did not strain for the *bon mot*, he did not define "schools" of cinema; he did not have a retinue of Little Vincents. What he had was a following of readers who trusted his views on how a film was written, directed, acted, and its human content. His prose was conversational with trenchant insights and wry humor.

> "It is guaranteed to put all teeth on edge, including George Washington's, wherever they may be."

> "Hack fiction exploits curiosity without really satisfying it or making connections between anything else in the world."

> "She was a woman attempting to make sense of, and get some satisfaction from a life that seemed to have no more logic than a roulette wheel."

And writing about fiction: "Good fiction reveals feeling, refines events, locates importance and, though its methods are as mysterious as they are varied, intensifies the experience of living our lives."

The word *gentleman* comes to mind in describing Canby—a Southerner, he had a hint of the Old South. Flamboyant he was not (Dartmouth graduate in tweed jacket, oxford shirt with button-down collar, gray or khaki trousers, and striped tie), but over and beyond, a man of grace, wit, and taste. If one were to say that we lived "behind the store" (a couple of blocks away), Canby lived in front. Dan had found him an apartment on Broadway and 89th Street, so it was easy to attend an early screening. He and I often ran into each other at Barzini's Fruit Store, on Broadway between 89th and 90th Street, and would tip each other off to some ripe avocados or fresh raspberries—dinner at his house that night with Penelope Gilliatt turned out to be an avocado salad, shrimp, and fresh raspberries. There was Penelope with her flaming red hair and Vincent in his tweeds. Vincent Canby: a modest man, a cultivated eye. He died on October 15, 2000.

Right: Dan Talbot and Alfred Hitchcock in front of the marquee (January 13, 1965)
Below: Alfred Hitchcock *(far right)* in the lobby of the New Yorker during a promotional tour in 1965, joined by *(left to right)* Dan Talbot, producer Lou Allen, and Toby Talbot

Top: New Yorker Theater marquee (January 13, 1965): Buster Keaton in "The General" and "Cops"

Middle: The New Yorker Bookstore (c. 1966)

Bottom: New Yorker Theater marquee (August 17–18, 1962): a repertory series that experimented with fragmented programming

Top (opposite): New Yorker Theater marquee (June 19–25, 1962): Visconti's *Rocco and his Brothers* (1960) was well received by critics and audiences alike in its American premiere.

Bottom (opposite): Cinema Studio marquee, Broadway and 66th Street (December 13–28, 1978): The opening program at our new twin theater.

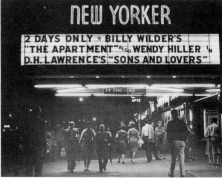

Left (opposite): Jules Feiffer's mural, created for the lobby of the New Yorker
Top left: Dan Talbot in the Lincoln Plaza projection booth (c. 2007)
Top right: Dan and Toby Talbot in Spain (1959)

Bottom left: Dan Talbot and Claude Lanzmann at the Berlin Film Festival (February 1987) where *Shoah* was presented
Bottom right: The Talbots in the late '60s, at fundraiser for Vietnam vets (photo: Richard Avedon)

Within the drawing:

ROBERT MILES PARKER · SEPTEMBER 11,1986

WEST 94TH STREET →

WEST 100TH STREET →

METRO

1 SPIKE LEE'S SHE'S GOTTA HAVE IT
'IRRESISTIBLY ENJOYABLE' DENBY NY MAG
2 WE WERE SO BELOVED THRU SEPT. 19

⊛ METRO ⊛

BEER · CIGARETTES · TOBACCO · CANDY

BROADWAY

Above: Drawing of Metro Theater
façade (Robert Miles Parker,
September 11, 1986)
Right (opposite): The Metro façade
was declared a landmark in 1989.

SAT LA STRADA AND JULIET OF THE SI

N. AMARCORD AND THE WHITE SH

ERY FRI AND SAT KINO JANUS FES

Top: Metro Theater, Art Deco interior refurbished by architect Peter Cohen, opening day (October 1, 1982)

Above left: Metro lobby, with candystand created by Peter Cohen in Art Deco style

Above right: Cinema Studio manager Carlos Canossa on the theater's last day (March 29, 1990)

Top (opposite): Metro Theater marquee (October 1, 1982)

Bottom (opposite): Cinema Studio 2 (185 seats) after the theater was twinned in 1978

MILOS FORMAN'S
'AMADEUS'
8 ACADEMY AWARDS

Opposite left: Metro Theater marquee and façade
(September 11–17, 1985)
Below (top): Bergman was misspelled in this New Yorker cartoon.

Below (bottom): Diane Keaton and Woody Allen in the Cinema Studio lobby (1977)

Senior-citizen ticket-holders on line for a 4 P.M. showing downstairs at the Lincoln Plaza Cinemas look forward to another grownups' movie — and also perhaps back to the bracing Truffaut and the ur-Woody Allen and the knockout Berman flicks they first caught at the Carnegie Cinema or the Beacon or the Thalia, when all the world and Anouk Aimée were fresh. — Roger Angell

THE NATIONAL SOCIETY OF FILM CRITICS

Annual Awards

1971

Special Award

to

DANIEL TALBOT

of the New Yorker Theatre for the contribution he has made to the cinema by
showing films that might not otherwise have been available to the public.

Hollis Alpert
Saturday Review

Gary Arnold
Washington Post

Harold Clurman
The Nation

Jay Cocks
Time

David Denby
The Atlantic

Penelope Gilliatt
The New Yorker

Philip T. Hartung
Commonweal

Pauline Kael
The New Yorker

Stefan Kanfer
Time

Stanley Kauffmann
The New Republic

Arthur Knight
Saturday Review

Robert Kotlowitz
Harper's

Joseph Morgenstern
Newsweek

Andrew Sarris
The Village Voice

Richard Schickel
Life

Arthur Schlesinger, Jr.
Vogue

John Simon
The New Leader

Bruce Williamson
Playboy

Paul Zimmerman
Newsweek

THE NEW YORK FILM CRITICS CIRCLE

63rd Annual Award 1997

Special Tribute

Presented to

Daniel Talbot

of

New Yorker Films

THELMA ADAMS
New York Post

JOHN ANDERSON
Newsday

DAVID ANSEN
Newsweek

JAMI BERNARD
Daily News

DWIGHT BROWN
Emerge

BOB CAMPBELL
Newhouse Newspapers

GODFREY CHESHIRE
New York Press

RICHARD CORLISS
Time

DAVID DENBY
New York Magazine

MARSHALL FINE
Gannett Newspapers

OWEN GLEIBERMAN
Entertainment Weekly

J. HOBERMAN
Village Voice

STEPHEN HOLDEN
The New York Times

DAVE KEHR
Daily News

STUART KLAWANS
The Nation

JANET MASLIN
The New York Times

JACK MATHEWS
Newsday

JOE MORGENSTERN
Wall Street Journal

TERRENCE RAFFERTY
GQ

REX REED
The New York Observer

LEAH ROZEN
People Magazine

ANDREW SARRIS
The New York Observer

RICHARD SCHICKEL
Time

LISA SCHWARZBAUM
Entertainment Weekly

JOHN SIMON
National Review

DAVID STERRITT
Christian Science Monitor

PETER TRAVERS
Rolling Stone

AMY TAUBIN
Village Voice

ARMOND WHITE
New York Press

BRUCE WILLIAMSON
Playboy

Above: Tributes to Dan in 1971 and 1997

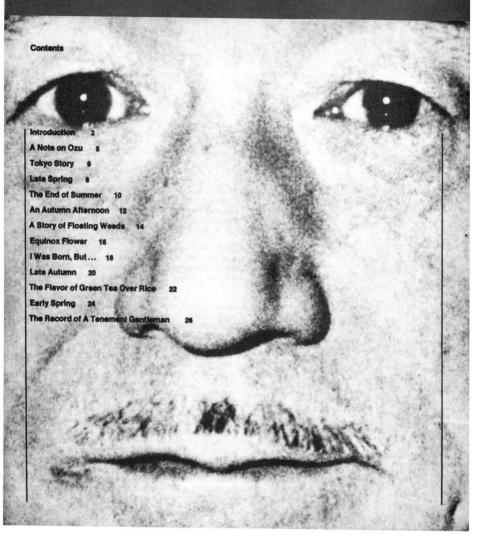

THE MAJOR WORKS OF YASUJIRO OZU

Contents

Above: Cover of a Yasujiro Ozu catalogue in 1974, with texts
on each film from Donald Richie's book on Ozu

American Premiere

JEAN-LUC GODARD'S

"LES CARABINIERS"

Screenplay by
ROBERTO ROSSELLINI · JEAN GRUAULT
and JEAN-LUC GODARD

·

Possibly the source of inspiration for Richard Lester's "HOW I WON THE WAR", and certainly a much better film than the latter, "LES CARABINIERS" drew this notice from Kenneth Tynan on its London premiere: "LES CARABINIERS" is probably the simplest study of war in the history of narrative cinema. But it is also for me the most potent of war films: a challenge to patriots and non-patriots alike, and missable by neither. It eats into the mind like acid. If this is not a masterpiece, it will do until one comes along."

Above: Lobby poster (22" x 28") for U.S. premiere of Godard's 1962 antiwar film at the New Yorker (April 25–May 15, 1968), as dissent against the Vietnam War was raging at Columbia University

VOL. II, NO. 6: JUNE 1962

SHOW

The Thirties Exhumed

The New Yorker Theater in Manhattan is America's most enterprising film revival house. Digging into the musty vaults on both coasts, founder-operator Dan Talbot has come up with "The Thirties," a double-bill-a-day program series of scarcely remembered Warner Brothers movies. The line-up, from May 29 through June 12, will include such treasures for the recondite film fancier as "Satan Met a Lady," which turns out to be a version of "The Maltese Falcon," sans Humphrey Bogart, but starring Bette Davis; "A Modern Hero," the German director G. W. Pabst's only U.S. production; and "50 Million Frenchmen," an early musical with a Cole Porter score; James Cagney in "Blonde Crazy." "Everyone went to the movies then," says Talbot. "A picture could not lose money. And the sheer output meant they never worried whether a picture might be a stiff. Consequently, some very interesting movies got sneaked across, and that's what I've tried to put into this program."

JOHN SPRINGER   "BLONDE CRAZY": CAGNEY

Above: Dan and the New Yorker got a nice mention in Huntington Hartford's glossy entertainment magazine (June 1962)

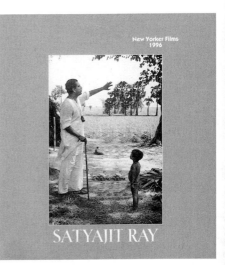

Above: Cast-iron medallion of
a sylvan art nouveau nymph from
lobby of the New Yorker
Top and bottom (right): New Yorker
Films catalogue covers of two
of our favorite directors

on Antonio Conselheiro, who together with thousands of followers held off an Army Expedition Force for months before being massacred at Canudos in 1893) and the possessed outlaw (based on the legendary cangaceiro Lampião) from a Marxist perspective that cries out for revolution and liberation from the culture of poverty imposed by imperialism. The folk songs which narrate the action also comment on it in a manner reminiscent of Brecht—like everything else in the film, they represent a living dialectic, a dynamic unity of ethnic and political forces. 110 min.

ANTONIO DAS MORTES
Glauber Rocha Brazil 1969 Thurs Aug 12
Rocha's color sequel to "Black God, White Devil" deals with the coming to political consciousness of the mercenary "jagunço" Antonio das Mortes, "the killer of cangaceiros," paid killer of rebels and bandits in the backlands. Even more stylized and operatic than "Black God," "Antonio das Mortes" is as much a revolutionary cultural expression as a political allegory. In its flamboyant transformation of native folk-art and mystical traditions, it is a highly original assertion of cultural values too long suppressed: its "tropicalist" style reflected newly formulated aesthetic principles in the Cinema Novo movement. 100 min.

DOCUMENTS OF STRUGGLE
Sun Aug 15
1: BRAZIL, REPORT ON TORTURE (color, 1971). Interviews with Brazilian political prisoners recently freed in exchange for the Swiss ambassador and re-enactments of standard tortures. Filmed in Chile by Saul Landau and Haskell Wexler. Excellent reportage. An essential document.
2. CHILE: INTERVIEW WITH SALVADOR ALLENDE (color, 1971). Saul Landau interviews the New Marxist president of Chile, eliciting fascinating personal and political statements. Filmed by Haskell Wexler.
3. MEXICO, THE FROZEN REVOLUTION (1970). Written and directed by Raymundo Gleyzer. With the Mexican Revolution of 1910 as its point of departure and continual frame of reference, this political documentary is a bold attempt to cover 60 years of historical experience, and analyze the present state of underdevelopment and repression in Mexico.

O PADRE E A MOCA
(The Priest and the Young Girl) Joaquim Pedro de Andrade Tues Aug 17
Brazil 1967
An elegaic film, "The Priest and the Young Girl" is set in an old diamond city in the interior, where only remnants of past splendor exist and the remaining population lives in an alienated world of slow death and ritualized despair. The only truly vital person in the village is a beautiful young girl. De Andrade narrates with much tenderness and poetry the story of her relationship with a priest whose spirit has been broken.

KILLED THE FAMILY & WENT TO THE MOVIES
Julio Bressane Brazil 1970 Thurs Aug 19
Julio Bressane is a leader of the "second wave" of Brazil's Cinema Novo. At 23, he has already made 6 films, most shot in 16 mm, and blown up to 35 mm. for release, like "Killed the Family," his second film, shot in 2 weeks. Taking off from the premises of yellow journalism, Bressane presents violent incidents from everyday life in Brazil: murder, suicide, torture and pentaposes these with highly personal flights of cinematic fancy, and idiomatic paraphrases of silent films and musicals. 80 min.

THREE FILMS BY SANTIAGO ALVAREZ
79 Springtimes   **LBJ**   **To take off at 18 Hours** Sun Aug 22
Perhaps the most creative talent in the new Cuban cinema is Santiago Alvarez, heir to Dziga Vertov as a master of didactic/informational revolutionary film practice. He has produced dozens of visually exciting newsreels and documentaries that combine art and propaganda in communicating the problems and achievements of the Cuban Revolution. A committed internationalist, he has also produced shorts about Vietnam, Laos, Africa and Black America. "To Take off at 18 Hours," which we will show in a new 35 mm. subtitled print, is his most ambitious work, a 75 minute essay on Cuban revolutionary achievements after 10 years of struggle. Employing visual and graphic techniques of startling originality, Alvarez even succeeds in making statistics cinematic, and entertaining. His impressionistic biography of Ho Chi Minh, "79 Springtimes," is one of the most beautiful and moving film portraits of all time. His "LBJ" (Luther, Bobby, Jack) is a dazzling montage experiment, as well as a devastating assault on LBJ's Amerika. 115 min.

BARRAVENTO
Glauber Rocha Brazil 1962 Thurs Aug 26
One of the first Cinema Novo efforts, "Barravento" is a semi-documentary study of Bahia fishermen, and their superstitions, embodied in Macumba, a mixture of Christianity and African tribal religions. The film was started by Paulino dos Santos, reorganized and finished by Rocha, with the help of Nelson Pereira dos Santos and a budget of $3,000. Rocha considers the film unfinished, "exploring mystical fatalism, political agitation, and the relationship between poetry and lyricism, a very complex relationship in a world that is still barbaric." 76 min.
PLUS: BERIMBAU (1971), world premiere of a short film on the Berimbau, a one-string instrument of African origin, demonstrated and played here by the Brazilian master Nana: a film by Toby Talbot and Alphonse Beato. 12 min.

THE LION HUNTERS
MEDINA BOE
Jean Rouch Mali/France Sun Aug 29
Like all of Rouch's ethnographic films, this cinema-verité document of men who hunt lions with bows and arrows in the remote bush country of Mali is a first-rate work of cinema. As a Third World film, it presents its subjects—a tribe of hunters and a tribe of herders—with dignity and respect: it also shows the level of their international consciousness in a most remarkable moment—the lion they hunt, the biggest and most clever of all the predators in the bush, is named the "American." 68 min.
PLUS: MEDINA BOE, a Cuban report on the revolution against Portuguese colonial oppression in Guinea Bissau. 40 min.

OS HERDEIROS
(The Heirs) Carlos Diegues Brazil 1969 Tues Aug 31
The destiny of one man, a leftist journalist, throughout 4 decades of Brazilian politics, is the focus of this tour-de-force of the new "tropicalist" cinema of Brazil. For all the hysteria it evokes, "The Heirs" is a calculated, anguished, polemical statement by a major talent in world cinema, Carlos Diegues. Its importance to the Cinema Novo's new direction cannot be over-stressed. Here is Glauber Rocha on "The Heirs": "The Heirs' is a key film in the Brazilian cinema. It is a dialectical sound/image montage of power corrupted by imperialism, but it is also a dialectical sound/image montage which projects, thru the strength of tropicalist sentiment, the first sign of a new civilization." 110 min.

A VIDA PROVISORIA
(Tentative Life) Mauricio Gomes Leite Brazil 1969 Thurs Sept 2
Like "O Bravo Guerreiro," Mauricio Gomes Leite's film debut - after 15 years of film criticism - is a political portrait distinguished by its anti-melodramatic treatment, and piercing references to the current public crisis in Brazil. The film's anti-hero is a journalist involved in the secret transfer of important papers documenting the interference of an imperialist organization in Brazilian state affairs. His personal life, involving 2 women he has loved, is probed via flashbacks to establish a link of conscience and consciousness to his actions as a political man. Part of the film's success can be attributed to sharp editing by the Italian cineaste Gianni Amico. 90 min.

BATTLE OF THE 10,000,000
CHILDREN OF THE REVOLUTION
Cuba 1970 Sun Sept 5
Chris Marker's second reportage from Cuba covers the period of last year's zafra, the harvest that was to have exceeded 10,000,000 tons but that proved a bitter disappointment. Starting with an acknowledgement that, "This year, Cuba is no longer so fashionable," the film examines critically many facets of Cuban life today, gradually building an argument that reaffirms its maker's solidarity with the on-going Cuban social experiment. The dialogue between Fidel Castro and Chris Marker provides Marker with dialectical base for the film's structure. The high point of this dialogue is, of course, Fidel's auto-critique before the people on July 26, 1970, which admitted the failure of the zafra and attempted a frank analysis of the basic reasons for the setback. Marker logically interrupts Fidel's speech with comments by workers, not only to present their criticisms, not only to underline the harmony between Fidel and the masses, but also to prevent the viewer from being swept up by Fidel's eloquence. Here and elsewhere, Marker refuses easy lyricism in favor of a strong, objective statement. 60 min.
PLUS: Jane Seller's CHILDREN OF THE REVOLUTION (Cuba, 1970), a study of Cuban youth by the British film-maker Jane Sellers. In the words of Guardian critic Irwin Silber: "A remarkable new film about Cuba . . . from infants in community creches to school children, teacher-trainees, university students and young workers, this film is about a generation coming to consciousness with values and a moral code shaped by a decade of socialist power." 30 min.

AL FATEH PALESTINIANS
PHELA - NDABA
Tues Sept 7
Produced by Unifele Film (Rome), this important new documentary presents the viewpoint of the Palestinian people on their removal from their land, and on the political/military methods they are developing to secure national and social justice. The film shows mass meetings in the refugee camps, social services of the Al Fateh, training combat footage, as well as interviews with doctors, fighters, military commanders, and political leaders, including Yasir Arafat. English version produced by Black Star Productions (Detroit). 30 min.
PLUS: PHELA-NDABA (End of Dialogue), South Africa, 1970. These searing images of Apartheid in South Africa were filmed by self-taught Black cameramen, and smuggled out of the country. Produced by the banned Pan-Africanist Congress of South Africa. 40 min.

DER LEONE HAVE SEPT CABEZAS
AMERICAN PREMIERE
(The Lion Has Seven Heads) Thurs Sept 9, Fri Sept 10
Glauber Rocha Congo Brazzaville 1970
Glauber Rocha brought the Cinema Novo to Africa for this Third World assault on the various imperialisms represented in the multi-lingual title. As in his Brazilian films, the agonies attending the birth of political consciousness in the Third World are expressed in operatic tableaux and stylized gestures. A Black revolutionary, a Portuguese mercenary, an American CIA agent, a French missionary (Jean-Pierre Leaud), and a voluptuous nude woman called the Golden Temple of Violence are among the characters in Rocha's violent allegory. Filmed on location in the Congo, "Der Leone Have Sept Cabezas" is a wild and undisciplined cry of anguish and liberation, but one that is impossible to ignore or dismiss. 97 min.

7:30 & 9:30 PM

ADMISSION 75¢
(EXCEPT SPECIALS)

Top left: The first of the three "American Premieres" series: June 15, 1966

Bottom left: The second in the "American Premieres" series: April 6–May 10, 1967

Opposite (left): 1972 ad for Louis Malle's *Phantom India* (1969)

Opposite (right): Susan Sontag text on a Godard retrospective at the New Yorker in 1967

Opposite (next pages over): Reprint of a full-page ad in the *New York Times* costing $5,000 in 1969. Pauline Kael helped Dan with the text, including the line: "The fact is, most of the films that are recognized as truly important movies—as influential, suggestive works that set people thinking along new lines—are not greeted with favor on their first showing. They may even irritate indeed." Reviews were generally favorable, but the series was a box office disaster.

Opposite (next pages over): The Metro Theater ran repertory from October 1, 1982, to July 8, 1987 (insert shows partial program for January 31– April 12, 1987).

NEW YORKER
Broadway & 88th Street
TR 4-9189

October 19 - November 1, 1967

GODARD

A crescendo of superlatives (all true):

Godard's work is, justly, being more passionately debated than that of any other contemporary director. Godard is the most important (and, in Europe, the most influential) film-maker of his generation. Godard is the greatest director working actively in the cinema today. Godard is one of the major artists of our age.

Happily, though, Godard remains "controversial." It's still possible, even common, for intelligent people to be irritated and frustrated by the films, even to find them unbearable. Godard's films haven't yet been elevated to the status of classics or masterpieces (as have those of Eisenstein, Griffith, Gance, Pabst, Renoir, Welles et al; or, to take some near contemporary examples, as L'Avventura and Jules and Jim already have been). That is, Godard's films aren't yet dead, embalmed, immortal, unequivocally (and merely) "beautiful." The films retain their youthful power to offend, to appear "ugly," incoherent, seditious, irresponsible, unpleasant, frivolous, pretentious, empty. Film-makers and audiences are still learning from them, still quarrelling with them.

Meanwhile, Godard manages to keep nimbly ahead of the inexorable thrust of cultural canonisation; continues exploring his language, questioning his artistic and intellectual resources, abandoning old problems and old solutions---making things ever more difficult for his audience, even those members of it now responding with pleasure to most of his work. His twelfth and perhaps greatest feature film, Deux ou Trois Choses que je sais d'elle, is certainly one of the most difficult and ambitious ever made. His fourteenth film, La Chinoise, opened in Paris this summer and took the first Special Jury Prize at the Venice Film Festival in September; but Godard didn't come to accept the award because he had just begun shooting his fifteenth film.

Fourteen films is a lot, but also only a beginning. While the eight features being shown at the New Yorker constitute a generous selection of Godard's work, many have either never been released commercially in the U.S. or have had no more than a brief token run in New York City only. This is unfortunate, because there's no substitute for seeing the whole work. And, like Resnais, one of his few serious near-peers among contemporary younger directors, but unlike most other directors whose artistic development is less conscious and experimental, Godard's work deserves, ultimately demands, to be seen in its entirety. Of course, not even the most passionate Godardist would claim that all the films are on the same level of accomplishment. Speaking for myself, I must admit to having almost an allergy to A Woman Is A Woman. Godard's sense of humor, for me, isn't one of his strong points. To make perhaps even clearer the slant and the limits of my own taste: after several viewings, I have yet to dispel some big reservations about Band of Outsiders, Alphaville, and Made in U.S.A., while my fondness and admiration for two films that few Godard fans rate as highly as I do, Contempt and Les Carabiniers, continues to grow. I also find it hard to look at Breathless in the same way as I used to, though I don't like it any less; but Breathless is, alone among Godard's films, almost a classic. About My Life to Live and Masculine Feminine every Godard fan agrees: they're great. And so on...

But the important point isn't the judgment upon this or that film, but a judgement about the sense and weight of Godard's work as a whole. Like many great modern artists (but, interestingly enough, few filmmakers), each individual work derives its final value from its place in a larger enterprise, which, in Godard's case, if we're lucky, will be the work of a long, prodigally creative lifetime. The nature of Godard's gifts promise much further, unpredictable development. On the extensive evidence already provided, it's a cinema characterised both by mind-teasing difficulty and a casual, sensuous energy---generous, aggressive, flippant, solemn, subtle, simplistic, egocentric, inexhaustibly vivacious.

The difficulties, of course, are what invite discussion. Godard's movies conflate a large number of seemingly unreconcilable elements. A fragmentation/collage method of narration drawn from modernist painting and poetry is combined with the bare, hard staring, "frontal," neo-realist aesthetic of television (cf. the interviews, all filmed in close-up and middle-shot, in Masculine Feminine and Deux ou Trois Choses). Alongside the propagandist zeal of the left-wing political tract and hortatory, non-realistic techniques of address by the actors adapted from the Brechtian political theatre (cf. Les Carabiniers, La Chinoise) are to be found an unmistakable, sentimental complicity with the strident mythologies of contemporary neo-American popular culture (cf. the comic strip plot of Alphaville, the gangster movies romanticism of Breathless, Band of Outsiders, Made in U.S.A.) as well as an ambivalent immersion in the allure of pop imagery and an only partly ironic display of the symbolic currency of urban capitalism---pinball machines, fast cars, neon signs, billboards, fashion magazine ads, airports. The gravity and controlled indignation of the sociological exposé (cf. the recurrent theme of prostitution in My Life to Live, A Married Woman, Deux ou Trois Choses, the recent short Anticipation) alternates with a slick, externalised energy frankly inspired by série noire novels and by Hollywood musical comedies and thriller films. Highly stylised visual compositions (using recurrent arrangements of primary colors in such films as Contempt, Pierrot le Fou, and La Chinoise) is promoted along with the "look" of improvisation and an unremitting search for the "natural" manifestation of personality before the truth exacting eye of the camera. (Incidentally, A Woman Is A Woman is the only one of Godard's films to be shot in a studio; all the rest, including the sci-fi situations of Alphaville, Le Nouveau Monde, and Anticipation, were done in "found" locations.) A feeling for the mundane facticity of the life of dislocated, urban persons like petty hoodlums, discontented housewives, students, prostitutes, solitary intellectuals (the everyday present) coexists with a fascination with the fable form (cf. Les Carabiniers) and with anti-utopian fantasies about the cruel future.

There's all this, and more. Godard's insouciant mixture of tonalities, themes, and narrative techniques suggest something like the union of Brecht and Robbe-Grillet, Gene Kelly and Francis Ponge, Gertrude Stein and David Riesman, Ray Bradbury and Robert Rauschenberg, Hegel and rock 'n roll.

What happens, then, to the familiar boundaries between moral passion and aestheticism? To the contrast between the fastidious, anti-hedonist code of "abstraction" regnant in the most prestigious modern art works and the inelegant, even sloppy demands of "realism"? To the difference between the casual jotting and the fully premeditated statement? To the difference between first person and third person narrative? To the gulf separating science fiction and other brands of pop fantasy (both apocalyptic and "cool") from documentary and quasi-scientific cinema verité? To the contradiction between political engagement and an apolitical stance verging on nihilist detachment? (Apropos of this last dualism, it seems worth mentioning that the four most recent features all include a scene in which the main characters denounce the war in Vietnam, and Godard has said that until the war ends he'll put such a sequence into every film he makes.)

What happens is that the boundaries are changed. That Godard characteristically requires his audience to violate a received system of standards, to disturb some useful network of expectations, is precisely what supplies the energy of his films. Given the quality of his work, these difficulties are to be cherished. Like every important body of work in the canon of modern culture, Godard's films are both simply what they are and also push their audience to reconsider the meaning and scope of the entire art form of which they are instances. They're not only works of art, but meta-artistic activities or projects aimed at the reorganization of our entire sensibility.

But, of course, the old forms of sensibility die hard. Film, both protected and patronized by virtue of its dual status as mass entertainment and art form, remains the last bastion of the values of the 19th century novel and theatre---even to many of the same people who have made room for plotless novels like Ulysses, The Unnameable, Naked Lunch, That Awful Mess on Via Merulana, and Pale Fire, or for the corrosive anti-spectacles of Beckett, Pinter, and the Happenings. Thus, the standard criticism levelled against Godard is that the stories in his films are undramatic, arbitrary, often simply incoherent; that his characters are flat or psychologically improbable; and that his films generally are emotionally cold, static except for a busy surface of senseless movements, topheavy with undramatized "ideas," unnecessarily obscure. Now, it's certainly true that, with the possible exception of his first feature, Breathless, Godard's films don't tell satisfying stories. But what his detractors don't grasp is that Godard doesn't want to do what they reproach him for not doing. His effort is to make movies which live in the actual present, to construct a language for films which speaks in a purer present tense, and not to tell something from the past, relate something that's already taken place. Godard thinks about movies from the standpoint of sight and sound and their relation to emotion and time rather than in relation to "story" and action.

Needless to say, Godard isn't the first director to disavow the novelistic or story-telling model for narration in feature films which use professional actors. Consider the work of Dziga Vertov and the two films of Buñuel-Dali from the silent period, not to mention a number of contemporary films, like Rossellini's Journey to Italy and Resnais' Muriel, collateral to Godard's enterprise. But it is Godard, with his varied "attempts at cinema," who has suggested more of the rich possibilities of an "unrealistic" system of narrative than any other director.

The reasons for this are at least three. First, Godard has boldly addressed the problem of directly representing or embodying ideas, including abstract ideas, as no director has done before him. Second, Godard is more ingeniously and persistently concerned with language: with speech not only as dialogue but as discourse and as recitation. (Cf. the stories in My Life to Live, the American producer's book of proverbs and the translator's doubling of the dialogue in Contempt, the oral commentary on the action delivered by Godard throughout Deux ou Trois Choses, the Maoist slogans in La Chinoise, the "broken" speech in Anticipation.) Godard's preoccupation with language is strongly reminiscent both of the efforts of certain contemporary painters and of Brechtian theatre, in which the word functions as an alternative, a complement, and a rebuke to the image. (Cf. the text of the ads in A Married Woman; the "titles" in My Life to Live, Les Carabiniers, Masculine Feminine.) And third, Godard has exploited the sense in which a visual image, a picture, can stand as exactly equivalent to a word, a sentence, a text. (Cf. the showing of the picture postcards in Les Carabiniers, the shots from the film about Ulysses in Contempt, the use of the monochromatic color photography in three "political" colors in Anticipation, the scenes in negative in A Married Woman and Alphaville.)

For Godard, the silent cinema, movies without language (except for titles), without heard speech, devoid of sound is almost an aberration---speaking unhistorically, of course. And Godard's position is a persuasive one. At the least, it seems clear that Godard's work has definitively undermined the idea that cinema is principally or essentially a "visual medium." This familiar critical dictum, in the sense usually meant intended to exclude "literary" cinema and so-called "theatrical films" such as Dreyer's Gertrud, amounts, at best, to an unnecessarily limiting view. There's no reason why one of the subjects of cinema can't be language itself---as language has become the very subject of poetry and, in a metaphoric sense, of some important painting, such as that of Jasper Johns.

At this point in Godard's stupendous body of work, it looks as if the concern with language is becoming his principal, over-arching motif. The effort to purify language of philosophical and cultural dissociation is the explicit theme (and provides the resolution) of Alphaville and Anticipation. But the concern with language must always, in the end, stand for all human concerns. Godard is reported to be fond of quoting Lenin's famous sentence, "Ethics are the aesthetics of the future." Godard's heroic, beautiful body of work tells us more than any other contemporary film director's something about what that sentence means.

Susan Sontag

A Sampler of Godard Quotes

"Beauty and truth have two poles: documentary and fiction. You can start with either one. My starting point is documentary to which I try to give the truth of fiction. That's why I've always worked with professional actors."

"The camera is not only a reproducing apparatus, the cinema is not an art which films life: the cinema is something between art and life. Unlike painting and literature, the cinema both gives to life and takes from it, and I try to render this concept in my films. Literature and painting both exist as art from the very start; the cinema doesn't."

"When I made Breathless, I knew very little about life and even less about gangsters. I could only copy from the films I had seen. And Breathless is modelled much more on Scarface and other American thrillers than on any direct knowledge I had of the underground milieu."

Speaking of Le Petit Soldat: "I wanted to show a confused mind in a confused situation. Well, that could be considered wrong, because perhaps one should not have been confused. But that's how it was. My film, in any case, was a kind of auto-critique."

"The whole New Wave can be defined, in part, by its new relation to fiction and reality..."

"I don't really like telling a story. I prefer to use a kind of tapestry, a background on which I can embroider my own ideas. But I generally do need a story. A conventional one serves as well, perhaps even best."

"The Americans know how to tell stories very well, the French, not at all. Flaubert and Proust don't know how to narrate; they do something else."

"I've found an idea for a novel. Not to write the life of a man, but only life, life itself. What there is between people, space... sound and colors.... There must be a way of achieving that; Joyce tried, but one must, must, be able... to do better." (spoken by Ferdinand/Pierrot in Pierrot le Fou)

"Literary critics often praise works like Ulysses or Endgame because they exhaust a certain genre, they close the doors on it. But in the cinema we are always praising works which open doors."

Writing about a film by Frank Tashlin: "The découpage of comic strips is aesthetically years ahead of film découpage. Within each strip, the change of shot is done with an inventive boldness that is missing now from the French cinema."

"I discovered in Breathless that when a discussion between two people became boring and tedious, one could just as well cut between the speeches. I tried it once, and it went very well, so I did the same thing right through the film."

"More and more with each film, it seems to me the greatest problem in filming is to decide where and why to begin a shot and where and why to end it."

"Pierrot le Fou isn't really a film, it's an attempt at cinema. Life is the subject, with 'Scope and color as its attributes.... Life on its own as I would like to capture it, using pan shots on nature, plans fixes on death, brief shots, long takes, soft and loud sounds, the movements of Anna and Jean-Paul. In short, life filling the screen as a tap fills a bathtub that is simultaneously emptying at the same rate. The whole ending was invented on the spot, unlike the beginning which was organized. It's a sort of Happening, but one that was controlled and dominated. Two days before I began I had nothing, absolutely nothing. Oh well, I did have the book. And a certain number of locations.... I've got a notion that when Bresson or Demy shoot a film they have an idea of the world that they are trying to put on to the screen; or, which comes to the same thing, an idea of the cinema they are trying to apply to the world. For them, cinema and the world are moulds to be filled, while in Pierrot there is neither mould nor matter."

"It may be true that one has to choose between ethics and aesthetics, but it is no less true that whichever one chooses, one will always find the other at the end of the road. For the very definition of the human condition should be in the mise en scene itself."

"Truth is in all things, even, partly, in error."

"You think I'm saying that because I'm in front of a camera, but it's not true: I really mean it." (spoken by Guillaume in La Chinoise)

On Richard Leacock: "There's no point in having sharp images if you've got fuzzy ideas. Leacock's lack of subjectivity leads him ultimately to a lack of objectivity. He doesn't even know that he is a metteur en scène, that pure reportage doesn't exist."

"You can start with fiction or with documentary. But whichever you start with, you will inevitably find the other."

"Alphaville is a fable on a realistic ground."

"The cinema can be physically defined as a double movement which projects us towards others at the same time that it takes us back to the depths of ourselves: inside out is only right side out."

"The big difference between the cinema and literature is that in the cinema the sky is there. One never has to say, is the sky blue or gray? It's just there.... I never have the feeling I am differentiating between life and creation. On the other hand, for someone like Flaubert, it was a great problem whether to describe the sky or the sea as blue or gray or blue-gray. If the sky is blue, I film it blue."

"I like people, especially women, who speak French with a foreign accent. It's always rather pretty, and it gives to ordinary words a certain freshness and value that they normally have lost."

"I built My Life to Live in tableaux to accentuate the theatrical side of the film. Besides, this division corresponded to the external view of things which best allowed me to give the feeling of what was going on inside. In other words, a contrary procedure to that used by Bresson in Pickpocket, in which the drama is seen from within. How can one render the 'inside'? I think, by staying prudently outside."

"I construct with the pieces that reality gives me. I like to think that I am a workman. I make an object which is 'me' and also 'independent of me.' Some of my effects crop up in the course of manufacturing the object. But isn't this also true of the artisan? He has an idea of the whole, but in details, he lets himself be guided by the grain of the wood. I also like to compare myself with a mathematician. When I was a lycée student, I wanted to study mathematics, or at least thought I wanted to. I liked the idea of pure research. What I've said is not very coherent, is it: a workman who creates a physical object and a mathematician who is only concerned with pure ideas. But perhaps both are compatible, after all. The two things working together produce, almost involuntarily, some kind of mystical inspiration."

"I prefer simply putting things side by side."

"Between Chardin and Braque, there is not so much difference. Some, but not so much."

The producer of the recent sketch-film Le Plus Vieux Métier du Monde, before Godard began work on his sketch about prostitution in the year 2000, Anticipation: "Listen, Monsieur Godard, it's going to be all right, isn't it? I mean, it's going to be exciting?" Godard: "Well, it all depends what you mean. I find Gertrud very exciting."

From a review of Renoir's Eléna et les Hommes: "This film is art and at the same time a theory of art; beauty and at the same time the secret of beauty; cinema and at the same time an explanation of the cinema...."

"Sometimes I have shots that were badly filmed, because I lacked time or money. Putting them together creates a different impression; I don't reject this; on the contrary, I try to do my best to bring out this new idea."

"We novelists and filmmakers are condemned to an analysis of the world, of the real; painters and musicians aren't."

"Right and left are a completely outmoded equation.... One must learn to pose the problem differently." (spoken by a character in Made in U.S.A.)

A description of Deux ou Trois Choses que je sais d'elle: "An attempt... to consider subjects as objects, a film in which chases would alternate with ethnological interview, where the spectacle of life would be finally blended with an analysis of life; in short, a free film."

"Objects exist, and if one pays more attention to them than to people, it is precisely because they exist more than these people. Dead objects are still alive. Living people are often already dead."

Apropos of Deux ou Trois Choses: "It seems to me that in and around Paris today, we are all living more or less in a state of prostitution. The increase in prostitution, literally speaking, is a partial proof of this statement because it calls into question the body, but one can prostitute oneself just as well with the mind, the spirit. I think it is a collective phenomenon, and perhaps one which is not altogether new. But what is new is that people now find it normal."

"More and more the people I see, and I meet many different kinds in the film milieu (one comes into contact with every level of society, from the banker to the electrician), don't really enjoy what they're doing. Like prostitutes, they just do it. All they really want is a car to take them to the seaside. Except that when they get the car there won't be enough roads to get to the sea, and if they do, the beaches will be too crowded. I don't think that you can find a single carpenter or plumber today who likes his job."

"The woman in A Married Woman is in fact already an inhabitant of Alphaville---woman reduced to an object by the pressures of modern life, incapable of being herself."

"There is just a moment when things cease to be a mere spectacle, a moment when a man is lost, and when he shows that he is lost."

Speaking of Contempt, which was based on Alberto Moravia's A Ghost at Noon: "Moravia's novel is a nice novel for a train journey, full of old-fashioned sentiments. But it is with this kind of novel that one can make the best films."

"To me, style is just the outside of content, and content the inside of style, like the outside and the inside of the human body---both go together, they can't be separated."

"The subject of A Woman Is a Woman is a character who succeeds in resolving a certain situation, but I conceived this subject within the framework of a neo-realistic musical: an absolute contradiction, but that is precisely why I wanted to make the film."

"I consider myself an essay-writer. I write essays in the form of novels, or novels in the form of essays. I'm still as much of a critic as I ever was during the time of Cahiers du Cinéma. The only difference is that instead of writing criticism, I now film it."

\+ + + + + + + + +

All the quotes are taken from Richard Roud's excellent book Godard (incidentally, the first full-length study of Godard in English) to be published in January by Doubleday.

Filmography

Jean-Luc Godard was born in Paris in 1930, was educated in Switzerland and Paris, published his first articles on movies in 1950, travelled in North and South America in 1951, made his first film (a short called Opération Béton) in 1954, collaborated regularly on Cahiers du Cinéma from 1956 to 1959, etcetera.

To date, fourteen feature films have been completed and released:

A Bout de Souffle (Breathless)	1959
Le Petit Soldat	1960
Une Femme est une Femme (A Woman is a Woman)	1961
Vivre Sa Vie (My Life to Live)	1962
Les Carabiniers	1963
Le Mépris (Contempt)	1963
Bande à Part (Band of Outsiders)	1964
Une Femme Mariée (A Married Woman)	1964
Alphaville	1965
Pierrot le Fou	1965
Masculin Féminin	1966
Made in U.S.A.	1966
Deux ou Trois Choses que je sais d'elle	1966
La Chinoise	1967

Plus five shorts:

Opération Béton	1954
Une Femme Coquette	1955
Tous les Garçons s'appellent Patrick	1957
Charlotte et son Jules	1958
Une Histoire d'Eau (with Truffaut)	1958

Plus seven sketches:

La Paresse (sketch in Les Septs Péchés Capitaux)	1961
Le Nouveau Monde (sketch in RoGoPaG)	1962
Le Grand Escroc (sketch for Les Plus Belles Escroqueries du Monde---cut when film was released, shown later that year in Paris as a short	1963
Montparnasse-Levallois (sketch in Paris vu par...)	1963
Anticipation, ou L'An 2000 (sketch in Le Plus Vieux Métier du Monde)	1967
section of Loin du Vietnam	1967
sketch from Gospel 70	1967

PROGRAMS

NEW YORKER

B'way & 88th St · TR 4 9989

Jan. 12-18
BLACK GIRL (La Noire De...) J. Ousmane Sembène

Jan. 19-25
PICKPOCKET

Jan. 26-Feb. 1
BAD COMPANY (Les Mauvaises Fréquentations)

Feb. 2-8
ME AND MY BROTHER Robert Frank

Feb. 9-15
IDENTIFICATION MARKS: NONE (Rysopis)

Feb. 16-22
LES CREATURES Agnès Varda

Feb. 23-Mar. 1
JEAN-MARIE STRAUB

Mar. 2-8
SIX IN PARIS (Paris Vu Par...)

Mar. 9-15
LE SOCRATE

Mar. 16-22
TROPICI Gianni Amico

Mar. 23-29
THE FIRE WITHIN

Mar. 30-Apr. 5
MORINE GRATIS

Apr. 6-12
CHRONICLE OF ANNA MAGDALENA BACH

Apr. 13-19
WALKOVER Jerzy Skolimowski

Apr. 20-26
THE SMUGGLERS

MASCULIN FEMININ (Feb. 18)

REAR WINDOW (Feb. 16-17)

ANNIE HALL (March 21-22)

THE PHILADELPHIA STORY (March 9-10)

METRO REPERTORY

FRI, JAN 31: MY NIGHT AT MAUD'S (*Eric Rohmer, 1969*) 2:15, 6:10, 10:05/THE AVIATOR'S WIFE (*Rohmer, 1980*) 12:20, 4:15, 8:10

SAT-SUN, FEB. 1-2: The Marx Brothers in DUCK SOUP (*1933*) 12:30, 3:15, 6, 8:45/and HORSE FEATHERS (*1932*) 1:55, 4:40, 7:25, 10:10

MON-TUES, FEB. 3-4: THE PASSENGER (*Michelangelo Antonioni, 1975*) 1:50, 5:50, 9:50/THE SPIDER'S STRATEGEM (*Bernardo Bertolucci, 1970*) 12, 4, 8

WED-THURS, FEB. 5-6: Humphrey Bogart in TREASURE OF THE SIERRA MADRE (*John Huston, 1948*) 2:55, 7:10/and CASABLANCA (*Michael Curtiz, 1942*) 1, 5:15, 9:30

FRI-SUN, FEB. 7-9: BARRY LYNDON (*Stanley Kubrick, 1976*) Fri-Sat: 2:10, 7:30; Sun: 1, 6:20/THE DRAUGHTSMAN'S CONTRACT (*Peter Greenaway, 1982*) Fri-Sat: 12:10, 5:30, 10:50; Sun: 4:20, 9:40

MON, FEB. 10: STRANGER THAN PARADISE (*Jim Jarmusch, 1984*) 12, 3:25, 6:55, 10:25/REPO MAN (*Alex Cox, 1983*) 1:40, 5:10, 8:40

TUES-WED, FEB. 11-12: MY DINNER WITH ANDRE (*Louis Malle, 1981*) 1:20, 4:45, 8:10/CHRISTMAS IN JULY (*Preston Sturges, 1940*) 12, 3:25, 6:50, 10:15

THURS, FEB. 13: LATE AUTUMN (*Yasujiro Ozu, 1960*) 12, 4, 8/A STORY OF FLOATING WEEDS (*Ozu, 1934*) 2:20, 6:20, 10:20

FRI-SAT, FEB. 14-15: BADLANDS (*Terrence Malick, 1974*) 12, 3:35, 7:10, 10:45/DAYS OF HEAVEN (*Malick, 1978*) 1:50, 5:25, 9

SUN-MON, FEB. 16-17: REAR WINDOW / (*Alfred*

WED, MARCH 5: THE SEARCHERS (*John Ford, 1956*) 1:50, 5:50, 9:50/RED RIVER (*Howard Hawks, 1948*) 12, 4, 8

THURS, MARCH 6: BIG DEAL ON MADONNA STREET (*Mario Monicelli, 1958*) 12, 3:25, 6:50, 10:15/THE WHITE SHEIK (*Federico Fellini, 1952*) 1:45, 5:10, 8:35

FRI-SAT, MARCH 7-8: Sam Shepard in THE RIGHT STUFF (*Philip Kaufman, 1983*) 1:15, 4:45, 8:15

SUN-MON, MARCH 9-10: Cary Grant and Katharine Hepburn in THE PHILADELPHIA STORY (*George Cukor, 1940*) 2, 5:50, 9:40/Cary Grant and Rosalind Russell in HIS GIRL FRIDAY (*Howard Hawks, 1940*) 12:15, 4:05, 7:55

TUES, MARCH 11: BOUDU SAVED FROM DROWNING (*Jean Renoir, 1932*) 2:20, 6:10, 10/DIARY OF A COUNTRY PRIEST (*Robert Bresson, 1951*) 12:10, 4, 7:50

MON, MARCH 17: THE EXTERMINATING ANGEL (*Luis Buñuel, 1962*) 1:40, 5:10, 8:40/TRISTANA (*Buñuel, 1970*) 12, 3:25, 6:55, 10:25

TUES, MARCH 18: TRISTANA (*Luis Buñuel, 1970*) 2:25, 6:05, 9:45/THAT OBSCURE OBJECT OF DESIRE (*Buñuel, 1977*) 12:30, 4:10, 7:50

WED, MARCH 19: THAT OBSCURE OBJECT OF DESIRE (*Luis Buñuel, 1977*) 2:15, 5:55, 9:35/VIRIDIANA (*Buñuel, 1961*) 12:30, 4:10, 7:50

THURS, MARCH 20: VIRIDIANA (*Luis Buñuel, 1961*) 12, 3:25, 6:50, 10:20/THE EXTERMINATING ANGEL (*Buñuel, 1962*) 1:40, 5, 6:55, 8:35

FRI-SAT, MARCH 21-22: ANNIE HALL (*Woody Allen, 1977*) 12:15, 3:45, 7:15, 10:45/MANHATTAN (*Allen, 1979*) 2, 5:30, 9

SUN-MON, MARCH 23-24: BIZET'S CARMEN (*Francesco Rosi, 1984, in Dolby*) 3:55, 9:05/THE MAGIC FLUTE (*Ingmar Bergman, 1975*) 1:30, 6:40

TUES, MARCH 25: W.C. Fields in NEVER GIVE A SUCKER AN EVEN BREAK (*1941*) 1:40, 4:30, 7:20, 10:10/and THE BANK DICK (*1940*) 12:15, 3:05, 5:55, 8:45

WED, MARCH 26: SANS SOLEIL (*Chris Marker, 1982*) 2:40, 6:15, 9:50/HIROSHIMA, MON AMOUR (*Alain Resnais, 1959*) 1, 4:35, 8:10

THURS, MARCH 27: THE ASPHALT JUNGLE (*John Huston, 1950*) 1:50, 5:45, 9:40/Burt Lancaster in SWEET SMELL OF SUCCESS (*Alexander Mackendrick, 1957*) 12, 3:55, 7:50

FRI-SAT, MARCH 28-29: Bogart and Bacall in THE BIG SLEEP (*Howard Hawks, 1946*) 2:25, 6:30, 10:35/and

THURS, FEB. 20: LA NOTTE (Michelangelo Antonioni, 1961) 1, 5:20, 9:40/BEFORE THE REVOLUTION (Bernardo Bertolucci, 1962) 3:15, 7:35

FRI-SAT, FEB. 21-22: STALKER (Andrei Tarkovsky, 1980) 2:40, 7:15/WALKABOUT (Nicolas Roeg, 1971) 1, 5:35, 10:10

SUN-MON, FEB. 23-24: A PASSAGE TO INDIA (David Lean, 1983, in Dolby) 12, 3, 6, 9

TUES, FEB. 25: THE PASSION OF JOAN OF ARC (Carl Dreyer, 1928) 2, 4:45, 7:30, 10:15/PICKPOCKET (Robert Bresson, 1959) 12:30, 3:15, 6, 8:45

WED, FEB. 26: WOYZECK (Werner Herzog, 1979) 2:30, 6:05, 9:40/STROSZEK (Herzog, 1977) 12:30, 4:05, 7:40

THURS, FEB. 27: NASHVILLE (Robert Altman, 1975) 12, 4:40, 9:20/HEALTH (Altman, 1980) 2:50, 7:30

FRI-SAT, FEB. 28-MARCH 1: BYE BYE BRAZIL (Carlos Diegues, 1980) 2, 6:05, 10:10/DONA FLOR AND HER TWO HUSBANDS (Bruno Barreto, 1977) 12, 4:05, 8:10

SUN-MON, MARCH 2-3: GHANDI (Richard Attenborough, 1982, in Dolby) 1:25, 4:50, 8:15

TUES, MARCH 4: DIMSUM (Wayne Wang, 1985) 12:30, 3:45, 7, 10:15/CHAN IS MISSING (Wang, 1982) 2:10, 5:25, 8:40

99th Street and Broadway

TEL: 222-1200

WED, MARCH 12: AMERICAN GIGOLO (Paul Schrader, 1980) 1:45, 5:45, 9:45/THE LADY EVE (Preston Sturges, 1941) 12, 4, 8

THURS, MARCH 13: MERRY CHRISTMAS, MR. LAWRENCE (Nagisa Oshima, 1983) 1:45, 5:45, 9:45/THE MAN WHO LEFT HIS WILL ON FILM (Oshima, 1970) 12, 4, 8

FRI, MARCH 14: GRAND ILLUSION (Jean Renoir, 1938) 2:40, 6:25, 10:10/PATHS OF GLORY (Stanley Kubrick, 1957) 1, 4:45, 8:30

SAT, MARCH 15: BADLANDS (Terrence Malick, 1974) 2:35, 6:30, 10:25/BONNIE AND CLYDE (Arthur Penn, 1967) 12:30, 4:25, 8:20

SUN, MARCH 16: Robert DeNiro in TRUE CONFESSIONS (Ulu Grosbard, 1981) 3:10, 7:25/Jack Nicholson and Jessica Lange in THE POSTMAN ALWAYS RINGS TWICE (Bob Rafelson, 1981) 1, 5:15, 9:30

TUES, APRIL 1: ALPHAVILLE (Jean-Luc Godard, 1965) 2:15, 6:05, 9:55/WEEKEND (Godard, 1967) 12:15, 4:05, 7:55

WED, APRIL 2: WHO'S AFRAID OF VIRGINIA WOOLF? (Mike Nichols, 1966) 12:40, 3:40, 6:40, 9:40/PULL MY DAISY (with Jack Kerouac, Larry Rivers, 1959) 12, 3, 6, 9

THURS, APRIL 3: Two from Senegal – EMITAI/(Ousmane Sembene, 1971) 1:35, 5:05, 8:35/JOM (Ababacar Samb, 1982) 12, 3:30, 7, 10:30

FRI-SAT, APRIL 4-5: LAST TANGO IN PARIS (Bernardo Bertolucci, 1973) 1, 5:45, 10:30/DEATH IN VENICE (Luchino Visconti, 1971) 3:20, 8:05

SUN-MON, APRIL 6-7: The Marx Brothers in ANIMAL CRACKERS (1930) 2:30, 6:10, 9:50/and MONKEY BUSINESS (1931) 12:40, 4:20, 8

TUES-WED, APRIL 8-9: PIXOTE (Hector Babenco, 1981) 1:35, 5:30, 9:25/LOS OLVIDADOS (Luis Buñuel, 1951) 12, 3:55, 7:50

THURS, APRIL 10: JONAH WHO WILL BE 25 IN THE YEAR 2000 (Alain Tanner, 1976) 3, 7:25/LA SALAMANDRE (Tanner, 1971) 12:45, 5:05, 9:30

FRI-SAT, APRIL 11-12: DIVA (Jean-Jacques Beineix, 1982) 2:15, 6:15, 10:15/BREATHLESS (Jean-Luc Godard, 1959) 12:30, 4:30, 8:30

THE BIG SLEEP (March 28-29)

THE WHITE SHEIK (March 6)

BONNIE AND CLYDE (March 15)

NASHVILLE (Feb. 27)

LAST TANGO IN PARIS (April 4-5)

OVER →

Upper left: Box office at Lincoln
Plaza Cinemas
(Broadway and 62nd Street)
Lower left: Escalators lead to entrance
to lobby of Lincoln Plaza Cinemas
(below street level)
Opposite (upper right): Toby and Dan
Talbot in front of Lincoln Plaza box
office (c. 2008)
Opposite (lower right): Lincoln Plaza
marquee showing program in
January 2009

Festivals

Cannes

Vittorio Mussolini, in 1936, on the Lido, invented the film festival. Now, with over five hundred of them, you could well become a cinema bum, attending a different one every day—Venice, London, Edinburgh, Rome, Tehran, Montreal, Toronto, Los Angeles, San Francisco, Sundance, Palm Springs, and New York. Movies, however, are a relative newcomer in the world of art. Not until 1924 was the first filmmaker elected to the French *Académie*. Not until 1947 was the theory of film art included in the Prague Art Academy. And, until the sixties, in our own universities, there were chairs for literature and all arts save film.

Our first festival was in Cannes in 1967. Cannes: a babel of producers, directors, agents, screenwriters, journalists, actors, stars, and would-be starlets teeming with ambition. Hordes of paparazzi roam with flashbulbs; camera hounds track topless girls on the beach; strollers gape at mute painted men on stilts and at bearded Tarzans pounding their chests—anything to attract attention. Senegalese vendors hawk caftans and pukka necklaces. All collect like seaweed on the Croisette, a crescent where Romans centuries ago likewise did commerce. Cafés and restaurants along the promenade serve bouillabaisse, pizza, steak and frites, and ice cream cones for two-and-a-half Euros. Hotels with names like Europa, Excelsior, Majestic, and the Grand get booked a year in advance. We always stay at the small Hotel Splendid, run by Mme Cagnat and her capable female staff. The selection committee of the New York Film Festival is there as well. Each year we occupy Room 501, facing the Grand Palais where films in competition are shown. The room overlooks yachts anchored in the Mediterranean, and a promenade with plane trees shorn each spring like poodles, and children riding a carousel, and retirees with berets and canes chatting on benches, and clochards taking their beauty sleep. The cinema of the old port unfolds right outside our window.

Each morning, well before eight-thirty, we hasten across the trafficked boulevard, present our badges to stern uniformed guards, evade film buffs imploring for an extra ticket, scurry up a red-carpeted stairway, and scramble for a seat. The earliest screenings are quickly filled by journalists and distributors. Once ensconced, we search for eyeglasses and eagerly await the film.

The weather is usually sublime. For good reason do folk sun themselves on benches on the promenade along the azure sea. In an unseasonably chilly and rainy year, with no one equipped for it, musty screening rooms stutter with coughs, sneezes, and the snores of jet-lagged viewers nodding in and out of films, ear-phones in various tongues plugged in dormant ears. The festival is divided into sections: Official Competition, Films Out of Competition, Un Certain Regard, the Quinzaine des Réalisateurs, Critics Week, and Market Screenings. Each day choices must be made. "So many movies, and so many failures," veterans grumble. It's part of the festival script. But Dan and I keep hunting for that golden nugget that will light up our screen. Each morning we scan the offerings. How to juggle attendance at the Grand Palais, Debussy, or the Hilton? How to allow ample time to join the queue that forms well before the scheduled hour? We split up at times to cover more films. A jury, each year different, consisting of directors, stars, screenwriters, and a president award the Palme d'Or for the best film, best director, best actors. Invariably, everyone wonders why a certain strong one was not in the official competition.

Each year a big Hollywood movie barges into the Cannes Film Festival. Whether the audience is disappointed may be less relevant than that the theater be filled, a scenario the Studio hopes to replicate when the movie opens across the globe. One year we went and were bored out of our minds. Our suitcase after that never held a tuxedo or formal gown.

At the award of the Grand Prize, stars in *décolleté* gowns, trumpeted by horsemen in gala uniform, ascend the red-carpeted stairway. Moviegoers in glittery dress and black tuxedos hurry for the evening screening. Paparazzi swarm behind ropes. Look, there's Catherine Deneuve—doesn't she look great? And Isabelle Adjani—is that jewelry real? And there's Marcello Mastroianni, and Daniel Toscan du Plantier, president of Unifrance. Dan and I never attend this ceremony—party poopers, we're here to look at movies.

A restored print of 1939's *Gone With the Wind* was the opening film of the 1968 Cannes Film Festival. Princess Grace of Monaco was the Mistress of Ceremonies, and the French writer André Chamson the jury president. A French newspaper summed up the first few days as "dozing in the sunshine, far from the barricades." In Paris, students from the Sorbonne were fighting pitched battles with the French police.

But Cannes's real problems that year were just around the corner. One of the first to get an inkling of this was Polish-born director Roman Polanski, who was in Cannes as a member of that year's jury. Polanski was staying at the Martinez, with his wife, actress Sharon Tate, when awakened by an early telephone call. It was his friend, François Truffaut, asking him to attend a press conference in La Salle Jean Cocteau in the former festival palace. Polanski rushed to the conference thinking it had something to do with Henri Langlois, who had recently been reinstated in his job after being unceremoniously fired by the French culture minister André Malraux. When Polanski arrived, he realized that it wasn't about Langlois at all, but about stopping the festival. He couldn't see any connection. Others thought like him, but some were vehement about closing the festival, like Louis Malle, who was also on the jury, and Truffaut, but not shouting as much as Jean-Luc Godard, the main agitator.

Godard announced that he wanted films to be shown, but for the festival to be totally overhauled, and no prizes awarded. Truffaut called for a complete halt. "Everything that has a shred of dignity and importance is stopping in France," said Truffaut. "I don't know how one must do it, but I know that this afternoon or tonight, at least through radio, it must be announced that the Cannes festival has stopped or at least substantially reformed."

Dominique Delouche was one of the first to reluctantly withdraw his film from the competition. Other directors such as Czechoslovakia's Milos Forman (*The Firemen's Ball*) and fellow Czech Jan Němec (*The Party and the Guests*), France's Michel Cournot (*Les Gauloises Bleues*) and Alain Resnais (*Je T'Aime, Je T'Aime*), Italy's Salvatore Samperi (*Thank You, Aunt*), and Mai Zetterling (*Doctor Glas*) followed suit. Resnais was one of three French directors with a film in the main competition. He had spent five years getting this sci-fi melodrama to the screen.

"Everybody was taking films out of the festival, so out of emulation and solidarity with the French filmmakers, I withdrew my film too," Forman explains. Then the jury began to resign, starting with Louis Malle and followed by Roman Polanski, Italian actress Monica Vitti, and British director Terence Young. Carlos Saura's *Peppermint Soda*, a surreal picture about repression during the Franco regime, was due to screen, but Saura, the film's star Geraldine Chaplin, Truffaut, and Godard all tried to stop the screening from taking place by holding on to the curtain as it was being pulled back. "The whole thing was quite funny," said Polanski. "The curtain was huge, and there must have been a very powerful motor, because they were hanging on to it like grapes." The screening of Saura's film was eventually cancelled, and arguments broke out between those who wanted the festival to continue and those who wanted it to stop. "It all started out nicely, and then there was fighting and people screaming at each other. Jean-Pierre Rassam, the French producer, got punched in the nose right in the middle of the stage."

The next day, May 19th, the festival was called off. Protesters crowded the Croisette in support. Three million French workers had gone on strike when the festival entered its second week. It had run for ten days. There were twenty-eight films in competition—seventeen were cancelled, eleven were screened. After three days riot police were dispatched to the Côte d'Azur.

Festivals provide an international tour of the cinematic world. They are the first place where important films get shown (sometimes the only ones). François Truffaut, Satyajit Ray, Bernardo Bertolucci, Lars von Trier, Steven Soderbergh, and Alejandro González Iñárritu were all launched with a landmark Cannes debut. "It's a festival film," you hear said. And, like a good wine, unable to travel—the intractable commercial structure of the system disallows it. What makes for a draw in a movie theater, or for a blockbuster? Does it have "sell" written on it? Quality, of course, doesn't guarantee success, and many fine movies are fated to remain on the cultural margins, unavailable to audiences that might appreciate them. What will induce people to go to a movie by an obscure Portuguese director such as Pedro Costa, or a challenging Jean-Marie Straub, or an unknown director from the Philippines, Turkey, Paraguay, or Mali?

At the Hotels Ambassade and the Carlton a core of agents, distributors, and exhibitors strike deals. It's as urgent as a camel market, minus the camels. Movies are an embattled collaboration: An individual sits at his or her desk, comes up with an idea, writes a script, seeks a producer, attempts to raise money (you're as good as your last movie), shoots the film, seeks a distributor, seeks an exhibitor, then prays for good reviews. An independent filmmaker may spend 90 percent of his time looking for money to make his film. If numbers go south, a theater may pull it in a week—the bottom line is what counts. Numbers get published immediately—there are no secrets in the industry. And movies are so expensive to make, international support is required. Banks, television channels,

Canal Plus, RAI (Italian Television) are all acknowledged in opening credits. France has a laudable system of film funding, supported by the CNCC (Centre National du Cinéma). Ten cents of each ticket sold goes into a fund, sufficiently large, to finance films with reasonable budgets. This encourages a filmmaker to think more about his art and not what will work at the box office.

Filmmakers have sales agents prowling the festivals, employing auction techniques, and trying to stick their fingers into a distributor's pocket. There have been occasions when Dan and I make an offer on a film and an agent will use it as bait for a larger company. This may be helpful for a filmmaker in raising funds on the next movie, but many "small" films get shoved under the carpet. In 2004, Dan made a bid on *Distant*, a Turkish film we both loved, directed by Nuri Bilge Ceylan. Dan offered our typical modest advance—we are a modest company. But rather than seek a percentage deal, Ceylan wanted to sell the film outright. Since there were two more screenings, Dan told him that if he could fetch more money from a larger company, to accept it. Taken aback as he was at this generosity, Ceylon decided to act on it. A few days later, after the last screening, he phoned. Was Dan's offer still standing? It was. No contract was signed, but they had a deal. A quiet film, it had a quiet run, but brought the director to American audiences. Next film around, two years later, Ceylan was represented by a swinging agent who quoted swinging advances. How could we win that contest? Discovering an artist is a thrill. And it has been gratifying to be the first or early distributor of artists like Ceylan, Marker, Fassbinder, Herzog, Godard, Rivette, and Kieslowski. But expectation of permanence is like applying for Cinema Heaven.

Every morning one reads *Variety*: OLD WAYS NO LONGER CUT THE MUSTARD. CANNES FEST SPIRES AGAIN—SETS POWERHOUSE SLATE. Every day there are new predictions on who will win the Grand Prize. The daily magazines offer critics' evaluations. And while we go to the movies, the real world is making news. But the *International Herald Tribune*, delivered at the hotel, is instantly stale. In a bookshop, I overhear a remark from an elderly Cannoise in a white cap: "Nous sommes obligés de dire des betises jusqu'a la mort" (We're compelled to blabber nonsense till death).

Sometimes I'll sneak away for an hour or so to the Fourvilles Market, a paradise of peonies and roses, dozens of varieties of baby salad, little green courgettes topped with their yellow blossom, *herbes-de-Provence*, green olive oil, oozy cheeses, fat sausages, and shimmering fish with mysterious names. I squeeze a golden melon from Apt, tuck a small basket of *frais de bois* into my handbag, admire a giant artichoke (wishing I could steam it,) and purchase flasks of lavender for everyone in our family. Suddenly, gazing in horror at my watch, I hasten to the next screening. I've been playing hooky.

No one can get to see a couple of hundred films. "What's the running time?" is the eternal question. When the lights go out in the Grand Palais, a voice in the darkness proclaims: *Mesdames et messieurs, la séance va à commencer.*

One doesn't attend Cannes in quest of three-star restaurants: meals are squeezed in between screenings. La Pizza is our canteen, its rotund *papa* dishing out pizza margarita, pizza with anchovies, pizza with eggplant, pizza with mushrooms—all baked in a brick oven. It's where those in the know go—"folk in the garlic" as the Spanish say. On our last night, we may treat ourselves to a bouillabaisse feast at Tetou, a restaurant in a nearby coastal village overlooking the Mediterranean. A steaming tureen of fish bouillon, redolent of garlic, fennel, saffron, and orange peel, comes accompanied by a piquant garlic-and-pepper *rouille* and toasted bread rounds, followed by a platter with the catch of the day—*rascasse, languouste, crevettes, galinette, murène, merlan, saint-pierre, lotte, dorade*—each identified by the "surgeon" who fillets them before your eyes. If you have room, you indulge in home-made apricot, currant, and peach preserves, accompanied by crispy beignets. We order a white Pedro Domecq—and the next day, do not eat.

One evening we drive up to Mougins, an old village with winding, cobbled streets, small plazas with bubbling fountains, and stone houses aflame with geraniums—a haven from the mayhem but kilometers away.

The three-star restaurant, Le Moulin de Mougins with its noted chef Roger Vergè, draws celebrities, though we favor the smaller Roger's Bistro for his superb *bacalao aux èpinards*, a codfish and spinach mèlange I've had small success in duplicating, and baby lamb chops sprinkled with rosemary and thyme, accompanied by a lusty red Domaine Ott. At the end of each festival, we allow ourselves to wander: one year to Grasse with its spectacular flower market; another to the glassmaking village of Biot with its Ferdinand Lèger Museum; another to Antibes with the Picasso Museum; and another to Nice to stroll its promenade, visit the Matisse Chapel, and have a lunch of *pistou* soup, roquette salad, and an oozy brie at Chez Marie, a thumbnail bistro. In the afternoon, we drive up to the perched village of Éze in the *pais arrière*. Dan, wary of heights, stays far from the precipice. One year at the end of our stay, we lodge overnight at La Colombe d'Or in St. Paul de Vence and catch a Giacometti retrospective at the nearby Maeght Museum. Lunching in its garden over a feast of twenty-odd hors d'oeuvres, we greet Simone Signoret, queenly in her cloak, and in the evening at the bar run into James Baldwin's brother, more at home in Provence than in the United States.

Berlin

On February 4, 2001, at 4:02 P.M., amidst formidable frost, Lufthansa Flight 450 ascends JFK: destination, the 50th Berlin Film Festival. This was not to be our typical *voyage à deux*, for Dan had left two days earlier while I finished the spring semester. Six hours after departure, our daughter will phone Lufthansa to verify the safe arrival of Flight 457, Kennedy to Tegel, carrying aboard passenger TT.

From Seat 11A, the dwarfed world vanishes beneath eiderdown clouds. As usual, I'd requested a window seat, to be undisturbed by a person climbing over me to reach the lavatory. Shifting sky, shifting time zones, and shimmering water induce daydreams. Settled in the aisle is a bearded orthodox man, two rows apart from his wife and their three young children (another tucked under her long-sleeved dress), and as the third occupant, a young woman, edges towards the middle seat, he leaps to his feet to avoid contact. Not so lucky am I. No sooner are seatbelts fastened than Middle-Seat turns to me: Where was I going? Hearing *Film Festival*, she bolts upright. What fun seeing movies all day! What'll you wear opening night? What are your ten favorite films? On and on she goes, an unhaltable Ancient Mariner. My mind wanders.

Years after World War II, Dan and I avoided the Berlin Film Festival. The sound of German evoked neither Goethe nor Heine, but concentration camps and the murder of six million. *Schult* encapsulates guilt and debt: after the war, the Germans strove to confront guilt and debt, examining their conscience. Not so in France regarding *conscience* (conscience, consciousness), as shown in Marcel Ophüls' *The Sorrow and the Pity* (1969), a scathing examination of the moral response of the French under the German Occupation. French television refused to show the film for it undermined the cherished mythology of French Resistance, but finally it was exhibited in theaters all over the country.

We began attending the Berlin Film Festival in the early seventies. Now it is our favorite, with excellent categories, politically engaged films, and welcoming young volunteers. Many close friendships have been formed, among them Jan Schütte, whose film *Dragon Chow* (1987) we took on for distribution. It is a moving story of Asian political refugees in Germany living on the edge of deportment. Two years later he and his fiancée Christina asked to be married on our Long Island lawn, Dan and I the sole attendants. We saw it as a blessing on our home.

Fassbinder

Dragon Chow recalled Rainer Werner Fassbinder's *Ali: Fear Eats the Soul* (1974). Also about an outsider, it is a touching story of the unlikely love affair between a German floor-washer in her sixties and an inarticulate Arab mechanic barely half her age: a perverse social comedy and a biting drama of social prejudice. By then, we were hooked on German cinema and hooked on Fassbinder. The prolific and daring director was the most torrential force in European cinema since Godard. When he died at the premature age of thirty-six he had directed over forty films. Once, when asked by a reporter why he didn't take more time, he said: "That's how I make them." Had anyone ever asked Lope de Vega, the Spanish dramatist of the Golden Age, the "prodigious monster," why *he* didn't take more time? No Fassbinder film is like the others. Each goes further than the last, moving from soap opera to social analysis to irony to politics to farce.

We wound up distributing many of his films. *The Merchant of Four Seasons* (1972) is a heart-breaking story of a fruit peddler who escapes from the Foreign Legion and returns home to watch his unexceptional life disintegrate. *The Bitter Tears of Petra Von Kant* (1972) describes the shifting relations between three lesbians: a successful fashion designer, her contented slave girl, and a sultry slug of a model. *The Marriage of Maria Braun* (1979) stars the magnetic Hanna Schygulla and established her as the most exciting German star since Marlene Dietrich. *Katzelmacher* (1969) is about a gang of youths in a Bavarian village who achieve a common purpose only in their hatred of a Greek immigrant who wanders into their territory. *Gods of the Plague* (1970) is an archetypical gangster story about two sleazy petty crooks who try to rise in life by pulling small-time jobs. *Why Does Herr R. Run Amok?* (1969) is about an ordinary guy with a family, job, and hobbies who calmly picks up a cudgel one day and bludgeons to death his wife, child, and neighbor. *The American Soldier* (1970), an homage to the world of Humphrey Bogart and great action directors like Raoul Walsh and Sam Fuller, centers on a gunman named Ricky, a charismatic figure in soft hat and white suit. Recently returned from Vietnamized America, he fulfills his assigned murders without emotion. *Effi Briest* (1974), based on Theodor Fontane's nineteenth-century classic, is a coldly detached and elegant kind of *Madame Bovary*, a mixture of anti-conformity and mediocrity about a young woman married to a much older Prussian diplomat. Carried away to a Baltic port, she drifts into a passionless affair, the full effects of which are felt only six years later in a chilling manifestation of the Prussian code. *Berlin Alexanderplatz* (1980) is a monumental adaptation of Alfred Döblin's novel about German life in the 1920s, focusing on a simple Everyman who has just been released from prison. It is one of my favorite Fassbinder films.

We acquired *The Marriage of Maria Braun* in 1979. It became one of our largest-grossing films with one of the longest runs at the Cinema Studio. What can one say about Fassbinder? A film addict, a drug addict, a homosexual, he married one of his leading ladies (Ingrid Craven). His films are soap opera, sexual politics, offbeat comedy, epic romance, contemporary history, analysis of postwar Germany from the fall of Hitler through the "economic miracle." He is outrageous, irreverent, and tender.

One Sunday after a family dinner, as we were sitting in our living room, the phone rang. It was Fassbinder, who had just arrived in town for the New York Film Festival, where his latest film was being premiered. Dan invited him to drop by, quite expecting him to decline. This man was noted for his reserve, meager threshold for social amenities, brusqueness with all but the closest intimates, and known to sit in stony silence at a luncheon in his honor, to fail to show up for an engagement, to be rude. To Dan's surprise, Fassbinder accepted the invitation and asked if he might bring a friend.

Hanging up, Dan casually mentioned that Fassbinder was coming by in half an hour, and scarcely noticing, we resumed our thread of conversation. Shortly after, my mother said she was tired and would be leaving. She didn't look a bit tired. It was her tactful way of not intruding. We insisted that she stay, though secretly I had my fingers crossed that she not witness some predictable curtness at worst, a stiff encounter at best. The man whose movies were caustic satires of every institution up and down the line, families not excluded, could not be counted on to be nice to your mama.

Fassbinder was punctual, arriving on the dot with his friend in matching black leather pants and leather zipped jackets. We introduced them to my mother and our daughters. Both spoke fluent English. Then, the usual queries one makes to a foreign visitor: When did you arrive? How was the flight? How long will you stay? The replies were brief. A conversation with Fassbinder required a slow massage to get underway.

Fassbinder, on a chair and Dan on the sofa, proceeded to speak in low tones about his next project, while I engaged his friend, a lively slender man from Frankfurt who'd done a variety of things, ranging from owning a florist shop to running a bar. Bella and the girls talked to each other and then drifted off, Bella to hear Emily play a new Liszt piece on the piano, Nina and Sarah to their rooms. From the living room we heard the scattered theme of the sonata.

In a short while, Bella returned, calmly seated herself, and was drawn into conversation with me and Fassbinder's friend. In a lull, Fassbinder turned to her, asked where she lived, how many children she had, where she originally came from. Not too many transitions, rather abrupt in that way of his. I nearly fainted. Never had I heard him actively initiate so much conversation at one clip. My mother replied easily, unselfconsciously. Soon the girls returned. One sat on the arm of her chair, the others on the window seat, gazing discreetly but curiously at the prodigious director, having seen his brilliant and outrageous *The Bitter Tears of Petra von Kant* and his moving *Ali: Fear Eats the Soul*.

The visit was drawing to an end. The two men had an appointment downtown. Fassbinder rose to his feet in that rather jolting way of his—leather jacket never removed. We stood up to say goodnight. He approached my mother, who was still seated, took her hand, kissed it, and told her how happy he was to meet her. She smiled her gentle smile and thanked him.

The next morning, Fassbinder called Dan, saying how touched he was to have been invited into "the heart of your family." Seldom had he come into people's homes, met their children and mother. So, even this "terrorist" was accessible. His presumed Teutonic arrogance may have been largely shyness, though in the face of Bella you couldn't be cruel.

Berlin provides the luxury of looking at films just to look at films. It can be a newcomer or "minor" director who won't "play" theatrically but makes "festival films," or an ethnographic documentary about Estonian villages or Mongolian nomads (latter four-and-a-half hours long). Less frantic than Cannes, there's time to see friends from abroad, among them

Andi Engel of London who began Artificial Eye, a distribution company akin to ours, and the indomitable Lia van Leer, who directs the Jerusalem Cinémathèque.

Post-Toronto: 2001

On Sunday, September 9th, 2001, I return from the Toronto Film Festival alone, in time for my first Fall class, scheduled next day. The empty apartment now feels far too big—once it held five. Two days later, on September 11th, lying on a mat for morning exercise, I watch CNN out of the corner of my eye. At 8:46, a plane crashes into the North Tower of the World Trade Center—an upside down, absurd, hallucinatory image. Blinking, I sit up. At 9:03 another crashes into the South Tower. At 9:59, the South Tower collapses; at 10:28 the North Tower hurtles down and the skyline turns into a billowing black cloud, people screaming and fleeing the fury. Numb, mouth dry, I stare at the chaos on the screen. Quickly dressing, I race downtown to 62nd Street and Broadway to shut down our Lincoln Plaza Cinemas. This is no time for movies. When I try to reach Dan in Toronto, all telephone lines are jammed.

I head uptown in a daze. Pedestrians, unexpectedly released from work, are strolling arm in arm along Broadway—like a *paseo* in a Spanish village. It was as if nothing had happened. Inside the shops and offices, people had not seen the horror. They simply had the day off. Where to go? What to do with myself? I head for the river, as if to verify Manhattan's coastline. On Riverside Drive at 72nd Street, the statue of a serene Eleanor Roosevelt peers down at pigeons flocking at her feet. On the waterfront, the pearl-gray template of the Hudson is without ripple. On this balmy day, it is as if nothing has happened. Yet every few minutes, fighter planes sinisterly buzz overhead, vigilant, circling this vulnerable island. Manhattan is a prime target. The smoke begins wafting uptown, you can smell it. I hurry home.

The phone rings as I enter. "Where were you? I kept calling," Nina asks, worried that this was a day I was teaching downtown. No, that was yesterday. Some employed in the Twin Towers didn't happen to go to work that day: a dental appointment, a sick child, but most did. The phone rings again: Dan, at last. The airports in Toronto and in JFK are closed. He is stranded.

The sun at its zenith over the Hudson floods the apartment with light. Automatically, I draw the shutters to protect the furniture from fading. My God, imagine worrying about furniture! But *that's* something I can protect. Strewn on the dining room table are accumulated newspapers and magazines, and on my desk unpaid bills, unanswered correspondence, postcards from friends summering abroad, and Fall catalogues: American Ballet, 92nd Street Y, Wayside Gardens, and the New School, listing my documentary film course, "The Human Condition Seen Through Film." The *inhuman* condition seems more like it. Nothing on the answering machine from Dan.

I head for the window seat to keep an eye out—that pathetic Anything May Happen Watchdog Syndrome. When one is not looking, there may be an electric short, a carrot not going down right, a parent's death. It takes but a moment. The towers fell in 102 minutes. On the slope of Riverside Park, trees flutter and boats ply peacefully beneath the George Washington Bridge. But the flag at the Soldiers' and Sailors' Monument flutters at half-mast, and a terrible thought occurs: *The bridge is another target!*

It is twilight, the hour when fretful babies cry, but in the playground children linger. "Leave the sandbox, swing, and see-saw!" I want to shout. Darkness falls and the inky river outlines the park like a burial announcement. Yellow sodium lamps punctuate a deserted landscape and white paths unfurl like ghostly bandages. The Soldiers' and Sailors' Monument rises like a funerary urn of stone. In bed, my hand reaches out to Dan's side of the bed.

R E E L

6

Demolition

One whistle, one minute to blasting
Two whistles, ready to blast
Three whistles, all clear.

On a hot July day in 1985, stores alongside the New Yorker have been reduced to a gaping hole, a cemetery of rubble and concrete slabs. A bulldozer with eight or nine jackhammers going all week had done their job. From the opposite sidewalk, I snatch a final glance—structures need blank space to be fully seen. Off go the whistles: pavement shudders, eardrums explode. Frozen in my tracks, heart pounding, movie images rush forth: Polish partisans in Wajda's *Kanal* emerging from Warsaw sewers; Renoir's clochard being fished from the Seine in *Boudu Saved from Drowning*; a boy running on the beach in Truffaut's *The 400 Blows*; Joan of Arc impaled on a stake in Dreyer's *The Passion of Joan of Arc*.

Girders swoon, beams careen. In slow motion a section of the balcony quakes, undulates, and hurtles forth. An entire structure collapses like a house of glass. Chicken Little, your house is falling. But the moon gives not a damn if a dog barks at it. Our northern wall, hitherto concealed, is suddenly exposed. I shut my eyes. The screen goes blank.

The yellow dragon pauses over its booty as if catching its breath. Chunks of plaster, dismembered pipes, and shards of mirror glitter at its feet under a spitfire sun. Four wreckers in green helmets and baseball bats gingerly pick their way through the debris like workers skirting landmines. From the second storey, a side door suddenly swings ajar—the projection booth clinging still to its DO NOT ENTER sign. And I picture Melvin our projectionist stepping out between reels for a breath of air and plummeting into the gully, trailed by a flying saucer of film.

From the fallen marquee, over a jigsaw of brick and slate, light bulbs flap on disconnected wires. Oh Dan, no more worries about change of marquee, archaic wiring, ancient air conditioner, suspect asbestos. Neon lights glint in memory only. The New Yorker is no more. Let the building inspectors come.

By next day, resourceful locals have posted signs over COMING ATTRACTIONS: French lessons from Columbia Ph.D., Piano Tuning, Fabulous Black-and-White Stills of Garbo. The uprooted turnstile lists to one side like an extracted tooth. Watching me try to right it, a worker on a folding chair, digging into a hero sandwich, shakes his head and points to an ax and sledge hammer propped against the box office.

Before I know it, a stockade fence girds the ruins, a neatly lettered sign planted on it:

IN MEMORIUM
THE NEW YORKER THEATER
BUILT 1933
ORIGINALLY THE ADELPHI,
LATER THE YORKTOWN
RENAMED THE NEW YORKER IN 1960
BY DAN TALBOT
SOLD—APRIL 1973
TORN DOWN—JULY 1985

LOVED BY MILLIONS, NOW GONE
ON TO THE WATERS OF CASABLANCA

Someone—a forlorn patron perhaps—has embellished it, dotting the i's with shiny blue, yellow, and purple stick-on hearts, and as a final touch a red lipstick kiss, the kind that might punctuate the last frame of a Betty Grable Technicolor movie: The End.

Each morning, a white-haired man in a cap shows up and peers into the excavation like an inspector, ears deaf to the clamor of machine claws and power shovels preparing a new foundation. Sorely tempted to squeeze that voyeuristic head through the *Citizen Kane*–like aperture, I finally designate him as a viewfinder establishing a shot. The New Yorker is dead space. I feel lonely.

The End of New Yorker Films

As this book was going to press, New Yorker Films, after forty-four years of distributing films, closed its doors. In the ultra-competitive corporate climate of the industry, it was impossible for this small, independent company to survive. Bernardo Bertolucci's *Before the Revolution*, our initial film in 1965, was followed by such landmark works as Rainer Werner Fassbinder's *The Marriage of Maria Braun* and Werner Herzog's *Aguirre, the Wrath of God*. The biggest successes among independent films were Louis Malle's *My Dinner with Andre*, which ran for one year in New York, and, in 1982, Wayne Wang's *Chan is Missing*. On March 30, 2009, over fifty people who had cut their professional teeth at New Yorker Films, and were still active in the industry, gathered for a last toast. Almost at the same time, Columbia University Press acquired our archive, and all the New Yorker Theater programs can be found on the Internet (see www.cup.columbia.edu/talbot).

Epilogue: An Ongoing Reel

For a long time, I avoided passing our New Yorker site (soon to be reincarnated as the Savannah high-rise apartment building). From the opposite sidewalk the block is a mirage: Joe Rosen's thumb still on the scale, Benny in white apron and sailor cap dishing out frankfurters with the works. "What the eyes have seen cannot be erased," says Dr. Pollack, the Holocaust survivor. Urban structures get leveled and razed—it's a pattern, it's progress. Nothing lasts, I repeat as a mantra. Manhattan, bounded by two rivers and spanned by multiple bridges, has no more permanence than its shore line. Replacement implies displacement—think of it as deconstruction and reconstruction, or first-runs and revivals.

In the sixties, if you went away for a while, you returned to Third Avenue minus its rumbling El and minus the Beverly Theater, a once penumbrous street having now been transformed into a glitzy boulevard of boutiques and ice-cube towers. And Sixth Avenue, with its second-hand bookstores and oddball wares, would become the Avenue of the Americas, a canyon of glass. Henry James on a return visit to America in

1904 was struck by the welter of construction and the onslaught of tall buildings: "The wantoness of wealth and greed."

The New Yorker was both venture and adventure. We set out in the dark. And in the dark played movies we loved and wanted to see. We were our best audience. We were lucky. The time was ripe, cinema was ripe, and audiences were ready. We traveled from Groucho to Godard.

A movie house is not just a structure of brick and stone. It is a chamber where images captured in a much smaller one (the camera) survive on a screen. Movie scenes and images haunt my mental landscape with the force of real life and dreams. Unbeckoned they surface.

Scene: Jimmy Cagney's crazed expression in Raoul Walsh's *White Heat* when told that his mother is dead, whereupon whimpering, lurching, and punching everyone in his way until, cornered by the cops, he climbs atop an oil refinery and shouts, "Made it Ma, to the top of the world!" then empties his gun into the gas tank to join her forever. *Scene*: a black soldier in Roberto Rossellini's *Paisan* who, before falling asleep, is warned by a child not to do so for "I'll steal your shoes," and the soldier does fall asleep and his shoes *are* stolen. *Scene*: the grief on a father's face in Satyajit Ray's *Pather Panchali* on learning that his child is dead, a zither wailing on the sound track. *Scene*: Michel Simon's luminous expression in Jean Vigo's *L'Atalante* as he sails down the Seine with his new bride. *Scene*: in Jean Renoir's *The Rules of the Game* where dead rabbits during a hunt forebode the scent of war. *Scene*: the crazed look of the conquistador in Werner Herzog's *Aguirre* as he sails down the Amazon on a raft with dead men and scampering monkeys. *Scene*: in Renoir's *Grand Illusion* when an aristocratic French officer (Pierre Fresnay) and a German officer (Erich von Stroheim) understand that duty destroys friendship. *Scene*: in Andrei Tarkovsky's *The Sacrifice* of a father planting a tree with his young son in the hope that his own life will spare the child from apocalyptic disaster. *Scene*: in *Ikiru* with Takashi Shimura, a minor bureaucrat, dying of cancer and swaying on a swing. *Scene*: in Kenji Mizoguchi's *Sansho the Bailiff*, of a mother on the banks of a river getting wrenched from her children by slave drivers.

What is it like for a director or actor to view his work with an audience? In 1964, Bernardo Bertolucci, a first-time director, ran up to the projection booth after the first show for a final cut on *Before the Revolution*. In 1965 a portly gentleman in proper suit and tie gazed admiringly at the letters on the New Yorker marquee announcing an Alfred Hitchcock Retrospective: it is Hitchcock himself. On August 6, 1966, an unshaven man stands anonymously at the rear of the New Yorker, watching *Red River* in its one-day run: it is Montgomery Clift, epitome of male perfection, now scarred by a car accident and ravaged by drink and drugs. He is watching an image of his former self—Howard Hawks's mythological, rugged cowboy. As the audience files out, no one notices the tearful figure in back, and no one can see the scars.

In 1973 we abandoned the New Yorker to devote ourselves to distribution. But running a store had gotten into our blood. Like homing pigeons we returned in 1977. A couple of blocks up from Lincoln Center, we spied a shut-down theater on Broadway and 66th Street. There Rudolph Valentino had lain in state until he and others passed through the portals for their final resting place in outlying cemeteries. What was missing in that location was sidewalk traffic, a near prerequisite for a movie house. And at night, the area was a ghost town. No matter. We took it over, repainted its sooty bricks white, and renamed it the Cinema Studio.

At the Cinema Studio, we premiered Federico Fellini's *City of Women*, Andrzej Wajda's *Man of Marble*, Jean-Luc Godard's *Every Man for Himself*, Werner Herzog's *Stroszek* and *Woyzeck*, Wim Wenders's *The American Friend*, Ermanno Olmi's *The Tree of Wooden Clogs*, Rainer Werner Fassbinder's *The Marriage of Maria Braun*, Satyajit Ray's *The Home and the World*, Andrei Tarkovsky's *The Sacrifice*, Claude Lanzmann's *Shoah*, Pedro Almodóvar's *Women on the Verge of a Nervous Breakdown*. Why list so many, why so few? So many do I want to re-see. Each time you look at something you see it differently. Every now and then Dan and I fetch out a 35mm print and quietly screen it before the theater opens.

In 1981 we built the Lincoln Plaza Cinemas on Broadway between 62nd and 63rd Streets. It took a year. You descend an escalator and enter a lobby with mauve walls, fleur-de-lis carpet, and a gurgling fountain encircled by faux foliage. A stand offers pastries plus more substantial smoked salmon, smoked turkey, and ham. A moviegoer may miss the show, while agonizing over gingerbread, ricotta cheesecake, ruggelech, or macaroons to accompany a cappuccino. If the film hasn't started, that person may linger on a banquette beneath introspective landscapes of trees, then file past a *tropicalista* canvas of urban dwellers and moviegoers. No one knows that these are the work of our daughters Nina and Sarah—after all, it's a family store. No one knows that I, inheriting my mother's candy-stand role as it were, am Selector of all confections. No one knows that the man often seated in our manager's office is Dan Talbot—still overseeing the store.

One evening in September 2008, my friend Judy Feiffer phoned: "I just got back from the New Yorker and saw *I Served the King of England*." Jiří Menzel's film had opened that day. "Judy," I broke in. "What *are* you saying? The New Yorker is gone." She paused: "Oh, that's right, but at the Lincoln Plaza, I *feel* that I'm back at the New Yorker. So, let me tell you about the movie … " My mind unspooled as she went on. When had we played Menzel's *Closely Watched Trains*—1966 or 1967? A picaresque coming-of-age story, it told of a naive apprentice train-dispatcher in Nazi-occupied Czechoslovakia. *I Served the King of England*, set in the 1930s and '40s under totalitarian regimes, is a dark and slapstick view of Czechoslovakian society. Menzel, a leading figure in the New Wave Czech cinema, was *still* making voluptuous films, still spoofing political regimes, still speaking through an ingenuous hero. And we are showing them.

Yes, Dan and I are *still* running films—at the Lincoln Plaza, in postal zone 10023. And we are still, as one friend puts it, a Double Feature. As a movie is about to begin, I stand in the aisle and see whitish faces turned in the dark toward the light of the screen. Trailers go on. A collective inhalation of breath gets released as the movie is about to start. And a distant voice from Cannes calls out: *Mesdames et messieurs, la séance va à commencer.*

Ladies and gentlemen, the show is about to begin!

APPENDIX 1

Program Notes

MOVIES: WINTER 60-61

GOLD DIGGERS OF 1933

1933 (sound)   American
Directed by Mervyn LeRoy; musical numbers staged by
Busby Berkeley; screenplay by Avery Hopwood; adaptation by Erwin Gelsey and James Seymour; dialogue by
David Boehm and Ben Markson; music by Harry Warren;
lyrics by Al Dubin; photography by Sol Polito; edited by George Amy; released by Warner Bros. Running
time: 96 minutes.

Carol................................Joan Blondell
Fay....................................Ginger Rogers
J. Lawrence..........................Warren William
Trixy................................Aline MacMahon
Polly..................................Ruby Keeler
Brad...................................Dick Powell
Barney.................................Ned Sparks
Peabody.................................Guy Kibbee
Don..............................Clarence Nordstrom
Dance Director.......................Robert Agnew
Eddie................................Tammany Young
Messenger Boy....................Sterling Holloway
Club Man.....................Ferdinand Gottschald

* * *

One can always be sure that when an old fan asks "Why don't they
ever bring back GIRL CRAZY or YOU CAN'T TAKE IT WITH YOU" he's talking
about the movies, not the plays.

No one starts movements to bring back the classic musicals or
vintage farces of Broadway. Broadway has made other adjustments and its
audience, gripe and bitch though they may, has not the faintest desire
to flock enmasse or even semi enmasse to a nostalgic revival of the
dear gone, golden past when a musical book was an alternate switch of
dirty jokes and romantic confrontations designed to serve as stage
waits between songs and dances. And while it's true that off-Broadway
has had some luck in recent revivals, it's a brand of luck helped
considerably by the substitution of past-period innocence for present-
period campiness. The old, original flavor would seem dated in today's

theatre and therefore, not desirable. On the screen the old flavor is, of course, just as dated and, strangely because of it, quite desirable.

GOLD DIGGERS OF 1933 is a depression movie. Like MY MAN GODFREY, MR. DEEDS, THE DEVIL AND MISS JONES, LIBELLED LADY, THE THIN MAN, the early Eddie Cantor musicals and others, no doubt many others, it practices a form of escapism that reeks of the spirit common to all good entertainment of that period; a romantic blend of the unresolved yacht club innocence of the 20's with the Rooseveltian idealism of the 30's. The mixture was always lots of rich for the dream factor and several poor to contrast where we've been with where we're going. I don't think it's reading anything into these films to say that they had a social consciousness about them. They couldn't very well avoid it. It was in the air and what's in the air always sneaks into our lower forms of entertainment.

Just as the sick jokes represented our sense of deadness in the early 50's and the Mort Sahls and Nichols and Mays represent our current re-awakening, so did the musicals and the romantic comedies of the 30's catch a flavor in many ways more representative than any dozen of the more serious Henry Fonda, Sylvia Sidney, "If you make a mistake once they never let you forget it" films of the same time.

Imagine a musical, any musical, opening with a luscious glamour queen astride the conventional million mile theatre stage of the day, adorned (in what has come to be known as Busby Berkeley traditional) only in bosom and crotch covering giant gold coins and singing with a mob of like minded editorialists — "We never see headlines about headlines today. And when we see the landlord we can look that guy right in the eye 'cause we're in the money, we're in the money. Old man depression is on his way."

The glamour queen is Ginger Rogers. Ned Sparks is the producer whose shows are always closed by his creditors and whose dream it is to put on a giant, glamorous, happy bubbling production dedicated to — who else? — the Forgotten Man. ("Remember my Forgotten Man. You put a rifle in his hand. You shouted hip hooray and you sent him away. Now look at him today.") How do you like that for a finale?

Naturally, there is Dick Powell and Ruby Keeler (who were in every musical ever made, up to my twelfth birthday) and there is Guy Kibbee playing the Edward Everett Horton role and Joan Blondell as the best friend, mistaken by stuffy rich older brother Warren William (later to be known as Ralph Bellamy) for suspected gold digger Ruby Keeler, who has her hooks into rich song writing younger brother Dick Powell. It's the familiar mixture and yet done with a lightness that

I don't remember in most of its successors. It has no wit, it has no Astaire, in truth it has no real talent, but it does have a lovely sheen of innocence, a constant youthfulness which never gets cute, which, even while steeped in what since have become cliches, seems fresher and far more alive than any musical Hollywood has done in years.

And that is one of the signs the good ones invariably have. No matter how many times their style may be lifted and imitated the good ones keep their glow. They sweep over you, instantly creating a mood that accepts no terms but its own, that engulfs with such finality that the plots cease being fantasies and become, instead, a substitute reality.

Movie fantasies have less durability in our time. It's because their makers have quit believing in them. Comden and Green will apply a veneer of sophistication to the same old musical book and because the application is an arbitrary one, from the outside in rather than from the inside out, the surface cracks easily and what was intended to be clever is simply stale.

Ben Hecht, in what must be one more of a series of long looks back on the picture business, wrote recently — "Movie making was an end in itself. Everything else including marriage, infidelity, riches, headlines, was secondary. They 'made' movies in restaurants, at dinner parties, in swimming pools, in bed, in bathrooms, on love hegiras, hunting trips, in theatre lobbies and in Doctor Menninger's Clinic for the Disturbed." Theirs was an attitude of sheer belief unlike anything we have in the 60's. Most of us are no longer that clear about anything. The texture of the times is fuzzy and a bit removed. And so is our humor. So are our comedies. So are our musicals.

Jules Feiffer

(Jules Feiffer, cartoonist, is the author of SICK,SICK, SICK, PASSIONELLA, and THE EXPLAINERS. His weekly syndicated cartoons appear in New York in THE VILLAGE VOICE. He is currently at work on a revue based on his cartoons, called THE EXPLAINERS, which will be presented on Broadway later this season. Probably the largest Feiffer in captivity can be found in the lobby of the New Yorker Theatre.)

All the fluffs and blow-ups in this short collection occured during the shooting of various Hollywood films made between 1936 and 1940. With the exception of MY MAN GODFREY, which was produced by Universal, the pictures were released by Monogram Pictures, now defunct. The people and the movies include:

Betty Blythe, Guy Usher in ROMANCE OF THE LIMBERLOST (1938);
Warren Hull, Claudia Dell, Ward Bond in A BRIDE FOR HENRY (1937);
Sally Blane, Mayo Mathot in NUMBERED WOMAN (1938);
Jack Randall, Charles King in DANGER VALLEY (1937);
Boris Karloff, Holmes Herbert in MYSTERY OF MR. WONG (1939);
John Carroll, Movita, Duncan Renaldo in ROSE OF THE RIO GRANDE (1938);
Dick Purcell, Jackie Cooper in STREETS OF NEW YORK (1939);
Robert Warwick in GANGSTER'S BOY (1938);
Grant Withers, Frankie Darro in BOY'S REFORMATORY (1939);
John Carroll in I AM A CRIMINAL (1938);
Movita, John Carroll, George Cleveland in WOLF CALL (1938);
Dennis Moore in CHEYENNE KID (1940);
William B. Davidson in PARADISE ISLE (1937);
Movita in THE GIRL FROM RIO (1939);
Carole Lombard, William Powell, Eugene Pallette in MY MAN GODFREY (1936).

SECOND PROGRAM MOVIES: WINTER 60-61 AT 7:00 & 9:30
NOTES BY JONAS MEKAS

Nov. 14 — SHORS
(Alexander Dovzhenko, 1939)

In this thundering, fast-paced film biography of a young hero of the 1919 Russian Revolution, Dovzhenko, director of ARSENAL and EARTH, splashes across the screen a rich, vibrant picture of strength, patriotism and humanity. Beautifully photographed, the film has a vital lyricism behind even its harshest battle scenes — the kind of tough poetry Griffith achieved in BIRTH OF A NATION. As James Agee said, speaking of SHORS: "Scenes like the silver blaze of ripe wheat and sunflowers, full of struggling men, crazed horses and black explosions, make any perceptive film-goer wonder, seriously, whether he has ever seen a real moving picture before."

THE MASSACRE (1912). The great D.W. Griffith's exciting, massive picturization of Custer's Last Stand. In twenty short minutes Griffith is able to put on the screen larger and more authentic scenes of strife than any current "spectacular" can in four hours.

NEW YORKER
FILM SOCIETY

MOVIES:
WINTER 60-61

SHORS

1939 (sound)   Soviet

Direction and scenario by Alexander Dovzhenko; assistants, J. Solntseva & Chmarouk; photography by Y. Ekelchik; second cameraman, J. Goldabenko; assistants, A. Mitchourine & V. Youtchenko; special effects by A. Likatchev; art direction by Maurice Umansky; make-up by L. Khazanov; music by D. Kabalevsky; lyrics by A. Malychko; sound by Toumartsev; assistant, A. Tchumakhan; editor, O. Skrypnik; production manager, Rogozovsky; produced by Ukrainfilm, Studios in Kiev. Running time: 85 minutes.

Cast: E. Samoilov (Shors), I. Skuratov (Bozhenko), V. Dukler (Isaac Tychler, Political Commissar), L. Iyaschenko (Polish soldier), P. Krasilitch (Gavritchenko), A. Gretchany (Mikhaliouk), N. Makarenko (Antoniouk), F. Ichtchenko (Petro Tchij), N. Nikitina (Nastia), D. Milioutenko, A. Kvyblia, A. Borisoglenskaia, D. Kadnikov, S. Komarov, G. Polezhayev, O. Glazounov, G. Klering, N. Komissarov (three German soldiers), Egorova (an old woman), N. Krioukov (a spy), J. Bantych, D. Barvinsky, D. Kostenko, P. Masokha, P. Radetsky, P. Tatarenko, A. Levtchenko, D. Milioutenko, G. Youra.

* * *

Women, crying like seagulls; wooden bridges; telephone poles in the white vastness of the winter landscape; black lines of trees; and the fields of rye, always fields of rye, and the sun flowers, and the women; and then the horses; and then the old men, ripe with age; and death. Yes, the soldiers too, as they ride, as they ride. "Riding, riding, riding, through the night, through the day..." Little dots in a wide space of snow, little black specks of death. The white space embraces everything: the soldiers, the revolution, the rye fields, death, and sun flowers.

SHORS was made under the supervision of Stalin himself, every step of it. And what are the soldiers fighting for? Yes, revolution. But Bozhenko cries: "They killed the mother!" The old general cries like a woman, in the empty room, alone: "They killed the mother!" And there they go, across the Ukraine, to avenge the mother!

And again the fields are singing; again the earth; again death. Yes, revolution, communism! Is Hemingway a chronologist of wars? Hemingway is a poet of death. And so is Dovzhenko. The poet of death and earth, Ukraine, Mother, Kiev.

The other night, we sat drinking, four of us, and Al said: "Let us drink to revolutions." And we sat there, and there were no revolutions. Revolts, yes, but how many revolutions were there, good revolutions? French? American? Russian? Cuban? Four, five? We need a good revolution to drink to. And what a noble action a revolution! Every poet dreams of overthrowing the government. No government is ever good.

SHORS is a memory of a revolution. Poetry. Like a Western. The basic heroic patterns—sacrifice, pathos, disorder of a revolution. Not a war. Only revolutions are just and only revolutions are capable of poetry and pathos and exaltation and sacrifice.

Propaganda? No, poetry. Let us criticize the living ones, and let us sing the dead ones! Were their dreams the same as ours? Yes, the dreams always are. Cruelties committed? We are always judging, always carrying the electric chairs of our minds. Yes, there was blood on the snow, I saw it, and it went deep down, burning the snow.

SHORS is just a fragment of a revolution, it has no beginning, no end, nothing closed, like the revolution itself. Wars end, but not revolutions, Dovzhenko knew that. In the very fragmentary form he chose for his film, revolution still continues. We know the reality of revolutions. We know the reality of politicians. But it is for the poet to sing the beautiful, heroic, exalted, as only the dreams of a revolution can be. No dirt here. No dirt was ever part of Dovzhenko. His people are beautiful.

"I am also an intellectual," shouts Shors. "I also went to universities!" And there he is, in the middle of the Ukrainian rye fields, nine days and nine nights without sleep, still carrying in his suitcase a blue summer suit—for what summers? when?—yes, yes, as they ride, as they ride, fulfilling the will of their times, themselves a will-less, wild passion—as they ride, through the winter, and the bridges, and the trees, and the clouds, and the telephone poles, and the rivers—and Shors himself, the fourth brother of the Karamazovs, or, perhaps, Ivan?

Says Dovzhenko: "Later, my mother came to live with me in Moscow. She was very unhappy. She did not like it. She kept standing by the window, looking into the street. She kept repeating to me: 'Who are those people, running around like that, always busy, worried?' When the evening came, she would say: 'Let us sing', and we sang, all together, the old Ukrainian songs. But still, this was not the country. So she went back to Kiev. She used to say to me: 'I don't have much more time to live. But don't cremate me. If you burn my body, I'll come back to earth to menace you. But put me into the ground, into the earth. I love the earth. I want to be with earth.'"

* * *

THE MASSACRE

1912 (silent)   American
Directed by D.W. Griffith; photography by G.W. (Billy) Bitzer; produced by the Biograph Studio. Two reels.
Cast: Blanche Sweet (the Girl), Charles West (her husband), Wilfrid Lucas (the Scout), Lionel Barrymore (Calvary Officer), Jack Pickford (a boy), Alfred Paget (Indian Chief), Mary Alden (Indian Squaw), Christie Miller (Preacher), Robert Harron (Trooper), Dell Henderson (the Gambler), Joseph Graybill (his associate).

* * *

It is good to see THE MASSACRE together with SHORS. On both the patina of time. Both are history. Both are poetry.

It was Dr. Kracauer who said in his THEORY OF FILM that it is impossible to show history in cinema. "The costumes fully belong to the past," says he, "while the actors are still half in the present."

THE MASSACRE proves otherwise. When one looks at THE MASSACRE today, it is not only because of its hardly surpassable battle scenes, those amazing long shots. If the audience of 1912 couldn't help seeing in Custer's soldiers the faces of their contemporaries—today, looking from a third level of time, from under the layer of another 50 years, both their costumes and their faces "belong to the past."

To a scientist, there will be mistakes in costumes and manners, but not to a straight viewer, like myself, who reacts to movies emotionally. There is no more discord between their dress, their gestures, and the times depicted. What was a non-realistic spectacular in 1912, becomes realistic in 1960. The very print, used up as it is, beaten up, and scratched, and dusty, and stepped upon, and what not, seems to add to the realism, authenticity, the truth.

We know that the story, the plot is partly concocted. But that doesn't bother us at all—the plot is of no consequence. We know that

massacres took place. And it must have been just as Griffith shows it.
THE MASSACRE today is as realistic as UMBERTO D. Details false
historically? Who cares about that! Don't the poets create history
anyway, if you know what I mean?

Jonas Mekas

(Jonas Mekas, poet and anarchist, is the Editor of FILM
CULTURE, movie critic for THE VILLAGE VOICE, leader of
the New American Cinema movement on the East Coast, and
is currently finishing his first film, an independently
financed feature shot in New York, called GUNS OF THE
TREES. Its intention is the overthrow of the government...)

THIRD PROGRAM MOVIES: WINTER 60-61 AT 7:00 & 9:30
NOTES BY CHANDLER BROSSARD

Nov. 21 — DEAD OF NIGHT
(Hamer, Cavalcanti, Dearden, Crighton, 1945)
We are showing the COMPLETE five-part version of this chilling British
supernatural shocker (usually shown with two stories chopped out). With
nightmarish intensity and a deft, never-too-serious outlook, the picture is
one of the most successfully weird movies every made, with a cast of excellent English actors including Michael Redgrave and Ronald Squire. To
quote Mr. Agee again: "In every way made with exceptional skill and wit
...its famous last shot is one of the most successful blends of laughter,
terror and outrage that I can remember."
THE DENTIST (1932). The fabulous W.C. Fields slaps his daughter around,
plays a couple of rounds of golf, then goes to his office and finishes off
three patients. An uproarious two-reel gem.

MOVIES: WINTER 60-61

NOTES: Nov. 21

DEAD OF NIGHT

1945 (sound)   British

Directed by Cavalcanti (hearse and ventriloquist sequences), Robert Hamer (all farm scenes and mirror sequence), Charles Crichton (golf sequence), Basil Dearden (party sequence); produced at Ealing Studios by Michael Balcon; associate producers, Sidney Cole & John Croydon; camera, Jack Parker & H. Julius; screenplay by John Baines & Angus Macphail, additional dialogue by T.E.B. Clarke, based on original stories by H.G. Wells, E.F. Benson, Baines & Macphail; art direction by Michael Relph; lighting by Stan Pavey & Douglas Slocombe; sound supervisor, Eric Williams; edited by Charles Hasse; special effects by C. Richardson & L. Banes; music by George Auric; make-up by Tom Shenton; production supervisor, Hal Mason; A J. Arthur Rank Presentation. Running time: 100 minutes.

Cast: Mervyn Johns (Walter Craig), Roland Culver (Eliot Foley), Mary Merrall (Mrs. Foley), Googie Withers (Joan Cortland), Frederick Valk (Dr. Van Straaten), Antony Baird (Hugh Grainger), Sally Ann Howes (Sally O'Hara), Robert Wyndham (Dr. Albury), Judy Kelly (Joyce Grainger), Miles Malleson (Hearse Driver), Michael Allan (Jimmy Watson), Barbara Leake (Mrs. O'Hara), Ralph Michael (Peter Cortland), Esmé Percy (Antique Dealer), Basil Radford (George Parratt), Naunton Wayne (Larry Potter), Peggy Bryan (Mary Lee), Allan Jeayes (Maurice Olcott), Michael Redgrave (Maxwell Frere), Elisabeth Welch (Beulah), Hartley Power (Sylvester Kee), Magda Kun (Mitzi), Garry Marsh (Harry Parker), Renee Gadd (Mrs. Craig).

* * *

THE DENTIST

1932 (sound)   American

Directed by Leslie Pearce; produced by Mack Sennett; written by W.C. Fields; released by Paramount Pictures. Two reels. With W.C. Fields.

PROBLEMS OF BEING THE REAL ME

At first I could hardly believe my eyes. Schweinkind! I hissed,
nudging myself. Just look at that! How did they know? Who gave them
the information? Not a smidgen of sickness was missing, not even a
mouse. There it was before me, as bold as a noodle factory—the
complete and truthful story of my life! Feigenwasser! I had to gulp
down three shrimp balls to calm myself. Oh, to be sure, they had tried
to bring my story to the silver screen before. SON OF FRANKENSTEIN,
GOOGIE THE WOLF BOY, MURDERS OF THE RUE MORGUE, MADCHEN IN UNIFORM—
each had been a self-conscious, fragmentary attempt to expose the real
me. Each had failed because of the sanity of the producers, the utterly
paralyzing reluctance of the writers to crawl into the unknown, for
fear they might go to jail for it. But now—oh, what cunning! what
mastery! (Quiet, Maxie. Put your sandals back on or I'll smash you!
Usher! Another helping of stuffed derma, please. And get yourself a
strudel or something.)

Well, as I was saying, the thrill of self-realization was almost
overwhelming. I cried into my parka sleeve. (Listen, Nicholas my boy,
I'll describe my emotions any way I please. Now go back to your
needlepoint.) At this juncture, however, I must confess something. Up
above, in the foregoing paragraph, I told a teensy-weensy lie. You
must forgive me. I said this movie was the complete story of my life.
That isn't so. Perhaps at the insistence of the authorities, there are
some things they left out. (Melvin, get your hands off that little
girl's ear!) For example—that part about the little boy in the hidden
room in the castle. Remember? Well, that wasn't really Christopher
Soames. It was J. Edgar Hoover, hiding out from his Mums. You see, he
had become an addict of a series called SMUT FOR SMALL FRY, and that
redecorated butler's pantry was the only place he could devour the
stuff in peace. Another thing, just to keep the record clear—that bit
about his mother being a murderess, that isn't true. The fact is, she
was having an affair with a celebrated chimney sweep, and one afternoon
when she was a bit tiddly on cooking sherry, she thoughtlessly lit up
a few logs in the fireplace. The rest is history. (Turn that radio
down, Igor! I don't give a damn if Caruso has returned from the grave.
Usher, there's a strip poker game going on in the orchestra. You'll
take care of it? Thank you.)

To continue—that part about me and the fiendish mirror. A few
corrections are needed. First of all, it was a damn lie; I didn't
really see that other room reflected in it, as I said I did. I was
looking for an excuse to get rid of that dumb quiff I was engaged to—

did you ever see such hats? I'm convinced she bought them off a mudlark—and I came up with that paranoia bit. Not top drawer, I'll admit, but not bad, really. Her conversation was incredibly limited. If it wasn't Cecil this, it was Chumbumbley that, and she would never allow me to eat pizza pies in bed. So she had to go, you can understand that. In the part they don't show you, I finally do get to her, in a tram station in Piccadilly. Almost no overhead, you might say.

(Pass me the Moxie, Grushenka. My throat's as dry as a hunchback's laugh. Mountjoy, I'm telling you for the last time, come down off that chandelier! You're not at home.)

Where was I? Oh, yes, pursuing the truth, as usual. Do you recall the part where I am a ventriloquist with a problem dummy? I must admit that that was one of the more engrossing periods in my life. Anyway, there was much more to that than the police reports show. First of all, I had literally plucked Hugo out of the gutter and made him what he was. From now on I'll pay more attention to blood lines. I didn't mind his stealing from me when I was drunk, or his insatiable forgeries at Hammacher and Schlemmer, but it was the last straw to discover that he was a fag, a common winking, smirking, camping, cruising garden variety fag. What would you have done? (I didn't ask you, Antonovich.) I didn't squash him as the movie says. I simply let him go off with whosis. The last I heard Hugo had become a transvestite and was peddling yams in Cadiz.

I could go on clearing up the minor details for days, but I don't have time. I have to report for work. I am currently employed in a Chinese Rumour Factory. Before I go, though, I want to say a few words about another cinematic pearl, dealing with the short dental career of an old friend, C.W. Gumnit, better known as W.C. Fields. The real tragedy of this story is that Gumnit, or Fields if you prefer, never wanted to be a dentist in the first place. He had tried out for and flopped at the college hammer-throw, and there was nothing else to do but become a dentist. Many a career has taken this turn. Also, there was that bit about his daughter... Psychodynamically speaking, she was not his daughter at all. She was Tony Perkins and that's why old Gumnit kept her locked up and away from the iceman. In any event...

All right, Mr. Orwell, I'm coming. You don't have to tug at my sleeve that way. I'm quite capable of walking by myself. Joselito, get out of that giraffe's cage!

Chandler Brossard

4

(Chandler Brossard, novelist, playwright, "bon vivant
and retired fantasist", is the author of THE BOLD
SABOTEURS and WHO WALK IN DARKNESS. Two of his plays,
LOVE'S SUCCESS and SOME DREAMS AREN'T REAL, were
produced recently in St, Louis. His latest novel,
published by Dial Press earlier this year, is THE
DOUBLE VIEW.)

FOURTH PROGRAM MOVIES: WINTER 60-61 AT 7:00 & 9:30

NOTES BY HAROLD HUMES

Nov. 28 – THE LAST LAUGH
(F.W. Murnau, 1924)
One of the most important films in cinema history, THE LAST LAUGH was
the first silent film to be made without any titles. As Paul Rotha says in
THE FILM TILL NOW: "By psychological understanding, every action
suggested a thought to the audience, every angle a mood that was unmistakable in meaning ... cine-fiction in its purest form...". Done in the
German expressionistic style, it tells the story of a proud hotel doorman,
humbled by ironic circumstances, with Emil Jannings at his moving best.
(Piano accompaniment by Arthur Kleiner).
THE MUSIC BOX (1932). Only Laurel & Hardy could make a simple task
like carrying a piano up a flight of stairs seem Herculean, impossible,
fiendish ... and unbearably funny.

NEW YORKER FILM SOCIETY

MOVIES:
WINTER 60-61

THE LAST LAUGH
(DER LETZTE MANN)

1924 (silent)   German

Directed by F.W. Murnau; scenario by Carl Mayer; photography
by Karl Freund; designed by Walther Roehrig & Robert Herlth;
produced by Erich Pommer for Union-Ufa; presented in America
by Carl Laemmle for Universal release. Running time: 85 mins.

The Man.......................................Emil Jannings
His Daughter..................................Mady Delschaft
Her Bridegroom................................Kurt Hiller
His Aunt......................................Emilie Kurz
The Manager...................................Hans Unterkircher
The Nightwatchman.............................Georg John

Music for THE LAST LAUGH arranged
and played by Arthur Kleiner.

* * *

　　　This film was screened for me about one month ago, and the thing
I find most striking now is how little I remember of the plot. I
suspect that this is due to a rather thin consistency of dramatic
line. Unless one happens to have been a hotel doorman of that epoch,
there is very little magic here to compel the memory. I think it
rather difficult to identify with the vicissitudes of the old cluck
played by Emil Jannings, and only an audience deeply hypnotized by
the externals of rank and authority could be deeply moved by the
jejune emotionalism that underlies the dramatic structure of the film.
The whole moral of this opus is that clothes (uniforms, medals,
moustaches, etc.) make the man; or, more precisely, no-clothes unmake
the man. From a dramatic point of view the film is absurd. That the
old doorman comes alive at all is a tribute to the astounding acting
drive of Jannings rather than to the dramatic idea. That he manages a
sympathetic portrait is more astounding, because any old gaffer so
lacking in the wisdom of age as to flip over the loss of his uniform

must be either a fool or a despot. Whoever wrote this film, I'll wager, never worked as a doorman. The condescension is too obvious.

I think some of the foregoing remarks help explain the curious broken-neck shape of the film, for the extra episode is the only thing that makes the whole thing bearable. It is almost as though the creators realized that they had won a false artistic victory as they closed in on the disaster which was to have ended the film. Turning as the story does on totally false motivations, the ending is bathetic rather than tragic. After an hour or so of diligent churning the whole mess curdles into bonneyclabber rather than into the good butter of tragedy, and the viewer is left holding the unhappy end of the stick. The only title in the entire film appears at this point, wherein it is announced rather cavalierly that the authors have taken pity on this noxious old fart. Actually they've taken pity on the disgruntled viewer. (It might be pointed out that THE LAST LAUGH was the first feature film to run its entire course without any explanatory or dialogue titles.) Having failed utterly to achieve a sad ending they thereupon embark upon a happy one. This time they make it, more or less, one jump ahead of the gun. Well, it was 1924, and that was a confusing year all over. In America we elected Calvin Coolidge, who started life as a tacked-on ending.

Technically speaking, THE LAST LAUGH is brilliant. This is a particularly good print as such things go, and it will pay you to watch carefully for the various technical surprises which these German filmmakers have laid out for your amusement. The use of the moving camera (particularly in the dining room scene near the end), the use (and overuse) of artificial light, the very effective use of subjective camera viewpoints (as in the drunken scene), all are worth your close attention. In this connection the weakness of the plot is a blessing, since there is very little to tease your attention from the business at hand. Also interesting is the timing of the takes. There are several extremely long takes interlarded with ordinary montage, the effect of which is to make the pacing of the film surefooted and well matched to the development.

There are certain symbols which serve as structural links between episodes; note particularly the use of doors, revolving, swinging, closed. The wedding scene appears first as a "flash-forward" (as opposed to a flashback). There is one point in the wedding scene where the guests are arranged as though in an Ensor painting. There are a great many other things I could point out, but why should I. Calvin Coolidge notwithstanding.

Just imagine you're the camera.

THE MUSIC BOX

1932 (sound)   American

Directed by James Parrot; produced by Hal Roach; story by
Leo McCarey; dialogue by H.M. Walker; edited by Richard
Currier; released by Metro-Goldwyn-Mayer. Three reels.
Cast: Stan Laurel (A thin piano mover), Oliver Hardy (A fat
piano mover), Billy Gilbert (the husband), Charles Rogers
(the mailman).

This film won the Academy Award in 1932 as the Best Short
Subject of the Year.

* * *

Laurel and Hardy belong, I think, in the top rank of American
comic artists. Repetition, resignation, and well meant disaster.
Surreal laughter. Ho Ho Ho.

And furthermore I resent the bad rapping these two have taken for
basing their efforts on sublimated sadism. After all, it's not <u>you</u>
the piano falls on, is it now?

And furthermore, their works are very classical. Mythic, some
idiots might say. This one is a dittybob version of the Labor of
Sisyphus. In case you didn't know.

Don't miss the hat trick. Try it yourself when you get home.
Use your spouse if you can't find a friend with a small head.

If you're not married you won't understand the hat trick anyhow.
It takes intimacy and love to make comedy out of the slow burn.

Pain, frustration, resignation. Affronted dignity. It's all in
the movement. Ho Ho.

And don't miss the dance sequence. It's even funnier run backwards.
I've asked the management to run it backwards, but they'll probably
cop out on technical grounds.

Harold Humes

(Harold Humes, novelist, and one of the founders of
THE PARIS REVIEW, is the author of THE UNDERGROUND
CITY and MEN DIE. He is currently shooting his first
film, DON PEYOTE, with his left hand and fighting
City Hall with his right. He is Chairman of the
Citizens' Emergency Committee, and in that capacity
recently spent a day in the pokey where he finished
these notes.)

4

(Note: I told Doc Humes that I disagreed with him on THE LAST LAUGH and he invited me to put in my two cents. I think he missed the point slightly by concentrating so much on the story-line, which isn't the primary interest of films anyway. It's the director's work that counts, and Murnau is not just a brilliant filmmaker, he's extraordinary. The fluidity and grace of his handling is superb and his narrative, with the imposed limitations of no help from titles, is vivid, taut, and continually exciting to the eye and convincing. On the other hand, the story isn't that bad, man; and the ending isn't simply tacked on, I think it's entirely premeditated—a kind of Pirandello finale in which you're left wondering as to what is the truth anyway. It also has that wry, post-war Brecht quality of cynical, reluctant romanticism. And that preoccupation with uniforms and everything is quite significant, it seems to me, considering Germany's entire history. I think Doc agrees with me on most of this. I screened the picture for him and he was equally as fascinated with the camera-work, lighting and acting as I was. But I agree that it's the cliche to praise a film in a program note—knocking it is far more interesting. And besides, why be so solemn? And furthermore, five in the morning is a hell of a time to write—right?   — Peter Bogdanovich.)

(A Final Note: Knocking it is easier too. — H.H.)

* * *

FIFTH PROGRAM MOVIES: WINTER 60-61 AT 7:00 & 9:30
NOTES BY ROBERT BRUSTEIN

Dec. 5 – NEVER GIVE A SUCKER AN EVEN BREAK *(Edward Cline, 1941)*

Like most W.C. Fields' comedies; SUCKER defies description — wild, grumbling, bumbling, delightful farce ... Fields himself — bulbous-nosed and unblushingly outspoken — wheels throughout the picture in his own inimitable fashion, going from mistake to mistake, ever positive that he's right.

ROOM SERVICE (William F. Feiter, 1938) The famous stage farce about a penniless play producer getting along by hook and crook, revamped to fit the talents of the Marx Brothers, which it does like a four-fingered glove. Lucille Ball and Ann Miller are the hapless chicks in their midst. An insane, zany (feature-length) romp.

NEVER GIVE A SUCKER AN EVEN BREAK

1941 (sound)   American
Directed by Edward Cline; screenplay by John T. Neville and
Prescott Chaplin, based on an idea by Otis Criblecoblis;
photography by Charles Van Enger; art direction by Jack
Otterson; edited by Arthur Hilton; released by Universal
Pictures. Running time: 71 minutes.
Cast: W.C. Fields, Gloria Jean, Leon Errol, Butch & Buddy,
Susan Miller, Franklin Pangborn, Charles Lang, Margaret
Dumont, Anne Megel, Mona Barrie, Nel O'Day, Irving Bacon,
Jody Gilbert, Minerva Urecal, Emmett Vogan, Charlotte Montie,
Bill Wolfe.

* * *

Though THE BANK DICK has more unity of conception, and TILLIE AND
GUS a greater number of boffos, NEVER GIVE A SUCKER AN EVEN BREAK is
unquestionably Fields' wildest, most extravagant, and most spontaneous
film. Liberated from even the minimal requirements of plot, logic, or
form, the Knight of the Bulbous Countenance here waddles unsteadily
through an outlandish series of picaresque adventures, juggling
elements of farce, vaudeville, satire, fantasy, and nightmare in a
virtuoso surrealist balancing act. As a result of this weird mixture
of forms, NEVER GIVE A SUCKER AN EVEN BREAK is less a conventional
Fields vehicle than a versatile exercise in the absurd which—despite
the fact that it was made in a particularly uncreative era (1941) by
an exceptionally mechanical studio (Universal)—rarely loses its air
of inspired improvisation.

For the old battler has now extended the area of hostilities
to include the rigid conventions of the Hollywood film, so as to make
a calculated assault on the spectator's grip on reality. The full
force of this assault is delayed—if you are familiar with most of
Fields' movies, you will not find in the opening frames anything
particularly surprising or new. It is a little unsettling, to be
sure, to discover that the action takes place within a movie studio
(Esoteric Pictures), and that most of the actors, including Fields
himself, are calling each other by their actual names. But aside
from a rather jarring alliance he has formed with a vacuous sub-
teenager (Gloria Jean), there is little here to stun you, for Fields

begins by rampaging across a traditional battlefield and waging war against a familiar group of enemies: the two monster children with freckled faces and a variety of lethal weapons who invariably goad him to violence; the cadaverous panhandler whose ghastly appearance jolts his nervous system; the leering, squinting, splenetic pansy Official who is always one of the prime objects of his aggression; and the fat-assed broad with a barrel of laconic wisecracks who reduces him to sotto voce imprecations. Here also is that conspiratorial army of things (horseflies, dogs, straw hats, menus, ice-cubes, golf clubs, coat-stands, etc.) which always seem to converge upon this embattled innocent with purely malicious intent, against which he must be perpetually alerted in order merely to survive. While Fields has never been known to repeat a routine, both his dramatis personae and his ornery response to them usually remain constant, and so for the first quarter of this film we are hardly prepared for the bedlam which is to follow.

After this deceptive prologue, however, Fields goes on to demolish all film conventions, including his own, embarking on a startling odyssey through his own rather demented unconscious. From the moment that he begins to assail his harrassed producer with a synopsis of his new scenario (Fields provided the idea for SUCKER, by the way, under the pseudonym of Otis Criblecoblis), the film assumes Pirandellian components, becoming a movie about a movie which takes place within an endless series of Chinese boxes. Inside these boxes, one can just discern Fields' comment on the difficulties he was having with Universal at the time, but beyond this all logic, coherence, and meaning are forced aside. Wafted back and forth between Fields' lunatic adventures and the producer's despairing expressions of disgust, the spectator is artfully suspended between laughter, bafflement, and sheer confusion until he is finally left gasping in the general dislocation and disorder.

For in the course of a crackbrained safari which wanders jerkily from one incredible location to another, we have been introduced to the most bewildering assortment of insane characters ever collected together on one screen, including a dumb virgin blonde out of Lost Island movies who plays "squidgulum" and breaks without warning into the "jumping jive", a corpulent Turk in an upper berth endlessly untying his belly sash, and a gorilla, sitting halfway up a mountain, who has an unaccountable affection for playing post office. Further, we have incredulously watched Fields 1) jump out of a moving plane in pursuit of his whiskey bottle, 2) test the local vintage of "nanny goat's milk" in a Russian Village from out of nowhere (probably used in the last Deanna Durbin movie), 3) push Leon Errol off a cliff after promising to show him a famous "hanging swimming pool", and 4) prepare for his wedding with Margaret Dumont (on loan from the Marx Brothers) by putting on a tailcoat so long it has to be held behind him like a bridal train. Finally, we have been yanked out of this nightmarish inner action to participate in one of the wildest, most destructive automobile chase

sequences ever filmed, during which not only Fields' car but the entire
outside world seems to be disintegrating beneath the sustained attack
of this violent, beserk, and uninhibited film comedian.

Here, in short, is farce bursting its seams under pressure from a
feverish, unpredictable imagination, a madbrained charade with no
organizing principle except the presence of Fields himself—serene,
boozy, lethargic, indestructible—his hobnail nose aloft as a monument
to his supreme indifference to the restrictions by which ordinary
mortals live. NEVER GIVE A SUCKER AN EVEN BREAK is a sustained image of
man in his natural state, unfettered by institutions, conventions, or
morality—man cavorting on the stage of the world before the world became
his prison. In its hilarious expression of our wilder unconscious
instincts, Fields' film is a rare nourishment for the daunted modern soul.

1938 (sound)   **ROOM SERVICE**   American
Directed by William F. Feiter; produced by Pandro S. Berman;
screenplay by Morris Ryskind, based on the stage play by
John Murray and Allan Boretz; photography by J. Roy Hunt;
art direction by Van Nest Polglase; musical direction by
Roy Webb; edited by George Crone; released by RKO Radio
Pictures. Running time: 78 minutes.

Cast: Groucho Marx, Harpo Marx, Chico Marx, Frank Albertson,
Donald MacBride, Lucille Ball, Ann Miller, Cliff Dunstan,
Philip Loeb, Philip Wood, Alexander Asro, Charles Halton.

* * *

ROOM SERVICE is an uninspired Broadway farce, only partially altered
to fit the uses of the Marx Brothers. Morris Ryskind is generally one
of their most dependable screenwriters, but he has sadly hobbled their
talents here. Except for a first-rate performance by Donald MacBride as
a sneering, disgusted, hoarse-voiced hotel manager, and an impressive
eating scene in which Harpo is momentarily permitted to display his
considerable gift for pantomime, the movie is plodding, dull, and
disappointing. The routines are flat, there is too much plot, and too
often Groucho is left silently staring into the camera when the situation
demands some devastating rejoinder. Once in a while an isolated sequence
will demonstrate Groucho's old affection for disintegrating logic
(Finance Man: "Where did he go?" Groucho: "To the maternity hospital."
Finance Man: "I thought you said he was crazy?" Groucho: "Well, if he
wasn't crazy, would he have gone to a maternity hospital?") but most of
the time the Brothers look like imposters. There is little suggestion
here of what Antonin Artaud called their "boiling anarchy" and "whole-
hearted revolt" or of those elements in their comedy which once
influenced the French avant-garde (especially Eugene Ionesco), for their
activities have been too thoroughly contained within the sturdy,
unyielding walls of a hotel suite. After ROOM SERVICE, Hollywood will

begin to employ the Marx Brothers primarily to support the love story, and then they will be exiled to TV: Groucho as a bourgeois quizmaster, Chico as an occasional player in television bridge games, and Harpo as a salesman for motor oil. Mass culture will suck them into its maelstrom, as it has consumed and domesticated every authentic comic talent in America, and only the fading prints of ANIMAL CRACKERS or NIGHT AT THE OPERA will remain to remind us of their unparalleled genius for liberation and revolt.

Robert Brustein

(Robert Brustein is assistant professor of dramatic literature at Columbia University and drama critic for THE NEW REPUBLIC. His articles on the theatre and movies have appeared in various publications, including HARPER'S MAGAZINE, ENCOUNTER, PARTISAN REVIEW, COMMENTARY, THEATRE ARTS, FILM QUARTERLY, HUDSON REVIEW. His latest piece, on repertory theatre, appears in the December issue of HARPER'S, and he is currently working on a book to be called THE THEATRE OF REVOLT.)

* * *

SIXTH PROGRAM MOVIES: WINTER 60-61 AT 7:00 & 9:30

NOTES BY EUGENE ARCHER

Dec. 12 — THE WOMAN ALONE (SABOTAGE)
(Alfred Hitchcock, 1937)

Just about everyone agrees that Hitchcock's best, most urbanely witty, devilish and suspenseful thrillers were done in the early thirties while he was still in England — LADY VANISHES, MAN WHO KNEW TOO MUCH, SECRET AGENT, 39 STEPS, — and probably the best of them all, the rarely-seen WOMAN ALONE (called SABATOGE in America). With Sylvia Sidney and Oscar Homolka, this brilliant murder-sex-comedy combination has more depth and truth than many "serious" films of its day.
THE LITTLE MATCH GIRL (1927). The famed Jean Renoir film, not seen for many years, a charming, strangely beautiful adaptation of the Hans Andersen story, with the irresistible Catherine Hessling.

MOVIES:
WINTER 60-61

THE WOMAN ALONE
(SABOTAGE)

1936 (sound)   British

Directed by Alfred Hitchcock; screenplay by Charles Bennett,
based on the novel, THE SECRET AGENT, by Joseph Conrad;
dialogue by Ian Hay and Helen Simpson; continuity by Alma
Reville; additional dialogue by E.V.H. Emmett; photography
by Bernard Knowles; art direction by O. Werndorff; edited
by Charles Frend; musical director, Louis Levy; cartoon
sequence by arrangement with Walt Disney; produced and
distributed by Gaumont-British Productions. Running time:
80 minutes.

Cast: Sylvia Sidney (Mrs. Verloc), Oscar Homolka (Her
husband), Desmond Tester (Her young brother), John Loder
(Ted), Joyce Barbour (Renee), Matthew Boulton (Superintendent
Talbot), S.J. Warmington (Hollingshead), William Dewhurst
(The Professor).

* * *

An innocent, only slightly obnoxious little boy is instructed
to deliver a package by 1:30. Naturally, that package contains a
bomb set to explode precisely at 1:45. With equally inexorable
cinematic logic, since this, after all, is an Alfred Hitchcock
picture, that boy is going to dawdle en route—watching a parade,
peering into store windows, acting as guinea pig for a toothpaste
salesman to the cynical amusement of a mocking crowd.

If any other director had made SABOTAGE, a viewer could settle
back in his seat with reasonable certainty that that little boy would
be rescued at 1:44. With Hitchcock, one can never be sure. Remembering
the arrogant contempt for humanity displayed in thinly veiled fashion
in his later films, plus his disconcerting habit of delivering on his
promises, a viewer is going to watch the hands of that clock with
increasing uneasiness, waiting for that smug little bastard to
receive his just deserts—apocalypse.

SABOTAGE, released here in 1937 as THE WOMAN ALONE, is based on
Joseph Conrad's SECRET AGENT, but is not to be confused with Hitch-
cock's preceding SECRET AGENT, a film based on Somerset Maugham's
ASHENDEN. It has little more relation to its source than the title

implies, for literary fidelity is not among the virtues of this dedicated anarchist. The film came fourth in the series of British thrillers begun with THE MAN WHO KNEW TOO MUCH and THE 39 STEPS, and indicates the director's increasing boredom with the stiff-upper-lip genre that had made his name. Already the stars—Sylvia Sidney and Oscar Homolka—are international, lacking the lightness associated with comic melodrama; the subject—exhibitionism for political ends—is disturbingly serious in its implications; the director's concern has turned to the unexpected, the deliberately perverse. The seeds of discontent were sown; a sterile England and a peurile British cinema had had its due. Three more increasingly hostile films remained—the ironically titled YOUNG AND INNOCENT, the deceptively conventional THE LADY VANISHES, and the baroque JAMAICA INN—before he flew the coop.

Since the New Yorker is offering a rare opportunity to see one of the most expert films from Hitchcock's so-called "vintage" period, it would be remiss to observe that, contrary to popular opinion, the master melodramatist grew steadily subtler, more meaningful, more formally accomplished in his later, infuriatingly commercial American works. The fast click-clack of cuts for effect, observed here in its most accomplished phase, soon gave way to the slow, tracking evocation of people and places in REBECCA, NOTORIOUS, ROPE, VERTIGO, THE WRONG MAN. To suggest that deep-focus master plans can be more profoundly symbolic in a talking film than the more elementary superficialities of montage, would mean challenging the most sacred cow—that myopic aesthetic dogma, widely promulgated since the basic treatises on film theory were written in the Nineteen Thirties, which maintains that cinema began with Griffith and ended with Eisenstein. (Not, of course, the later Eisenstein of IVAN THE TERRIBLE, who startled his advocates by contradicting his own earlier principles of montage and tracking to his heart's content—but, then, no books have been written to explain that.)

Since basic critical theory has gone unchallenged in the last three noisy decades, let it rest in peace—along with that other eminently quotable cliché that "Hollywood inevitably corrupts". It's far easier to disregard the troublesome implications of PSYCHO and UNDER CAPRICORN and I CONFESS, and instead sit back and enjoy the fast and funny and relatively uncomplicated Hitchcock of SABOTAGE, letting him set a pace too fast to provoke that disturbing suspicion that cinema might be an intellectual medium after all. Besides, it may only be an accident that in this elementary little thriller innocence is decisively punished and murder promptly pays.

* * *

THE LITTLE MATCH GIRL
(La Petite Marchande D'Allumettes)

1927 (silent)   French

Direction and scenario by Jean Renoir, based on the short
story by Hans Christian Andersen; produced by Renoir and
Jean Tedesco; photography by Jean Bachelet; designed by
Erich Aes; post-production musical score directed by Manuel
Rosenthal. Running time: 30 minutes.

Cast: Catherine Hessling (Karen), Jean Storm (The Young Man),
Manuel Raaby (Policeman), Amy Xells (The Doll).

* * *

As Hitchcock blithely pursues his cynical path toward the nether
regions of personal cinema in PSYCHO, Jean Renoir, with humanistic
tolerance for the ignorance of an unappreciative public, continues
the most distinguished unsuccessful film career since the days of
Erich von Stroheim by growing more violently unpopular than ever.
Hitchcock, by turning to interior content expressed through a
viciously ironic symbolic technique, merely challenged the purists
and the Puritanical. Renoir, by daring to suggest that technique
doesn't matter an iota in the cinema, any more than good acting or a
believable plot, has managed to offend everyone in sight.

What, one might reasonably ask, does matter? Merely conception,
the artist would answer: merely a personal vision of the world.
Certainly Renoir's work in the film conveys the personality of the
man if nothing else—and, ultimately, nothing more is required. LA
REGLE DU JEU is either a masterpiece or trash, and so is PICNIC ON
THE GRASS. So, indeed, are GRAND ILLUSION, PARTIE DE CAMPAGNE, TONI,
LE CRIME DE M. LANGE, LA BETE HUMAINE, THE SOUTHERNER, DIARY OF A
CHAMBERMAID, WOMAN ON THE BEACH, THE RIVER, THE GOLDEN COACH, FRENCH
CANCAN, ELENA AND THE MEN.

THE LITTLE MATCH GIRL, made nearly at the end of the silent era
and near the beginning of Renoir's imagistic stream of subconscious-
ness in the cinema, shows the artist in an experimental mood. Hans
Christian Andersen's simple tale of a dying waif's last dreams of
romance becomes, in his hands, a slight ballet on the theme of
illusion and reality—obviously the most intensely personal of
subjects for any director worthy of the name.

Of course, everyone knows that fantasy is not an appropriate
genre for a film. The cinema, after all, is a realistic medium, too
penetrating in its intimate observation of detail to permit the
viewer to exercise his imagination by looking beyond the pores. Only
realism, if these truths be self-evident, is proper material for our
socially significant screen—just as Ibsen's box-set with its
invisible fourth wall was inevitably the one and only theatrical

technique, Shakespeare notwithstanding.

Under this accepted gospel, of course, THE LITTLE MATCH GIRL should never have been made. Neither should LOLA MONTES, UGETSU, WILD STRAWBERRIES, THE GOLD RUSH, or HIROSHIMA, MON AMOUR. Our enlightened, socially conscious modern cinema leaves room only for such classics as THE BICYCLE THIEF and the films of Stanley Kramer.

Fortunately, no one ever bothered to tell that to Renoir.

Eugene Archer

(Eugene Archer is a reporter and reviewer in the motion picture department of THE NEW YORK TIMES. He has written critical articles on the movies for FILM QUARTERLY, FILMS AND FILMING, BIANCO E NERO, and other cinema publications. A year overseas, spent in the screening rooms of the Cinematheque in Paris, the National Film Theatre in London, and various film festivals, gave him an inside scoop on many different European picture theories.)

* * *

SEVENTH PROGRAM MOVIES: WINTER 60-61 AT 7:00 & 9:30
NOTES BY TERRY SOUTHERN

Dec. 19 — A STAR IS BORN
(William Wellman, 1937)

Not seen in many years, this is the original Janet Gaynor — Fredric March version of the famous drama about a big star and a struggling starlet — the former on the way down and the latter on the way up — who passed each other on the way and fell in love. Stirring, beautifully acted, vigorously directed, this was the first definitive picture of Movieland people — the SUNSET BOULEVARD of the 30's. As Richard Griffith said, "a devastatingly frank study of Hollywood".

LIZZIES OF THE FIELD (1924). An absolutely mad Mack Sennett one-reeler — cars, cops, mechanics, dames — all thrown together into a sped-up, intoxicated auto-race. The prize: just laughs.

A STAR IS BORN

1937 (sound)   American
Directed by William Wellman; produced by David O. Selznick;
screenplay by Dorothy Parker, Alan Campbell, Robert Carson,
from a story by William Wellman & Robert Carson; photography
by W. Howard Greene; music by Max Steiner; a Selznick-
International production released through United Artists.
Running time: 110 minutes.
Cast: Janet Gaynor, Fredric March, Adolphe Menjou, Lionel
Stander, May Robson, Andy Devine, Edgar Kennedy, Elizabeth
Jenns, Owen Moore, J.C. Nugent, Clara Blandrick, Peggy Wood,
Arthur Hoyt, Guinn Williams, Vince Barnett, Paul Stanton,
Franklin Pangborn.

* * *

At a time now when the standard serious image of The Actor includes
the sensibilities of a poet and a psyche as complex as a deranged chess-
player's, the general viewer may be hard put to understand how a waspish
ninny like Janet Gaynor could be involved in the personification at all,
much less the title-role. What is not actively enough realized, however,
is that the title A STAR IS BORN was intended to be wholly and wistfully
ironic—that the ascension or "birth" of the new star is quite incident-
al to the real drama: the slow and horrible death of the old star. For it
is, of course, only through the figurative death of the old star that the
new one can be born; a corner-stone of Studio economics.

The confusion here, between the motif of the story and its foil,
originally came about when two irrelevant sequences were spliced into the
film: the first and the last—both mere sops for evading the story's real
and disturbingly negative conclusion. The resulting distortion was then
given its finite emphasis by a 1954 rehash of the movie, with Judy Garland,
which actually attempted to reverse the two roles completely.

This does not mean to say that the peripheral account, the rise of
the new star, is entirely without interest, but rather that it pretends
to no dramatic value of itself; its interest lies simply in the picture
it gives of the various machinations and attitudes which in those days
went into creating a film-celebrity—all of which is by now pretty stale
stuff. Actually it is fairly remarkable that "Vicky Lester" manages to

evoke the degree of sympathy that she does from certain of the scenes—explained in part, one may believe, by Eisenstein's so-called "theory of empathetic-reflection", that process whereby an audience supposes itself to be evaluating one character but is in fact re-responding to another through the one consciously seen. In any case, it should be acknowledged that (aside from the absurd opening and closing episodes) Vicky Lester, despite her non-Studio, non-Old Vic (ergo, "non-serious") background, occasionally does succeed in suggesting that she just well <u>might</u> contain the seeds of a genuine talent (especially at the moment when he accidentally slaps her). However, this does not strengthen the story but detracts from it; dramatically she is no more than a cipher in the tragic equation of Norman Maine. Otherwise there is no tragedy; and here we encounter the principal difficulty—that of recognizing the basic seriousness of the protagonist's situation when he is through as an actor. After all, there he is, still relatively young, obviously a man of means, energy, experience...it is even suggested (generally, by his manner, and specifically, by his denunciation of his last three films) that he is also a person of considerable taste and intelligence. Why then, one may wonder, doesn't he at least <u>consider</u> some other phase of the medium—directing or producing—before beginning his slow swim towards the moon? To understand his ambivalence, or ultimately the lack of it, about applying his own peculiar qualities (taste, intellegence, etc.) to directing or producing, one must simply remember that in 1937 the film was not considered to be (as certain aspects of this one—notably the photography—will attest) an art form; consequently, it would not have been psychologically possible for him to want to become a director or producer, and to still retain the sympathy of the audience of that period.

It is only within the framework of these limitations that one may begin to perceive the essential strength of the film, which is its persuasive credibility—not as a whole, but within individual scenes, curiously self-contained and independent of context, or seen each as a vignette of speculative ethic and personality—an approach which Wellman was to develop and bring to full fruition several years late in THE OX-BOW INCIDENT. It is, in fact, a film which in more than one respect is well in advance of its time; there are instances, almost, of "throw-away lines", which, if they do not emerge as such technically, are there in effect—the sort of muttering delivery, for example, that Fredric March uses in the clubhouse scene with Lionel Stander, or the eloquent "O.K." spoken by Menjou (at a point where he should have said much much more) when finally agreeing to let the girl have the big role opposite Maine. And here, concerning Menjou's interpretation of the producer, it is in order to note that it is <u>probably flawless</u> throughout—

far superior to his celebrated role in FRONT PAGE, which is nothing less than ham-fat by comparison. As for Lionel Stander's role, whether it is believable is certainly open to question—alongside the three principals he is a mere caricature—and yet surely there are few scenes in cinema more successful than the one between himself and March in the clubhouse bar.

Too bad about the ending. Ideally the film would end in chaos, like DAY OF THE LOCUST, with Janet at the premiere, being majestically engulfed (slow-motion) by a tidal wave of avid fans, and presumably torn to pieces; or better, that she should appear to be carrying it off, smiling bravely down the aisle on Menjou's arm, until, with that last minute "accidental" glimpse of Maine's footprints, she goes stark raving mad, screaming at the top of her lungs.

CLOSE UP ON SCREAM AND CUT TO BLACK.

* * *

(A STAR IS BORN was originally photographed in color, but such prints, unfortunately, are extremely difficult to come upon. After an extensive search, this black-and-white print was the only one we were able to locate.   — NYFS)

* * *

LIZZIES OF THE FIELD

1924 (silent)   American
Directed by Del Lord; produced by Mack Sennett; released by Pathe Films. One reel.
Cast: Billy Bevan, Sid Smith, Andy Clyde, Jack Lloyd, Barbara Pierce, John Richardson.

* * *

Note the fine surrealist opening (none of this sneaky, obscene "pushing out West as a young girl" crap).

The best parts of this film are superb examples of pure cinema; there is nothing flat about the use of camera here. We have motion and counter-motion, motion within motion, spacial and textural compositions to compare with the good German films of the period. When a Mack Sennett car leaps with such seeming abandon through the frame in a long shot, the movement is executed not simply in the frame but in precisely the right part of the frame; if you were to

freeze the action at any point, you might have an abstract painting.
But why freeze it? Why not freeze Porky Pig instead? After suitably
mutilating his fat snout!

Terry Southern

(Terry Southern, novelist, short story writer, and
essayist, is the author of FLASH AND FILAGREE and
THE MAGIC CHRISTIAN. His stories have appeared in
such magazines as THE PARIS REVIEW, NEW STORY, THE
EVERGREEN REVIEW, HARPER'S BAZAAR. His celebrated
essay on humor appeared recently in THE NATION.)

* * *

EIGHTH PROGRAM MOVIES: WINTER 60-61 AT 7:00 & 9:30
NOTES BY JACK KEROUAC

Jan. 9 — NOSFERATU (DRACULA)
(F.W. Murnau, 1922)
The classic German horror film and the first to bring vampires to the screen.
Full of misty woods, wolves, eerie birds, phantom ships and coaches,
blood-thirsty monsters, and grotesque figures, this brilliant silent film, as
a famous critic once said, seems as if "a chilly draft from doomsday"
passed through its scenes.
A CORNER IN WHEAT (1909). D.W. Griffith's most famous short film —
an incisive social document with a revolutionary use of parallel construction.
MIGHTY LIKE A MOOSE (1926). A delightfully ridiculous vintage Charlie
Chase comedy — mistaken identity, disguises, unfaithful husbands and
wives. (Piano accompaniment for the evening by Arthur Kleiner).

---

* * *

We hope to see you again on January 9th; till
then have a very nice Christmas and a pleasantly
insane New Year. — New Yorker Film Society.

* * *

MOVIES:
WINTER 60-61

NOTES: Jan. 16

FOOLISH WIVES

1922 (silent)   American
Directed by Erich von Stroheim; screenplay by Erich
von Stroheim; produced by Carl Laemmle; released through
Universal Pictures. 9 reels.
Cast: Erich von Stroheim, Mae Busch, Maude George, Miss
Dupont, Rudolph Christians, Dale Fuller, Caesare Gravina,
Malvina Polo and Louis K. Webb
**

The movies are generally divided into two broad categories;
the personal film in which the director molds the entire experience, and the film of sterotypes in which the director attempts
to convey his message (if any) through the unusual use of conventi
al characters and of plot. (Any discussion with me of which way i
best will be at your expense at the bar of your choice.)

All Hollywood films are of the latter category. FOOLISH
WIVES has several disarming performances and the corniest plot.
Erich von Stroheim has been feted for his manical drive in the
meticulous reproduction of reality. Certainly this obsession
accounts for the marvelous portrayals, but it doesn't seem to cove
up the plot---or for that matter von Stroheim's inability "to see"
in film.

FOOLISH WIVES came into being after Stroheim's first film,
BLIND HUSBANDS, scored at the box office. Universal Films sent
out releases during 1921 extolling the mad genius of Erich von
Stroheim. There were countless delays in turning out the film.
Sets crashed down or weren't accurate, there were endless front
office discussions concerning the sex angle (Mr. Fatty Arbuckle
had caused a sensation in San Francisco), and one of the players
died with half the picture finished. (Randolph Cristians plays
Miss Dupont's husband. Robert Edeson replaced him and I can't

tell the difference.)

After one year, $1,103,736.38, and 320 reels of film shot, the movie opened in New York on January 12, 1922--- a hollywood extravaganza with hand-tinted red flames in the fire sequence. It ran fourteen reels (3½ hours) with a five minute intermission. There were some provocative reviews and the picture went on to make money.

A few days later Carl Laemmle, the producer, announced that the picture was too long and that he was cutting it. He also said that his cutting it had nothing to do with the New York Censorship Boards request for deletions. And so it went: everywhere it was chopped down. (Don't ask me what version you are seeing or which ones I've seen---Idon't know.)

And here is the place for Dan Talbot to have grimy little men in white coats passing among you selling postcard size stills from the picture. You'd make a fortune, Dan. Erich von Stroheim biting Mae Busch's hand whilst she pulls his ear. Old Erich,the master voyeur, watching Miss Dupont undress in his pocket mirror. Don't forget to include one of those long lingering looks between Mae Busch and Maude George.

Von Stroheim is a fake and a bore---a con man conned. I don't think this thought will enhance your seeing the movie--- but what will?

Perhaps a clue to the deepest meaning of FOOLISH WIVES is its relationship to the segment of SALOME that is being shown with it.Maybe it is in the rational process that led the management in putting the two on the same bill. I couldn't even laugh at the damn thing.

I could do that and watch a few other things in FOOLISH WIVES. After all, that's what the old magic box is about: to settle bets on whether horses ever have all four legs off the ground; to see the mushroom cloud; to see Erich strip off a pair of gloves. My guess is,that is what is meant when you hear the phrase, "in the tradition of Griffith."

These are moments. In movies that's all there is--- there ain't no more. Generally the theatrical plot is the villain, but Isuspect it is only a wart on an acned face. The reasoning behind a meretricious plot is beyond me: apparently the audience, aged 8, will respond to the lessons shown (and pictures have tackled the toughest didactics) and the moviemaker (Erich von)

will have serviced the community and future generations and
at the same time will have made money. There is something to
be said for making money, as I understand it is very good pro
paganda to increase our gross national product.
    But it is 1961 and we know what happened to Von S. He
didn't fill the producer's pockets with bread (GREED) and tha
was virtually the end (SUNSET BLVD.)of him. No doubt his
unique gift and conscious concern for fetishism added fuel
under the pot in which he boiled.

Jack Gelber

(Jack Gelber is the author of the off-
Broadway hit, THE CONNECTION,a Living
Theatre production. His latest play
THE APPLE will be opening soon at the
Living Theatre.)

SALOME

1922 (silent)   American
Directed by Charles Bryant; scenario by Peter N. Winter from
a play by Oscar Wilde; produced by Allied Productions &
Distributing Corp.
Cast: Alla Nazimova, Rose Dione, Mitchell Lewis, Nigel de
Brulier, Earl Sckenck, Arthur Jasmina, Frederick Peters,
Louis Dumar. 4 reels.

(PIANO ACCOMPANIMENT FOR THE EVENING BY ARTHUR KLEINER)

Jan. 23 — NANOOK OF THE NORTH
(Robert Flaherty, 1922)
The greatest and most famous documentary ever made — a remarkable picture of life among the Eskimos, made with Flaherty's unique blend of vivid imagery and harsh reality.
THE RIVER (Pare Lorentz, 1937) A "tragedy of land twice impoverished", this memorable document depicts, with compassion and strength, the terrors and destruction of the Mississippi floods.
THE BATTLE OF SAN PIETRO (John Huston, 1945) Without doubt the most shocking and powerful anti-war indictment ever made. Done as a government assignment during World War II, the Army considered it too horrifying to show and censored it. But the guts are still there, and it is one of Huston's most vibrant, angry, deeply human achievements.

American Theatrical Premieres
at the Cinema Studio

1977

STROSZEK   Werner Herzog
THE AMERICAN FRIEND   Wim Wenders

1978

WOMAN OF PARIS (Reprise)   Charles Chaplin
WOMEN   Márta Mészáros
PERCEVAL   Eric Rohmer

1979

THE TREE OF WOODEN CLOGS   Ermanno Olmi
EL SUPER   Leon Ichaso and Orlando Jiménez-Leal
WOYZECK   Werner Herzog
THE MARRIAGE OF MARIA BRAUN   Rainer Werner Fassbinder

1980

ANGI VERA   Pál Gábor
KNIFE IN THE HEAD   Reinhard Hauff
THE CHANT OF JIMMIE BLACKSMITH   Fred Schepisi
EVERY MAN FOR HIMSELF   Jean Luc-Godard
LOULOU   Maurice Pialat

1981

MAN OF MARBLE   Andrzej Wajda
CONFIDENCE   Istvan Szabo
CITY OF WOMEN   Federico Fellini
CAMOUFLAGE   Krzysztof Zanussi
PIXOTE   Hector Babenco
TAXI TO THE LOO   Frank Ripploh

1982

THE TRAGEDY OF A RIDICULOUS MAN
    Bernardo Bertolucci
MARIANNE AND JULIANE   Margarethe von Trotta
CHAN IS MISSING   Wayne Wang
BOB LE FLAMBEUR   Jean-Pierre Melville
XICA DA SILVA   Carlos Diegues
LE BEAU MARRIAGE   Eric Rohmer
VERONIKA VOSS   Rainer Werner Fassbinder

1983

MUDDY RIVER   Kohei Oguri
THEY DON'T WEAR BLACK TIE   Leon Hirszman
WAYS IN THE NIGHT   Krzysztof Zanussi

LONELY HEARTS   Paul Cox
REAR WINDOW (Reprise)   Alfred Hitchcock
VERTIGO (Reprise)   Alfred Hitchcock

1984

ENTRE NOUS   Diane Kurys
THE TROUBLE WITH HARRY (Reprise)
    Alfred Hitchcock
THE MAN WHO KNEW TOO MUCH (Reprise)
    Alfred Hitchcock
ROPE (Reprise)   Alfred Hitchcock
IN THE WHITE CITY   Alain Tanner
CARMEN   Francesco Rosi
STRANGER THAN PARADISE   Jim Jarmusch

1985

THE HOME AND THE WORLD   Satyajit Ray
SHEER MADNESS   Margarethe von Trotta
SHOAH   Claude Lanzmann

1986

QUILOMBO   Carlos Diegues
TRACKS IN THE SNOW   Orlow Seunke
SHE'S GOTTA HAVE IT   Spike Lee
DOWN BY LAW   Jim Jarmusch
MÉNAGE   Bertrand Blier
TANGOS, THE EXILE OF GARDEL   Fernando Solanas
EL AMOR BRUJO   Carlos Saura

1987

OPERA DO MALANDRO   Ruy Guerra
SWIMMING TO CAMBODIA   Jonathan Demme
LAW OF DESIRE   Pedro Almodóvar
TAMPOPO   Juzo Itami
SAMMY AND ROSIE GET LAID   Stephen Frears
THE FUNERAL   Juzo Itami
REPENTANCE   Tengiz Abuladze

1988

THE FAMILY   Ettore Scola
FRIDA   Paul Leduc
BABETTE'S FEAST   Gabriel Axel
HIGH TIDE   Gillian Armstrong
WINGS OF DESIRE   Wim Wenders
PLAYING AWAY   Horace Ove
MATADOR   Pedro Almodóvar
HOTEL TERMINUS: LIFE AND TIMES OF KLAUS BARBIE
   Marcel Ophüls
WOMEN ON THE VERGE OF A NERVOUS BREAKDOWN
   Pedro Almodóvar
NOBODY LISTENED   Nestor Almendros

1989

CHOCOLAT   Claire Denis
A TAXING WOMAN'S RETURN   Juzo Itami
SEX, LIES, AND VIDEOTAPE   Stephen Soderbergh
STORY OF WOMEN   Claude Chabrol
MYSTERY TRAIN   Jim Jarmusch

1990

THE PLOT AGAINST HARRY   Eric Rohmer
TOO BEAUTIFUL FOR YOU   Bertrand Blier

American Theatrical Premieres at the Lincoln Plaza Cinemas

1981

CITY OF WOMEN   Federico Fellini
VOYAGE EN DOUCE   Michel Deville
LA DRÔLESSE   Jacques Doillon
MODERN ROMANCE   Paul Viachelli
MESSIDOR   Alain Tanner
HEART TO HEART   Pascal Thomas
THE AVIATOR'S WIFE   Eric Rohmer
THE CONTRACT   Krzysztof Zanussi
MY DINNER WITH ANDRE   Louis Malle
THE THIN LINE   Michal Bat-Adam
THEY ALL LAUGHED   Peter Bogdanovich

1982

DAVID   Peter Lilienthal
PASSION   Jean-Luc Godard

GREGORY'S GIRL   Bill Forsythe
LOLA   Rainer Werner Fassbinder
SWEET HOURS   Carlos Saura
COME BACK TO THE FIVE AND DIME, JIMMY DEAN . . .
    Robert Altman
LA FEMME ENFANT   Raphaël Billetdoux

1983

THE STATIONMASTER'S WIFE   Rainer Werner Fassbinder
THE GIRL WITH THE RED HAIR   Ben Verbong
THE NIGHT OF THE SHOOTING STARS
    Paolo and Vittorio Taviani
PETRIA'S WREATH   Srdjan Karanovic
THE NIGHT OF VARENNES   Ettore Scola
PRIVILEGED   Michael Hoffman
ANGELO, MY LOVE   Robert Duvall
PAULINE AT THE BEACH   Eric Rohmer
BERLIN ALEXANDERPLATZ   Rainer Werner Fassbinder
DANTON   Andrzej Wajda
STREAMERS   Robert Altman
BOAT PEOPLE   Ann Hui

1984

BASILEUS QUARTET   Fabio Carpi
NOSTALGHIA   Andrei Tarkovsky
THAT SINKING FEELING   Bill Forsythe
L'ARGENT   Robert Bresson
SUGAR CANE ALLEY   Euzhan Palcy
BIQUEFARRE   Georges Rouquier
ERENDIRA   Ruy Guerra
IREZUMI   Yoichi Takabayashi

AFTER THE REHEARSAL   Ingmar Bergman
ANOTHER TIME, ANOTHER PLACE   Michael Radford
FIRST NAME: CARMEN   Jean-Luc Godard
FULL MOON IN PARIS   Eric Rohmer
THE FAMILY GAME   Yoshimitsu Morita
A NOS AMOURS   Maurice Pialat
A LOVE IN GERMANY   Andrzej Wajda
DIARY FOR MY CHILDREN   Márta Mészáros
MAN OF FLOWERS   Paul Cox

1985

FAVORITES OF THE MOON   Otar Iosseliani
WHERE THE GREEN ANTS DREAM   Werner Herzog
STOP MAKING SENSE   Jonathan Demme
STREETWISE   Martin Bell
FLASH OF GREEN   Victor Nuñez
LE PÉRIL   Michel Deville
DETECTIVE   Jean-Luc Godard
WETHERBY   David Hare
DANCE WITH A STRANGER   Mike Newell
SUGARBABY   Percy Adlon

1986

WHEN FATHER WAS AWAY ON BUSINESS   Emir Kusturica
KAOS   Paolo and Vittorio Taviani
THE CRAZY FAMILY   Sogo Ishii
ANGRY HARVEST   Agnieszka Holland
VAGABOND   Agnès Varda
TEA IN THE HAREM   Mehdi Charef
THE GIRL IN THE PICTURE   Cary Parker
A GREAT WALL   Peter Wang

MEN Doris Dörrie
SUMMER Eric Rohmer
POLICE Maurice Pialat
THE SACRIFICE Andrei Tarkovsky
DOWN BY LAW Jim Jarmusch
THÉRÈSE Alain Cavalier

1987

COMIC MAGAZINE Yojiro Takita
MÉNAGE Bertrand Blier
SCENE OF THE CRIME André Téchiné
FACES OF WOMEN Désiré Ecaré
SOREKARA Yoshimitsu Morita
PRICK UP YOUR EARS Stephen Frears
ROSA LUXEMBURG Margarethe Von Trotta
MY LIFE AS A DOG Lasse Hallström
WISH YOU WERE HERE David Leland
LIVING ON TOKYO TIME Steven Okazaki

1988

EL SUR Victor Erice
HALF OF HEAVEN Manuel Gutierrez Aragon
MÉLO Alain Resnais
GIRL FROM HUNAN Xie Fie and U Lan
SUBWAY TO THE STARS Carlos Diegues
THE POINTSMAN Joe Stelling
BAGDAD CAFÉ Percy Adlon
"38" Wolfgang Glueck
A TAXING WOMAN Juzo Itami
DRAGON CHOW Jan Schutte
COMMISSAR Aleksandr Askoldov

BOYFRIENDS AND GIRLFRIENDS   Eric Rohmer
THE THIN BLUE LINE   Errol Morris
SALAAM BOMBAY   Mira Nair
RED SORGHUM   Zhang Yimou
PELLE THE CONQUEROR   Billie August

1989

36 FILLETTE   Catherine Breillat
VOICES OF SARAFINA   Nigel Noble
HIGH HOPES   Mike Leigh
UNDER THE SUN OF SATAN   Maurice Pialat
LITTLE VERA   Vassili Pitchul
LA BOHEME   Luigi Comencini
KUNG FU MASTER   Agnès Varda
THE MUSIC TEACHER   Gérard Corbiau
THE 4 ADVENTURES OF REINETTE AND MIRA-
BELLE   Eric Rohmer
THE LITTLE THIEF   Claude Miller
HIGH FIDELITY   Alan Miller
YAABA   Idrissa Ouédraogo
MY LEFT FOOT   Jim Sheridan

1990

VERÓNICO CRUZ   Miguel Pereira
SWEETIE   Jane Campion
CINEMA PARADISO   Giuseppe Tornatore
TIE ME UP! TIE ME DOWN!   Pedro Almodóvar
MAY FOOLS   Louis Malle
ICICLE THIEF   Maurizio Nichetti
LIFE AND NOTHING BUT   Bertrand Tavernier
L'ATALANTE (Restored Version)   Jean Vigo

THE NASTY GIRL   Michael Verhoeven
TILAÏ   Idrissa Ouédraogo
FREEZE-DIE-COME TO LIFE   Vitali Kanevsky

1991

RIKYU   Hiroshi Teshigahara
TAXI BLUES   Pavel Lounguine
AY CARMELA!   Carlos Saura
OPEN DOORS   Gianni Amelio
JUDOU   Zhang Yimou
KORCZAK   Andrzej Wajda
EVERYBODY'S FINE   Giuseppe Tornatore
PAPER WEDDING   Michel Brault
EUROPA, EUROPA   Agnieszka Holland
URANUS   Claude Berri
LA BELLE NOISEUSE   Jacques Rivette
CITY OF HOPE   John Sayles
THE DOUBLE LIFE OF VERONIQUE   Krzysztof Kieslowski
HIGH HEELS   Pedro Almodóvar
RHAPSODY IN AUGUST   Akira Kurosawa

1992

VOYAGER   Volker Schlondorff
TOTO THE HERO   Jaco Van Dormael
RAISE THE RED LANTERN   Zhang Yi-Mou
DELICATESSEN   Jean-Pierre Jeunet and Marc Caro
ADAM'S RIB   Viatcheslav Krichtofovitch
THE ADJUSTER   Atom Egoyan
MONSTER IN THE BOX   Spalding Gray
THE HAIRDRESSER'S HUSBAND   Patrice Leconte
A TALE OF SPRINGTIME   Eric Rohmer

LA DISCRÈTE   Christian Vincent
A BRIEF HISTORY OF TIME   Errol Morris
SWOON   Tom Kalin
DANZÓN   Maria Novaro
VAN GOGH   Maurice Pialat
WATERLAND   Stephen Gyllenhaal
CLOSE TO EDEN   Nikita Mikhalkov
THE MATCH FACTORY GIRL   Aki Kaurismaki
TOUS LES MATINS DU MONDE   Alain Corneau
INTERVISTA   Federico Fellini
INDOCHINE   Régis Wargnier

1993

THE OAK   Lucian Pintilie
OLIVIER, OLIVIER   Agnieszka Holland
IL LADRO DI BAMBINI   Gianni Amelio
LÉOLO   Jean-Claude Lauzon
THE STORY OF QUI JU   Zhang Yimou
MUCH ADO ABOUT NOTHING   Kenneth Branagh
UN COEUR EN HIVER   Claude Sautet
ORLANDO   Sally Potter
JACQUOT   Agnès Varda
THE WEDDING BANQUET   Ang Lee
TITO AND ME   Goran Markovic
SAMBA TRAORE   Idrissa Ouédraogo
RUBY IN PARADISE   Victor Nuñez
DIVERTIMENTO   Jacques Rivette
FAREWELL MY CONCUBINE   Chen Kaige
CHASSE AUX PAPILLONS   Otar Iosseliani
THE PIANO   Jane Campion
THE SNAPPER   Stephen Frears
BLUE   Krzysztof Kieslowski

THE ACCOMPANIST   Claude Miller
FARAWAY, SO CLOSE   Wim Wenders

1994

THE SCENT OF GREEN PAPAYA   Tran Anh Hung
FIORILE   Paolo and Vittorio Taviani
BELLE EPOQUE   Fernando Trueba
IVAN AND ABRAHAM   Yolande Zauberman
A TALE OF WINTER   Eric Rohmer
THE BLUE KITE   Tian Zhuangzhuang
32 SHORT FILMS ABOUT GLENN GOULD
    François Girard
KIKA   Pedro Almodóvar
THE SLINGSHOT   Ake Sandgren
WHITE   Krzysztof Kieslowski
A PLACE IN THE WORLD   Adolfo Aristarain
EAT DRINK, MAN WOMAN   Ang Lee
PRISCILLA, QUEEN OF THE DESERT   Stephen Eliott
CAFE AU LAIT   Mathieu Kassovitz
FRESH   Boaz Yakim
CARO DIARIO   Nanni Moretti
HOOP DREAMS   Steve James
VANYA ON 42ND STREET   Louis Malle
BULLETS OVER BROADWAY   Woody Allen
OLEANNA   David Mamet
HEAVENLY CREATURES   Peter Jackson
TO LIVE   Zhang Yimou
RED   Krzysztof Kieslowski
PRÊT-À-PORTER   Robert Altman
A MAN OF NO IMPORTANCE   Suri Krishnamma
THE MADNESS OF KING GEORGE   Nicholas Hytner

1995

STRAWBERRY AND CHOCOLATE   Tomás Gutiérrez Alea
WINDOW TO PARIS   Yuri Mamin
BEFORE THE RAIN   Milcho Manchevski
MINA TANNENBAUM   Martine Dugowson
MURIEL'S WEDDING   P. J. Hogan
9 FILMS BY SATYAJIT RAY (Reissues)   Satyajit Ray
   PATHER PANCHALI
   APARAJITO
   THE MUSIC ROOM
   THE WORLD OF APU
   DEVI
   TWO DAUGHTERS
   THE BIG CITY
   CHARULATA
   THE MIDDLEMAN
RED FIRECRACKER, GREEN FIRECRACKER   He Ping
BURNT BY THE SUN   Nikita Mikhalkov
ERMO   Zhou Xiaowen
LOVE AND HUMAN REMAINS   Denys Arcand
SMOKE   Wayne Wang
THE POSTMAN   Michael Radford
BANDIT QUEEN   Shekhar Kapur
LIVING IN OBLIVION   Tom DiCillo
KIDS   Larry Clark
I CAN'T SLEEP   Claire Denis
THE PROMISE   Margarethe von Trotta
AUGUSTIN   Anne Fontaine
BLUE IN THE FACE   Wayne Wang and Paul Auster
MIGHTY APHRODITE   Woody Allen
NOBODY LOVES ME   Doris Dörrie
GEORGIA   Ulu Grosbard

CRY THE BELOVED COUNTRY   Darrell James Roodt
LAMERICA   Gianni Amelio
SHANGHAI TRIAD   Zhang Yimou

1996

GAZON MAUDIT (FRENCH TWIST)   Josiane Balasko
THE WHITE BALLOON   Jafar Panahi
ANGELS AND INSECTS   Philip Haas
ANNE FRANK REMEMBERED   Jon Blair
THE FLOWER OF MY SECRET   Pedro Almodóvar
LAND AND FREEDOM   Ken Loach
THE CELLULOID CLOSET   Rob Epstein and Jeffrey Friedman
DENISE CALLS UP   Hal Salwen
NELLY AND MONSIEUR ARNAUD   Claude Sautet
MA SAISON PRÉFÉRÉE   André Téchiné
WALLACE AND GROMIT   Nick Park
I SHOT ANDY WARHOL   Mary Harron
SOMEONE ELSE'S AMERICA   Goran Paskeljevic
LONE STAR   John Sayles
MAGIC HUNTER   Iidiko Enyedi
WALKING AND TALKING   Nicole Holofcener
MANNY AND LO   Lisa Krueger
RENDEZVOUS IN PARIS   Eric Rohmer
KANSAS CITY   Robert Altman
MABOROSI   Hirokazu Koreeda
BIG NIGHT   Stanley Tucci and Campbell Scott
SECRETS AND LIES   Mike Leigh
BEAUTIFUL THING   Hettie MacDonald
THREE LIVES AND ONLY ONE DEATH   Raúl Ruiz
LOOKING FOR RICHARD   Al Pacino
THE GARDEN OF THE FINZI-CONTINIS (Reissue)
   Vittorio de Sica

SLING BLADE   Billy Bob Thornton
LE RIDICULE   Patrice Leconte
LA CEREMONIE   Claude Chabrol
LES VOLEURS   André Téchiné

1997

KOLYA   Jan Severak
PRISONER OF THE MOUNTAIN   Sergei Bodrov
SUBURBIA   Richard Linklater
THE DAYTRIPPERS   Greg Mottola
THE EIGHTH DAY   Jaco Van Dormael
A MONGOLIAN TALE   Xie Fei
FLAMENCO   Carlos Saura
DIARY OF A SEDUCER   Danièle Dubroux
LA PROMESSE   Luc and Jean-Pierre Dardenne
THE PILLOW BOOK   Peter Greenaway
TEMPTRESS MOON   Chen Kaige
WHEN THE CAT'S AWAY   Cédric Klapisch
GABBEH   Mohsen Mahkmalbaf
SHALL WE DANCE?   Masayuki Suo
GUANTANAMARA   Tomás Gutiérrez Alea and Juan Carlos Tabio
IN THE COMPANY OF MEN   Neil LaBute
LOVE SERENADE   Shirley Barrett
MON HOMME   Bertrand Blier
THE FULL MONTY   Peter Gattaneo
A SELF-MADE HERO   Jacques Audiard
THE ICE STORM   Ang Lee
UNDERGROUND   Emir Kusturica
TELLING LIVES IN AMERICA   Guy Ferland
BEAUMARCHAIS   Edouard Molinaro
KISS OR KILL   Bill Bennett
THE SWEET HEREAFTER   Atom Egoyan

MA VIE EN ROSE   Alain Berliner
OSCAR AND LUCINDA   Gillian Armstrong

1998

LIVE FLESH   Pedro Almodóvar
THE DRESS   Alex Van Warmerdam
FOUR DAYS IN SEPTEMBER   Burno Barreto
THE APOSTLE   Robert Duvall
MRS. DALLOWAY   Marleen Gorris
MEN WITH GUNS   John Sayles
LOVE AND DEATH ON LONG ISLAND   Richard Kwietniowski
POST COITUM   Brigitte Roüan
A TASTE OF CHERRY   Abbas Kiarostami
THE SPANISH PRISONER   David Mamet
WILD MAN BLUES   Barbara Kopple
TWENTY FOUR SEVEN   Shane Meadows
MARIUS AND JEANNETTE   Robert Guédiguian
A FRIEND OF THE DECEASED   Vyacheslav Krishtofovich
SHOOTING FISH   Stefan Schwartz
THE HANGING GARDEN   Thom Fitzgerald
CHINESE BOX   Wayne Wang
THE LAST DAYS OF DISCO   Whit Stillman
INSOMNIA   Erick Skjoldbjærg
BEYOND SILENCE   Caroline Link
COUSIN BETTE   Des McAnuff
UN AIR DE FAMILLE   Cédric Klapisch
HENRY FOOL   Hal Hartley
BUFFALO '66   Vincent Gallo
NIGHTS OF CABIRIA (Restored Version: Reissue)   Federico Fellini
THE THIEF   Pavel Chukhrai
WESTERN   Manuel Poirier
GADJO DILO   Tony Gatlif

REGENERATION   Gillies Mackinnon
YOUR FRIENDS AND NEIGHBORS   Neil Labute
THE EEL   Shohei Imamura
A MERRY WAR   Robert Bierman
LOLITA   Adrian Lyne
SLAM   Marc Levin
THE CELEBRATION   Thomas Vinterberg
THE INHERITORS   Stefan Ruzowitzky
HAPPINESS   Todd Solondz
GODS AND MONSTERS   Bill Condon
DANCING AT LUGHNASA   Pat O'Connor
CENTRAL STATION   Walter Salles
LITTLE VOICE   Mark Herman
THE GENERAL   John Boorman
HILARY AND JACKIE   Anand Tucker
AFFLICTION   Paul Schrader

1999

THE SWINDLE   Claude Chabrol
THE HARMONISTS   Joseph Vilsmaier
DR. AKAGI   Shohei Imamura
MY NAME IS JOE   Ken Loach
CHILDREN OF HEAVEN   Majid Majidi
TANGO   Carlos Saura
THE APPLE   Samira Makhmalbaf
THE SCHOOL OF FLESH   Benoit Jacquot
COOKIE'S FORTUNE   Robert Altman
DREAMLIFE OF ANGELS   Erick Zonca
LOVERS OF THE ARCTIC CIRCLE   Julio Medem
NÔ   Robert Lepage
THE WINSLOW BOY   David Mamet
THREE SEASONS   Tony Bui

ENDURANCE   Leslie Woodhead
ETERNITY AND A DAY   Theo Angelopoulos
AFTER LIFE   Hirokazu Koreeda
THE RED VIOLIN   François Girard
RUN LOLA RUN   Tom Tykwer
RED DWARF   Yvan Le Moine
BUENA VISTA SOCIAL CLUB   Wim Wenders
MY SON THE FANATIC   Udayan Prasad
AUTUMN TALE   Eric Rohmer
ROSIE   Patrice Toye
CABARET BALKAN   Goran Paskaljevic
TWIN FALLS IDAHO   Michael and Mark Polish
GRAND ILLUSION (Restored Version: Reissue)   Jean Renoir
MARCELLO MASTROIANNI: I REMEMBER   Anna Maria Tato
BLACK CAT, WHITE CAT   Emir Kusturica
EARTH   Deepa Mehta
LUCIE AUBRAC   Claude Berri
BOYS DON'T CRY   Kimberly Peirce
L'ENNUI   Cédric Kahn
SAME OLD SONG   Alain Resnais
LAST NIGHT   Don McKellar
FELICIA'S JOURNEY   Atom Egoyan
ROSETTA   Luc and Jean-Pierre Dardenne
ALL ABOUT MY MOTHER   Pedro Almodóvar
SWEET AND LOWDOWN   Woody Allen
THE EMPEROR AND THE ASSASSIN   Chen Kaige
THE THIRD MIRACLE   Agnieszka Holland
MR. DEATH   Errol Morris

2000

TITUS   Julie Taymor
HOLY SMOKE   Jane Campion

LIFE IS TO WHISTLE   Fernando Pérez

THE CUP   Khyentse Norbu

THE STRAIGHT STORY   David Lynch

REAR WINDOW   Alfred Hitchcock

NOT ONE LESS   Zhang Yimou

MIFUNE   Søren Kragh-Jacobsen

THE CLOSER YOU GET   Aileen Ritchie

WINTER SLEEPERS   Tom Tykwer

THE COLOR OF PARADISE   Majid Majidi

BEAU TRAVAIL   Claire Denis

JOE GOULD'S SECRET   Stanley Tucci

ME MYSELF I   Pip Karmel

EAST IS EAST   Damien O'Donnell

BOSSA NOVA   Bruno Barreto

THE IDIOTS   Lars von Trier

UP AT THE VILLA   Philip Haas

CROUPIER   Mike Hodges

HAMLET   Michael Almereyda

THE DISCREET CHARM OF THE BOURGEOISIE (Reissue)
    Luis Buñuel

KIKUJIRO   Takeshi Kitano

EAST/WEST (Move-over)   Régis Wargnier

THE DECALOGUE   Krzysztof Kie lowski

TIME REGAINED   Raúl Ruiz

BLOOD SIMPLE (Reissue)   Joel and Ethan Coen

SHOWER   Zhang Yang

THE FIVE SENSES   Jeremy Podeswa

ALICE AND MARTIN   André Téchiné

THE WIND WILL CARRY US   Abbas Kiarostami

THE TAO OF STEVE   Jenniphr Goodman

AN AFFAIR OF LOVE   Frédéric Fonteyne

RIFIFI (Reissue)   Jules Dassin

ORFEU   Carlos Diegues

AIMÉE AND JAGUAR   Max Farberbock
SOLAS   Benito Zambrano
GOYA IN BORDEAUX   Carlos Saura
DANCER IN THE DARK   Lars von Trier
TABOO   Nagisa Oshima
RATCATCHER   Lynne Ramsay
CALLE 54   Fernando Trueba
A ROOM FOR ROMEO BRASS   Shane Meadows
GEORGE WASHINGTON   David Gordon Green
KIPPUR   Amos Gitai
BOESMAN AND LENA   John Berry
A TIME FOR DRUNKEN HORSES   Bahman Ghobadi
QUILLS   Philip Kaufman
YI YI (Move-over)   Edward Yang
CROUCHING TIGER, HIDDEN DRAGON   Ang Lee
POLLOCK   Ed Harris
BEFORE NIGHT FALLS   Julian Schnabel
STATE AND MAIN   David Mamet
CHUNHYANG   Im Kwon-taek

2001

FAITHLESS   Liv Ullmann
IN THE MOOD FOR LOVE   Wong Kar-wai
THE TASTE OF OTHERS   Angès Jaoui
ME YOU THEM   Andrucha Waddington
MEMENTO   Christopher Nolan
AMORES PERROS   Alejandro Iñárritu
SMELL OF CAMPHOR, FRAGRANCE OF JASMINE
    Bahman Farmanara
THE CIRCLE   Jafar Panahi
WITH A FRIEND LIKE HARRY   Dominik Moll
UNDER THE SAND   François Ozon

THE KING IS ALIVE   Kristian Levring
FAST FOOD, FAST WOMEN   Amos Kollek
THE ROAD HOME   Zhang Yimou
DIVIDED WE FALL   Jan Hřebejk
SEXY BEAST   Jonathan Glazer
THE PRINCESS AND THE WARRIOR   Tom Tykwer
EVERYBODY'S FAMOUS   Dominique Deruddere
LOST AND DELIRIOUS   Léa Pool
THAT OBSCURE OBJECT OF DESIRE (Reissue)
   Luis Buñuel
GHOST WORLD   Terry Zwigoff
HEDWIG AND THE ANGRY INCH   John Cameron Mitchell
UNDER THE SUN   Colin Nutley
INNOCENCE   Paul Cox
FIGHTER   Amir Bar-Lev
TURANDOT PROJECT   Allan Miller
TOGETHER   Lukas Moodysson
L.I.E.   Michael Cuesta
OUR LADY OF THE ASSASSINS   Barbet Schroeder
LIAM   Stephen Frears
VA SAVOIR   Jacques Rivette
MULHOLLAND DRIVE   David Lynch
FAT GIRL   Catherine Breillat
SOBIBÓR, OCTOBER 14, 1943: 4:00 P.M.   Claude Lanzmann
WAKING LIFE   Richard Linklater
THE TOWN IS QUIET   Robert Guédiguian
TAPE   Richard Linklater
THE DEVIL'S BACKBONE   Guillermo del Toro
IN THE BEDROOM   Todd Field
NO MAN'S LAND   Danis Tanovic
THE BUSINESS OF STRANGERS   Patrick Stettner
BARAN   Majid Majidi
KANDAHAR   Moshen Makhmalbaf

LANTANA   Ray Lawrence
DARK BLUE WORLD   Jan Sverák

2002

MONSTER'S BALL   Marc Forster
WHAT TIME IS IT THERE?   Tsai Ming-liang
ITALIAN FOR BEGINNERS   Lone Scherfig
STORYTELLING   Todd Solondz
BEIJING BICYCLE   Wang Xiaoshuai
THE SON'S ROOM   Nanni Moretti
LAST ORDERS   Fred Schepisi
PAULINE AND PAULETTE   Lieven Debrauwer
Y TU MAMÁ TAMBIÉN   Alfonso Cuarón
TIME OUT   Laurent Cantet
LES DESTINÉES SENTIMENTALES   Olivier Assayas
THE KOMEDIANT   Arnon Goldfinger
HUMAN NATURE   Michel Gondry
MURDEROUS MAIDS   Jean-Pierre Denis
NINE QUEENS   Fabián Bielinsky
SADE   Benoît Jacquot
WARM WATER UNDER A RED BRIDGE   Sh hei Imamura
BARAN (RETURN)   Majid Majidi
THE LADY AND THE DUKE   Éric Rohmer
THE BELIEVER   Henry Bean
LATE MARRIAGE   Dover Kosashvili
13 COVERSATIONS ABOUT ONE THING   Jill Sprecher
CHERISH   Finn Taylor
THE FAST RUNNER   Zacharias Kunuk
SUNSHINE STATE   John Sayles
A SONG FOR MARTIN   Bille August
MY WIFE IS AN ACTRESS   Yvan Attal
TADPOLE   Gary Winick

THE KID STAYS IN THE PICTURE   Brett Morgen and
    Nanette Burstein
HAPPY TIME   Zhang Yimou
THE CHÂTEAU   Jesse Peretz
THE DECALOGUE (Revival)   Krzysztof Keiślowski
HOW I KILLED MY FATHER   Anne Fontaine
THE LAST KISS   Gabriele Muccino
IN PRAISE OF LOVE   Jean-Luc Godard
ALIAS BETTY   Claude Miller
QUITTING   Zhang Yang
8 WOMEN   François Ozon
HEAVEN   Tom Tykwer
BOWLING FOR COLUMBINE   Michael Moore
AUTO FOCUS   Paul Schrader
REAL WOMEN HAVE CURVES   Patricia Cardoso
ALL OR NOTHING   Mike Leigh
FAR FROM HEAVEN   Todd Haynes
THE CRIME OF FATHER AMARO   Carlos Carrera
TALK TO HER   Pedro Almodóvar
RUSSIAN ARK   Alexander Sokurov
NICHOLAS NICKLEBY   Douglas McGrath

2003

THE SON   Jean-Pierre and Luc Dardenne
BLIND SPOT—HITLER'S SECRETARY
    Othmar Schmiderer
CHAOS   Coline Serreau
LOST IN LA MANCHA   Keith Fulton and Louis Pepe
CHI-HWA-SEON   Im Kwon-teak
OPEN HEARTS   Susanne Bier
LAUREL CANYON   Lisa Cholodenko
NOWHERE IN AFRICA   Caroline Link

BEND IT LIKE BECKHAM   Gurinder Chadha
UNDER THE SKIN OF THE CITY   Rakhshan Bani-Etemad
CET AMOUR-LÀ   Josée Dayan
THE MAN WITHOUT A PAST   Aki Kaurismäki
LILYA 4 EVER   Lukas Moodysson
MAROONED IN IRAQ   Bahman Ghobadi
THE DANCER UPSTAIRS   John Malkovich
L'AUBERGE ESPAGNOLE   Cédric Klapisch
SWEET SIXTEEN   Ken Loach
RESPIRO   Emanuele Crialese
TOGETHER   Chen Kaige
CAPTURING THE FRIEDMANS   Andrew Jarecki
WHALE RIDER   Niki Caro
TYCOON   Pavel Lounguine
SWIMMING POOL   François Ozon
THE CUCKOO   Alexander Rogozhkin
THE HOUSEKEEPER   Claude Berri
CAMP   Todd Graff
THE MAGDALENE SISTERS   Peter Mullan
AMERICAN SPLENDOR   Shari Berman and Robert Pulcini
AUTUMN SPRING   Vladimir Michalek
TAKING SIDES   István Szabó
DEMONLOVER   Olivier Assayas
TO BE AND TO HAVE   Nicholas Philibert
MY LIFE WITHOUT ME   Isabel Coixet
THE STATION AGENT   Tom McCarthy
THE FLOWER OF EVIL   Claude Chabrol
SYLVIA   Christine Jeffs
ELEPHANT   Gus Van Sant
THE BARBARIAN INVASIONS   Denys Arcand
IN AMERICA   Jim Sheridan
THE TRIPLETS OF BELLEVILLE   Sylvan Chomet
GIRL WITH PEARL EARRING   Peter Webber

THE STATEMENT   Norman Jewison
THE FOG OF WAR   Errol Morris

2004

BAD EDUCATION   Pedro Almodóvar
BROKEN WINGS   Nir Bergman
CONTROL ROOM (Move-over)   Jehane Noujaim
CRIMSON GOLD   Jafar Panahi
DOGVILLE   Lars von Trier
FACING WINDOWS   Ferzan Özpetek
FAHRENHEIT 9/11   Michael Moore
GOODBYE, LENIN!   Wolfgang Becker
HOUSE OF FLYING DAGGERS   Zhang Yimou
I'M NOT SCARED   Gabriele Salvatores
INTIMATE STRANGERS   Patrice Leconte
IT'S EASIER FOR A CAMEL   Valeria Bruni Tedeschi
KINSEY   Bill Condon
KITCHEN STORIES   Bent Hamer
MARIA FULL OF GRACE   Joshua Marston
MOOLAADÉ   Ousame Sembène
MY ARCHITECT   Nathaniel Kahn
OASIS   Lee Chang-dong
OSAMA   Siddiq Barmak
RECONSTRUCTION   Christoffer Boe
RED LIGHTS   Cédric Kahn
ROSENSTRASSE   Margarethe von Trotta
SIDEWAYS   Alexander Payne
SINCE OTAR LEFT   Julie Bertuccelli
SPINGTIME IN A SMALL TOWN   Tian Zhuangzhuang
SPRING, SUMMER, FALL, WINTER, SPRING   Kim Ki-duk
STRAYED   André Téchiné
THE AGRONOMIST   Jonathan Demme

THE MERCHANT OF VENICE   Michael Radford

THE MOTHER   Roger Michell

THE MOTORCYCLE DIARIES   Walter Salles

THE RETURN   Andrei Zvyagintsev

THE STORY OF THE WEEPING CAMEL
    Byambasuren Davaa andLuigi Falorni

TOUCHING THE VOID   Kevin Macdonald

VODKA LEMON   Hiner Saleem

WILBUR WANTS TO KILL HIMSELF   Lone Scherfig

YOUNG ADAM   David Mackenzie

ZATÔICHI, THE BLIND SWORDSMAN   Takeshi Kitano

ŽELARY   Ondřej Trojan

ZHOU YU'S TRAIN   Sun Zhou

2005

NOBODY KNOWS   Hirokazo Koreeda

LOST EMBRACE   Daniel Burman

MY MOTHER'S SMILE   Marco Bellocchio

TURTLES CAN FLY   Bahman Ghobadi

UP AND DOWN   Jan Hřebejk

INTIMATE STORIES   Carlos Sorin

MELINDA AND MELINDA   Woody Allen

NINA'S TRAGEDIES   Savi Gabison

KONTROLL   Nimród Antal

LOOK AT ME   Agnès Jaoui

ENRON: THE SMARTEST GUYS IN THE ROOM
    Alex Gibney

3 IRON   Kim Ki-duk

THE HOLY GIRL   Lucrecia Martel

BROTHERS   Susanne Bier

KINGS AND QUEEN   Arnaud Desplechin

TELL THEM WHO YOU ARE   Mark S. Wexler

SEQUINS   Éléonore Faucher

5 × 2   François Ozon

MY SUMMER OF LOVE   Pawel Pawlikowski

MARCH OF THE PENGUINS   Luc Jacquet

THE BEAT THAT MY HEART SKIPPED   Jacques Audiard

SARABAND   Ingmar Bergman

JUNEBUG   Phil Morrison

RITTENHOUSE SQUARE   Robert Downey

2046   Wong Kar-wai

GRIZZLY MAN   Werner Herzog

THE EDUKATORS   Hans Weingartner

THE MEMORY OF A KILLER   Erik Van Looy

THE WEEPING MEADOW   Theo Angelopoulos

CAPOTE   Bennett Miller

THE SQUID AND THE WHALE   Noah Baumbach

USHPIZIN   Gidi Dar

PROTOCOLS OF ZION   Marc Levin

PARADISE NOW   Hany Abu-Assad

THE PASSENGER (Reissue)   Michelangelo Antonioni

BREAKFAST ON PLUTO   Neil Jordan

MRS. HENDERSON PRESENTS   Stephen Frears

CACHÉ   Michael Haneke

GOOD NIGHT, AND GOOD LUCK (Move-over)
    George Clooney

2006

WHEN THE SEA RISES   Yolande Moreau and Gilles Porte

WHY WE FIGHT   Eugene Jarecki

MANDERLAY   Lars von Trier

DUCK SEASON   Fernando Eimbcke

TAKE MY EYES   Icíar Bollaín

DON'T COME KNOCKING   Wim Wenders

TSOTSI   Gavin Hood
THREE BURIALS OF MELQUIADES ESTRADA
    Tommy Lee Jones
L'ENFANT   Jean-Pierre and Luc Dardenne
IRON ISLAND   Mohammad Rasoulof
THE BEAUTY ACADEMY OF KABUL   Liz Mermin
THE NOTORIOUS BETTIE PAGE   Mary Harron
FREE ZONE   Amos Gitai
LOOK BOTH WAYS   Sarah Watt
SOMERSAULT   Cate Shortland
THREE TIMES   Hou Hsiao-hsien
CLEAN   Olivier Assayas
DOWN IN THE VALLEY   David Jacobson
BELLE DE JOUR(R)   Luis Buñuel
THE PROMISE   Chen Kaige
RUSSIAN DOLLS   Cédric Klapisch
SKETCHES OF FRANKGEHRY   Sydney Pollack
PULP FICTION (Reissue)   Quentin Tarantino
LEMMING   Dominik Moll
JACKIE BROWN (Reissue)   Quentin Tarantino
ART SCHOOL CONFIDENTIAL   Terry Zwigoff
THE HEART OF THE GAME   Ward Serrill
WORDPLAY   Patrick Creadon
THE ROAD TO GUANTÁNAMO   Michael Winterbottom and
    Mat Whitecross
A PRAIRIE HOME COMPANION   Robert Altman
WHO KILLED THE ELECTRIC CAR?   Chris Paine
HEADING SOUTH   Laurent Cantet
TIME TO LEAVE   François Ozon
EDMOND   Stuart Gordon (David Mamet screenplay)
GABRIELLE   Patrice Chéreau
SCOOP   Woody Allen

HALF NELSON   Ryan Fleck
THE HOUSE OF SAND   Andrucha Waddington
WOMEN ON THE VERGE OF A NERVOUS BREAKDOWN
   (Reissue)   Pedro Almodóvar
ALL ABOUT MY MOTHER (Reissue)   Pedro Almodóvar
FACTOTUM   Bent Hamer
QUINCEAÑERA   Richard Glatzer and Wash Westmoreland
RIDING ALONE FOR THOUSANDS OF MILES
   Zhang Yimou
TALK TO HER (Reissue)   Pedro Almodóvar
SHERRYBABY   Laurie Collyer
LE PETIT LIEUTENANT   Xavier Beauvois
FLOWER OF MY SECRET (Reissue)   Pedro Almodóvar
LIVE FLESH (Reissue)   Pedro Almodóvar
AL FRANKEN: GOD SPOKE   Nick Doob and Chris Hegedus
LAW OF DESIRE (Reissue)   Pedro Almodóvar
THE LAST KING OF SCOTLAND   Kevin Macdonald
THE QUEEN   Stephen Frears
MATADOR (Reissue)   Pedro Almodóvar
BAD EDUCATION (Reissue)   Pedro Almodóvar
INFAMOUS   Douglas McGrath
REQUIEM   Hans-Christian Schmid
ABSOLUTE WILSON   Katharina Otto-Bernstein
VOLVER   Pedro Almodóvar
FUR   Steven Shainberg
FAST FOOD NATION   Richard Linklater
THE HISTORY BOYS   Nicholas Hytner
FAMILY LAW   Daniel Burman
THE PAINTED VEIL   John Curran
VENUS   Roger Michell
PERFUME: THE STORY OF A MURDERER
   Tom Tykwer

2007

THE ITALIAN   Andrei Kravchuk
THE SITUATION   Philip Haas
MAFIOSO (Reissue)   Alberto Lattuada
THE LIVES OF OTHERS   Florian Henckel von Donnersmarck
OFFSIDE   Jafar Panahi
AVENUE MONTAIGNE   Danièle Thompson
DAYS OF GLORY   Rachid Bouchareb
CLOSE TO HOME   Dalia Hager and Vidi Bilu
THE WIND THAT SHAKES THE BARLEY   Ken Loach
AMAZING GRACE   Michael Apted
AFTER THE WEDDING   Susanne Bier
THE PAGE TURNER   Denis Dercourt
BLACK BOOK   Paul Verhoeven
PRIVATE FEARS IN PUBLIC PLACES   Alain Resnais
RED ROAD   Andrea Arnold
THE VALET   Francis Veber
JINDABYNE   Ray Lawrence
AWAY FROM HER   Sarah Polley
THE TREATMENT   Oren Rudavsky
BRAND UPON THE BRAIN!   Guy Maddin
GOLDEN DOOR   Emanuele Crialese
PRIVATE PROPERTY   Joachim Lafosse
ANGEL-A   Luc Besson
CRAZY LOVE   Dan Klores
BELLE TOUJOURS   Manoel de Oliveira
PIERREPONT—THE LAST HANGMAN   Adrian Shergold
GYPSY CARAVAN   Jasmine Dellal
LADY CHATTERLEY   Pascale Ferran
BROKEN ENGLISH   Zoe Cassavetes
THE REAL DIRT ON FARMER JOHN   Taggart Siegel
VITUS   Fredi Murer

RESCUE DAWN   Werner Herzog
MY BEST FRIEND   Patrice Leconte
INTERVIEW   Steve Buscemi
GOYA'S GHOSTS   Milos Forman
MOLIÈRE   Laurent Tirard
THE WILLOW TREE   Majid Majidi
2 DAYS IN PARIS   Julie Delpy
SUNFLOWER   Zhang Yang
THE 11TH HOUR   Nadia Conners and Leila Conners Petersen
EXILED   Johnnie To
SICKO (Move-over)   Michael Moore
NO END IN SIGHT (Move-over)   Charles Ferguson
THE BUBBLE   Eytan Fox
GREAT WORLD OF SOUND   Craig Zobel
LUST CAUTION   Ang Lee
MY KID COULD PAINT THAT   Amir Bar-Lev
THE GOOD NIGHT   Jake Paltrow
SLEUTH   Kenneth Branagh
TERROR'S ADVOCATE   Barbet Schroeder
RESERVATION ROAD   Terry George
WRISTCUTTERS: A LOVE STORY   Goran Duki[LATIN SMALL LETTER C WITH ACUTE]
JIMMY CARTER: MAN FROM PLAINS   Jonathan Demme
BEFORE THE DEVIL KNOWS YOU'RE DEAD   Sidney Lumet
DARFUR NOW   Ted Braun
WAR/DANCE   Sean Fine and Andrea Nix Fine
MARGOT AT THE WEDDING   Noah Baumbach
REDACTED   Brian De Palma
I'M NOT THERE   Todd Haynes
THE SAVAGES   Tamara Jenkins
THE BAND'S VISIT   Eran Kolirin
THE DIVING BELL AND THE BUTTERFLY
    Julian Schnabel

NO COUNTRY FOR OLD MEN (Move-over)
  Joel and Ethan Coen
PERSEPOLIS   Marjane Satrapi and Vincent Paronnaud

Guest Book/Sample Pages

IF YOU WISH TO BE NOTIFIED
OF OUR FORTHCOMING PROGRAMS
PLEASE LEAVE YOUR NAME AND
ADDRESS ...
DO NOT HESITATE TO SUGEST
PICTURES YOU WOULD LIKE TO SEE.

14

ROBERT LOEFFLER
11 PAYSON AVE
NEW·YORK 34, N.Y

JACK ROSEN
622 E·20 ST.
N.Y. 9 N.Y.

Lillian CHARNES
440 WEST END AVE
N.Y. 24 N.Y.

Mrs Betty Cutler
545 West End Ave
N·24 Cuy

Susan Sontag
350 West End Ave.
NY 24

→ { Queen Christina (Ga
{ Zero de Conduite (V
{ Germany Year Zero (Ros

LES ADAMS
640 E. 6TH ST.
APT 25
New York 9, N.Y.

A. LEAR
43-08 40th St.
Sunnyside 4, N.Y.
George Gority   118 E 88

Al Kap
3722-48 W. 189 St.
BOSTON MASS.

Evelyn Brody   30 West 90 St

We would like to see "Heaven can wait"

with Don Amache & June Tierney

and all Alee prisons pictures
          Thank you

Name & Address

Remo Cosentino - 1573 38th St., Bklyn

Avalon + Paul Kato — 314 E. 2nd St. N.

KRISTNE

(William Metro)
31 W. 87th St.
N.Y.C.

Mrs. Helen Hacker
29 West 88 Street
N Y C

Joseph Wesly
375 Riverside Drive
New York 25 N. Y.

Pictures   I would like to see

our theatre great idea! But: screen has a hole
too wide for most pre-cinemascope films.
Not only the "classics" but current good
European films that other distributors
don't show: La Terra Trema – Visconti ✓
I'll think of more when I come to
see shoe shine! READ Sight & Sound

Eliza WIDICAN
154 W. 88 St

Monsieur Verdoux

DITTO The above criticism of
the wide screen

Paragon Place
Lollie Lundy
Mrs Joseph B Cohn
255 West 84 St
70, NY

28

Name & Address →

Paul Ledwig
145 Fort Washington Ave,
N.Y.C. 32

Joseph Lebo, 145 West 88,
NYC 24

William Shakespeare Stratford on Avon
Eng

Bring back the old screen

Please make screen wider!

So that we can see a complete
image

The great Dictator by Chaplin
Wedding and Babies by Morris Engel
Dieu a besoin des hommes by Jean Delannoy

Faust D. Polliaino
315 West 107 Street-

Pictures Darrell Crocker

The Blue Angel / Fury
City Lights Best Years
Great Dictator of our Lives
The Westerner The Little Foxes
The Breaking Point Long Voyage Home (complete)
The Proud Rebel Citizen Kane

Mailing list — Pierre Laguirat
442 East 20 St
NYC. 9. n.y.

Romeo & Juliet (Laurence Harvey)
Julius Caesar (Marlon Brando)
requested by J. Imagin
666 5th avenue

J. Neill
177 W 58 St. N.Y.C.

"MONSIEUR VERDOUX"
Ditto

34

Augustus Pigman
527 West 121 st.
N Y City 27
also
Walden School 1 West 88

Jim Scott
161 East 90 St.
N. Y. C. 32

Ingemar Bergman films!!
chaplin Films!
Bernice L. Cornyetz
225 W 86th St.
N. Y. 24 N. Y

Agnes C. Benjamin
120 Convent Avenue
New York 27, N. Y

35

Victor Seastrom Swedish & American Films
Hans Richter — Viking Eggeling
"The Last Laugh", "Joyless Street", "Sunrise"
"Hallelujah"

Phillys. Lopate 636 Brooklyn Ave, Brooklyn 3,
Mailing List   New York

Young Mr. Lincoln
Grapes of Wrath   Johnny
Le Million   Belinda

Possessed with Joan Crawford
and Clark Gable.
Jean Schliasel,
    214 W 91 St.

Intermezzo with Leslie Howard.
Sophie Weinstein
    214 W 91 St.

400 Blows!

Name & Address →

melvin Klotz
Otto Frurd

Robert Senkewicz 446 W 26 St.

Simon Flinn   382 East 10 St   NYC
JAMES E. NAGEL 138 W. 91 st

— R. E. Walker III - 124 W 75 th St

CHANGE
SCREEN
RATIO
DAMN IT!

Pictures I would like to see

The   Letter to Three Wives

Hamlet

Queen of Spades

Brgelowis Stenonski

80

Ibid.

81

List #2:

ORDET — The Bakers Wife — LIMELIGHT!
— City lights — M. Verdoux —
Vitelloni — Amici Per La Pelle — Sunset Blvd
The Childhood of Maxim Gorky —
Les Mistons — NY, NY — African Queen
— TREASURE OF Sierra Madre — Asphalt Jungle
— Touch of Evil — Tuesday Brown — VIGO!
— (+ Bravo for Henry V's statement above).

NOT STARTING TIMES IN NEWSPAPER AD?

W. C. Thomaier   185 HAMILTON AVE.   FAIRVIEW N.J.

       Like See :   ZERO DU CONDUITÉ
                     VAMPYR (REMARKABLY GOOD PRINT)
                     LOUISIANA STORY
                     LES MISTONS
                     PABST'S Three Penny Opera
                     EARTH
                     HUSTON'S LET THERE BE
                                        LIGHT
                     FARREBIQUE
                     CLOUZOT'S The RAVEN

Congratulations for showing
      "Day of Wrath" by
         one of the few
         great directors. Carl Dreyer.

ROBERT CATO / Emily Garbo
502 E 84
NY 28

VALERIE ALDRICH / BRIEF ENCOUNTER
25 RIDGE ST. APT 4D / ALEXANDER NEVSKY
N.Y. 2, N.Y. / ROMEO & JULIET (BOLSHOI BALLE
TEN DAYS THAT SHOOK THE WOR

BORIS GODUNOV
EUGENE ONEGIN

Marlon Brando in "Gone with the Wind" YEAH.

ROBERT GLATZER
600 WEST END AVE
NY 24
1. The Great Dictator
2. Program of unusual or exce
shorts.
3. Correct screen ratio, please

Foreign, old + new. Please ignore the big, flashy American films. The other places will take care of that. Give us films from abroad. We read about all the exciting things that happen there in films, but so rarely / see for ourselves.
Bergman, too, let's have plenty of Bergman

last angry man   either version of
Jeanne d'Arc   Joan of Arc   "SHADDOWS"

NUTS TO BERGMAN LET THE FLASHY ART
PLACES TAKE CARE OF THAT TOO.
        The Vigo films — L'ATALANTE, ZERO DE
                            CONDUITE, RIVIERA —
NANCY BELLAMY   200 WEST 107 ST.
            and   "ORDET"

Dufman   414 W 120th St — Send Program

    Chaplin, Eisenstein + some
of the new Polish films.

    Especially by Chaplin:
            Monsieur Verdoux, The Dictator
+ King in N.Y.

NAME & ADDRESS →

LEONARD LOPATE
636 BROOKLYN AVE
BROOKLYN 3, N.Y.

Mrs. Ce Bongartz, 310 W. 99 St., Apt. 805., N.Y.C. 25, N.

G. NELSON
57 W. 82.

Robert Silverberg   915 West End Ave NY X

Alfred Trachtenberg   10 W 93rd ST NY 25

RICHARD GORR
18 W 76th St   NYC 23

PICTURES I
WOULD LIKE TO SEE

"AGE D'OR" ANGERS "FIREWORK"
...TER + EGGELING FILMS, SEASTROM
...MS (WIND), "GREED," "ASPHALT"
...ST LAUGH," JOYLESS STREET"
...ty 'Light   chaplin FILM
... FALL OF THE HOUSE OF USHER
...+ DEATH OF A HOLLYWOODERAN"
...EL'S "CRIMINAL LIFE OF ARCHIBALDO
...A CRUZ", "SUPRIZE", + FRITZ
...'S MASTERPIEZES "CHILDREN
...HIROSHIMA" 'HIROSHIMA MON AMOR"
...s General"

...van Sale

...e Angel (Detrich version)
...venture for Two" - Laurence Olivier
...ie Angel (Dietrich version) + flunk
...e bookmark)
...Blue Angel (Dietrich)
...UT CUT SOME PICTURES FROM
...E MOVIE YOU ARE PLAYING,
... ENABLE YOUR CUSTOMERS
... RECOGNIZE WHETHER THEY
...AVE SEEN THE PICTURE
...he Death Parade 1934
...e Little Flower Girl
...y Dssica 1940

...Queen of the Jungle 1933

PLEASE LEAVE THIS
COLUMN BLANK FOR
MANAGEMENT'S RESPONSE

Swan Lake

A master list of films.

We'll try our best.

This film stinks.
Blue Angel is great.

OK.

?

120

Ibid.   I continue to be very grateful for your programs. I would be even more grateful if you could list starting times in your ads. Some further suggestions — Ace In The Hole, French version of Mon Oncle, Together, Man Escaped, Lovers + Lollipops, Renoir's The River, Cocteau's Orpheus, Fear + Desire; films by Val Lewton.

I renew my requests, as expressed in a letter which I thank you for answering, for La Terra Trema if you can get it, for the Pabst 3 Penny Opera, for L'Atalante, for Satyajit Ray — if not #3 in the trilogy, then #1 and #2 TOGETHER

For your mailing list:
    Mr & Mrs. E. L. Friedman
    650 W. 172 St. N.Y. 32, N.Y.

M. Verdoux, Gold Rush.
Theresa, Black Narcissus

Thanx for the great shows — How about a rerun of Disney's Fantasia
Please put my name on the mailing list:
    Merilee Oakes
    898 Helen St.
    Teaneck, N.J.

121

A. P. Hayna 4, Gertrude St. Hempstead N.Y.
Bravissimo!

M. Jorrin 88 East First St. NYC

THE RED BADGE
OF
COURAGE

~~David Keillor~~   Four D Man
                          Sink The Bon Man

Vic Ziegel - 675 Walton Ave. NY 51

BRING BACK FELLINI'S "THE WHITE SHIEK"

                          East of
                              Eden

Suggest "Salt of the Earth"
Hugh _____
_____ Crew

Bill together remakes + originals, e.g.
Dietrich's + Britt's Blue Angel
Chaney + Laughton's Hunchback
The McHex Italian Versions of Postman
Always Rings Twice

J _____
68 Stuart St. Lynbrook, N.Y.

"Flesh" by John Ford starring
Wallace Beery   1932

Garbo and Hepburn anything

Devil in the Flesh (Original version)
No more Daisy's, please

MORE W-C FIELDS ———!

Don't ever <u>show</u> anything like
     The Magnificent Ambersons!!!!

MORE PICTURES AS (GREAT) AS
"MAGNIFICENT AMBERSON"

The Original "SHADOWS"
Monsieur Verdoux

<u>Garbo</u> films

<u>Intolerance</u>
The Great Dictator
Modern Times

Modern Times

NAME and ADDRESS

J. GISTIRAK   54 E 1st St NYC 3
B. Epstein   Gate Hill Rd. Stony Pt.
   FROST   37 SPRING #15   NY

FILMS I WOULD LIKE TO SEE

PLEASE ALLOW THIS SPACE

BRING BACK POPCORN MACHINE!!

& THE GOLDEN" COACH (JEAN RENOIR

"The Cabinet of Dr Caligari
Any really good re-releases

NAME, ADDRESS, ZONE No. (PIEA
PRIN

Michael R. Widener   54 Riverside Drive NY
Charles A. Gretsch   593 2nd Ave. N.Y.

—

ANNE HELLEBUYCK
344 W 88 St. Apt 3 F

—

4/25

MONSIER VERDOUX   SUNSET BOULEVARD   THE SEARCH
MIRACLE AT MORGAN'S CREEK   FORBIDDEN GAMES
THE LITTLE FOXES   WUTHERING HEIGHTS
THE LADY EVE   HAIL THE CONQUERING HERO

DON LEHMEIER
65 PARK TERRACE WEST
N. Y. 34, N. Y.

F. G. LEHMEIER
515 EAST 88 ST.
N. Y., N. Y.

FILMS I WOULD LIKE TO SEE.

The "UNINVITED"
Nights of Cabiria."

FORBIDDEN GAMES
LOVERS & LOLIPOPS

YOUR CAMERA IS NOISY !!

The Bespoke Overcoat

The Dybbuk
The Golem

Please Print Clearly

Name	Address	Zone
Charley Chaplin	Mons. Verdoux and all the others	
W. Hooper	28 W 88th St.	Manhattan
J. Tharp	64 Thompson	NY 12 NY
Shanghai		

Who needs the Red rat — Chaplin?

I for one am not interested in his political life. I like his work as an performer. To me a movie house is to enrich art not to have a political discussion

Films I would like to see

Up in Arms
Wonder Boy
The Kid from Brooklyn ⎫ Danny
The Secret Life of Walter Mitty ⎭ Kaye

The original "Imitation of Life" - C. Colbert

Pinnochio
Snow White
Gulliver's Travels
Wizard of Oz
The Outlaw
Casablanca again (every 6 months)

Dreyer's Day of Wrath — Yes !!

Farewell to Arms with - Rock Hudson & Jennifer Jones

Sargeant York Gary Cooper

"We were Strangers" — John Garfield & Jennifer Jones

Please Print Clearly

Name   **Address**   **Zone**

Sigfried Krakauer

H. Meyer

And you, my friend, are a totally monumental moron!

and you are a totally monumental Communist

Cranes Are Flying was Monumental Junk, Trash, Claptrap!

Films I would like to see

~~Gervaise~~
~~The Last Bridge~~
~~S. Clay Trilogy~~ ✓✓ ✓✓
~~LOOK BACK IN ANGER~~
✗ ~~Renoir's "The River"~~
~~Umberto D~~
✗ ~~The Roof~~
~~Bambi~~
~~Ballad of a Soldier~~ ✓✓✓
~~"The man between" with James Mason and~~
~~Claire Bloom~~
✗ ~~Senator~~ ✓✓
~~Gate of Hell~~ ✓✓
~~Cabiria~~
~~Renoir's film on P/~~
~~H. Fellini~~ ✓✓
~~The Heiress~~
✗ ~~Renoir's films on Nazi Camps~~

~~The Left Hand of God~~
✗ ~~A King in New York~~

~~SCIENCE FRICTION~~
~~Hamlet~~

Uh (The) Girl in Black
~~Gentlemen's Agreement~~

Please Print Clearly

Name   **Address**   Zo

Films I would like to see

24 66

Some More MUSICALS
Please — Don't Be afraid
To show Two Musicals on one
Show. COMBINE THE 30's 40's
50's. And you Will not regret

How About Band Wagon &
                    FUNNY FACE
Probably Two of the Best.
            or
Guys & Dolls &
Porgy Bess   } My Show

        etc. ETC.

More Fred Astaire — Cyd charisse

Camilo Montaña   97 2ND Ave Apt 3
Fidel Montaña   "
Richard LASSLO   2124   31St 9/3

SKIN FLICKS

Jon Demme
Rockville Centre, L I

Films I would like to see

Surely only three:
"LAWRENCE OF ARABIA"
(with Peter O'toole)
Eisensteins "TEN DAYS THAT
SHOOK THE WORLD"
Orson Welles' "THE TRIAL"
— but express solid agreement
with others:
DEFINITELY LOWER (
PRICES!
(PLEASE!)

Simians

F.W. MURNAU FESTIVAL
TRIUMPH OF THE WILL

"Dodsworth" with Walter Huston
"Underworld" – Joseph Von Sternberg

The Exterminating Angel – Bunuel
Sansho the Bailiff – Mizoguchi

LET'S HAVE A LOOK AT
PECKINPAH'S "DEADLY COMPANIONS"
"DEADLY COMPANIONS"

Please Print Clearly

	Name	Address	Zo
u/2	Andrew Kull	140 W. 76	10023

Films I would like to see

Ray, Apu Trilogy   "M"
Chaplin   "Room at the Top"
"Intolerance"   "Les Cousins"

PUBLICATION OF FEATURE TIMES IN YOUR
NEWSPAPER ADVS IS MUCH APPRECIATED—
PLEASE CONTINUE IT WHERE POSSIBLE.

STILL HOPING TO SEE

     LE FEU FOLLET
     SANSHO THE BAILIFF

AND MANY THANKS FOR MURIEL AGAIN

L'AGE D'OR

EARLY RUSSIAN COMEDIES—
    ESP. OF BORIS BARNET
     (GIRL WITH A HAT BOX, etc.)

ROGOPAG

Le Feu Follet: for me
is it possible that is commercially
feasible to have
showings (perhaps
during the week) of
a SINGLE FILM
say, like MURIEL: so one
can look at
part again

Please Print Clearly

Name	Address	Z
John Neptune	25-39 44th St. LI.City 3, N.Y.	

Films I would like to see

Norma Shearer film festival

Gospel According to St. Mathew

Last Laugh

Katharine Hepburn Series

$1.75

Shit

Nelson Eddy - Jeanette McDonald series

Les Dimanches et Cybèle

ANNA MAGNANIS
Festival

Le Beau Serge

Variety

Joyless Street

Name   Address   Z

Films I would like to see

"Cyrano deBergerac"

"Drums"

"Four Feathers"

"Kim"

"Freud"

~~Monkey in the~~ Winter

"A Long Days Journey Into Night"

"Sandra"

All of W.C. Field's films.

How's about some happy stuff —
'The Thin Man' series

Dick Powell
Myrna Loy

A face in the Crowd

"Jesse James" Tyrone Power
Return of Jesse James

1/1/67

URGENT

SUGGESTION:

LET UP on the movies

THAT APPEAR HERE week

AFTER week AFTER week

E.G. — "CASABLANCA," "BIG SLEEP,"

MARX BROTHERS, W.C. FIELDS, ETC.

AD INFINITUM. THEY'RE GREAT —

DISCOUNT

BUT SO ARE A LOT OF OTHE[R]

movies WHICH YOU NEVE[R]

SHOW, most notably

"COME BACK, LITTLE S[...]

a Letter to 3 wives

Films I would like to see

Le Beau Serge

High Noon

Vera Cruz

Fury

Around the World in 80 Days

Sunset Blvd

Umbrellas Again!!

~~The Seven Magnificent~~

Monsieur Vincent

The Fire Within

a John Derek festival

Modern Times

The Great Dictator

anything by W.C. Fields

Please Print Clearly

Name   **Address**   Z

Kitty K.   EN·2-7360

1/14/67

Films I would like to see

Monkey in the Winter *"monkey in winter" you fool!*

FLAMES of PASSION

7 seven Magnificent

Some Came Running
Not as a Stranger

Order – "The Penny Arcade"
54 minute film
show at Finch College
Trestle + San Francisco first.
(Brandon Films Dist)

┌─────────────────────────┐
│ The room on the top   │ *"ROOM AT THE TOP", you IDIOT!*
└─────────────────────────┘

dr Pichard
400 E 77
NYC 10021

(Zorba the Greek)

A Letter to 5 Wives

Please Print Clearly

Name   Address   Z

Jack Fucks
11 5th Ave.
N.Y.C. , N.Y.

Woman in The Dunes

Jan 14 '67
Thank you for a lovely evening
Joan Baez

Films I would like to see

Gone with the Wind

The Horse's Mouth

Trader Horn

Bugs Bunny ~~Estato~~ Festival
Please!!

POSSIBLE

"THE MASK OF DEMITRIOS"

+

"4 FEATHERS"
WITH (CALPH RICHARDSON

Camille

Please Print Clearly

Name   Address   Z

Films I would like to see

Bergman — the seventh seal
Bergman Bergman Festival

Just more Mae!

Carnival in Flanders

Bringing Up Baby

Triumph of The Will

Films of Satyajit Ray

Welles — Touch of evil, Ambersons
Cairo (if comes back in circulation?)

Alexander Nevsky without Potemkin

The Fire Within   the Criminal
Therese   Chance Meeting
Muriel   Losey's "   "
South At Long distance

How About a
Prison Movie —
Gangster Movie
Double Feature

[from the 30's

James Cagney

Geor. Raft
R. Robinson,
Bogey
and all the other
swine

Frank Babary (6D)
4836 — 44-St,
Woodside, (Queens), N.Y, 11377

SHORTS

Pauline Kael, who you often quote in your newspaper and poster ads, has called Katharine Hepburn "the greatest actress of the sound era." Yet, you have never honored her with a festival and rarely show her films. I, personally, would love to see some of the rarely-seen, non-Tracy films such as "Bringing Up Baby" and "Holiday."

Ditto ↗

Chaplin films.
The new wave french films.

french films in color
also B+W
no good B+W

Italian films in Cinerama

Lithuania films in Cinemascope!!

Ledger from the New Yorker Theater

From March 7, 1960, to December 20, 1973, Dan Talbot kept a ledger (measuring 10 ½" x 13 ½"), noting every film shown at the New Yorker Theater. The following section shows sample pages from that ledger. After each title the distributor of the film is listed, followed by film rental, advertising cost, and daily gross. The entire ledger can be viewed on the Internet at www.cup.columbia.edu/talbot.

Of Special Interest

Ledger Page 2 (1960): The Yorktown Theater closes and the New Yorker Theater opens with Olivier's *Henry V* and Lamorisse's *The Red Balloon*.

Ledger Page 10 (1961): The first "Forgotten Film" series opens with Howard Hawks's *The Crowd Roars* and Robert Aldrich's *Kiss Me Deadly*.

Ledger Page 11 (1962): Cycle of D. W. Griffith's films begins with *Birth of a Nation* and continues with *Intolerance, Broken Blossoms, Way Down East,* and *Orphans of the Storm*.

Ledger Page 36 (1963): John Ford series opens with *The Informer* and *Rio Grande*.

Ledger Page 37 (1963): Science fiction series of SF films mostly from the 1950s opens with *The Fly* and *The Creeping Unknown*.

Ledger Page 44 (1964), bottom: Roy Export was Charlie Chaplin's agent who dealt with Dan and me on his films.

Ledger Page 45 (1964): One of the earliest Bogart retrospectives in the United States opens with *The Maltese Falcon* and *The Petrified Forest*.

Ledger Page 53 (1964–1965): *Henry Geldzahler* (in our "American Dada" cycle) is an early film by Andy Warhol during which its entire 90-minute length Geldzahler, then curator for the Metropolitan Museum of Art, smokes a cigar and cleans his eyeglasses.

Ledger Page 67 (1966): The first Premier Series opens with Claude Chabrol's *Les Bonnes Femmes* and Satyajit Ray's *The Music Room*.

Ledger Page 81 (1967): Godard retrospective opens with *Breathless* and *Masculin Féminin*.

Ledger Page 124 (1971): Rossellini retrospective opens with *Paisan* and *Open City*.

Ledger Page 130 (1972): Ozu's *Tokyo Story* begins eight-week run.

<u>1960</u>

			YORKTOWN THEATRE					
3/7	M.	Operation Petticoat	U-I	110.00		133.20		
3/8	Tu.	Girl's Town				126.85	260.05	
3/9	W.	Gate of Hell	Harrison	349.03		185.40		
3/10	Th.	The Medium	"			224.15		
3/11	F.					354.00		
3/12	Sa.					632.55	1396.10	
3/13	Su.	The Great Man				621.05		
3/14	M.	Face On The Crowd				210.45		
3/15	Tu.					205.80	1036.50	
3/16	W.	C L O S E D						
			NEW YORKER THEATRE					
3/17	Th.	Henry V	Lopert	1432.21		424.85		
3/18	F.	Red Balloon	Lopert	50.00		1053.89		
3/19	Sa.	Goya	Harrison	25.00		1973.06		
3/20	Su.					1831.77		
3/21	M.					596.81		
3/22	Tu.					588.57		
3/23	W.					574.98	7048.93	
3/24	Th.	Henry V	Lopert			405.16		
3/25	F.	Red Balloon	"			651.15		
3/26	Sa.					1146.06		
3/27	Su.					895.13		
3/28	M.					282.95		
3/29	Tu.					335.05		
3/30	W.					400.80	4116.30	
3/31	Th.	Day of Wrath	Brandon	799.87	479.99	308.68		
4/1	F.	Harvest	"	150.00		604.51		
4/2	Sa.	3rd Ave. El		57.50		1167.39		
4/3	Su.					758.05		
4/4	M.					233.75		
4/5	Tu.					350.91		
4/6	W.					326.19	3749.48	

1960

			F.R.	Adv.			
7 Th	Pull My Daisy	De Antonio	380.20	1195.29	477.17		1
2 F	Magnificent Ambersons	Principal	275.00	224.16	842.78		2
Se	Harlem Wednesday	Harrison	36.05		1156.89		3
Su					886.44		4
M					426.39		5
Tu					319.71		6
W					511.43	4620.81	7
							8
4 Th	Pull My Daisy	De Antonio	100.00	753.38	3488.38		9
5 F	Magnificent Ambersons	Principal	75.00	91.00	618.36		10
6 Se	Little Fugitive		51.50		961.59		11
7 Su	Fatal Glass of Beer	Union	20.00		611.74		12
M					312.74		13
Tu					309.80		14
W					262.50	3424.61	15
							16
Th	Shoeshine	Brandon	828.54	328.94	394.95		17
2 F	Strangers On a Train	W.B.	75.00		577.64		18
3 Sa	Neighbors		15.45		1157.00		19
4 Su					879.88		20
5 M					274.35		21
6 Tu					299.25		22
7 W					231.10	3814.15	23
							24
8 Th	Come Back Africa	Rogosin	400.00	699.89	358.93		25
9 F	My Own Yard To Play On	Harrison	50.00	286.34	639.09		26
0 Sa	Return To Glennascaul	Union	25.00		956.80		27
Su					1030.46		28
M					313.78		29
Tu					317.81		30
W					224.72		31
Th					167.68	4009.27	32
							33
F	Paths of Glory	U.A.	50.-	188.27	493.73		34
Sa	Touch of Evil	U.I.	50.-		965.29		35
Su	Fiddle-de-dee		12.36		1036.94		36
M					357.80	2853.76	37
							38
0 Tu	All About Eve	Fox	40.-	240.23	315.80		39
1 W	Treasure of Sierra Madre		40.-		375.35		40
Th					287.50		41
F					737.45	1716.10	42
Sa	Symphonie Pastorale		50.-	139.80	831.76		43
Su	Golden Age of Comedy		50.-		570.95		44
M	History of Cinema		25.-		190.00		45
Tu					272.15		46
W					283.08	2147.94	47

1961

#	Date	Day	Title	Distributor					
1	1/12	Th	Birth of a Nation (16m.)			400.-	87988	32863	
2	1/13	F	Cry of Jazz (16m)	DeCantonio		350.-		75943	
3	1/14	Sa.		tape —		743.-		140542	
4	1/15	Su						84902	
5	1/16	M	(9) FOOLISH WIVES	809.44				77925	
6	1/17	Tu.						41849	
7	1/18	W.						35228	434252
8	1/19	Th	Birth of a Nation (16m.)			250.-	28298	24441	
9	1/20	F	Cry of Jazz (16m.)			200.-		41165	
10	1/21	Sa						79873	
11	1/22	Su						65993	
12	1/23	M	(10) Nanook	790.38				230.-	
13	1/24	Tu						316.50	
14	1/25	W.						35421	301543
15			FORGOTTEN FILM, I						
16	1/26	Th	The Crowd Roars	U.A.A.		50.-	496.88	36382	
17			Kiss Me Deadly	U.A.		25.-	7262		
18	1/27	F	The Letter	U.A.A		50.-	2933	10508	
19			Outward Bound	U.A.A.		50.-			
20	1/28	Sa.	Strangers (Voyage To Italy)	U.M.Po		25.-		959.14	
21			Dawn Patrol	U.A.A.		50.-			
22	1/29	Su	Flirtation Walk	"		50.-		729.72	
23			Ceiling Zero	"		50.-			
24	1/30	M	Air Force	"		50.-		310.46	
25			Last Flight	"		50.-			
26	1/31	Th	Bringing Up Baby	Principal		25.-		726.79	
27			Thieves Highway	Fox		15.-			
28	2/1	W.	White Heat			20.-		292.14	
29	2/1		One Way Passage			50.-	550.-		443225
30	2/2	Th	Journey Into Fear	Principal		25.-	37346	493.40	
31			Tiger Shark			20.-			
32	2/3	F	French Can-Can	U.M.P.O.		20.-		62381	
33			Across The Pacific	U.A.A.		50.-			
34	2/4	Sa.	Europa '51			20.-		60797	
35			Five-Star Final	U.A.A.		50.-			
36	2/5	Su	Show of Shows	"		50.-		1012.14	
37			Two Seconds	"		50.-			
38	2/6	M	High Sierra			20.-		54684	
39			The Thing	Principal		15.-			
40	2/7	Tu	They Drive By Night			20.-		333.52	
41			H, Nellie	U.A.A.		50.-			
42	2/8	W.	Big Sleep			20.-		526.54	
43			Wagonmaster	Principal		15.-	435.-		414422

1961

Date	Title	Dist.				
9 Th.	Eye For An Eye	Ajay	150.–	573.88	330.55	
10 F.	I Meet Brendan Behan			70.–	508.62	
11 Sa.					965.79	
12 Su.					686.15	
13 M.					322.75	
14 Tu.					251.56	3065.42
15 W.	Anatahan		500.–	273.60	214.25	
16 Th.	Sins of Lola Montes		60.–		228.02	
17 F.					324.46	
18 Sa.					510.55	
19 Su.					494.26	
20 M.					184.69	1956.13
21 Tu.	Asphalt Jungle	MGM	1533.30	695.66	704.03	
22 W.	Julius Caesar	"			1009.30	
23 Th.					428.85	
24 F.					931.63	
25 Sa.					1278.–	
26 Su.					1051.73	
27 M.					342.44	5765.98
28 Tu.	Asphalt Jungle	"	103.–	53.50	289.55	
29 W.	Julius Caesar	"			327.47	617.02
30 Th.	An American in Paris	"	1902.87	53.29	557.94	
3 F.	Red Badge of Courage	"			1164.80	
4 Sa.					1840.50	
5 Su.					1605.79	
6 M.					440.10	
7 Tu.					507.20	
8 W.					389.41	6499.74
9 Th.			837.88	172.38	368.72	
10 F.					863.98	
11 Sa.					1531.19	
12 Su.					1152.25	
13 M.					307.27	4223.41
14 Tu.	Rules of the Game	Janus	463.50	431.83	438.36	
15 W.	None But the Lonely Heart	Principal	92.70		286.23	
16 Th.					279.22	
17 F.					530.94	
18 Sa.					944.49	
19 Su.					799.68	
20 M.					209.73	3493.65
21 Tu.				59.37	230.05	
22 W.					260.05	* 490.10

Date	Day	Title		Amt	Amt	Amount	Total
10/5	Th.	M		412.-	385.70	382.83	
10/6	F.	Key Largo				662.54	
10/7	St.					1008.42	
10/8	Su.					290.13	
10/9	M.					339.61	
10/10	Tu.					304.25	
10/11	W.					263.46	3691.24
10/12	Th.	Freaks (Col. Day)	Nillie Wenti	1140.-	448.11	724.94	
10/13	F.	Passage to Marseilles				894.42	
10/14	St.					1273.91	
10/15	Su.					989.36	
10/16	M.					429.76	
10/17	Tu.					430.46	
10/18	W.					372.93	5112.18
10/19	Th.	Double Indemnity	U-I	1500.-	1005.02	594.37	
10/20	F.	It's a Gift	"			1002.27	
10/21	St.					1374.27	
10/22	Su.					1177.81	
10/23	M.					479.50	
10/24	Tu.					448.20	
10/25	W.					328.26	5404.76
10/26	Th.	Horse Feathers	U-I	2546.44	431.15	864.49	
10/27	F.	I'm No Angel	"			1506.24	
10/28	St.					1880.73	
10/29	Su.					1590.27	
10/30	M.					732.65	
10/31	Tu.					813.15	
11/1	W.					668.35	8055.58
11/2	Th.	Horse Feathers	U-I	1000.-	399.77	402.31	
11/3	F.	I'm No Angel	"			702.32	
11/4	St.					1327.38	
11/5	Su.					929.06	
11/6	M.					445.2	
11/7	Tu.	(Election Day)				655.18	
11/8	W.					364.25	4775.82
11/9	Th.	Million Dollar Legs	U-I	2041.20	458.95	643.49	
11/10	F.	Desire	"			1165.82	
11/11	St.	(Armistice Day)				1893.95	
11/12	Su.					1325.64	
11/13	M.					521.40	
11/14	Tu.					531.58	
11/15	W.					468.38	6500.26

1961

Th.	A Day At The Races	MGM	1660.08	600.08	475.03		1
F.	Meet Me In St. Louis	"			1006.22		2
Sa.					1485.24		3
Su.					1385.25		4
M.					411.62		5
Tu.					457.32		6
W.					598.64	5849.44	7
							8
Th.	A Day At The Races	"	515.-	277.16	725.34		9
F.	Meet In St. Louis				823.57		10
Sa.					967.03		11
Su.					710.32		12
M.					299.72	3525.98	13
							14
Tu.	Devil Is A Woman	U-I	1508.03	480.58	494.98		15
W.	Trouble In Paradise	"			532.66		16
Th.					602.92		17
F.					1034.53		18
Sa.					1477.64		19
Su.					1274.63		20
M.					544.23	5962.59	21
							22
Tu.	Grand Hotel	MGM	1961.75	644.71	757.04		23
W.	At The Circus				687.88		24
Th.					694.05		25
F.					1362.57		26
Sa.					1863.41		27
Su.					1773.12		28
M.					554.84	7695.01	29
							30
Tu.	Grand Hotel	"	386.25	398.51	509.80		31
W.	At The Circus				370.37		32
Th.					324.-		33
F.					509.48		34
Sa.					978.28		35
Su.					885.05		36
M.					288.57	3965.95	37
Tu.			51.50	9684	278.03		38
W.					301.52	579.55	39
							40
							41
							42
							43
							44
							45
							46
							47

<u>1962</u>

Date	Title	Dist.				
7/17 Tu	The 400 Blows	Zenith	772 50	294 09	679 07	
7/18 W	Hiroshima, Mon Amour				639 31	
7/19 Th					481 42	
7/20 F					802 79	
7/21 Sa					1016 91	
7/22 Su					878 75	
7/23 M.mat	GRIFFITH CYCLE				67 30	
1 M.eve	Birth of a Nation (1)				1202 41	5767.96
7/24 Tu	Breakfast at Tiffany's	Par.	72 25	140 40	520 23	
7/25 W	Purple Noon	Times	51 50	242 06	574 88	
7/26 Th	Casque D'Or	F.Rep	25 75	242 73	393 90	
1 1	The Hustler	Fox	51 50		1	
7/27 F	Ninotchka	Allura	51 50		609 50	
7/28 Sa	Suspicion	RKO	25 75		804 87	
7/29 Su	Meet Me In St Louis	Allura	51 50		588 01	
7/30 M.mat	Hot Spell	Par.	36 05	370 80	36 85	
	M.eve Intolerance (2)				1525 52	4993.76
7/31 Tu	Stalag 17	Par.	51 50	249 96	540 55	
8/1 W	The Kitchen	Union	36 05		504 50	
8/2 Th	Too Late Blues	Par.	25 75		460 89	
1 1	To Have + Have Not	F.Rep	25 75		590 49	
8/3 F	Rififi	U.M.P.O	30 90		1	
8/4 Sa	The Misfits	U.A.	41 20		995 09	
8/5 Su	La Belle Americaine	Continental	61 20		1208 74	
8/6 M.mat	Big Deal on Madonna St	U.M.P.O	30 90	303 25	76 65	
1 M.eve	Broken Blossoms (3)				820 38	5197 29
8/7 Tu	Nights of Cabiria	Lopert	41 20	237 86	518 31	
8/8 W	Gen. della Rovere	Cont.	36 05		494 28	
8/9 Th	The Matchmaker	Par.	25 75		328 21	
1 1	Hoodlum Priest	U.A.	25 75		1	
8/10 F	Sapphire	U-I	41 20		516 91	
8/11 Sa	And God Created Woman	Union	51 50		633 07	
8/12 Su	Five-Day Lover	Unite	51 50		718 53	
8/13 M.mat	Look Back In Anger	Warners	36 05	309 -	49 30	
	M.eve Way Down East (4)				681 23	3939 92
8/14 Tu	The Cousins	F.G.W.	51 50	235 36	451 57	
8/15 W	Rules of the Game	Janus	51 50		412 99	
8/16 Th	The Entertainer	Cont.	25 75		535 42	
1 1	Breathless	F.G.W.	25 75		1	
8/17 F	The Apartment	U.A.	51 50		474 64	
8/18 Sa	Sons & Lovers	Fox	36 05		752 72	
8/19 Su	The Goddess	Col	36 05		930 36	
8/20 M.mat	It Started In Naples	Par.	36 05	314 15	79 05	
1 M.eve	Orphans of the Storm (5)				2465 7	4383 32

1962

A Night at the Opera	Altura	5150	23959	57648		1
The Joker	Lopert	4120		40748		2
Rocco + His Brothers	Astor	5150		60497		3
The Immigrant		—				4
L'Avventura	Janus	5150		63277		5
Touch of Evil	U-I	3090		88450		6
Sweet Smell of Success	U.A.	3605		68081		7
not The Truth	Cont.	5150	31415	7020		8
ew. America (6)				70412	456143	9
						10
Panic	F.R.	3605	231.12	65360		11
Casablanca	F.R.	3605		57936		12
Odds Against Tomorrow	U.A.	2575		49612		13
1984	Col.	2575				14
Love + The Frenchwoman	Union	3605		47003		15
The Innocents	Fox	3605		60344		16
Tiger Bay	Cont.	3605		106276		17
My Uncle (Labor Day)	Cont.	3605		67087	455618	18
						19
Mata Hari (1.50)	Altura	353013	107865	185056		20
Red Dust			1084	180480		21
				144420		22
				174679		23
				230578		24
				197969		25
				110968	1,204150	26
						27
Mata Hari	Altura	83784	48178	76170		28
Red Dust				55355		29
				46785		30
				78340		31
				115917		32
				94483		33
				55303	519053	34
						35
Lady Vanishes	Rank	1000.-	35683	75586		36
Odd Man Out			6006	54562		37
				43875		38
				89002		39
				123601		40
				87686		41
				44278	518590	42

1963

Date	Title		Amount			
6/18 Tu	If I Had a Million	O-I	1560.-	27435	4752	
				7495	51076	
6/19 W	Christmas in July				42435	
6/20 Th					66913	
6/21 F.					8357/	
6/22 Sa.					60498	
6/23 Su					4180	
6/24 M mat.					90871	46/586
	Meur. Dr. Jeeyll & the Hyde + Lost World (5)					
6/25 Tu	When a Woman Ascends The Stair	TOHO	500.-	2x.-	311 11	
6/26 W.	The Big Sleep	F.R.	78.-		24477	
			65.-		25323	
6/27 Th.					40989	
6/28 F.					59104	
6/29 Sa.					57112	
6/30 Su.					4980	
7/1 M mat.					76357	319447
	Meur. Comedy Shorts (6)		1040			
	JOHN FORD					
7/2 Tu.	The Informer	Principal	26.-	79849	46173	
	Rio Grande	Pancwood	26.-			
7/3 W mat					3400	
	Weur. MARCH OF TIME	T.L.	125.-		60137	
7/4 Th.	Horse Soldiers	UA	26.-		57833	
	Gideon of Scotland Yard	Col	3640			
7/5 F.	Long Voyage Home	Enterl.	72.-		59971	
	She Wore a Yellow Ribbon	Principal	1820			
7/6 Sa.	Stagecoach	Enfurt.	72.-		76630	
	The Searchers	WB	26.-			
7/7 Su.	The Quiet Man	Pancwood	26.-		7011	
7/8 M mat.	Wagonmaster	Principal	1820	36780	4845	
	Meur. Cat & the Canary (7)				79376	4608 76
	Fall of House of Usher	WB	52.-	252.04	2x.x	
7/9 Tu.	Rising of the Moon	WB	26.-		35164	
	Sergeant Rutledge				3315	
7/10 W mat					46706	
	Weur. THE MARCH OF TIME	T.L	125.-			
7/11 Th.	Fort Apache	Principal	1820		32338	
	Two Rode Together	Col.	26.-	247.20		11763
7/12 F.	Eclipse	Times	7020		54987	
7/13 Sa.	The Stranger	S. Lake	3640		86935	
7/14 Su					94196	
7/15 M mat.					5865	
	1 Meur. Kismet (8)				39567	3990.73
	Ella Cinders					

1963

	Title	Studio					
6 Tu	Horse Feathers	U-I	1560 -	209.4	84392		1
7 W.	Big Broadcast of 1938				63825		2
8 Th					58552		3
9 F.					75928		4
10 Sa.					92532		5
11 Su.					82457		6
12 Mnd					4520		7
Move.	an Cire of Serials (9)				65098	527344	8
							10
	SCIENCE - FICTION						
13 Tu	The Fly	Fox	1560	48977	68150		11
	The Creeping Unknown	UA	2600				12
14 W.	The Incredible Shrinking Man	U-I	1560		57775		13
	The Mysterians	RKO	1820				14
15 Th	The Thing	RKO	1820		77126		15
	Transatlantic Tunnel	BE	—				16
16 F.	Rodan	Valiant	1820		43536		17
	It Came From Outer Space	U-I	1560				18
17 Sa.	Mars Attacks the World	RKO	1820		161338		19
	Planet Outlaws	RKO	1820				20
	Rocket Ship	RKO	1820		195872		21
18 Su	War of the Worlds	Par.	2600		190.-		22
19 Mnd	Things To Come	BE	2600				23
Move.	Don Juan + voice that thrilled world (10)	Standard	3530	243.30	66308	688905	24
30 Tu	This Island Earth	U-I	1560	28578	90984		25
	The Time Machine	MGM	26.-				26
31 W	Invasion of Body Snatchers	Ideal	2250		56470		27
	Conquest of Space	Par.	26.-				28
1 Th	Day Earth Caught Fire	U-I	15.60		48701		29
	Battle In Outer Space	Col.	26.-	131.70			30
							31
2 F.	Alexander Nevsky	Artkino	52.-		44503		32
3 Sa.	Pather Panchali	Harrison	78.-		59783		33
4 Su.	Ivan the Terrible (2)	Janus	52.-		49347		34
5 Mnd	Aparajito	Harrison	52.-		4555		35
Move.	Lilac Time + The Bond	F.B.Y.	52.-	286.-	50094	404437	36
6 Tu.	Potemkin	Artkino	52.-	294.73	36266		37
7 W.	World of Apu	Harrison	78.-		37031		38
8 Th	Rebecca	Opex	416.-		79825		39
9 F.	Notorious				100493		40
10 Sa.					116452		41
11 Su.					108161		42
12 M.					53073	458504	43
13 Tu.					60866		44
14 W.					39748		45

1964

Date		Title		Amount				
2/28	F	I'm No Angel	U-I	1040.-	30992	70525		
2/29	Sa	Klondike Annie	"			111130		
3/1	Su	Batman - Ch. 8	Col.	780		99940		
3/2	M					44018		
3/3	Tu					45186		
3/4	W					37342		
3/5	Th					38845	447589	
3/6	F	Belle of the 90's	U-I	78.-	25444	70244		
3/7	Sa	Night After Night	"	78.-		92575		
3/8	Su	Batman - Ch. 9	Col.	780		103621		
3/9	M					40389		
3/10	Tu	Shanghai Express	U-I	52.-		56736		
3/11	W	Blonde Venus	"	52.-		49288		
3/12	Th				26780	46664	459770	
3/13	F	Morocco	U-I	1040.-	21986	73594		
3/14	Sa	Everyday's a Holiday	"			94430		
3/15	Su	Batman - Ch. 10	Col.	780		94591		
3/16	M					33270		
3/17	Tu					33589		
3/18	W					26513		
3/19	Th					34422	390714	
3/20	F	Brief Encounter	Cont.	45970	9088	61447		
3/21	Sa	I Know Where I'm Going	"			92862		
3/22	Su	Batman - Ch. 11	Col.	780		89938		
3/23	M					46511		
3/24	Tu	The Chaplin Revue	Roy Export	193427	78452	87871		
3/25	W					61353		
3/26	Th					71971		
3/27	F					85089		Good F...
3/28	Sa					113177		Passo...
3/29	Su					125566		East...
3/30	M					53125	598152	
3/31	Tu	The Chaplin Revue	Roy Export	161484	31004	57249		
4/1	W					57878		
4/2	Th					43070		
4/3	F					70381		
4/4	Sa					112186		
4/5	Su					92189		
4/6	M					34691	467644	

1964

	BOGART						
Tu	Maltese Falcon	Apex	236.—	196.—	120174		
	Petrified Forest	"	125.—	6545			
W.	King of the Underworld	"		49196	54071		
	Black Legion	"					
Th.	You Can't Get Away With Murder	UAA			42271		
	They Drive By Night	Apex					
F.	One Fatal Hour	UAA.			61325		
	Racket Busters	"					
Sa.	To Have & Have Not	Apex			212476		
	Big Sleep	"					
Su.	All Through the Night	UAA			96711		
	San Quentin	Apex					
M.	Wagons Roll at Night	UAA			27654		Aca Event
	San Quentin	Apex				614652	Night
Tu.	Across the Pacific	UAA	236.—	22026	67016		
	Oklahoma Kid	Apex	125.—				
W.	Key Largo	"			52728		
	Bullets or Ballots	"					
Th.	Crime School	"			26551		
	Great O'Malley	UAA					
F.	Chain Lightning	"			55723		
	Roaring 20's	Apex					
Sa.	Casablanca	"			187902		
	High Sierra Ch.15 Batman	"			101454		
Su.	Treasure of Sierra Madre	"					
	Brother Orchid	UAA			37215	529094	
M.	Action in the No. Atlantic	UAA					
	Marred Woman	Apex					
Tu.	To Have & Have Not	"		32168	75654		
	The Big Sleep	"					
W.	Casablanca	"			57252		
	Key Largo	"					
Th.	Treasure of Sierra Madre	"			50519		
	Maltese Falcon	"					
F.	All About Eve	Fox	1300.—		82788		
Sa.	Laura				94718		
Su.					76138		
M.					36536		
Tu.					34064		
W.					30336		
Th.					54009	388989	

_1964_

Date	Day	Title	Source				Running	Total	Note
Elec Day	11/3 Tu	Chronicle of a Summer	P-C	26.-			47795		Election
		Therese	P-C	26.-					
1	11/4 W	Hiroshima, Mon Amour	Zenith	36.40			30183		
		Earrings of Madame De	V.14.P.O.	26.-	291.20			287057	
5									
6	11/5 Th	Limelight	Ray Efport	171029	47618		52063		
7	11/6 F	(1.50)			6457		92980		
8	11/7 Sa						150762		
9	11/8 Su						114739		
10	11/9 M						41131		
11	11/10 Tu						47084		
12	11/11 W						68451	567210	Veterans
13	11/12 Th	Limelight	Ray Efport	141206	20074		37345		
14	11/13 F	(1.50)					77981		
15	11/14 Sa						137124		
16	11/15 Su						79981		
17	11/16 M						44485		
18	11/17 Tu						54174		
19	11/18 W						55568	483658	
20									
21	11/19 Th	Il Bidone	Mario De Vecchi	500.-	61805		47785		Thanksgiv.
22	11/20 F	Breath-Death	Vanderbeek	75.-	75140		88983		
23	11/21 Sa	(1.75)			10260		118393		
24	11/22 Su						96585		
25	11/23 M						34302		
26	11/24 Tu						34644		
27	11/25 W						47475	468167	
28									
29	11/26 Th	Point of Order	Cont.	124452	458.02		79590		
30	11/27 F	Shoot the Piano Player	Gerand	104.-	7266		130638		
31	11/28 Sa	(1.50)					162680		
32	11/29 Su						106120		
33	11/30 M	New American Cinema (1)-midnight					47011		
34	12/1 Tu						47178		
35	12/2 W						50873	624090	
36									
37	12/3 Th	La Strada	Trans-Lux	130.-	26316		38380		
38	12/4 F	Forbidden Games	Fleetwood	125.-			75587		
39	12/5 Sa	(1.25)					120599		
40	12/6 Su						87478		
41	12/7 M	N.A.C. (2)					26643		
42	12/8 Tu						37496		
43	12/9 W						34985	421168	

1964-1965

Th	Beat The Devil	Col.	338.—	24743	31741		
F.	Some Like It Hot	U.A	130.—		65629		
Sa.					101928		
Su					78703		
M	N.A.C. (3)				28453		
Tu					22960	3575.15	
W							
	AMERICAN DADA						
M	Trouble With Harry	Par.	26.—	33323	25931		
	Manchurian Candidate	U.A.	26.—				
	A La Mode	F.M.C.	15.—				
F.	A Damsel In Distress	Principal	36.40		47507		
Sa.	My Little Chickadee	U-I	36.40		73044		
	Munro	Par.	3/2				
Su	Day At The Races	Jason	26.—		74656		
M.	Bank Dick	U-I	36.40		41426		N.A.C.4
	Popeye In Gym Jam	Par.	3/2				
Tu	Mask of Dimitrios	F.R.	26.—		31941		
W	King Kong	Principal	36.40		25776		
	Science-Friction	F.M.C.	30.—	300.84	?	324685	
Th	Strangers On a Train	W.B.	26.—	24582	27591		
	Will Success Spoil Rock Hunter?	Pan-world	26.—				
	The Last Clean Shirt	Leslie	25.—				
F.	Million Dollar Legs	U-I	36.40		78985		
Sa.	Duck Soup	U-I	36.40		133558		
	Pull My Daisy	Leslie	50.—		68515		
Su	Swingtime	Principal	36.40		40405		
M.	Gay Divorcee	"	36.40				
	The Hole	Brandon	26.—				
Tu	The Lady Eve	U-I	36.40		36013		
W.	Christmas In July	"	36.40		31504		
	A Movie	F.M.C.	20.—	391.40		416576	
Th	Love Me Tonight	U-I	26.—	20435	47838		
	Gold Diggers of 1935	UAA	25.—				
	Henry Geldzahler	FMC	15.—				
F.	Night At The Opera	Jason	36.40		1298.—		
Sa.	You Can't Cheat Anout Man	U-I	36.40		104324		
	Sunday	De And.	25.—				
Su	I'm No Angel	U-I	36.40		72543		N.A.C.5
M.	Sullivan's Travels	U-I	36.40		34205		
	Popeye Makes A Movie	Par.	3/2				
Tu	Palm Beach Story	U-I	36.40		314478		
W.	Easy Living	"	36.40		33935	454128	
	Eyewash	F.M.C.	10.—	32252			

1966

1	3/22 Tu.	Scarlet Empress	U-I	5250	30275	55710	
2	3/23 W.	Naked Autumn	U.M.P.O.	5250		48190	
3	3/24 Th.					44970	
4	3/25 F.	If I Had a Million	U-I	3675		69320	
5	3/26 Sa.	An American In Paris	Pau-Werd	5250	19425	120275	
6	3/27 Su.					108150	
7	3/28 Mat.					5575	
8	1 Meve. L+H (2)		Embassy	3675		94050	545840
9	3/29 Tu.	8½	Kevand	5250	28590	49340	
10	3/30 W.	Forbidden Games				43375	
11	3/31 Th.					480.-	
12	4/1 F.	Lolita	MGM	5250		48070	
13	4/2 Sa.	Old-Fashioned Way	U-I	3675		79125	
14	4/3 Su.				17850	657.-	
15	4/4 Mat.					5090	
16	1 Meve. L+H (3)					87450	425350
17	4/5 Tu.	Naked Kiss	Allied	2625	30515	307.-	
18	4/6 W.	Wild Seed	U-I	2625		27525	
19	4/7 Th.	Moment of Truth	Rizzoli	210.-		30040	
20	4/8 F.	Kiss Me Deadly	U.A.	15750	420.-	50860	
21	4/9 Sa.					68450	
22	4/10 Su.					546.-	
23	4/11 Mat.					3660	
24	1 Meve. L+H (4)					1024.-	368735
25	4/12 Tu.	All Quiet On Western Front	U-I	3675	32689	476680	
26	4/13 W.	I Am a Fugitive From Chain Gang	Dominant	26.-		43190	
27	4/14 Th.	Arise My Love	U-I	5250		25750	
28	4/15 F.	Will Success Spoil Rock Hunter	Goldstone	3675		47720	
29	4/16 Sa.	It's A Gift	U-I	3675		85725	
30	4/17 Su.	Till the Clouds Roll By	Pau-Werd	3675	22550	738.-	
31	4/18 Mat.					4750	
32	1 Meve. L+H (5)					875.-	
33	4/19 Tu.	Compulsion Children Paradise	P-C	3675	31766	38030	
34	4/20 W.	The Hustler Trial of Joan of Arc	"	26.-		40425	4017.-
35	4/21 Th.	Time Machine Compulsion	Fox	3675		33360	
36	4/22 F.	Village of the Damned Hustler	7 Arts	2625		60185	
37	4/23 Sa.	Time Machine	MGM	2625		77025	
38	4/24 Su.	Village of Damned	"	2625	17825	96450	
39	4/25 Mat.					3795	
40	4/26 Meve. L+H (6)					90750	
41	4/26 Tu.	La Notte	Lopert	5775		39480	
42	4/27 W.	My Life To Live	P-C	3675		33235	434280

24 Th	Before The Revolution	N.Y.F	26250			34235		1
29 F.	Diary of a Chambermaid	Fox	315 -			59205		2
30 Sa.						82750		3
1 Su.						69675		4
2 M.						24775		5
3 Tu.						29745		6
4 W. mat.						3230		7
W. eve.	Intolerance					34050	337605	8
5 Th	Treasure of Sierra Madre	Downing	2625		64160	48375		9
6 F.	Fields Trilogy					90740		10
7 Sa.						147925		11
8 Su.	Meet Me In St. Louis	Pan World	3675			101550		12
9 M. mat.	World of Henry Orient	U.A.	3675			5280		13
M. eve	Dead of Night	-				81750		14
10 Tu.	Morocco	U-I	360			48205		15
11 W.	Damsel In Distress	Principal	2625		16275	42785	566610	16
	PREMIERE SERIES (1)							17
12 Th	Les Bonnes Femmes	Harim	1000 -		41508	720 -	subscription tix sold	18
13 F.	The Music Room	Harrison	26250		227575	143775	3/24,00	19
14 Sa.	(1.75)					238950		20
15 Su.						138950		21
16 M.						58825		22
17 Tu.						59275		23
18 W.						59175	770950	24
19 Th	Les Bonnes Femmes	"	-			46275		25
20 F.	The Music Room	"	26250		52732	66925		26
21 Sa.						109975		27
22 Su.						78975		28
23 M.						31750		29
24 Tu.						448 -		30
25 W.						50375	429075	31
								32
26 Th	Lofna	Pol-Ton	300 -		59051	48275		33
27 F.	Salvatore Giuliano	Royal	26250		2472	605 -		34
28 Sa.					53130	99675		35
29 Su.					14653	70875		36
30 M.						69775		37
31 Tu.						316 -		38
1 W.						42575	423275	39
								40
2 Th	Gertrud	P-C	525 -		53436	79175		41
3 F.	Third Lover	Atlantic	250 -			910 -		42
4 Sa.						137675		43
5 Su.						92550		44
6 M.						57675		45
7 Tu.						572 -		46
8 W.						60875	570150	47

1967

Date		Title						
8/28	M.	Nothing But a Man	Cinema 5	36 25		576. –		
8/29	Tu.	East of Eden	W.B	26 25		736 25		
8/30	W.	Mark of Dimitrios	Cyay	36 75	736 25	770 25	5241 75	
8/31	Th.	Little Caesar		36 75	338 20	753 50		
9/1	F.	Juliet of the Spirits	Rizzoli	78 25		867 –		
9/2	Sa.	Big Deal on Madonna St.	U. 4 PO	52 50		1009. –		
9/3	Su.	Kind Hearts + Coronets	Cont.	52 50		935 –		Return
9/4	M.	Bunny Lake Is Missing	Col.	36 75		483. –		
9/5	Tu.	M. Hulot's Holiday	Cont.	52 50		661 75		
9/6	W.	The Entertainer	Cont.	52 50	325 50	661 75	5913 50	
9/7	Th.	Shakespeare Wallah	Cont.	630. –	390 23	595 25		
9/8	F.	Dutchman	"			864. –		
9/9	Sa.					1504 50		
9/10	Su.					1117 75		
9/11	M.					553 50		
9/12	Tu.					662 50		
9/13	W.					581 25	5878 75	
		REPERTORY						
9/14	Th.	The Servant	AIP	105. –	298 08	381 50		
9/15	F.	Muriel	Lopert	36 75		907. –		
9/16	Sa.	Peppy	U-I	52 50		2144 50		
9/17	Su.	Day At The Races	Paul World	47 25		1360 50		
9/18	M.	Billy Budd	Allied	26 25		585 25		
/	/	Sons + Lovers	Fox	26 25				
9/19	Tu.	King + Country	AIP	105. –		652 75		
9/20	W.	Before The Revolution	N.Y.F.	50. –	449 –	662 50	6694 –	
9/21	Th.	Eclipse	Times	52 50	316 88	336 75		
9/22	F.	Brief Encounter	Cont.	52 50		690 25		
9/23	Sa.	Cocoanuts	U-I	52 50		2351 75		
9/24	Su.	You Can't Cheat an Honest Man	"	52 50		1842 –		
9/25	M.	Hud	Par.	26 25		579 50		
/	/	Point of Order	Cont.	36 75		1		
9/26	Tu.	Seconds	Par.	36 75		321 25		
9/27	W.	Major Dundee	Col.	36 75	346 50	203 50	6327. –	
					201 40			
9/28	Th.	Long Day's Journey Into Night	Embassy	26 25		395 25		
9/29	F.	A Day In The Country	P-C	26 25		914 25		
9/30	Sa.	International House	U-I	52 50		1430 50		
10/1	Su.	W.C. Fields Trilogy	–	–		1075 –		no a
10/2	M.	Landru	Embassy	26 25		406 –		
/	/	Luck of Ginger Coffey	W.R.	36 75		~~~~~~		
10/3	Tu.	The Great McGinty	U-I	105. –		390 50		
10/4	W.	North By Northwest	MGM	54 50	325 50	443 –	5054 50	

1967

	Title	Dist.					
Tu	La Notte	Lopert	3675	34520	443 —		Rich Hochman
W	Loneliness of Long Distance Runner	W-R	5250		83850		
	Monkey Business	U-I	5250		1988 —		
Tu	Million Dollar Legs	"	5250		148350		
	Birdman of Alcatraz	U-A	2625		298 —		
	The Killing	"	2625				
Tu	Soft Skin	Cinema V	3675		38075		
W	Modesty Blaise (M.F.)	Fox	3675	32025	42350	584625	
Th	M	Jerand	5250	31968	54275		Col. Day
F	Fantastic Voyage	Fox	5250		75325		Kol Nidre
Sa	My Little Chickadee	U-I	5250		251750		Yom Kippur
Su	Duck Soup	"	5250		170725		
M	Leda	Times	2625		425 —		
T	Doulos The Finger Man	P-C	3675				
Tu	Quiller Memorandum	Fox	3675		25425		
W	X-Man With X-Ray Eyes	Pan-World	2625	336 —	357 —	6550 —	
	GODARD						
Th	Breathless	P-C	105 —	49275	34925		
F	Masculin-Feminin	Royal	105 —		731 —		
Sa					108475		
Su					84850		
M	Married Women	Col.	5250		25325		
Tu	My Life To Live	P-C	5250		32350		
W				315 —	33850	392875	
Th	Alphaville	"	105 —	18375	29850		
F	Band of Outsiders	Royal	105 —		677 —		
Sa					78250		
Su					774 —		
M	Woman As a Woman	P-C	5250		32450		
Tu	Contempt	Embassy	5250	315 —	40775		
					358025	362250	
	WINTER REPERTORY						
	Cartouche	Embassy	2625	34260	24575		
	The Love Game	P-C	3675		57250		
	Grand Illusion	W-R	5250		189925		
	Blue Angel	—	2625		132225		
	Strawberry Blonde	Ajay	2625		272 —		
	The Trouble With Harry	Par	2625				
Tu	The Young Lions	Fox	3675		34975		Alexandra Day
W	Lonely Boy	Cinema V	2625	231 —	18375	477525	

1971

			Reporting						
1	5/30	R	Little Caesar	Ajay		6360	809.95	377.-	
2			Strawberry Blonde				2947		
3	✓	5/30 F	Strawberry Blonde	Ajay		6360	2257	691.-	
4			The General – The Blacksmith	McGen		150.-	8674.5		
5	✓	5/30 Sa	The General – The Blacksmith					853.50	
6			Go Into Your Dance	Ajay		6360			
7		5/30 Su	Go Into Your Dance					605.50	
8			West Side Story	U.A.					
9	✓	5/30 M	West Side Story	U.A.		53.-		561.25	
10			Jimmy The Gent	U.A. 16					
11	✓	5/30 Tu	Jimmy The Gent	-		7950		1032.25	
12			Streetcar Named Desire	U.A.		53.-			
13	✓	5/30 W	Streetcar Named Desire					1106.50	
14			Outward Bound	U.A. 16			526.30		5275.-
15	✓	5/30 Th	Outward Bound	U.A. 16		7950	402.83	525.50	
16			African Queen	Tran-Lux		106.-	1360		
17		5/30 F	African Queen				41653	771.-	RAIN
18			Midsummer Night's Dream	Ajay		6360			RAIN
19		5/30 Sa	Midsummer Night's Dream	Ajay				1300.-	RAIN
20			Adventures of Robin Hood	Ajay		6360			
21	✓	5/30 Su	Adventures of Robin Hood					1287.75	RAIN
22			Her Majesty's Love	U.A. 16		7950			
23	✓	5/31 M	Her Majesty's Love (One Day)					963.-	
24			How To Succeed In Business	U.A.		53.-			
25		6/1 Tu	How to Succeed In Business					387.50	
26			Charade	U-I		53.-			
27		6/2 W	Charade					472.25	
28			Topaz	U-I			498.20		5707.-
29		6/3 Th	Topaz	U-I		7950	386.31	523.-	
30			Quiller Memorandum				1360		
31		6/4 F	Quiller Memorandum	Fox		37.15	399.91	507.50	
32			Fortune Cookie	U.A.		53.-			
33		6/5 Sa	Fortune Cookie					1226.25	
34	✓		Gold Rush – Dentist	LeGen		150.-			
35		6/6 Su	Gold Rush – Dentist					877.25	
36			Countess From Hong Kong	U-I		53.-			
37		6/7 M	Countess From Hong Kong					501.75	
38			Tom Jones	U.A.		53.-			
39		6/8 Tu	Tom Jones					688.-	
40	✓		Hard To Handle	U.A. 16		7950			
41		6/9 W	Hard To Handle					492.-	
42			Charge of Light Brigade	U.A.		7950	505.10		4815.75

1971

	Title	Dist.					
Th	Charge of the Light Brigade	U.A.	53.50	403.44	482.50		
	Beast with 5 Fingers	Ajay	63.-	12.59			
F	Beast with 5 Fingers			416.03	588.50		
	Thief of Bagdad	16mm	150.-				
Sc	Thief of Bagdad				1,157.75		
	Dr. Strangelove	Col.	53.50				
Su	Dr. Strangelove				1305.50		
	Hunchback of Notre Dame	16mm	150.-				
M	Hunchback of Notre Dame				1145.-		
	Fearless Vampire Killers	MGM	53.-				
Tu	Fearless Vampire Killers				1255.-		
	Pretty Poison	Fox	37.10				
W	Pretty Poison				1056.25		
	Rosemary's Baby	Par.		559.10		7020.50	
Th	Rosemary's Baby	Par.	37.45	359.60	685.75		
	Cincinnati Kid	MGM	80.25	15.73			
F	Cincinnati Kid			375.33	475.-		
	Kremlin Letter	Fox	53.50				
Sa	Kremlin Letter	UA			841.25		
	The Killing	U.I.	53.-				
Su	The Killing				452.-		
	Beloved Rogue	16mm	150.-				
M	Beloved Rogue				544.-		
	Isadora	U.I.	53.-				
Tu	Isadora				592.-		
W	Days of Wine + Roses	W.B.	37.45				
W	Days of Wine + Roses	W.B.			362.75		
	12 Angry Men	U.A.	53.-			3952.75	
Th	12 Angry Men	U.A.		359.60	459.25		
	The Letter	UA 16	82.80	12.59			
F	The Letter			372.19	524.75		
	Sweet Smell of Success	U.A.	53.-				
Sa	Sweet Smell of Success				455.75		
	Wild Boys of the Road	UA 16	82.80				
Su	Wild Boys of the Road				467.75		
	These Are The Damned	Col.	53.50				
M	These Are The Damned				373.-		
	Mickey One	Col	53.50				
Tu	Mickey One				467.25		
	The Crowd Roars	UA 16	82.80				
W	The Crowd Roars				439.25		
	Little Caesar	Ajay	+25 (see later)			3161.-	

1⁰⁰ - Students & Golden Age
starting 11/4   1971

	Date		Title					
1	10/26		Middhouse	Wildflr	131047	215144	347 -	
2	10/27		Thank You, Masse Man	Grove	50 -	33188	30450	
3	10/28					2490 32	42250	
4	10/29						95025	
5	10/30						152425	
6	10/31						110050	
Elec Day	11/1						48275	512175
7	11/2						66525	
8	11/3				+ 153 (Rosselleni)		28150	6071 -
9	"							
11	11/4	Th	RAISAN	N.Y.F	20039	43659	275 -	
12	11/5	F	Open City	Open City	26750	2490 09	538 50	
13	11/6	Sc	75 → 6500 ; also 5050			148568	591 -	
14	11/7	So	100 cofeature deduction				708 -	
15	11/8	M					208 -	
16	11/9	Tu					267 -	
17	11/10	W					433 -	332050
18								
19	11/11	Th	The Miracle	N.Y.F	44298	73427	31650	
20	11/12	F	Stromboli	R++	500 -	102.74	570 -	
21	11/13	Sc			94298	837.01	951 -	
22	11/14	So					598 -	
23	11/15	M					300 50	
24	11/16	Tu					338 -	
25	11/17	W					353 -	3429 -
26								
27	11/18	Th	Voyage To Italy	N.Y.F	72521	528.73	333 50	
28	11/19	F	Rise of Louis XIV	Oltura	458 -	98 63	62050	
29	11/20	Sc				62436	1011 -	
30	11/21	So					804 -	
31	11/22	M					432 50	
32	11/23	Tu					338 -	
33	11/24	W					53150	4071 -
34								
35	11/25	Th	Socrates	N.Y.F	887.67	450.36	630 -	
36	11/26	F	(2.50-2.00)			242.95	960 -	
37	11/27	Sc				69331	1024 -	
38	11/28	So					81550	
39	11/29	M					259 -	
40	11/30	Tu					390 -	
41	12/1	W					58450	4705 -
42								
43	12/2	Th	The Servant	AIP	535 -	26583	172 -	
44	12/3	F		Grove X			416 -	
45	12/4	Sc	Accident	Grove X	133.75	58762	782 -	
46	12/5	So					582 -	
47	12/6	M				28344	196 -	
48	12/7	Tu					188 -	
49	12/8	W					258 -	2618 -

Student discounts discontinued 1/3/72

1971-2

19 Tu	Z	Cinema V	214 –	27030	202 –			1
10 F	Senso (m.f.)	Albina	326 –	1826	300 50			2
1 Sa			535 –	28856	512 –			3
2 Su					856 –			4
3 M					149 50			5
4 Tu					161 50			6
5 W					180 –	185550		7
								8
6 Tu	Calcutta (on Ol. 13 – 12/7)	E YR	267 50	17279	3/150			9
7 F	Viva Maria	UA	166 50	2184	536 –			10
8 Sa	Zazie	N Y F	107 –	19443	879 50			11
9 Su	Fire Within	N Y F	107 –		734 50			12
10 M			642 –		337 –			13
11 Tu					454 50			14
12 W					323 50	357650		15
								16
13 Tu	Adventures of Robin Hood	UA 16	267 50	18046	367 –			16
14 F	Rabbit y Seville (holid price)	WB	16 05	3472	438 50			17
15 Sa	The Frog	Fox	10 70	21518	550 –			18
16 Su	Toy Man	Fox	10 70		555 –			19
17 M	Juggling Lady	Fox	10 70		470 –		no ads	20
18 Tu			31 35		401 50	3203 –	no ads	21
19 W					424 50	3203 –	no ads	22
								23
20 Tu	Caufornia	Pan	535 –	13340	966 50			24
21 F	B T R	N.Y.F	267 50	1494	793 –			25
22 Sa	(holiday prices)		80250	15834	1539 –			26
23 Su					1155 –			27
24 M	Student discounts discontinued				411 50		no ads	28
25 Tu					481 50		no ads	29
26 W					492 50	5041 –	no ads	30
								31
27 Tu	Rio Bravo	W. B	80 25	15558	227 50			32
28 F	Rio Lobo (M.F)	N.G.	53 50	2184	411 50			33
29 Sa			133 75	17722	618 –			34
30 Su					899 –			35
31 M	Utamaro	N Y F			423 50			36
32 Tu	Teorema	Goldstone			526 –			37
33 W					446 50	3354 –		38
								39
34 Tu	Utamaro	N Y F	200 –	51187	591 –			40
35 F	Teorema	Goldston	133 75	2824	992 50			41
36 Sa	450 = lowa deal 90/10			54011	1196 –		very cold	42
37 Su	distrib pays all advertising				876 –			43
38 M					343 –		no ads	44
39 Tu					464 50		no ads	45
40 W	89 pays – Theatre 88 348 41				920 –	4835 –	no ads	46
								47

1972

#	Date	Day	Title	Venue					Notes
1	3/2	Th	La Collectionneuse	—			108.12	422.50	Spring weather
2			Elvira Madigan	Cinema II	60.-		17.32		
3	3/3	F.	Elvira Madigan	—			125.44	537.-	Rain-sleet-Cold
4			Downhill Racer	Par.	50.-			671.-	
5	3/4	S.	Downhill Racer	—					
6			Gimme Shelter	Cinema II	60.-			737.-	Cold
7	3/5	Su	Gimme Shelter	—					
8			Gold Diggers of 1933	Ajay	75.-			230.50	
9	3/6	M.	Gold Diggers of 1933						
10			Cul-de-Sac	Altura	150.-			334.50	
11	3/7	Tu.	Cul-de-Sac	Altura				328.-	
12			Simon of the Desert	Altura	100.-				
13	3/8	W.	Idiot	New Yorker					
14			Simon of the Desert	Altura	—			326.50	
15									
16	3/9	Th	La Hora de los Hornos	J. Diaz	200.-		130.44	169.50	
17	3/10	F.					28.32	245.50	
18	3/11	Sa.					158.36	510.50	
19	3/12	Su						677.50	
20									
21	3/13	M.	Tokyo Story	NYF			3026.21	747.-	
22	3/14	Tu	(2.50)				970.01	774.50	Snow-cold
23	3/15	W.					3996.22	890.50	
24	3/16	Th						908.50	
25	3/17	F.	(12th Anniversary)					1837.50	Heavy Rain all day
26	3/18	Sa.						3101.50	good weather
27	3/19	Su						2082.50	10,342.-
28									
29	3/20	M.	Tokyo Story	NYF			2363.28	705.-	
30	3/21	Tu	(2.50)				412.02	766.-	
31	3/22	W.					2775.30	781.-	RAIN all day
32	3/23	Th.						727.50	
33	3/24	F.	"					1513.50	Co
34	3/25	Sa.	"					2302.50	Co
35	3/26	Su.	"					1938.-	8733.50	Co
36									
37	3/27	M.	Tokyo Story	NYF			1419.80	661.-	COLD
38	3/28	Tu	(2.50)				683.10	615.-	
39	3/29	W.	1st Seder night				2102.98	554.-	
40	3/30	Th	Passover (3/30-4/6)					730.-	Dear Shepard item
41	3/31	F.	Good Friday					1662.-	
42	4/1	Sa.						1747.50	warm
43	4/2	Su	Easter Sunday					1054.-	7023.50

1972

3 M.	Tokyo Story	N.Y.F.	1332.70	529.-		1
Tu	(2.50)		28462	455.-	Jeffrey Lyons (WPIX)	2
W.			162372	52550		3
Th.				437.-	Spring-like	4
F				917.50	New York morning review - cold	5
Sa.				156750	Cold. Sunny	6
Su				108050	5515.-	7
9 M.	Tokyo Story (Acad Award)	N.Y.F.	60343	327.-		9
Tu	(2.50)		9083	405.50		10
W.			69406	407.-		11
Th.				358.-		12
F.				88750	warm	13
Sa.				174150	Rain - good snow weather	14
Su				1018.-	514450	15
17 M.	Tokyo Story	N.Y.F.	517.74	327.50		17
Tu	(2.50)			307.-	Spring weather	18
W.				24250		19
Th				30250	Rain	20
F.				85690	Rain N.Y. Times morning Pt.	21
Sa.				136050	Rain	22
Su				75250	417940	Sunny - warm	23
M.	Tokyo Story	N.Y.F.	67820	307.-		25
Tu	A Full Life	N.Y.F.		31350	Chilly	26
W.	(2.50)			249.-		27
Th.				36950		28
F				831.-		29
Sa				112750		30
Su.				52450	3722.-	Warm Beautiful	31
M.	Tokyo Story + A Full Life (land day)	N.Y.F.		328.-		33
Tu	(2.50)			46150		34
W.				322.-	Rain all day	35
Th.				68350		36
F.				1367.-	3162.-		37

INDEX

Initial articles in all languages, e.g., *The, La, El,* are ignored in sorting of titles. NYT in subheadings refers to New Yorker Theater.

Stanley Theater, 26

Sternberg, Josef von, 38

Straub, Jean-Marie, 65–66, 82, 108

Strick, Joseph, 97

Stroheim, Erich von, 192

Stroszek (Herzog, 1977), 109, 193

student protests. *See* protests of 1968

Students for a Democratic Society (SDS), 15, 44

Sturges, Preston, 9

Styron, William, 94

subtitled films, resistance to, 82

Suchomel, Franz, 130, 133

The Sudden Wealth of the Poor People of Kombach (Schlondorff, 1970), 108

Sugimura, Haruko, 122

Sullivan's Travels (Sturges), 9

Sunset Boulevard (Wilder, 1960), 6, 14, 18

Swanson, Gloria, 6

Swerdlow, David, 149

Talbot, Dan: dialogue with audience, 33; father's attitude toward career choices, 7–8; New York Film Critics Award for Lifetime Achievement, 69; as NYT manager, 5, 11; *Point of Order*, 72–74, 76–79; pre-NYT career of, 3–4, 26; travel to Cuba, 83

Talbot, Emily, 2, 37, 184

Talbot, Nina, 21, 42, 48, 49, 119, 184, 185, 194

Talbot, Sarah, 28, 48, 184, 194

Talbot, Toby: *Berimbau*, 76, 88–89; as cultural editor of *El Diario de Nueva York*, 26; Fifth Avenue Cinema course on Latin American films, 91–93; inspiration for children's books, 50; as movie-house matron, 11; as Spanish professor and translator, 2, 3–4, 82, 90, 92–94; travel to Cuba, 83

Talbot relationship and family life: accidental meeting of Dan and Toby,

24; daughters' life in New York, 29–31, 48–50; life in Spain, 1–3; movies' importance in, 25–26; as Upper West Side residents, 27–33

Tanner, Alain, 107, 110–11, 125, 128

Targets (Bogdanovich), 43

Tarkovsky, Andrei, 127, 192, 193

Tate, Sharon, 175

Tati, Jacques, 116–19

Tauw (Sembene, 1970), 71

Les Temps Modernes (journal), 129

termite art, 162

Terra em Transe / Land in Anguish / Earth Entranced (Rocha), 89

Tharp, Twyla, 52

theaters *See* movie theaters

Theodore Huff Society, 33

They Don't Wear Black Tie, 89

The Thin Blue Line (Morris), 93

The Tree of Wooden Clogs (Olmi), 135

Timerman, Jacobo, 86, 93–94

Tokyo Story / Tokyo Monogatari (Ozu), 120, 121, 127

Tolpen, Bella: as candy counter manager, 10, 12, 149, 152, 154–56, 158–59, 161; Fassbinder's meeting with, 183–84; relationship with granddaughters, 29

Tolpen, Joseph, 10, 153–54

Tout Va Bien (Godard), 69

Traffic (Tati, 1971), 117

The Traveling Players (Angelopoulus), 127

The Tree of Wooden Clogs (Olmi), 193

Tresca, Carlo, 143

Trier, Lars von, 177

Triumph of the Will (Riefenstahl), 39, 93

Tropici (Amico, 1969), 64

Trotta, Margarethe von, 108

Truffaut, François, 177; cancellation of 1968 Cannes Film Festival and, 175–76; New Wave and, 98–99, 106; *politique d'auteur* and, 36; protests against closing of Cinémathèque Françoise, 47